The Action-ori
Approach

NEW PERSPECTIVES ON LANGUAGE AND EDUCATION
Founding Editor: Viv Edwards, *University of Reading, UK*
Series Editors: Phan Le Ha, *University of Hawaii at Manoa, USA* and
Joel Windle, *Monash University, Australia.*

Two decades of research and development in language and literacy education have yielded a broad, multidisciplinary focus. Yet education systems face constant economic and technological change, with attendant issues of identity and power, community and culture. This series will feature critical and interpretive, disciplinary and multidisciplinary perspectives on teaching and learning, language and literacy in new times.

All books in this series are externally peer-reviewed.

Full details of all the books in this series and of all our other publications can be found on http://www.multilingual-matters.com, or by writing to Multilingual Matters, St Nicholas House, 31-34 High Street, Bristol BS1 2AW, UK.

NEW PERSPECTIVES ON LANGUAGE AND EDUCATION: 72

The Action-oriented Approach

A Dynamic Vision of Language Education

Enrica Piccardo and Brian North

MULTILINGUAL MATTERS
Bristol • Blue Ridge Summit

To the memory of John Trim and Leo van Lier

DOI https://doi.org/10.21832/PICCAR4344
Names: Piccardo, Enrica, author. | North, Brian, 1950- author.
Title: The Action-oriented Approach: A Dynamic Vision of Language Education
   /Enrica Piccardo and Brian North.
Description: Blue Ridge Summit, PA: Multilingual Matters, [2019] | Series:
   New Perspectives on Language and Education: 72 | Includes bibliographical
   references and index.
Identifiers: LCCN 2019003483 (print) | LCCN 2019013389 (ebook) | ISBN
   9781788924351 (pdf) | ISBN 9781788924368 (epub) | ISBN 9781788924375
   (Kindle) | ISBN 9781788924344 (hbk :alk. paper) | ISBN 9781788924337
   (pbk: alk. paper)
Subjects: LCSH: Second language acquisition – Methodology. | Second language
   acquisition – Study and teaching. | Language and languages – Study and teaching.
Classification: LCC P118.2 (ebook) | LCC P118.2 .P533 2019 (print) |
   DDC 418.0071–dc23
LC record available at https://lccn.loc.gov/2019003483

Library of Congress Cataloging in Publication Data
A catalog record for this book is available from the Library of Congress.

British Library Cataloguing in Publication Data
A catalogue entry for this book is available from the British Library.

ISBN-13: 978-1-78892-434-4 (hbk)
ISBN-13: 978-1-78892-433-7 (pbk)

Multilingual Matters
UK: St Nicholas House, 31-34 High Street, Bristol BS1 2AW, UK.
USA: NBN, Blue Ridge Summit, PA, USA.

Website: www.multilingual-matters.com
Twitter: Multi_Ling_Mat
Facebook: https://www.facebook.com/multilingualmatters
Blog: www.channelviewpublications.wordpress.com

The policy of Multilingual Matters/Channel View Publications is to use papers that
are natural, renewable and recyclable products, made from wood grown in sustainable
forests. In the manufacturing process of our books, and to further support our policy,
preference is given to printers that have FSC and PEFC Chain of Custody certification.
The FSC and/or PEFC logos will appear on those books where full certification has
been granted to the printer concerned.

Typeset by Riverside Publishing Solutions.
Printed and bound by CPI Group (UK) Ltd, Croydon, CR0 4YY

Contents

Tables and Figures

Tables

Figures

1 The Emergence of a New Vision

Les sciences humaines ne savent pas qu'elles sont inhumaines,
non seulement à désintégrer ce qui est naturellement intégré, mais
à ne retenir que le quantitatif et le déterministe.

– Edgar Morin

1.1 From Practice to Theory to Practice

The term Action-oriented Approach (AoA) has increasingly circulated in the world of language education since the publication of the *Common European Framework of Reference for Languages* (CEFR) (Council of Europe, 2001) and particularly in the last decade. At first it was somehow mentioned between the lines, almost whispered in teacher education workshops and language teaching conferences, but little by little it started to be mentioned more often and a discussion on its main tenets began. A debate soon appeared as to whether the AoA could be considered a new approach or simply old wine in a new bottle – namely the communicative approach – with strong advocates on both sides (Beacco, 2007; Bento, 2012; Puren, 2009a; Richer, 2009). As is often the case when practice is involved as well as theory, this issue was not central for practitioners, who were once again looking for support in their difficult everyday mission to teach languages more effectively and improve the proficiency of their students. Thus, the AoA started to be the object of increased attention from language educators and curriculum developers and consequently a body of knowledge started to be created. Materials that claimed to be action-oriented, some more correctly than others, started to be produced in different languages and contexts. More recently, interesting projects have been carried out, often resulting in targeted web resources that acted as trailblazers (e.g. the FIDE project in Switzerland: www.fide-info.ch, Schleiss & Hagenow-Caprez, 2017; the Durham project in Canada, Durham Immigration Portal, 2016; Piccardo & Hunter, 2017; Hunter *et al.*, 2017) sometimes providing a first hint at theorisation (Piccardo, 2014a). Other ongoing projects focus exclusively on classroom practice (e.g. Hunter *et al.*, forthcoming).

1

This effervescence has already produced some positive effects: the action-oriented perspective has been widely accepted, particularly in relation to teaching languages other than English. It is recognised as a new vision in language education, which is rooted in the notion of action (Denyer, 2009; Puren, 2004, 2009a, 2009b; Richer, 2008, 2009, 2012, 2017). This vision aligns with a socio-constructivist perspective on the one hand and, on the other hand, encompasses and goes beyond the achievements of the earlier innovations in language education, particularly but not exclusively the communicative approach based on Hymes' (1972a) ground-breaking work, and the task-based approaches (Ellis, 2003; Nunan, 1989, 2004; van den Branden *et al.*, 2009; Willis, 1996; Willis & Willis, 2007). The AoA has triggered powerful innovation at a practical level in the teaching of different languages, with materials and examples of AoA-based scenarios, which show noticeable similarities beyond differences in pedagogical cultures. We are now at a moment in which we can capitalise on this rich reflection and practice to highlight the tenets of the AoA and investigate its conceptual depth and its implications for the classroom. This is precisely what this book intends to offer.

1.1.1 The issue at stake: The action-oriented approach, a practice in search of a theory

Languages are a key aspect of human life, they are crucial in human development both cognitive and social, they are the vehicle of our cultural, political and economic existence in society. In our globalised world, where exchanges and contacts are exponentially increasing, the role of languages stands out as a fundamental element. Languages are able to determine effective communication, are a major element for fostering cultural awareness and sensitivity, and eventually for enhancing peaceful coexistence. It is no surprise, therefore, that the stakes around language education are very high and they are perceived as such by the different stakeholders. Language policies and language-related educational policies are a very sensitive domain in every country and the socio-political demands are therefore high. Language teachers usually feel under particular pressure to deliver the best possible 'product', as they are called upon to bring their students to the highest possible level of proficiency, which will be mercilessly tested by every speaker of the target language these students will come into contact with.

In this climate, it is certainly not surprising that teachers are constantly in search of the most effective approaches and techniques for their daily work. Teachers are called on to be at the forefront of social change and they do not hesitate to use all they judge effective in their mission, without necessarily worrying about the underlying theory or the conceptual development of the notions, approaches and techniques that they select for their practice. However, the theorisation of professional know-how and action is essential if we want to avoid fragmentation, lack of coherence, and ultimately a proliferation of different things that all claim to belong to the same founding concept, but that often do not do so, or do so only partially. The relation between practice and theory is a reciprocal one, where developments help give flesh and blood to abstract conceptualisation and where in turn the theoretical discussion helps steer the practical development by providing reference points that cast light on the reasons behind the professional action. As a matter of fact, in the history of language teaching, practice has often been ahead of theory. On the other hand, as Kurt Lewin reminds us, there is nothing as practical as a good theory (1952: 169). This can apply to what has increasingly become known by practitioners as the action-oriented approach (AoA), which we are tempted to define as a practice in search of a theory. In reality, as we will explain in this book, things are a bit more complex than that, but it is certainly not incorrect to say that teachers operating at different levels and in different contexts have seen the potential of the AoA for their practice and have proceeded to some form of conceptualisation, if not of real theorisation, over the past few years. Certainly they have been inspired by this term to produce examples of practices that all present similar characteristics, beyond the obvious differences due to educational contexts and cultures/traditions. This phenomenon of having similar methodological developments occurring almost at the same time in different contexts is a clear sign that in the case of the AoA we are faced with a major (methodological) paradigm shift that calls for deeper theorisation and conceptualisation of the approach itself, of its roots and of its implications in language education as a field.

Let us see what the AoA is and where it comes from. The term 'action-oriented approach' is introduced in the Common European Framework for Reference (CEFR) (Council of Europe, 2001), a key resource for all those involved in language education (teachers, researchers, curriculum developers, and policy makers).

The AoA is mentioned upfront in the CEFR when the key concepts of this document are laid down and its philosophy and vision of language education are presented. There is no pose of methodological neutrality. The term 'action-oriented approach' appears in the CEFR to flesh out the 'very general view of language use and learning' (Council of Europe, 2001: 9) that is deemed necessary in order for a frame of reference to be comprehensive, transparent and coherent as the CEFR intends to be. As is the case with several definitions contained in the CEFR, the definition of the AoA embeds various concepts that need to be unpacked in order to capture all their theoretical depth and density. In fact, the AoA 'views users and learners of a language primarily as "social agents", i.e. members of society who have tasks (not exclusively language-related) to accomplish in a given set of circumstances, in a specific environment and within a particular field of action' (Council of Europe, 2001: 9). This first statement is further elaborated by three more sentences that specify the way individuals act with languages. They refer to the relationship between language activities and the social context, the vision of tasks adopted, and the role of resources of diverse nature (cognitive, emotional, volitional) and of different individual abilities.

The term 'action-oriented approach' refers to the choice made by the CEFR itself to reach its mission, i.e. to contribute transparency and coherency to the vast and complex field of language use and language education; it does not intend to push a particular methodological agenda. However, it is very symptomatic that the initial preamble we have mentioned lays the foundations for the following box that tries to describe 'any form of language use and learning' (Council of Europe, 2001: xi). This box contains, in fact, a syntactically dense and challenging paragraph that basically presents all the core elements of the new vision proposed by the CEFR.

Language use, embracing language learning, comprises the actions performed by persons who as individuals and as social agents develop a range of **competences,** both **general** and in particular **communicative language competences.** They draw on the competences at their disposal in various **contexts** under various **conditions** and under various **constraints** to engage in **language activities** involving **language processes** to produce and/or receive **texts** in relation to **themes** in specific **domains,** activating those **strategies** which seem most appropriate for carrying out the **tasks** to be accomplished. The monitoring of these actions by the participants leads to the reinforcement or modification of their competences. (Council of Europe, 2001: 9)

What we would like to stress here is that by presenting its view of language use and learning as action-oriented, the CEFR provides a powerful foundation that relates individuals to the social context, and that suggests real-life situations with their implications and outputs. It is not surprising, therefore, that practitioners felt in tune with this vision and that they could relatively easily see its potential for the classroom. In a sense, these few lines summarised a lot of what they had been trying to do in their everyday class: reproduce real-life situations, assign tasks, take into account the different resources and capabilities of their learners, and develop their competences and ability to learn.

Thus, even though the CEFR claims that it does not 'embody any one particular approach to language teaching to the exclusion of all others' (Council of Europe, 2001: 18) and later stresses that 'it is not the function of the Framework to promote one particular language teaching methodology, but instead to present options' (Council of Europe, 2001: 142), the AoA started to be increasingly associated with the CEFR, not only to indicate its view of language use and learning, but also to refer to a methodological approach in the true sense of the term that as such has started to develop in a bottom-up, rhizomatic way in the different contexts where the CEFR has been implemented.

The intuition of practitioners has been key in helping to overcome the alleged methodological neutrality of the CEFR and enhance its innovation potential in language education. What is particularly interesting to note is that, in spite of context-related differences, a certain generic understanding is visible throughout the practical developments of the AoA, which demonstrates that a transparent basis for development had been provided by the formulation of the concept in the CEFR. However, being as we said a bottom-up, rhizomatic process, not only did the development and definition of the AoA take time but the little differences also risk being magnified in the absence of a proper theorisation of the approach itself and an analysis of its roots and implications. This is precisely what this book sets out to do.

1.1.2 Who is this book for and how is it organised

This text aims to theorise the AoA in terms of origins, development and conceptual underpinnings. For this reason, the main target audience is researchers and graduate students in language education. At the same time, it also aims to provide a clear insight into the practical implications of the AoA in language education. As such, it is also addressing practitioners and prospective teachers who are trying to understand how the AoA fits in the development of second/foreign language methodologies and what it contributes to the field.

In addition, this book targets a crucial and unfortunately often neglected audience, i.e. curriculum developers and directors of studies, in other words all those that are responsible for curricula and curriculum planning. As the AoA is not an off-the-shelf methodology that can be applied as an add-on to any type of curricula, but is rather a comprehensive philosophy that relates curriculum planning, teaching and assessment in a coherent – and therefore more effective – ensemble, it is crucial that people involved in curriculum development have a clear understandings of the tenets of the AoA as they have a pivotal role to play in educational innovation. Thus, this book addresses their needs too.

As we said, the AoA has developed in a rather 'naturalistic' way so far, in the sense that the ideas that it presented and the vision it proposed, simply on the basis of the few paragraphs and occurrences in the CEFR, have acted as grains that have germinated in different contexts. However, precisely as in nature – grains do not produce standardised clones but rather recognisable plants belonging to the same species, which may differ according to the nature of the soil, the climate they grow in, and the care they receive – the AoA-inspired practices are influenced by context-related factors. This aspect calls on the one hand for systematisation and clarification; on the other hand it is a proof that the AoA is both lively and robust.

The methodological developments in language education bear major consequences not only in terms of practices and education policies but also in terms of social implications, since proficiency in languages is increasingly becoming crucial to individual and societal development. A book that tries to link theory and practice not only has the ambition to provide food for thought to all those involved in language education, but also contributes to overcoming the hiatus that presently still exists between researchers and practitioners. As the aim of applied linguistics should be that of conducting research that inspires and helps conceptualisation of practice, and data from research should feed back into practice too, a book that spans a broader audience by presenting the necessary theoretical and conceptual underpinnings of a dynamically emerging approach in plain and accessible language offers a vehicle for this synergy between theory and practice, thus potentially making a real contribution to the advance of the field.

We consider that we need to go back thirty years to a very established and productive tradition that saw key publications which pursued precisely this aim and presented both theory and practice in a positive and thought-provoking feedback loop. To be effective though, a feedback loop of this kind, between theory and practice, needs to be direct and not mediated later through interpretations and syntheses. We hope that this book will be considered in a similar light to texts like Widdowson's *Teaching Language as Communication* (1978) or Moirand's *Enseigner á communiquer en langue étrangére [Teaching to Communicate in a Foreign Language]* (1982), or Piepho's *Kommunikative Didaktik des Englischunterrichts Sekundarstufe I: Theoretische Begründung und Wege zur Praktischen Einlösung eines Fachdidaktischen Konzepts [Communicative Methodology for English Language Teaching: Lower Secondary Level: Theoretical Rationale and Paths towards Practical Implementation of a Teaching Approach]* (1979). These books are just a few examples of the intense and rich conceptualisation and discussion of language teaching and learning that took place from the late 1970s throughout the 1980s and that produced the communicative paradigm shift. The phenomenon we are experiencing now with the AoA is potentially equally rich and stimulating as it builds on that deep innovation and brings it to another level by incorporating not only the advances in research in fields such as language acquisition, discourse analysis, and brain-related language processing, but also insights from broader theories such as complexity theory and the sociocultural theory.

The awareness that language education situates itself in the field of complexity, since it involves several actors interacting within different contexts and focuses on change over time, brings a new vision of the respective roles of researchers and practitioners. The contribution of theories to practical action is not trivial and there is an increasing consensus on the need for the practitioner to act in a strategic way (Piccardo, 2010a; Tudor, 2001) in order to be effective in the ever-changing reality we are confronted with. Since the paradigm shift represented by the communicative approach, it is no longer viable to apply a ready-made all-encompassing method. Complexity and diversity have increased at the different levels: from societies, to classes to individuals. There is no longer a 'one-size-fits-all' solution, and luckily so.

Strategic action is a principled way of acting (Borg, 2006; Freeman, 2002) and, as such, it is inevitably informed by theory. This theory in turn needs to be accessible and clear in order to be useful, and not to remain in the ivory tower of academia. Besides clarity, coherence is also an important factor that helps convey the message more effectively. In order to reach such coherence, the structure of this book has been conceived in a way that brings the different dimensions together and aims to create a multiple perspective that casts light onto the specific features of the AoA, the reasons for their emergence and evolution, and their innovation potential.

The present chapter aims to help the reader to get acquainted with the AoA, to position it within the socio-educational context, to provide a first link to the founding document of the AoA, the CEFR, and to get a first general overview of the core elements that need to be considered in the theorisation of the AoA. The chapter consists of three sections. In the first, we present the reasons for a theorisation and conceptualisation of the AoA and the perspective adopted by the book. In the second section, the move towards the AoA since the paradigm shift of the communicative approach is situated in a broader perspective, which encompasses the role of languages in today's societies, alongside the rapid change itself that societies – and with them the individuals that constitute those societies – are presently undergoing. That section anticipates some of the core pillars of the AoA as it focuses on the synergies between the contributions of cognition and socialisation in the understanding of language education on the one side, while also embedding these synergies within the complexity of the sociological landscape characterised by increased mobility, *métissage* and change on the other. As is the case for all educational evolutions, the AoA is a creature of its time; thus it is crucial to help readers understand the position and role of languages within the socio-economic transformations of our time and their implications for language teaching and learning. As we will be following the pattern that has characterised the emergence of the AoA, the third section is dedicated to a brief overview of the CEFR, which is at the origin of the AoA. This offers a very first introduction to the core of the AoA to enable readers to situate the AoA in the conceptualisation of language education and to grasp its foundational notion, that of the social agent.

The second chapter of the book then tackles the notion of competence, which is key in understanding the AoA. This notion has been used in different disciplines and contexts, thus acquiring different meanings and connotations. The chapter discusses the notion of competence and its implications in the domains of linguistics and the world of work and education. The final section of the chapter shows the complementarity of these two perspectives by introducing the notion of competence in the CEFR. In doing so, it explains the descriptive scheme of the CEFR, which sees competences in terms of general and communicative ones and articulates their relationships and interdependence. It then explains the role of competences in the AoA. The third chapter of the book retraces the development of theories that have informed language education over time and complements them with theories developed in other scientific domains that have proved relevant for language learning and teaching alike. The chapter brings them all together by showing how the AoA is informed by and builds upon different theories, and explains the reasons for this multiple theoretical framework. Chapter 4 then links the practical methodological side to the theoretical overview provided in Chapter 3. Once again the AoA builds upon previous reflection on how languages should be taught and learned; thus, the chapter is organised into two sections: a historic overview of language teaching methodologies and a focus on the features characterising the AoA. The book continues with Chapter 5, which provides an in-depth analysis of the CEFR with the aim of highlighting the multifaceted nature of a document that enabled a paradigm shift in language education through synergic work at the level of informing language policies, bringing new insights into language education and paving the way for methodological reform through the AoA. Afterwards, Chapter 6 embeds the AoA in the present dynamic, sociological landscape by bringing readers to reflect upon a broader view of the AoA that encompasses plurality and creativity both at the linguistic and the cultural level. In doing so, it positions the AoA within the new developments in the CEFR: plurilingualism and mediation. The chapter shows how the AoA can be deepened and enriched by explicitly building upon and expanding the linguistic and cultural capital of learners and the dynamic process of mediation both at the individual and at the social level. After accompanying the reader through all the different conceptualisations and developments that underlie the AoA, the final substantive chapter of the book, Chapter 7, brings the different elements together and provides a synthesis of the AoA, relating theory and practice. In particular, it deals with the way the implementation of the AoA implies renewing language education all the way from planning to assessment. In order to make this shift clear and concrete, the chapter also includes some guidance for practice.

1.2 The Evolving Landscape of Language Education: From Communication to Action

As with all human activities, language education does not happen in a vacuum. Rather it is highly dependent on the vision of what constitutes learning and teaching in general and, more specifically, on what characterises learning and teaching a language, as well as using it, on an everyday basis. Along the same lines, the vision of what a language is modifies itself under the impact of societal evolution and change.

Languages have a double nature: they are the means through which things are accomplished, transactions are done, contacts are established or ended, and by which tastes, goals, dreams, and feelings are expressed. But whilst serving such different purposes, they also structure themselves as entities, albeit constantly evolving ones. Languages are in the modality of becoming, they take shape, or rather shapes, which are themselves very composite. In our increasingly linguistically and culturally diverse societies, languages undergo a double movement: they both take shape at the level of each individual and at the level of communities, be they large or small. Cultures and identities, like languages, are also structured at different levels similarly to the way fractals are. They also have different levels of variability. Both languages and identities look like neat, stable, delineated entities from the outside, but once they are seen from the inside they reveal themselves as unstable aggregates.

A great debate has emerged recently on the role of languages in society and on the nature of languages themselves. Sociolinguistic research has made us increasingly aware of the fact that languages are what their users produce; languages are not something existing out there that one simply applies in a situation, but are by nature a ductile tool that takes multiple forms according to both the nature of the situations in which they are used and the particular characteristics and goals of the speakers/writers concerned. At the same time, research into the functioning of the brain is also making us aware that languages are more than simple tools for expressing ourselves as they carry layers of intricate features, connections and implications that are all dynamically evolving. Finally, educational research has explored and tried to come to terms with this variability and the ever-changing nature of language, language use and language learning and has developed theories and practices that stress the role of co-construction of meaning, the potential of crossing linguistic and cultural borders, and the ability to see the continuum of languages and cultures. This represents a movement of constant expansion from a strict Cartesian vision of languages as defined and codified entities, to a vision of languages as the fluid in which societal change is immersed in an osmotic relationship. It is also a shift away from Cartesian thinking in the sense of 'mind over matter, cognition over context, individual over society' (Canagarajah, 2013: 23).

In all three research areas (language, language use, language learning), borders are increasingly being overcome and all levels, social, individual and educational are concerned with the need to de-conceptualise and re-conceptualise languages and language education to ensure that they are a means to understand our evolving way of living together. The switch from a linear to a complex perspective brings the situated nature of language and language use to the fore, calling for the concept of 'action' in both its generic and theoretically framed senses (Engeström, 1995) to be given a prominent role. As will be discussed throughout the book, the action-oriented approach aims to enable the concept of action to play the key role in language education that it has the potential to do.

1.2.1 Social complexity, mobility and change: A dynamic vision of societies and individuals

The process of globalisation gives rise to different forms of mobility and change, resulting in dynamic sociological landscapes where plurality and diversity are the norm rather than the exception. Post-industrial societies are characterised by a high degree of mobility and exchange in terms of both people and ideas in all domains of knowledge. Societies are undergoing phenomena of deterritorialisation and reterritorialisation (Defert, 2012) and this process is the key sign of postmodernity, or, to use Baumann's term, of liquid modernity (2000). Liquidity, as a metaphor, provides a powerful explanation of the lack of limits and barriers in our postmodern societies, in which phenomena of different nature spread everywhere without any real possibility of limiting or even classifying them. For Baumann, liquidity extends to every realm of human life, as everything is increasingly becoming uncertain and uncontrollable. Modernity and change come together in every aspect of our individual and collective lives. This increase in diversity leads to change and renewal of cultural and linguistic forms. In education, classes are increasingly diverse with students' life trajectories characterised by plurality both in languages and cultures, which then interact with the languages and cultures of the host societies, thus producing further change (Piccardo, 2013a).

In our societies, which are certainly diverse and have even been defined as superdiverse (Vertovec, 2007), language education needs to be revisited and reconceptualised. At the societal level, one reaction could be acceptance of and an active interest in diversity, but unfortunately one noticeable tendency is to gloss over, or even try and eliminate, cultural and linguistic differences through a more or less hidden process of introducing an impoverished form of English as a *lingua franca* in economic and political exchanges and institutions on the one hand, while at the same time reducing cultural differences to a simulacre through a process of folklorisation and essentialisation of cultures. For instance, we witness the reductive idea of sprinkling cultural elements in a substantially globalised and standardised vision, something that reminds us of McDonald's' offer of an olive oil and balsamic vinaigrette in Italy and a coffee accompanied by a little *macaron* in France, alongside the ubiquitous hamburger. One can see this type of minor accommodation to local cultures in such diverse domains as business, sports, architecture, etc. This choice underestimates the profound implications that cultural diversity has on people's lives. This process reinforces a tendency to oversimplification that assumes transparency and equivalency between languages and cultures, with the core message being easily conveyed with a little embellishment added to make it more attractive. This tendency is in fact increasingly common with the spread of English as a *lingua franca* (ELF) being presented as a historically inevitable form of 'progress.' In this view, other languages are seen as layers of complication and obfuscation, as obstacles to efficiency and effectiveness in both transactions and everyday life.

In such a context, what would then be the motivation for valuing linguistic diversity, enhancing proficiency in a variety of languages, and building on the linguistic and cultural capital and trajectories of increasingly mobile and diverse individuals and communities?

1.2.2 The place of language education within the developing socio-political context: Towards a new conceptualisation

The challenging and contradictory socio-economic landscape we have presented calls for reflection on the role and the place of languages and consequently of language education. Learning a language has in fact implications for both individuals and societies.

At the individual level the process of being exposed to linguistic diversity alongside that of learning additional languages has an impact in the mental sphere. Languages are lenses through which we make sense of the world: through languages we interpret and act upon the world. Having multiple languages means having multiple lenses and embracing a wider perspective. The awareness that glossodiversity is not equal to semiodiversity (Halliday, 2002) is a major leap forwards, opening up a new range of possibilities, potentially providing enhanced creativity and innovation. It is not surprising that recent studies have started to cast light on the benefits of multiple languages on the functions of the brain (e.g. Doidge, 2007; Malafouris, 2015). Languages are a powerful form of capital in several possible meanings of the word, from cognitive to affective, from social to economic. However, there is more to it than that at the individual level. The complexity of liquid societies require a *'homo complexus:'* someone whose *forma mentis* is shaped by semiodiversity, who is not afraid of opacity. They are even at ease with the unknown and willingly ready to explore it, to embrace nonlinearity, and reflect and capitalise on all forms of mixing and meshing. In a word, complex societies need people who are able to thrive in a complex paradigm.

At the societal level, precisely this complexity requires phenomena to be studied from different angles, from different perspectives. This in turn calls for people to be able see things from different perspectives, to use different lenses. Diversity of species – biodiversity – and linguistic diversity have a lot in common. As Halliday points out there is even an extra layer in language: the diversity of meaning: 'Is it glossodiversity we should be concerned with, or semiodiversity: diversity of forms as well as meanings, or just diversity of meanings? And exactly what is the value that attaches to such diversity, for the human race as a whole?' (2007: 14).

The alternative, reductionist vision that languages and communication are exclusively used for information exchange is not only an impoverished, sterile exercise, but also an illusion. If languages were used only to exchange information we would gain nothing that one of us did not already have. Knowledge is not a finite commodity to be exchanged and bartered in a zero-sum game. Languages are instead tools for (co)constructing meaning, as sociocultural theory has widely demonstrated, and as we discuss in Chapter 3. They are the main artefacts for interpreting the world and developing both individual knowledge and collective intelligence. The use of a common, reduced code, such as ELF, can be detrimental to all this potential, both individual and societal. Rather than examining a phenomenon from richly articulated different perspectives, there is a danger of linear, monocular vision.

1.2.3 Cognition and socialisation: The need for a new approach

If languages are potentially such door-opening tools, it follows that language education has a role to play when it comes to creating conditions conducive to positive social integration and innovation based on the synergies of different cultures, world visions and collective intelligence.

Now, as we know, learning a language, or even just avoiding language loss, is a challenging endeavour. Success requires multiple factors to work in an interdependent way, from individual engagement through effective support all the way to a positive attitude towards linguistic diversity on the part of society. It requires, above all, a shift at the pedagogic level. In particular, it requires an approach able to articulate both the individual and the societal dimensions we mentioned above, and to embed these dimensions in a broader educational frame where all the phases of pedagogic intervention contribute in an iterative, spiral pattern to awareness raising, enhancement of proficiency, and eventually autonomy. The AoA provides an ample enough perspective to encompass both the individual and the societal dimensions whilst being at the same time rooted in a clearly defined vision of what using and learning a language involve. Whilst we are fully conscious that for years there has been a quest for the methodological Holy Grail, with the consequent inevitable disillusion, we claim that the AoA has the potential to make the difference that is needed in order to overcome the substantially linear vision that still underpins most language education.

The AoA sees a user/learner who acts as a social agent always dealing with both the individual dimension, that of cognition, and the social dimension, that of communication and socialisation. As we will see in greater depth while talking about the CEFR in Chapter 5, the source of the AoA, the interdependence and cross-fertilisation of the cognitive and social dimensions is at the core of the approach. It is a vision that does not deny the complexity of language as a phenomenon in its linguistic, sociolinguistic and pragmatic manifestations, and that conceives of language education as a process operationalised through different types of communicative activities and related competences, in a conscious, strategic, way. This contrasts with previous methodologies and approaches, which tended to be linear in nature as they were informed by one specific view of what learning a language means, as we will explain later in the book.

1.3 Laying the Foundations for Methodological Innovation

Before getting into the specifics of the emergence and conceptualisation of the AoA, alongside its key concept of 'social agent,' and before highlighting its innovation potential in language education, we need first to introduce the CEFR, which, as we just mentioned, constitutes the founding document of the AoA.

1.3.1 The Common European Framework of Reference for Languages (CEFR): A turning point in language education

As the title (*Common European Framework of Reference for Languages: Learning, Teaching, Assessment*) suggests, the CEFR is primarily concerned with the structuring of effective learning and teaching. Its main objective is to provide a common metalanguage to assist language professionals in their respective practices and missions. It provides a common foundation upon which to organise the entire range of language proficiency with six general levels (A1, A2, B1, B2, C1 and C2), expressed using positive descriptors of communicative language activities of reception, production, interaction, and mediation that learners perform through meaningful tasks that draw on a variety of competences, both communicative language competences and general competences, for example acquired through general education and experience. The CEFR was developed in the mid-1990s, was published in 2001 (Council of Europe, 2001) and is now available in 40 languages.

The CEFR is a sophisticated if somewhat unwieldy 200+ page reference document made up of policy statements, explanatory text, taxonomic lists, descriptor scales and appendices which 'is exceptional in the exhaustiveness with which it sets out to list all the conceivable functional goals of foreign language teaching and all the known individual items that make up language knowledge. It is also refreshingly modest in its insistence that it is merely a guide to be used to develop a curriculum or test for specific purpose and context' (Spolsky, 2008: 15). The CEFR represented a turning point in language education and has already had a considerable and positive impact on language teaching and learning in Europe and beyond, as documented by Martyniuk and Nojons (2007), Jones and Saville (2009), North (2010), Piccardo *et al.* (2011a), Byram and Parmenter (2012), Figueras (2012), Huta (2013), Takala (2013), Little and Erickson (2015), O'Dwyer *et al.* (2017) and Arnott *et al.* (2017) among others. Initially, users focused on the levels and the descriptors before discovering the conceptual richness of the AoA, the lessons for curriculum design and assessment, and – more recently – innovative notions such as mediation and plurilingual/pluricultural competence. As is always the case for processes of innovation, it took time for the field to digest the complexity of the CEFR, which is not a straightforward document. As people have realised that there is more to the CEFR than levels, they have started to experiment with the more complex aspects of the CEFR in curricula and practice. In response to this continued and growing interest, the Council of Europe undertook a 4-year development project to more fully elaborate the concepts and operationalise them in descriptors (North & Piccardo, 2016a, 2016b). The result of this project is a *CEFR Companion Volume with New Descriptors* which explains the key aspects of the CEFR related to teaching and learning and which provides a considerably extended version of the CEFR illustrative descriptors (Council of Europe, 2018). The CEFR Companion Volume supplements the foundations to the AoA laid by the CEFR with an expansion of aspects that will further clarify and support the paradigm shift that the AoA has the potential to introduce.

As we hope will become clear in the course of the book, the CEFR initiated a broad movement towards a more complex, holistic view of language education, informed by the advances in research of the last decades, which the CEFR Companion Volume takes further. The proof of the impact of the CEFR has been the constant cross-fertilisation between the action of practitioners, curriculum developers and applied researchers working in different languages and contexts. This has created a virtuous circle in which innovative notions (e.g. mediation, plurilingualism, intercomprehension) have been tried out in the field, which in turn has fed back into conceptualisation – as one can see with the CEFR Companion Volume. This process has been assisted by several policy documents related to the CEFR, particularly two guides to plurilingual and intercultural education at a policy level (Beacco & Byram, 2007a, 2007b) and curriculum level (Beacco *et al.*, 2015), conceptual texts (e.g. Coste & Cavalli, 2015; Coste *et al.*, 1997/2009), plus projects coordinated by the European Centre for Modern Languages (e.g. FREPA/CARAP: Candelier *et al.*, 2011) and other institutions and associations. Taken together, these developments initiated by the CEFR and its action-oriented, plurilingual, intercultural approach have brought about substantial change in the vision of language education in Europe and beyond.

Unfortunately, the CEFR is often 'applied' by superimposing the CEFR levels on a traditional curriculum organised around the four skills and a grammatical progression. Confusion reigns between the CEFR, the European Language Portfolio (ELP) (with its Language Passport, Language Biography and Dossier). The ELP is intended as a tool for lifelong learning that (a) promotes language awareness, learner autonomy and plurilingual personal profiles and (b) reports such learner proficiency profiles in relation to the CEFR levels. Many people think they know what the CEFR is without having actually read it; some even think that the ELP self-assessment grid *is* the complete CEFR. The grid (included in the CEFR as Table 2) defines listening and reading ('understanding'), spoken interaction and spoken production ('speaking'), plus writing for the six levels.[1] As a result of widespread familiarity with this grid in at least Europe, it is unfortunately not uncommon even for researchers to refer to what they suppose to be the CEFR five skill model, for example:

> 'As is commonly known, the framework distinguishes five profi-
> ciencies (speaking, listening, reading, writing, and interaction) and
> describes six levels of these proficiencies with regard to one language.'
> (Backus *et al.*, 2013: 191)

The misapprehension that the CEFR proposes five skills (i.e. just splits speaking into spoken interaction and spoken production) shows just how difficult it is for people to move on from the traditional model of the four skills plus three elements: grammar, vocabulary, pronunciation (Lado, 1961). In reality the CEFR replaces the four skills with four *modes* of communication (reception, production, interaction and mediation), as explained in Chapter 5.

To summarise, the CEFR offers:

- a sophisticated model of language use;
- a rich, structured hierarchy of descriptor scales (50 in 2001; 80 in 2018);
- a discussion of the organisation of language learning and teaching, and the role of tasks;
- an educational philosophy promoting flexible curricula for plurilingual and intercultural education.

These points are elaborated in Section 5.1.4.

1.3.2 Action-orientation in the CEFR

The CEFR can be considered to be 'action-oriented' in a number of mutually supporting ways. Fundamentally, it completes the shift away from 'forward design' in curriculum planning: the systematic teaching of 'the language' from simple grammatical structures and usage to more complex and unusual structures and usage, towards 'backward design:' planning back from real-world action involving language (Richards, 2013). With the CEFR, the starting point for any planning is its view of the user/learner as a social agent with an individual profile and personal goals. What do the users/learners concerned need and want to *do* in the language(s) concerned, in terms of their interaction with other speakers, their appropriation of knowledge through language, their integration into the relevant community/ies? This perspective permeates the CEFR descriptive scheme. In communication, the user/learner's *general competences* (e.g. sociocultural competence, intercultural competence, emotional competence, professional experience) are always combined with *communicative language competences* (linguistic, sociolinguistic and pragmatic competences) and strategies (some general, some *communicative language strategies*) in carrying out the combination of *communicative language activities* necessary in order to complete a real-life, action-oriented task.

Thus, the CEFR firstly promotes a pragmatic, functional view of language and of the selection of language learning objectives. As Sickinger and Schneider (2014: 114) highlight in discussing the place of pragmatic competence in the CEFR: 'The view of language use and learning that ... [the CEFR] ... endorses is explicitly action-based, focusing on "acts of speech [that] occur within language activities" which in turn "form part of a wider social context" (Council of Europe, 2001: 9).' This is reflected in the 'can do' descriptors in the many descriptor scales, which, as Green (2012) points out, are predominantly for a range of functional language activities. Consequently, the CEFR promotes the idea of needs-based pedagogy. Which language activities (often called 'target situations') are relevant to the learner(s) concerned? The CEFR descriptor scales for language activities can be very useful as a starting point for needs analysis (see North *et al.*, 2018) and for creating needs profiles for different groups (Council of Europe, 2018). Which 'can do' objectives are suitable at the level of the learners? Which functions and notions, which microskills and language exponents, which strategies are needed? These issues are discussed further in Chapter 5.

Secondly, as mentioned above, CEFR Chapter 2 highlights the collaborative co-construction of meaning to accomplish a given task, mobilising competences and strategies that are in themselves further developed through the experience of the task. This collaborative model recognises the centrality of the social dimension in language. Interaction is not just the sum of reception and production, but introduces this new factor: the co-construction of meaning. Mediation in turn takes the dynamic nature of meaning making to another level, by underlining the constant link between the social and individual dimensions in language use and language learning (see Council of Europe, 2018; North & Piccardo, 2016a; Piccardo, 2012a). Although the 2001 CEFR text did not develop the concept of mediation to its full potential, through its vision of the user/learner as a social agent, it emphasised key notions in the socio-constructivist/sociocultural view of learning (Lantolf, 2000; Schneuwly, 2008). This laid the foundations for a thorough development of the concept of mediation activities and strategies that is now prominent in the CEFR Companion Volume. In this way, although it is not stated explicitly in the 2001 text, the CEFR descriptive scheme *de facto* gives mediation and agency key positions in the AoA, similar to the role that other scholars give them when they discuss the language learning process. These issues are discussed further in Chapters 6 and 7.

Finally, the CEFR give tasks a prominent role from an organi-sational and methodological point of view. The focus is on real-life, action-oriented tasks. Such tasks are seen as having the potential to provide coherence to the entire process of planning, teaching/learning and assessment; they are the backbone of the curriculum. Language learning happens both in a formal context and process and in informal and non-formal contexts and ways (OECD, n.d.) through meaningful iterative action. The CEFR view of tasks tries to capture this breadth of the learning process by overcoming the limits of the classroom and bringing real life into the teaching/learning process, thus fostering learners' awareness and autonomy. Purposeful outcome-oriented tasks involving realistic action as well as language, agency, personal engagement and collaboration as well as practice, are implicit in the AoA. These issues are discussed further in Chapters 4 and 7.

Taken together, the three aspects discussed above (functional perspective; collaborative co-construction; action-oriented tasks) imply a shift of approach that is in fact happening on the ground in different contexts. But to what extent do practitioners engaged in this shift have a rationale to support it? How does this shift reflect developments in the conceptualisation and theorisation of language learning? How is it more than the 'communicative approach'? These are the issues we discuss in this book.

1.3.3 Theorising a new notion: The action-oriented approach (AoA)

As we have just seen, the CEFR planted several seeds that would germinate in the years following its publication. However, in the same way that this happens in nature, in order to germinate, seeds need to find fertile soil, the right conditions of light and temperature, and to receive the right amount of water. Furthermore, little plants often need to be taken care of in order to grow strong. It is clear that most if not all of the seeds planted by the CEFR found good soil and the right conditions – the very recent publication of the CEFR Companion Volume is proof of this. In turn that soil has been nurtured and those conditions favoured by the new sensibility and vision that can be observed at different levels, in society, in scientific theorisations and epistemologies, and in practices at the level of the class. In all these areas, there has been a shift towards a more complex and dynamic view, fostered by the need to respond to increasing diversity in social spaces and to consider socially enhanced forms of collaborative work and learning. The correspondent need for all actors involved to be able to purposefully and strategically exert their agency in an informed way calls for a clear understanding of the new notions and models that can help them in this process. Not only was the AoA one of those seeds that would germinate, but it also proved to be a broad and solid enough concept to put the contributions of different theories, epistemologies and conceptualisations at the service of innovation in Second Language Education (SLE). This book is an attempt to make this complexity and multiplicity visible and to provide a broad and coherent theorisation of the AoA.

1.3.3.1 Emergence of the AoA

In the English version of the CEFR the term 'action-oriented' occurs only five times (including once where it is used in a paragraph title). The French version alternates the term *'approche actionnelle'* with the term *'perspective actionnelle'*, something which seems to suggest a wider angle. However, one would expect that the upfront use of the term in Chapter 2, which announces the 'view of language use and learning' adopted by the CEFR (Council of Europe, 2001: 9) would make for a much stronger impact of the AoA in the field, immediately triggering a series of reflections and studies on the subject, something which has not necessarily happened in these terms, as we mentioned above.

Several reasons can explain this slow start of the AoA. One is the CEFR itself, which claims more than once to be methodologically neutral, presumably for political reasons considering that the CEFR would be used in numerous contexts characterised by diverse educational and pedagogical cultures. A second, rather banal, issue that for a long time masked the AoA was the near exclusive use of the CEFR for assessment purposes, and the very unbalanced visibility of the different aspects of the CEFR in the field, with the levels being by far the most prominent and the pedagogical dimension being relegated to the back of the picture. However, these are only superficial explanations, as in reality the AoA in a sense provided a name for something that had not yet been invented, and at the same time – as is often the case – helped create that something precisely by naming it.

It is not surprising that there was the debate we mentioned above – concerning whether the AoA was indeed something new or just the continuation of something already existing, only presented with a new label. Neither is it surprising that this same debate took place in France, homeland of the famous 17th century *'Querelle des anciens et des modernes'* where the alleged perfection of the ancient, the classics, was opposed to the danger and lack of balance of the modern, the innovative. With the AoA the CEFR suggests that established approaches, even when they are very good, are not untouchable, but can be revisited, renewed and even replaced, since innovation is at the core of language education and language education needs to be in line with societal developments and new visions of teaching and learning. In general, the AoA was especially forward-looking as it built on advances in the conceptualisation of teaching and learning that had been informed by major social and educational theories, as we will see in Chapter 3. However, as happened with other innovative concepts that the CEFR introduced, namely mediation and plurilingualism, the theoretical density behind the AoA was not elaborated in the CEFR, thus leaving the concept underdeveloped and at the mercy of varying interpretations.

Finally, there was a more general reason for the AoA not to immediately take off, a practical one: the idea of acting together in order to produce something, rather than just communicating and exchanging information and opinions, was greatly boosted by the massive introduction of technologies in all aspects of human life and especially in the professional world. It is now extremely common to work at a distance on a collective project with a specifically defined outcome. Project work has become the bread and butter of an increasing number of professions and has been fully integrated into educational practice. We are witnessing an expansion of this way of working and learning, which overcomes linguistic and cultural barriers. This way of thinking, including the concepts of 'beta versions', 'pooled partial competences' and 'work in progress' – all essential features of the AoA in practice – were not yet so common in the 1990s.

In spite of all these hindrances and the relatively small space it was given in the CEFR text, as we suggested above, the AoA was a seed that would germinate in the following years. The time would, in fact, soon be ripe for the paradigm shift that the CEFR announced with the AoA.

1.3.3.2 The user/learner as a social agent – (and the AoA)

The idea that students should be seen as fires to be lit rather than vases to be filled has a very long history, coming to us from Plutarch through Rabelais. So is the idea that learning cannot be a passive endeavour, something that has been more recently strongly advocated and has been at the basis of constructivism. However, the consideration of learners as social agents, the core concept of the AoA, takes this idea of personal engagement and active participation and involvement to another level.

While the term 'learners' usually conveys a rather neutral and unidimensional idea of the different human beings that are engaged in the process of learning a language, we all know that each of those human beings has multiple 'faces', i.e. multiple roles, connections and identities, which interplay and overlap in the most diverse modalities, constellations, roles, and socialisations (Coïaniz, 2001; Lahire, 1998). 'As a social agent, each individual forms relationships with a widening cluster of overlapping social groups, which together define identity' (Council of Europe, 2001: 1). This multiplicity of relationships, which contributes to the shaping of unique individual personalities, is not a trivial characteristic. It can precisely spark a process of (co)construction of learning and meaning-making. As the adjective 'social' underlines, the way language learners operate is as individuals who act, alone or in groups (Carson, 2012), who indeed show initiative and willingness to act, and in doing so make mindful decisions about the type of language or languages they use. But they are also accountable for their actions and they are aware of the way their actions might – and actually do – affect others (van Lier, 2010). In a nutshell, social agents are individuals (learners) who exert their agency in a defined sociocultural context. Social agents are defined by the CEFR as 'members of society who have tasks (not exclusively language-related) to accomplish in a given set of circumstances, in a specific environment and within a particular field of action' (Council of Europe, 2001: 9). This definition is provided by the CEFR precisely in relation to the AoA, which in fact brings to the fore the need for language learning in real-life situations that are communicatively meaningful and require a strategic decision-making process (Bourguignon, 2010; Piccardo, 2010a, 2014a; Piccardo & Galante, 2018).

The real-life task, where social agents are engaged, is the core of the AoA, since it provides the unifying frame within which all actions make sense and serve a purpose. As we will see more in detail later in the book, action-oriented tasks do not equate to the tasks of Task-based Language Teaching (TBLT), as they have been described in, for example, the work of Ellis (2003), Nunan (2004), Skehan (1998) and Willis and Willis (2007). The AoA goes further than classic TBLT, insofar as it is informed not only by communication theories and discourse analysis, but by multiple theories (e.g. communication, discourse, activity, sociocultural, and complexity).

As 'communication calls upon the whole human being' (Council of Europe, 2001: 1), the rational and emotional dimension are both called on, exactly as they are in real life. Fundamentally, interpersonal language use is at least – if not more – important than transactional use, since every transaction is embedded in a sociocultural situation that calls for a social interaction which will, in very many cases, determine the success – or failure – of the transaction. The need to consider all dimensions, functions and aspects of language and language use linked to the different vision of what constitutes real-life orientation has an impact on the view of the individual who uses and learns those languages. Here comes a fundamental characteristic of the social agent: action is not strictly reduced to language, and is socially situated, thus greatly influenced by all sort of pragmatic elements and goals. For Richer (2009), the social agent and the vision of action which characterise the AoA align with attempts in linguistics to develop a general theory of action (Vernant, 1997) which aims to 'elaborate a pragmatics not just as the study of effective uses of the language, but defined as a real general theory of action, encompassing its language and non-language dimensions' (Vernant, 1997: 20, our translation). It is precisely this move away from a strictly linguistic perspective, in the most traditional sense, that characterises the action of the social agent, and thus the AoA.

As we will see more in detail in Chapter 3, a major shift has taken place in recent decades in research on (language) education, which brought to the fore the social and situated nature of all human phenomena and thus the difficulty of embracing a 'one-size-fits-all' model of learning, one that only considers the cognitive side. Poehner identifies different philosophies of science developed during the twentieth century that informed the development of theoretical reflection in second/foreign language education, namely post-positivism and more recently interpretivism. As Poehner points out 'post-positivism represents the clearest effort to emulate a natural science model and is easily identifiable as the dominant orientation to SLA. Interpretivism, with its emphasis on the social construction of individual meanings and advocating of qualitative research methods, is arguably the preeminent counter to post-positivism' (2016: 135). To these two philosophies he adds Marxian dialectical-materialism, which 'concurs with the position of interpretivism that human beings are meaning-making agents. Within dialectical materialism, however, agency is understood as changing the world while also changing humanity, both at a collective and individual level' (Poehner, 2016: 141). By doing this he proposes a move from the vision *humans as natural objects* (post-positivism) through *humans as meaning-making individuals* (interpretivism), to *humans as historical agents of change* (Marxian dialectical-materialism).

The fundamental rejection of thinking in discrete and often contrasting entities and concepts (e.g. internal vs external, individual vs social), and the opposite idea that one needs to think of all these entities and concepts in terms of dialectic units if one wants to capture the complexity of any human phenomenon and learning, is a fundamental feature of sociocultural theory, one that actually provides it with its cohesiveness. In the same way, the impossibility of thinking of any one of the concepts and aspects involved in the process of teaching and learning languages in isolation without engaging with all the others is what characterises the AoA and its innovation potential in language education.

1.3.4 The AoA in the conceptualisation of language education

Where does the AoA position itself in this shift of conceptualisation of language, language use and language education in general? What kind of theoretical framework does it draw inspiration from? Finally what educational philosophy does it embrace?

The quest for a methodological Holy Grail (Piccardo, 2016a) has haunted the development of language education for over a century, if we consider the opposition between the traditional grammar translation method and the new 'direct' method that appeared at the turn of the 20th century. This quest has manifested itself in sterile contrasts between absolute positions, which usually aimed to wipe away all that had been constructed beforehand. Attempts to maintain an interdisciplinary attitude and perspective have usually been isolated as the mainstream embraced an 'either-or' game, though they have continued to exist. The same type of strong opposition between incompatible poles that has characterised the development of methodologies in language education has also marked other scientific domains that nurture reflection in language education, namely linguistics and psychology. In linguistics, the era of structural linguistics (going from Saussure's work at the beginning of the 20th century to structuralism in the 50s and early 60s) still had a strong connection with other human sciences, particularly anthropology, as it was interested in the study of the different environments, the different 'worlds'. 'In such a context it was natural that the relation between language and the environment, and between languages, played an important role in linguistic theorizing' (van Lier, 2004: 167). This remained the case even though structural linguistics was greatly influenced by the behaviouristic theories which were dominant in the mid-century.

It was the harsh criticism of behaviourism by Chomsky and the subsequent cognitive revolution that wiped all that away and 'built an impermeable wall between the individual and the social' (van Lier, 2004: 167). This put linguistics in the realm of the brain alongside cognitive sciences and left all the context-related human sciences, including sociolinguistics, exclusively on the social side. This dichotomy has been very powerful ever since, even though some linguists raised critical voices. One of the most prominent and relevant for the AoA has been Halliday (1973, 1975, 1978) who stressed how linguistics cannot be conceptualised independently from the context, and who developed a social-semiotic perspective, which we will discuss in greater depth in Chapter 3. Finally in psychology, a similar process of pendulum oscillation has taken place, giving rise to opposite views and powerful clashes from the very beginning. Reed (1996) identifies four crises and corresponding revolutions in the development of psychology. For our field it is interesting to notice how the rise of behaviourism was immediately challenged by all those who called for a more holistic view (van Lier, 2004: 165, mentions in particular Gestalt psychology, Vygotsky's sociocultural-historical approach, and Piaget's genetic epistemology). However, behaviourism continued to dominate the field until its intrinsic limitations became visible and it was swept away by the cognitive revolution. It is also important to see how cognitivism also showed its limitations, namely its lack of consideration of environmental and social factors, which gave rise to what Reed (1996) saw as a revolution towards a more ecological perspective that adopted a holistic view of psychology as a science that studies all that is human. It is not surprising, therefore, that Vygotsky's theories have received a new boost of interest, giving rise to the sociocultural theory, which aims to provide a holistic and dialectic framework to such complex, human phenomenon as the development of language in general and the learning of new languages in particular.

We will see in Chapter 3 that this shift towards a more articulated, situated and flexible view of all human phenomena draws upon the contribution of different theories and conceptualisations. This shift helps us to provide some answers to the three questions we asked earlier: Where does the AoA position itself in this shift of conceptualisation of language, language use and language education in general? What kind of theoretical framework does it draw inspiration from? And finally, what educational philosophy does it embrace?

As we will see throughout the book, the AoA positions itself precisely within this new complex, holistic and ecological paradigm of language education, which alone can provide the necessary coherence to the different aspects that come into play in the delicate process of teaching and learning languages.

1.3.5 Potential of the AoA: Agency and mediation

The notions of action, mediation and action, mediation and agency (Bandura, 1989, 2001) recur throughout the book as they are central to the AoA. Action is at the basis of the AoA and the notion of agency is subsumed in the CEFR's view of the learner as a 'social agent', as we will explain. Mediation, which was briefly introduced in the CEFR descriptive scheme, has recently been the object of extensive further conceptualisation with the CEFR Companion Volume, which informed the creation of a wealth of specific descriptors for different aspects of mediation. Both concepts – social agent and mediation – have great innovation potential for SLE. However, considering the extent of the shift in perspective that the AoA implies, it is not surprising that it took time for the depth of the AoA to emerge. These two key notions which inform the AoA and constitute the turning point of methodological innovation – agency and mediation – themselves needed some 20 years to be fully conceptualised and then operationalised for practitioners.

The AoA itself took years to take shape within the teaching community through a process of bottom-up experimentation among practitioners and reflection among scholars through articles, edited books, journal issues, etc. (e.g. Byrnes, 2007; Goullier, 2007a; Lion-Olivieri & Liria, 2009; Morrow, 2004; North, 2014; Piccardo, 2006,

2014a; Piccardo *et al.*, 2011a; Rosen, 2009). In fact, the concepts presented in the CEFR published in 2001 prompted a shift in language education that needed time to be fully understood and even more time to be implemented, a process that is certainly still in its inception. Very often those concepts were still in a very initial form (Piccardo, 2012a). The time is now ripe to see all those concepts as interrelated and cross-fertilizing. It is not by chance that a new Council of Europe project has just been completed that produced the CEFR Companion volume (Council of Europe, 2018), which developed precisely all those dimensions that were left incomplete in the CEFR 2001, namely the crucial areas of mediation and plurilingualism, of literature appreciation, and areas for which research and conceptualisation has moved further, like phonological competence. In this sense, the CEFR (2001) and the CEFR Companion Volume (2018) need to be considered as a unified tool, one that has evolved and refined itself on the basis of the advances in SLE and of the paradigm shift towards a more holistic, complex and ecological turn. As such it has fostered, nourished and accompanied the development of the AoA, as we will see in the various chapters of this book.

Note

(1) The original version of the self-assessment grid in the draft CEFR (Council of Europe, 1996, 1998) and the prototype *European Language Portfolio* (Schneider *et al.*, 2000) contained reception, interaction and production, each divided into spoken and written. But in the process of finalising the ELP Passport, this was changed to the current version, which for the sake of coherence was then substituted for the original in the CEFR at publication in 2001.

2 The Notion of Competence: An Overview

This chapter will outline the way different views of 'competence' are united in the CEFR and AoA, and will discuss the impact of this broader and more complex vision of competence on pedagogy. The expression 'competence' comes from the Latin *competens*, present participle of *competō* meaning both to be sound, capable, applicable and to coincide, to happen at the same time. The Middle English *competent* is borrowed from the 14th-century Old French term *compétent* meaning sufficient, appropriate, suitable. In the late 15th century the term was applied to jurisdictions: an institution was, or was not, competent to give a judgement in a specific case (Concise Oxford Dictionary of English Etymology; Richer, 2012). This meaning is still given by the Oxford English Dictionary and is common in expressions like 'I'm afraid that's outside our/my competence' (meaning area of expertise). From the 18th century the meaning generalised again, the German adjective *kompetent*, for example, coming to mean responsible *(for)* or *decisive* (Grebe & Drosdowski, 1963: 350, cited in Pikkarainen, 2014: 623).

In the Chomskyan tradition of applied linguistics, competence, in opposition to performance, was considered as an invisible trait. The move from an idealised, innate competence to a series of socially situated communicative competences, developed since Hymes' publication in 1972, has still not overcome the competence/performance opposition. A parallel tradition has developed since the 1960s in applied psychology and in the world of work, aiming to break with the idea of a static relationship between qualification(s) and tasks at work by stressing the capacity of the individual to take initiatives and operate autonomously. Competence in this sense corresponds to the mobilisation of resources in a specific situation. In this vision, competence is seen as being contextualised, plural, complex, possibly social, and implying a 'meta' dimension as individuals reflect on their choices. In a word, competence is seen as the capacity to deal with unforeseen situations. The CEFR unites and extends Hymes' notion of communicative competence and the view of competence as mobilisation of resources, typical of the world of work, in a clear vision of multiple competences including general competences (*savoir, savoir-faire, savoir-être*) and communicative language competences (pragmatic, linguistic, sociolinguistic) that are interdependent and expressed through a multidimensional set of descriptor scales. The model shows how in action-oriented tasks, competences are supplemented by communicative language strategies in order to accomplish a task by performing one or more communicative language activities (reception, interaction, production and mediation) in one – or a combination of – language(s) under specific conditions and constraints. In turn, the accomplishment of the task contributes to the further development of the individual's competence, in an iterative process.

2.1 Competence: Evolution of an Elusive Notion

It is very challenging to produce a definitive description of the notion of competence. It does not help that competence is often defined in ways that are mutually contradictory, even within the same academic discipline (e.g. psychology, education, world of work and professional training) as Castellotti (2002) points out. One group of authors suggest there are almost as many definitions as users of the term (Miller *et al.*, 1988). As a result it has often been stated to be a 'fuzzy' notion – but at the same time one that is becoming more and more central in education.

Things are further complicated by different traditions in the US, UK and Europe and by the fact that the English concept of 'proficiency' does not find an adequate translation in many other languages. At the time the CEFR was written, it was common in English to talk of 'language proficiency scales' or 'scales of language proficiency' and the term 'proficiency' is in fact used 138 times in the CEFR itself. But 'proficiency scale' translates as *échelle de compétence* in French and *Kompetenzskala* in German, to give just two examples. The lack of a consistent distinction between competence and proficiency throughout a work with multiple authors was in fact criticised at the time (Vollmer, 2003). However, Vollmer himself, in what became a classic definition of language proficiency, only defined it as 'what language proficiency tests measure' (1981: 152) adding that it was 'somewhere in between the performance and competence (in the Chomskyan sense of the terms)' (1981: 160).

The term 'language proficiency' also has the connotation of a person having a certain global proficiency level. This idea shows the enduring influence of the concept of General Language Proficiency (GLP) and the Unitary Competence Hypothesis (UCH) related to it (Oller, 1983a, 1983b) that held sway in the 1970s and led to the development of cloze tests. Language proficiency scales before the CEFR continued this tradition, having, at most, scales for each of the four skills. This unidimensional view contrasts with the way the term 'competence' is used today. There is a move towards a more articulated vision of 'competence profile,' reflecting the new, contextualised, situated view of language – and of competences in general. Today, the word 'competence' also brings with it an overtone of action, in the sense of the ability to do something. As Pikkarainen (2014: 622) writes in relation to the philosophy of education the 'concept of competence is central in understanding all action and thus an essential but neglected part of any viable theory of action.' An action is always situated, it takes place in a context, of which any person either does or does not have experience. It is difficult to claim competence in something you have never experienced. This experiential perspective is nowadays shared in the worlds of education, work and therapy, and is reflected in both language teaching/learning and increasingly in competence-based curricula for other disciplines.

2.2 Competence in Linguistics and Applied Linguistics

Before we turn to competence as understood in the worlds of work and education, let us look in a little more detail at the (applied) linguistic perspective. It is widely known that Chomsky introduced the term competence as 'the underlying system of rules that has been mastered by the speaker-hearer' (1965: 4). Chomsky saw competence as a mental state *excluding* ability: 'it does not seem to me to be quite accurate to take 'knowledge of English' to be a capacity or ability, though it enters into the capacity or ability exercised in language use' (1975: 23). Later, he says: 'To know a language, I am assuming, is to be in a certain mental state' (Chomsky, 1980: 48). For Chomsky, being competent is a question of knowing rules and theoretically knowing how to use them, but does not include actual use, as this is of the realm of performance.

2.2.1 Competence vs performance

Right at the beginning of his seminal work, Chomsky makes the 'fundamental distinction between *competence* (the speaker-hearer's knowledge of his language) and *performance* (the actual use of language in concrete situations' (Chomsky, 1965: 4). Performance 'obviously could not directly reflect competence' (Chomsky, 1965: 4) because of all the false starts, slips and changes of plan that characterise natural speech. Linguistic theory, for Chomsky, 'is mentalist, since it is concerned with discovering a mental reality underlying actual behaviour' (Chomsky, 1965: 4). In such a perspective, competence is an abstract and perfect concept. Natural language is just the imperfect data with which the linguist (or child learning a language) has to work in order to divine the generative structure of the language. In spite of its conceptual limitations, 'native speaker competence' was for long seen as the theoretical goal of all language learners, who were seen as developing through stages of interlanguage (Corder, 1981; Selinker, 1972) on their route towards it. This was reflected in language proficiency scales before the CEFR, which all took the proficiency of a native speaker (or educated native speaker, or well-educated native speaker) as their top level (Liskin-Gasparro, 1984, 2003; Lowe, 1985; Wilds, 1975; Wylie & Ingram, 1995).

2.2.2 Communicative competence

With his concept of communicative competence, Hymes (1972a) overcame the Chomskyan dichotomy of competence and performance. Hymes expands the notion of competence by listing four aspects of which grammaticality, i.e. that something is formally possible (roughly corresponding to Chomsky's notion of competence) is but one. The others are feasibility (i.e. that something can be reasonably processed by human beings), appropriateness (i.e. that is adequate in relation to the context) and, finally, accepted usage (i.e. whether or not something is in fact done), since in fact 'a sentence maybe be possible, feasible, appropriate and not occur' (Hymes, 1972a: 286). Furthermore and fundamentally, for Hymes 'competence is dependent upon both (tacit) *knowledge* and (ability for) *use*' (1972a: 282) and: 'The specification of *ability for use* as part of competence allows for the role of noncognitive factors, such as motivation, as partly determining competence' (1972a: 282–283).

Hymes' concept of communicative competence includes a range of factors that have little to do with knowledge, but reflect interactional rituals: '... capacities in interaction such as courage, gameness, gallantry, composure, presence of mind, dignity, stage confidence ...' that Hymes takes from Goffman (Goffman, 1967: 224, cited in Hymes, 1972b: 64). A person's repertoire of communication behaviours includes 'ways of speaking' within a community (Hymes, 1974: 199): 'The communicative competence of persons comprises in part a knowledge of determinate ways of speaking' (Hymes, 1986: 58), which would be characterised by pragmatic, semantic, morphological, paralinguistic and sociolinguistic aspects. As Widdowson summarises: 'For Chomsky, competence is knowledge. For Hymes, competence is knowledge and ability' (1989: 132).

Habermas (1970) also criticised Chomsky's approach, calling it 'monological' (Habermas, 1970: 366); he also said it was related to an 'information transfer' perspective (Habermas, 1970: 367). Rather than starting from the ideal native speaker he posited the ideal speech situation, with a focus on culturally-determined, inter-subjective semantics and pragmatics:

In order to participate in normal discourse the speaker must have at his disposal, in addition to his linguistic competence, basic qualifications of speech and symbolic interaction (role-behaviour), which we may call communicative competence. Thus communicative competence means the mastery of an ideal speech situation. (Habermas, 1970: 367)

He also said that 'a theory of communicative competence can thus be developed in terms of universal pragmatics' (Habermas, 1970: 368). Finally, Habermas rejected Chomsky's idea that competence was innate or mentalist in humans, independently of socialisation through speech situations:

> Universal meanings, which arise in all natural languages, neither automatically precede all experience, nor are they necessarily rooted in the cognitive equipment of the human organism prior to all socialization. (Habermas, 1970: 363)

For Hymes too, social factors are not only characteristic of performance, they are intrinsic to competence as well. In discussing Hymes' view, Coste *et al.* (2012) put it like this: 'The differentiated nature of competences and the inherent heterogeneity of linguistic communities requires that social factors need to be taken into consideration, not just at the level of performance, but most of all in relation to competence itself' (2012: 106, our translation).

Hymes and Habermas' contextualised, dialogical view of competence aligns with Halliday's concept of *meaning potential* (what a speaker *can mean*), which we will discuss in Chapter 3, which Halliday himself claimed to be 'not unlike Dell Hymes' notion of "communicative competence"' (Halliday, 1973: 54).

2.2.3 Different competences, different models

The debate between Chomsky and Hymes sparked a period of intense reflection and exchange in applied linguistics, which would lead to the development of a number of models of communicative competence, as we will see below. Chomsky himself started the process by further developing his own model with the introduction of a distinction between linguistic competence and pragmatic competence. However, he still claimed to be talking only about knowledge: 'knowledge of conditions and manner of appropriate use in conformity with various purposes' (Chomsky, 1980: 224). This distinction is picked up by Davies (1989: 169) with *knowledge what* and *knowledge how* and Spolsky who prefers *knowing a language*, and *knowing how to use a language* (Spolsky, 1989: 50–51). However, Widdowson criticised Chomsky's new position saying he was being 'inconsistent in his use of terms' since 'it is evident that by pragmatic competence he means a kind of *ability*' (1989: 130) and not just knowledge. This view was clearly shared by Levinson, one of the fathers of the discipline of pragmatics, who introduced his book with that title by saying: '... to invoke Chomsky's distinction between competence and performance, pragmatics is concerned solely with performance principles of language use' (1983: 3). As such it concerns itself with such areas as conversational management, discourse organisation, speech acts and implicature from contextual and co-textual cues.

A series of models of communicative competence appeared in applied linguistics during the 1980s and early 1990s. Sometimes these were called models of communicative language proficiency, but as can be seen, they all focused on similar characteristics in declining communicative language competence into constitutive aspects like linguistic competence, pragmatic (or discourse) competence, sociolinguistic and/or sociocultural competence, and sometimes referential competence (= knowledge of the world) and strategic competence. Most authors shuffled the grouping of categories in succeeding versions of their models, reflecting the difficulty of arriving at a definitive version. Table 2.1 compares the main models.

As can be seen in Table 2.1, all models contain linguistic/language competence (grammar, vocabulary, pronunciation). In addition, van Ek also includes language functions in this category, and Bachman includes textual competence here, since there is no separate discourse category in at least that version of his model. All the models include sociolinguistic and/or sociocultural competence, sometimes with one subsumed in the other. Canale and Swain (1980) included discourse competence under sociolinguistic (separated out in Canale's later 1983 version) – while Bachman (and Palmer) include sociolinguistic competence, together with illocutionary/functional competence, under pragmatic competence. This really shows the difficulty of drawing any definitive line between these three closely related aspects. Bachman (1990) is the first to use the distinction made by Chomsky (1980) between linguistic and pragmatic competence and to reflect the development of pragmatics during the 1980s. Half the models contain knowledge of the world, half do not – presumably because it is considered a general competence (as it is in the CEFR). Moirand is the only one to specifically mention 'ability for use;' her definition for each component starts with the phrase: 'knowledge of and ability to use ...', explicitly rejecting Chomsky's division between competence and performance. Ability for use is obviously included in Bachman's model, since this is a model of proficiency – which includes use – and this also shows itself in both the psycho-physiological mechanisms and the broad view taken of strategic competence. Bergeron et al. (1984) are the first to broaden the concept of strategic competence and Celce-Murcia et al. (1995) are the first to put functional competence, which is so central to the AoA, in a separate category 'actional competence' – but curiously take the older, more reductionist view of strategic competence.

Table 2.1 Applied linguistics models of communicative competence and language ability

Canale & Swain, 1980; Canale, 1983	Moirand, 1982	Bergeron et al., 1984	van Ek, 1986 & Trim, 1990/2001	Bachman, 1990	Bachman & Palmer, 1996	Celce-Murca et al., 1995
Grammatical competence: (lexical items, rules of word formation, sentence formation, literal meaning, pronunciation and spelling)	Linguistic competence: - phonetic models - lexical models - grammatical models - textual models of the system of the language	Linguistic competence	Linguistic competence - Language functions - General notions - Specific notions - Grammar & intonation - Vocabulary and idiom	Language competence - Grammatical competence (Lexis, morph., syntax) - Textual competence	Organisation knowledge - Grammatical knowledge (including vocabulary and phonology) - Textual knowledge	Linguistic Knowledge
Sociolinguistic competence (*including Discourse in Canale & Swain, 1980*)	Sociocultural competence - including interactional norms	Sociolinguistic competence (including Discourse)	Sociolinguistic competence	Pragmatic competence - Illocutionary comp - Sociolinguistic competence.	Pragmatic knowledge - Functional knowledge - Sociolinguistic knowledge	Actional competence
		Sociocultural competence	Sociocultural competence			Sociocultural competence (including sociolinguistic)
Discourse competence (*Not in Canale & Swain, 1980*)	Discourse competence (in context of situation)	*(included in Sociolinguistic)*	Discourse competence			Discourse knowledge

Knowledge of the world (Referential)	Knowledge of the world (Referential)	-	Knowledge of the world	Knowledge of the world	-
-	Strategic competence (interactional: maintain and manage)	Compensatory competence	Strategic competence (Assessment, Planning, Execution)	Metalinguistic strategies (Assessment, Planning, Execution)	Strategic Competence (seen as compensatory)
Strategic competence (compensatory)			Psycho-physiological Mechanisms: (Mode: recep, prod.; Channel: oral/aural, visual)		

As we will see later in this chapter, these models influenced the presentation of communicative language competence in the CEFR (CEFR 5.2). There are considerable similarities between the presentation in the CEFR and that in the final two models (Bachman & Palmer, 1996; Celce-Murcia *et al.*, 1995), which were all three produced at the same time. Indeed the reporting of the Bachman and Palmer model in Celce-Murcia *et al.*'s article is incorrect on several points, indicating that they were working with a draft. This points yet again to the fluidity of these models and the overlap between categories. Celce-Murcia herself later provides a substantially revised version of her own model (Celce-Murcia, 2007), underlining this point.

The earlier models chose to maintain Chomsky's competence/performance distinction. For example, Canale and Swain talk of communicative competence and communicative performance, listing aspects included in each (Canale & Swain, 1980), and therefore considering it unnecessary to include psycholinguistic processes in their model of communicative competence). Gumperz in his extension to discourse-processing conventions, knowledge of cultural norms etc. (Gumperz, 1982, 1984) does much the same. Loveday at that time criticised this representation of communicative competence as 'etiquette; speech acts; routine situational language; discourse machinery' etc. He felt that one of the most fundamental points of Hymes' argument was being ignored, namely: 'the sociocultural framework in which all linguistic behaviour is embedded' (Loveday, 1982: 124).

Despite such criticisms, all these models were certainly helpful in broadening the perspective of applied linguistics and curriculum developers, and in highlighting the multifaceted nature of communicative competence. However, as with every form of categorisation, they cannot avoid being in a way artificial by deciding to place boundaries here rather than there, as it is extremely difficult to neatly separate aspects of something as holistic, individual and context-dependent as communication. Not surprisingly, therefore, an attempt in Toronto to validate the Canale and Swain model by operationalising the different components in separate tests (Harley *et al.*, 1990) demonstrated the impossibility of isolating individual components. Indeed, it became increasingly accepted that all the different aspects overlap and interrelate.

Besides formal models, there were also other attempts to conceptualise communicative competence in SLE. Savignon in 1972 focused in her assessment criteria on the sociocultural and pragmatic aspects that Hymes had highlighted, for example *naturalness* and *poise* (= 'the capacity to suppress and conceal any tendency to become shamefaced' Goffman, 1972: 321). Her 'accuracy' was message precision; grammatical knowledge wasn't mentioned at all. In a later work she said one should study experts to identify 'the behaviours of those considered successful at what they do, specifically, the identification of the characteristics of good communicators' (Savignon, 1983: 4). As we will see below, this approach of Savignon's reflects more the approach adopted outside linguistics, particularly in the world of work. The idea of studying the characteristics of good communicators is also fundamental in communication theory.

As a matter of fact, from a communication theory perspective, it has always been clear that competence included both knowledge and ability. Wiemann (1977) followed Goffman and Hymes and posited a model of communicative competence that included '(1) affiliation/support, (2) social relaxation, (3) empathy, (4) behavioural flexibility, and (5) interaction management skills.' This approach was relational: focused on the relationship between the speaker and the conversational partner(s). In 1980, Wiemann and Backlund explained that: 'unlike the linguistic view of competence and performance, the communication view considers performance as part of competence – not as a separate concept' (1980: 188). It is worth noting that they mention empathy, behavioural flexibility and interaction management as 'the most clearly defined' dimensions of communicative competence (Wiemann & Backlund, 1980: 185). Recently, Canagarajah (2018) has also criticised the narrow view of competence taken in applied linguistics, pointing out that communicative competence involves far more than simply verbal language and that in practice it also tends to involve the exploitation of and mobilisation of resources – even from different periods of time – ('bricolage:' 2018: 282) and combination with aspects of the context ('assemblage:' 2018: 271). This idea that competence is always situated, and that what one can mean is dependent on what is available in the context, echoes the ideas of Halliday and of related ecological approaches that stress the importance of 'affordances' in the environment, which we will address in Sections 3.4 and 3.9 respectively. Such broader, situated views of competence, involving mobilisation and collectivity, are not uncommon in the worlds of work and education, to which we now turn.

2.3 Competence in the World of Education and Work

Wiemann and Backlund state that competence is 'a combination of knowledge and skill' and that 'proficiency in skills ... is required for the manifestation of communicative competence' (1980: 190). They tied this to effective behaviour. This type of definition of competence as a combination of knowledge and skills has become standard in the Anglo-Saxon world in the worlds of education and work. In this connection, 'skills' means practical abilities, such as being able to draw, use a computer, swim, drive a car, use a machine or program, etc. In an educational context, 'skills' could mean, among other things autonomous learning skills, analytical and critical thinking skills, listening and observing skills, flexibility and adaptability, cooperation skills, etc. (from Barrett, 2016).

Competence models with the categories (a) knowledge, (b) skills and (c) attitudes have become common in professional training (the KSA model: Delamare le Diest & Winterton, 2005: 29) and education. This traditional, tripartite division can be traced back through Bloom and Krathwohl's (1956) taxonomy and even further to Pestalozzi's concept of Head, Hand and Heart. In several European documents and taxonomies produced over the last two decades, the KSA model has been used as an organising principle. For example, in one of the studies leading up to the CEFR, Byram *et al.* (1996) and Byram (1997) divided sociocultural competence (taken as general competence in the CEFR) into knowledge, skills and attitudes. 'Values' has recently appeared as a fourth category to KSA in several projects. *The European Profile for Language Teacher Education* (Kelly & Grenfell, 2004), for instance, uses (a) knowledge and understanding, (b) skills and strategies and (c) values; the Council of Europe's recent Competences for Democratic Culture (Barrett, 2016) uses (a) values, (b) attitudes, (c) skills, (d) knowledge and critical understanding. In all of these models, there is an assumption that these various aspects of competence are integrated in any action. As Barrett puts it, competence is a dynamic process involving: 'the ability to mobilise and deploy relevant values, attitudes, skills, knowledge and/or understanding in order to respond appropriately and effectively to the demands, challenges and opportunities that are presented by a given type of context' (Barrett, 2016: 23).

In the European Union, the notion of key competences for citizens has become a central policy issue. As opposed to simply transmitting knowledge, the purpose of education is to prepare students for social and professional life. This is a continuation of the 'modernist' approach to education that started in the latter part of the nineteenth century, with the development from education seen as the transfer of knowledge in an elite to mass education for personal mobility in a meritocracy (Dolz, 2002). John Trim's (2012) description of the conflict since the 1880s between the 'modern' and 'classical' approaches to education in general and foreign language learning in particular, and the place of the CEFR in that process, is a reminder of just how slow the pace of any such change can be. In recent decades, there have been a number of initiatives launched by the European Commission in order to integrate traditional education, professional training and experiential development, partly by 'providing "ladders" for those who have had fewer opportunities for formal education and training but have nonetheless developed competence experientially' (Delamare le Diest & Winterton, 2005: 28).

The EU Key Competences Recommendation (European Commission, 2006)[1] sets out eight key competences each stated to be a combination of knowledge, skills and attitudes. On the EU's website it is explicitly stated that '[m]any of the competences overlap and interlock. Transversal skills, such as critical thinking, creativity, initiative or problem solving are present throughout the framework'.[2] The eight key competences are:

(1) Communication in the mother tongue;
(2) Communication in foreign languages;
(3) Mathematical competence and basic competences in science and technology;
(4) Digital competence;
(5) Learning to learn;
(6) Social and civic competences;
(7) Sense of initiative and entrepreneurship, and
(8) Cultural awareness and expression.

There are, however, very different professional and educational traditions with regard to competences, which causes complications, as Pikkarainen explains:

> There seem to be at least three different broad and established uses of the concept. The first is the behaviourist US tradition initiated by psychological studies about the personality characteristics behind superior performance. ... Central to this discourse is the concept of competency (plural: competencies) as behaviourally defined, task-based skills, and models for competency-based training (CBT). This thinking is then partly superseded by a more UK-centred Anglo-Saxon conception, which is broader and more functional, but still quite limited. Many writers regard continental German and French conceptions to be more fruitful because of their broader view on occupations instead of specific jobs and separate skills. (Pikkarainen, 2014: 623; see also Delamare le Diest & Winterton, 2005: 33–38 for more detail)

A 'competency' approach is usually associated with checklists of requirements, expressed as descriptors of behaviours, for a specific job. This is particularly the case in British vocational education, which has a narrow focus on training for employer-led skills of a low intellectual level and 'contains very little input of any formal knowledge' with 'no notion of an integration of different forms of knowledge, and thus of experiential learning and knowledge creation' (Brockmann *et al.*, 2008: 555). Developing *competences* should not be a process of utilitarian teaching directed towards only specific, short-term training goals in that way. Instead it should provide long-term core knowledge and intellectual tools, so that learners can cope with a variety of tasks and situations (Roegiers, 2000: 286, our translation).

At this point we need to clarify a very common misunderstanding that 'competence' and 'competency' are synonyms. This is certainly not the case: the former is a holistic concept, with transversal aspects that overlap and intermesh; the latter is one of a series of discrete items that can be checked off on a list. Woodruffe (1991) 'offers the clearest statement, contrasting areas of competence, defined as aspects of the job which an individual can perform, with competency, referring to a person's behaviour underpinning competent performance' (Delamare le Diest & Winterton, 2005: 29). Jolly (2012) echoes this distinction, talking of 'a trend to see "competencies" as tools to be selected for specific tasks and "competence" as an overarching concept involving the integration of multiple capacities and abilities' (Jolly, 2012: 347). Blömeke *et al.* (2015) confirm the distinction again saying: 'that "competence" (plural "competences") is the broader term whereas "competency" (plural "competencies") refers to the different constituents of competence. The first term describes a complex characteristic from a holistic viewpoint whereas the latter takes an analytic stance' (2015: 5).

Another definition of the distinction is the following, given in the context of literature on the subject for the nursing profession:

> Although they may sound similar, competence and competency are not necessarily synonymous. Competence refers to a potential ability and/ or a capability to function in a given situation. Competency focuses on one's actual performance in a situation. This means that competence is required before one can expect to achieve competency. Thus, competence makes one capable of fulfilling his/her job responsibilities. (Schroeter, 2008: 2)

The competency view is a very reductionist and atomistic one that is at best not helpful in an educational context. In sharp contrast to the holistic and developmental view of competence taken in, for example, Germany and the Netherlands (Brockmann *et al.*, 2008: 555; Delamare le Diest & Winterton, 2005: 27), in the way competence has been interpreted in Britain 'this notion has been whittled down to the ability to undertake specific tasks; it has been largely stripped of its social, moral and intellectual qualities. ... In the current discourse competence as a fully human attribute, has been reduced to competencies – series of discrete activities that people possess the necessary skills, knowledge and understanding to engage in effectively' (Smith, 1996: n.p.).

The problem of the distinction between competence and competency is further complicated by a confused usage of the two terms in some official documents. For instance, Kennedy *et al.* (2009), in a guide related to the Bologna process, claim that the words 'competence' and 'competency' are now used in English as synonyms – or are given definitions of the difference between them that directly contradict each other. Unfortunately, this is to some extent the case. For example, whereas the EU (see above) uses the expression 'competence' the OECD prefers 'competency', though it is clear that they are using the term in a broad, holistic sense as a synonym of competence:

> A competency is more than just knowledge and skills. It involves the *ability to meet complex demands*, by drawing on and *mobilising psychosocial resources* (including skills and attitudes) *in a particular context*. For example, the ability to communicate effectively is a competency that may draw on an individual's knowledge of language, practical IT skills and attitudes towards those with whom he or she is communicating. (OECD, 2005, our emphasis)

The distinction between *competence* and *competency* could be useful because the former – *competence* – emphasises a holistic yet multi-dimensional, transversal personal or group attribute, whereas the latter – *competency* – refers to demonstrated professional capability of an individual in relation to a set of standards.

2.3.1 From qualifications to competences

From ancient times until very recently, the emphasis in both education and training was on acquiring, and demonstrating through an examination, a mastery of a body of knowledge in order to receive a qualification, which had a gatekeeping function. London taxi drivers still have to pass 'The Knowledge,' an oral examination of their knowledge of the streets and routes of London, for example. In many white collar occupations, it was possible after leaving school to climb through a series of such qualifications, each permitting one to apply for a position with a higher function, but the emphasis remained demonstration of a mastery of knowledge. Once mastery had been demonstrated, that was sufficient for the rest of one's career; what counted was seniority (Le Bianic, 2001: 2). A move away from this static concept started in the 1970s. Workplaces and production lines were starting to change, slowly becoming more flexible rather than confining the employee to the single task for which they were qualified. Employees were increasingly expected to deal with the unforeseen and face the uncertainty of permanent change (Le Boterf, 2010; Richer, 2008, 2012). This development accelerated during the 1980s and 1990s (de Terssac, 1992), in line with the development from static quality control (= reject imperfect products) to Total Quality Management (= optimise processes and staff involvement so as to improve products), with a corresponding switch from the exercise of knowledge and experience to the mobilisation and development of professional competence (Zarifian, 2001) and its evaluation through defined management procedures (Le Bianic, 2001). To a considerable extent, business owners and managers had in fact always tended to promote people whom they thought were 'competent,' so rather than a complete revolution, this paradigm change was really more a move to base such judgements on explicit criteria (Le Bianic, 2001).

Today we realise that, with the accelerating pace of technological development, young people will probably have several occupations during their working lives and therefore the development of transversal competences is what they need, not mastery of a static body of knowledge. As Richer therefore explains, the notion of competence in the world of work has been recently further developed in two main ways. The first, more American in origin, is the expectation to improve oneself constantly, to do more and more, and to do it more quickly; the second, more French in origin, is to see competence above all as a means to allow the development of creative potential, empowerment to action and capacity to find meaning and personal engagement in the issues one handles in daily professional situations (Richer, 2017).

In the following sections, we will discuss the development of the concept of competence primarily in the world of work. We will also focus more on continental conceptions of competence in so doing, for the reason Pikkarainen (2014) and Brockmann *et al.* (2008) give, particularly the French version, which Delamare le Diest and Winterton (2005: 37) confirm is the most comprehensive.

2.3.2 The notion of situated action

In the world of work, competence is inseparable from action – intellectual or physical (Richer, 2012, 2017). Competence 'is realised in action. It does not pre-exist the action. There is no competence other than competence in action' (Le Boterf, 1994: 16, cited in Richer, 2012, our translation). The action is complex action: competence is 'related to a social practice of a certain complexity' (Perrenoud, 1997: 44, our translation). This action is always situated, taking place in a context, always characterised by the specific demands of each situation concerned. One is always competent in relation to a situated action, that is to say an action for which the planning includes a consideration of improvisation in the face of unexpected developments (Richer, 2012). One doesn't know in advance what exactly one will have to do and how one will have to do it – it is necessary to be inventive, innovative, managing complex, unstable situations (Le Boterf, 2010). Competence is thus linked to complex action and is realised in practice in that action. Castellotti (2002) summarises that, seen from the perspectives of different disciplines, competence is inseparable from action and situation, and that there is usually, in addition, an authority to recognise the competence shown.

In the world of work, therefore, competence is thought of in the plural with *savoirs déclaratifs* (declarative knowledge), *savoir-faire procéduraux* (procedural knowledge: knowing how things are done), and *savoir-être* (knowing how to comport oneself, handle relationships with other people – the relational and psychological sphere) (Richer, 2012, 2017). Readers familiar with the CEFR will notice that these three expressions (*savoir, savoir-faire, savoir être*) appear there as the framework for general competences, though they are translated differently into English, showing the strength of the more habitual model of knowledge, skills and attitudes. But *savoir-être* means far more than attitudes and values. It also encompasses the ability to be a good listener, to be welcoming, to know when to take the initiative, when to be tenacious and above all to have self-confidence (Le Boterf, 2010). In addition, in the humanistic interpretation of s*avoir-être* common in France, it also includes an autonomy of action, to engage oneself with the permission and the capacity to take the initiative in order to improve the result – i. e. to take responsibility (Richer, 2017; Zarifian, 2001).

Finally, *savoir-être* also includes a *savoir coopérer* (teamwork), which refers to the way individual and collective competences interact. In any collaborative work context, there is a constant interplay between the individual and social level. On the individual side, apart from the question of autonomous competence (the ability to work alone, structuring one's work effectively: Canale, 1984), many aspects of competence concern relationships with others. Working with others involves *savoir-être*: having a cooperative attitude, a willingness to share and compromise, but it also involves a *savoir relationel* (Le Boterf, 2010; Richer, 2017), i.e. knowing how to manage relations with others, like colleagues, clients, assistants, superiors, etc.

2.3.3 A dynamic view of competences: Mobilising resources

These different competences, or aspects of 'competence', are never used separately, but always in combination as they interact with each other. Therefore, it is difficult to observe or assess a single competence, because any action requires the interaction and integration of several competences (de Montmollin, 1996; Leplat, 1991). None of these concepts are foreign to applied linguistics. Various language testers have tried to develop models that would take account of this interaction (e.g. Bachman & Palmer, 1996; Skehan, 1995). Weir (2005) even talks of 'interactional authenticity' as an aspect of the validity of a language test: does the test create a performance situation in which different competences interact in a way that they would in the real world?

However in the development of the concept of competence, in the '*sociologie du travail*', the capacity to effect this mobilisation and integration is itself seen as a competence: *savoir mobiliser*: 'Competence does not reside in the resources to be mobilised (knowledge, skills etc.) but rather in the actual mobilisation of these resources. The competence is of the order of being able to mobilise (*savoir mobiliser*)' (Le Boterf, 1994: 17, our translation). It is not a question of addition or assembly like with Lego, but rather of dynamic integration in context through a *savoir combinatoire* (being able to combine). In all this discussion, we also have to bear in mind that '*savoir*', as in all Romance languages, is not restricted to the meaning 'to know', but has an element of 'to be able to'. Clearly knowledge of appropriate schemata for the situation at hand is necessary, but mobilising resources goes even beyond 'knowing how to'. There is a strategic aspect to it. To return to the discussion of linguistic models of communicative competence, Skehan (1995: 16) in developing an interaction model proposed that *ability for use* was separate from both competence and performance, and related to Bachman's (1990) interpretation of strategic competence. *Savoir mobiliser/combiner* (being able to mobilise/combine) is thus a strategic capacity to activate and integrate in real time other relevant, equally transversal, competences.

But as Bourguignon points out, it is not enough to see competence, or even *savoir mobiliser* as 'mobilisation of knowledge and application of skills in the context of situation' (Bourguignon, 2006: 65, our translation), a definition she herself used earlier. The problem with such a concept of savoir *mobiliser* is, as she points out, that it suggests that competences are something fixed for all time – like in the qualifications paradigm that preceded the competence paradigm in the world of work. It interprets competence as an object, rather than as a permanent process of personal development (*en éternel devenir*). As she says, it is necessary to add to the concept of competence 'a dynamic of construction, modification, adaptation of knowledge and skills in action' (Bourguignon, 2006: 65, our translation).

2.3.4 The continuous process of building and refining competences

As Bourguignon suggests, competences, are not static: either they develop or they atrophy. There is a meta level which has a dimension of reflection and strategic development. Richer (2012) emphasises the importance of reflection, both during and after any particular action, a *savoir analyser* one's successes and setbacks. The competent professional can turn his/her actions into experience, and hence collect a conscious repertoire of experiences, examples, insights and actions: *savoirs expérientiels* (Le Boterf, 1994: 176; Richer, 2017: 9). Collective reflection can lead to the sharing of such knowledge and insights and bring a new collective competence, around which a community of practice (see Section 3.8) can be built to further develop them. However, effective reflection requires verbalisation, what Richer calls *savoir dire*, the ability to explain what one can do, what one has learnt. 'Skills (*savoir-faire*) do not acquire the status of competence until they have been articulated and communicated to other members of the group' (de Terssac & Chabaud, 1990: 134, our translation). This social dimension is central to the idea of collective competence: 'competence is the ability to mobilise a network of social agents around situations that are common to the group, share the stakes and assume areas of responsibility' (Zarifian, 2001: 71, our translation).

In order for competences to further develop, at an individual or social level, Le Boterf (2010) posits that those involved need to know how to act (*savoir agir*) to mobilise the relevant knowledge and skills and put into place the appropriate procedures, need to want to act (*vouloir agir*), having sufficient motivation, and need to be able to act (*pouvoir agir*), to be given a positive context, a management climate and social conditions that make it possible for people to take responsibility, take risks and innovate, to be able to go beyond what has been prescribed, to *savoir affronter l'imprévu* (be able to confront the unexpected).

Richer (2017) completes his description of this 'humanist version of competence' (Richer, 2017: 9, our translation) with the diagram given as Figure 2.1. At the top we have the conditions necessary for

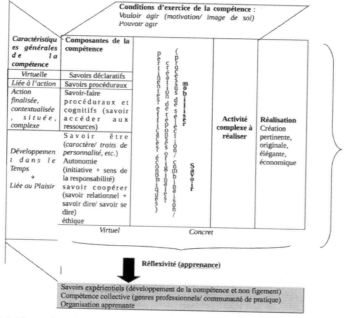

Figure 2.1 The traits of a humanist version of competence. Richer (2017: 9)

the continuous development of competence that are mentioned just above. On the left, one has the general characteristics: that it is linked to complex, situated action, that it develops across time and above all that it is linked to satisfaction and pleasure. Then the elements of competences – *not* seen as separable 'components' – that we have discussed throughout the whole of this Section 2.3: declarative and procedural knowledge, procedural and cognitive skills to access resources, existential competences (*savoir-être*), autonomy and initiative, and finally collaborative and relational competences: the ability to work with others, to articulate what one can do, has learnt (*savoir dire*). All these aspects are abstract, in the sense that they cannot be seen directly. Then in the centre of the chart comes '*savoir mobiliser*', the ability to put all these things together in concrete, efficient, action: the creation of appropriate, original responses to any given situation, through a process of selection and combination. On the right one has the context of the complex task to be accomplished and finally the realisation of the competence in the creation of a relevant, original, elegant and economical – one could say ergonomic, ecological – solution. All this is concrete and visible – in a specific professional situation, one sees in the end whether someone is competent or not. Finally, at the bottom of the chart, we see that the result of this experience of realising competence in concrete, situated action brings reflection, learning and experiential competence at both the individual and collective/social levels.

Richer (2017) summaries by saying that this model:

(a) reintroduces a cognitive element in two ways, firstly with the interface to mobilise resources and secondly with the reflection;
(b) gives a key role to socio-psycho-affective aspects at the individual and collective levels;
(c) is doubly dynamic, both with the selective implementation of elements of competence and personal resources through their mobilisation, and also through the analysis of and reflection on this implementation afterwards.

He concludes that the implications for the use of strategies in choice, and of creativity in deciding how to approach the complex task involved, plus the meta-dimension of reflexivity (Zarifian, 2001), distances this humanistic vision of competence from any atomistic, behaviourist one.

The humanistic view of competence that we have outlined here is very compatible with the theories that we will consider in Chapter 3, especially complexity and ecological theories and theories of situated action and learning. It is also very compatible with the approach to competence taken in the CEFR, which we discuss below, and with the tenets of the AoA. Individuals and groups, are no longer seen as passive vessels that should be filled up with knowledge; nor are they seen as objects that should acquire a set of task-specific abilities (be able to operate this machine, be able to spell their name) – 'competencies'. As Coste *et al.* (2012) remind us, communication is profoundly holistic and there is a real danger in atomising competences into long lists of attributes. The chance to document language competence in ways other than just formal qualifications was one of the main ideas behind the development of the European Language Portfolio associated with the CEFR (Council of Europe, 1992; Schärer & North, 1992).

At the end of a review of the interpretation of competence in the USA, UK and continental Europe, Delamare le Diest and Winterton (2005) propose a model of competence that is considerably simpler than that of Richer, but that also incorporates the humanistic, dynamic view of competence discussed above and avoids the atomisation criticised by Coste *et al.* (2012). Of their 4-part model, shown in Figure 2.2, they say that the 'first three dimensions, cognitive, functional and social competences, are fairly universal and are clearly consistent with the French approach (*savoir, savoir faire, savoir-être*) as well as the longstanding KSA (knowledge, skills and attitudes) of the training profession' (Delamare le Diest & Winterton, 2005: 39). The fourth category, meta-competence is concerned with 'facilitating the acquisition of the other substantive competences' (2005: 39). Although it clearly relates to the professional domain, whereas the CEFR is concerned with the educational domain, this model is similar to the approach taken to general competences in the CEFR (Council of Europe, 1998, 2001), as we will see in the next section.

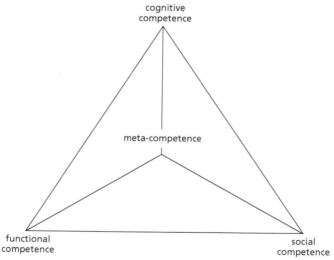

Figure 2.2 A holistic model of competence
Source: Delamare le Diest and Winterton, 2005: 40.

2.4 Competences in the CEFR and in the AoA

Let us now look at the concepts underpinning the CEFR's vision of language teaching and learning, bearing in mind what we have just said about the concept of competence. In the above discussion, we first outlined the development of the concept of communicative competence, and we then moved to the treatment of the concept of competence itself in the world of education and work, focusing more on the latter since the competence tradition in education is derived from it. In this process we explained the difference between 'competence' and 'competency', echoing some of the reservations made by various writers about the reductionist interpretation common in many Anglo-Saxon contexts and underlining the dynamic, humanistic and potentially empowering nature of the interpretation of competence in other European contexts.

The CEFR defines competence as: 'the sum of knowledge, skills, and characteristics that allow a person to perform actions' (Council of Europe, 2001: 9). This definition aligns with the conceptual framework of the CEFR upon which the AoA approach is based: it links the notion of competence inextricably to the notion of action, as discussed in Section 2.3.2 above. In its view of communicative language proficiency, the CEFR incorporates the idea of competence in four complementary ways, which relate to different aspects of the discussion earlier in this chapter: (a) in relation to general competence; (b) in relation to communicative language competence; (c) with the operationalisation of its descriptive scheme with 'can do' descriptors, and (d) with the concept of plurilingual and pluricultural competence.

Firstly, the CEFR embeds the idea of communicative language competence in a broader and deeper fourfold scheme for **general competence**. This is rooted in the concept of 'existential competence' (*savoir être*), in which learners are able not only to display declarative knowledge (*savoir*) by means of targeted skills and know-how (*savoir-faire*), but to increase and self-develop through the ability to learn how to learn (*savoir apprendre*). These correspond closely to Delamare & Winterton's social competence, cognitive competence, functional competence and meta-competence. Secondly, this complex vision of general competence is paralleled by a complex vision of **communicative language competence**, which includes linguistic, sociolinguistic and pragmatic competences. Thirdly, by its provision of a wealth of **'can do' descriptor scales** (50 in 2001; 80 in 2018) for communicative language activities, strategies and competences, the CEFR suggests what is generally described as a 'competence-based approach'. Finally, and most importantly, the CEFR introduces the concept of dynamically unstable 'partial competences', most notably **plurilingual and pluricultural competence**.

2.4.1 General and linguistic competences

The CEFR defines general competences as 'those not specific to language, but which are called upon for actions of all kinds, *including language activities*' (Council of Europe, 2001: 9, our emphasis). Various overlapping aspects of general competence are explained. The boundaries between knowledge of the world (CEFR Section 5.1.1.1), sociocultural knowledge (CEFR Section 5.1.1.2) and intercultural awareness (CEFR Section 5.1.1.3) are not really clear cut, as the CEFR aptly explains. Nor are those between practical skills and know-how (CEFR Section 5.1.2.1) – the latter including social skills – and sociocultural knowledge or intercultural skills and know-how (5.1.2.2). What is more important than possible overlap between categories is the fact that the user/learner calls on all these various aspects, merged with the appropriate communicative language competences, in the creation of meaning in a communicative situation. Categories cannot be considered to exist in isolation. In reality, all communicative activity involves integrating language competences with general competences and relevant strategies. The fact that we bring one aspect into focus in order to describe it does not imply in any way that it enjoys a separate existence.

Savoir-être (existential competence) in the CEFR is defined as comprising attitudes, motivations, values, beliefs, cognitive styles and general personality factors (CEFR 5.1.3: 105–6), though – as always in the CEFR – the list of factors is intended to be illustrative and open-ended. *Savoir-être* can be also interpreted to include other factors mentioned above in relation to it, such as how to comport oneself, be a good listener, be welcoming, be cooperative, know when to take the initiative, when to be tenacious and when to compromise: in other words, being open to other perspectives and being able to establish and manage relationships with other people. This clearly relates to concepts like emotional competence and empathy, and overlaps with sociocultural knowledge (CEFR 5.1.1.2), intercultural awareness (CEFR 5.1.1.3) and intercultural skills and know-how (CEFR 5.1.2.2). Indeed, when discussing *savoir-être*, the CEFR states: 'The development of an "intercultural personality" [*see Section 6.2*] involving both attitudes and awareness, is seen by many as an important educational goal in its own right' (Council of Europe, 2001: 106). *Savoir-être* and *savoir apprendre* (ability to learn: meta-competence) are the dynamic parts of the CEFR's model of general competences, – considerably more dynamic than the rather static knowledge, skills and attitudes of the American training model. Under *savoir-apprendre* are listed aspects like language, communication and phonetic awareness, study skills and heuristic skills (the ability to handle new experiences, new information, and new technologies). These are the kinds of competences necessary for successful lifelong learning.

Communicative language competences themselves are, as mentioned before, presented under linguistic, sociolinguistic, and pragmatic competence. The six scales under pragmatic competence are: flexibility, turn-taking, thematic development and coherence/cohesion (for discourse competence: CEFR 5.2.3.1), plus spoken fluency and propositional precision (for functional competence: CEFR 5.2.3.2). Table 2.2 summarises competences as they are presented in the CEFR.

General competences are essential for the exercise of communicative language competences; the two cannot be separated. The way Richer summarises this is as follows:

> The general competences of the individual comprise *savoirs* (declarative knowledge), *savoir-être* (existential competence) forms of *savoir-faire* (skills and knowhow) that are necessary in order to exercise communicative language competence and in addition integrate key elements (autonomy and capacity for reflection) that come from the conception of competence in the world of work. (Richer, 2012: 60, our translation)

2.4.2 Relationship between competences and communicative activities

The CEFR descriptive scheme (see Section 5.1.4) introduced a distinction between general competences (CEFR Section 5.1), communicative language competences (CEFR Section 5.2), and communicative language activities and strategies (CEFR Section 4.4). Communicative strategies are seen as a kind of hinge between competences and activity, attached to the four modes of communication: reception, production, interaction, and mediation. CEFR Chapters 4 and 5 are complementary and between them make up the CEFR's detailed descriptive scheme. Essentially CEFR Chapter 4 is concerned with WHAT the user/learner can do (in which domains, under what conditions) and can inform the development of communicative objectives, the selection and/or development of tasks and materials. CEFR Chapter 5, on the other hand, is concerned with HOW the learner does it: qualitative aspects of competences of different kinds.

Different types of communicative language activities require the activation of different types of both general and language competences. Language users/learners who are all at the same overall level of proficiency (e.g. B1) will find certain communicative activities more difficult. This reflects the differences in their personal profile of general competences as a result of their age, experience of the world and individual cognitive and interpersonal competences. Some learners may find relatively easy certain cognitively-demanding activities like *Listening and notetaking, Reading for information and argument,*

Table 2.2 Schematic organisation of competences according to the CEFR

General Competences				Communicative Language Competences		
Declarative Knowledge	Skills and Know-how	Existential Knowledge	Ability to Learn	Linguistic Competences	Sociolinguistic Competences	Pragmatic Competences
- knowledge of the world - sociocultural knowledge - intercultural awareness	- practical skills - intercultural skills		- language and communication awareness - general phonetic awareness and skills - study skills - heuristic skills	Competences: - lexical - grammatical - semantic - phonological - orthographic - orthoepic	- social relations - politeness - conventions - expressions of folk wisdom - register differences - dialect and accent	- discourse competence - functional competence

Source: Piccardo et al., 2011b: 35.

Addressing audiences, Processing text and producing *Reports and essays*. Other learners may find such activities very difficult, but find relatively easy other, interpersonally-demanding activities like *Goal-oriented cooperation, Facilitating collaborative interaction with peers, Facilitating communication in delicate situations and disagreements* (Council of Europe, 2018).

Different types of communicative language activities also require the activation of different types of communicative language competences. For example in certain interactive types of activities *Spoken fluency, Vocabulary range* and interaction strategies like *Cooperating, Taking the floor (Turntaking)* and *Asking for clarification* are very important. In other, monologic productive activities *Thematic development, Propositional precision, Coherence and cohesion* and *Grammatical accuracy* are more central. From the point of view of judging the quality of learner language, the teacher should vary the teaching emphasis, and be selective in choosing the relevant categories to develop assessment criteria for feedback.

A user/learner acts and accomplishes tasks in order to learn; he or she does not learn in order to act. The goal is successful action and the different communicative activities involved serve the action. Communicative activities are not the end goal of teaching/learning. It is by engaging in communicative language activities that learners/users build up their competences.

2.4.3 Strategic development of competences

New knowledge gained is not simply added to the knowledge one had beforehand but is conditioned by the nature, richness and structure of one's previous knowledge and, furthermore, serves to modify and restructure the latter, at least partially. Clearly, the general declarative and procedural knowledge that an individual has already acquired is directly relevant to language learning. This conceptualisation is consistent with the overarching competence fostered by the CEFR, the existential competence (*savoir être*), which draws on what van Ek (1986), in one of the studies that was a precursor of the CEFR, referred to as *optimal personal ability*, embracing culture, language and learning, and therefore learner autonomy, language competence and intercultural awareness.

The CEFR deals with the strategic dimension in two complementary ways: firstly in terms of learning strategies and secondly in terms of communication strategies. However, it only provides descriptors for the latter. Nonetheless, the discussion of the need for a reflective, strategic attitude throughout the learning process is clearly apparent and presented in the descriptive scheme under general competences as 'learning to learn' (*savoir apprendre*).

Learning to learn (*savoir apprendre*) is a strategic undertaking. Strategies and language awareness are crucial to learners becoming autonomous (Dam, 2001; Holec, 1981; Little, 1991; Little *et al.*, 2017; Wolff, 2003) or self-directed (Dickinson, 1987). Unless a learner is self-directed – which includes seeing him/herself as a language user, with an idea of where he/she is starting from, where he/she wants to go (self-assessment) as well as motivation (*vouloir agir*) – he/she will be unable to take the initiative necessary to exert agency and thus profit from the learning opportunities offered. Learning to learn skills are useful for education and throughout life (European Parliament, 2006). The dynamic notion that links all these aspects in the CEFR is this educational aim of learning to learn. This goes beyond the traditional vision of autonomy as an exclusively individual capacity, embedding it instead in a more social and interactive perspective. Social exchange and interaction, together with a reflective individual attitude, allow learners to improve their language competence and to increase their cultural awareness.

The second way the CEFR handles the strategic dimension is through communicative strategies which are defined as 'a means the language user exploits to mobilise and balance her or his resources, to activate skills and procedures, in order to fulfil the demands of communication in context and successfully complete the task in question in the most comprehensive or most economical way feasible' (Council of Europe, 2001: 57).

Completion of a complex task, with the help of strategies, then itself leads to further development of the competences involved. 'The monitoring of these actions by the participants leads to the reinforcement or modification of their competences' (Council of Europe, 2001: 9). It is a virtuous circle, since by engaging in communicative activities in order to accomplish tasks, users/learners further develop competences, which includes extending the range and improving the quality of their language. This is turn allows them to perform other more challenging tasks in a spiralling process with feedback and feedforward.

2.4.4 The CEFR descriptive scheme and the AoA

In the CEFR, the term 'proficiency' encompasses the ability to perform communicative language activities (can do...), whilst drawing upon both general and communicative language competences (linguistic, sociolinguistic, pragmatic) and activating appropriate communicative strategies.

> The acquisition of proficiency is ... seen as a circular process: by performing activities, the user/learner develops competences and acquires strategies. This approach embraces a view of competence as only

existing when enacted in language use, reflecting both (a) the broader view of competence as action from applied psychology, particularly in relation to the world of work and professional training and (b) the view taken nowadays in the sociocultural approach to learning. The CEFR 'Can do' descriptors epitomise this philosophy. (Council of Europe, 2018: 33)

This reflects both the broader view of competence as action discussed in Section 2.3, plus Hymes's ability for use discussed in Section 2.2.2. In addition, it reflects the vision of competence as opposed to competency that we discussed in relation to the world of work and professional training.

The heuristic model of the action-oriented approach that outlines this vision of enacted competences was introduced in Section 1.1.1. It is a rather dense paragraph from Chapter 2 of the CEFR that summarises the CEFR descriptive scheme. Each of the elements presented in bold in that paragraph is later defined in detail in CEFR Chapters 4 and 5, which lay out the scheme in more detail, providing illustrative descriptor scales for those aspects of the scheme that have proved scaleable. The vision is one of dynamic development of competences through integration in action:

> Language use, embracing language learning, comprises the actions performed by persons who as individuals and as social agents develop a range of **competences**, both **general** and in particular **communicative language competences**. They draw on the competences at their disposal in various contexts under various **conditions** and under various **constraints** to engage in **language activities** involving **language processes** to produce and/or receive **texts** in relation to **themes** in specific **domains**, activating those **strategies** which seem most appropriate for carrying out the **tasks** to be accomplished. The monitoring of these actions by the participants leads to the reinforcement or modification of their competences. (Council of Europe, 2001: 9, original emphasis)

The CEFR descriptive scheme is explained in more detail in Section 5.1.4. We will investigate in Chapter 7 the pedagogic implications of developing competences dynamically through integration in action. What we would like to highlight here is the paradigm shift that the AoA implies: i.e. the move from a paradigm of linearity and simplification focusing on knowledge to a paradigm of complexity focusing on competence, where the object of study (language), the subject learning it (language user), the action (language use) and the reflection (metacognitive/metalinguistic phase) are interconnected and interdependent (Bourguignon, 2006). The AoA adopts a holistic, whole person perspective that rejects working in silos, with different elements taken in isolation. Competences only exist and make sense in action. Action being by nature not fully predictable, different competences need to be mobilised at different moments and for different purposes both in a proactive and a reactive way. Furthermore, action is conceptualised as social in the CEFR, thus requiring some form of collaborative work in which the social agent is engaged.

However, one important point to stress is that the CEFR does not just consider the external context of language use in which the user/learner operates. The CEFR underlines a constant movement between the social and individual levels during the process of language learning. The CEFR stresses how the external context must always be interpreted and filtered by the user/learner in relation to several characteristics (Piccardo *et al.*, 2011b), but also the mental context of both the user/learner and their interlocutor(s). It points out that:

> The mental context is … not limited to reducing the information content of the immediately observable external context. Line of thought may be more powerfully influenced by memory, stored knowledge, imagination and other internal cognitive (and emotive) processes. In that case the language produced is only marginally related to the observable external context. External conditions and constraints are also relevant mainly in so far as the user/learner recognises, accepts and adjusts to them (or fails to do so). This is very much a matter of the individual's interpretation of the situation in the light of his or her general competences (see Chapter 5.1) such as prior knowledge, values and beliefs. (Council of Europe, 2001: 50–51)

The articulation of competences into general competences and communicative language competences that the descriptive scheme proposes is aptly schematised in the CEFR Companion Volume, where it is underlined that:

> In any communicative situation, *general competences* (e.g. knowledge of the world, sociocultural competence, intercultural competence, professional experience if any: CEFR Section 5.1) are *always* combined with *communicative language competences* (linguistic, sociolinguistic and pragmatic competences: Section 5.2), and *strategies* (some general, some communicative language strategies) in order to complete a *task* (CEFR Chapter 7). (Council of Europe, 2018: 29, original emphasis)

The term 'always' is highlighted twice to stress the interdependence of linguistic and non-linguistic competences but also the dynamic nature of the mobilisation process which is by nature strategic, recursive and cyclical.

The action-oriented tasks and scenarios, as we will see in Chapter 4 and further in Chapter 7, situate all these competences in a dynamic context and relationship where they are constantly under construction, through action, and revised and modified through subsequent reflection. This dynamic process is itself a complex one, and it requires some form of mediation that takes place both at individual and at the social level. The central role of mediation in the entire process of using and learning the language and thus of (further) developing competences is particularly stressed in the CEFR Companion Volume, which '[i]n addition to cross-linguistic mediation, ... also encompasses mediation related to communication and learning as well as social and cultural mediation. This wider approach has been taken ... because mediation is increasingly seen as a part of all learning, but especially of all language learning' (Council of Europe, 2018: 34).

Thus the situated action at the core of the AoA fuels the entire process of using, constructing, and developing competence, which in turn steers the action itself towards further improvement of language proficiency.

2.4.5 Action-oriented tasks: A dynamic, systemic view of competences

The language learner's ability to communicate is realised through complex, collective and collaborative tasks, where speaking and doing are intermingled, thus putting into practice an action-oriented perspective on language. The notions of communicative language competence and task are 'absolutely inseparable, (*indissociables*) exactly like in the world of work' (Richer, 2012: 58, our translation). The notion of task, central in the CEFR, brings together the complexity of language learning and teaching and can also be used to organise learning modules or the entire syllabus. Nevertheless, tasks are not something artificially created for the purpose of teaching the language, they are instead a naturally occurring feature of everyday life in the personal, public, educational or occupational domains (Council of Europe, 2001: 157).

The term 'task' refers to concrete experiences: 'Task accomplishment by an individual involves the strategic activation of specific competences in order to carry out a set of purposeful actions in a particular domain with a clearly defined goal and a specific outcome' (Council of Europe, 2001: 157). Some tasks are relevant at different levels, even all levels. Progress in such tasks is cyclical as users/learners acquire and are able to use more competences to improve their performance. Other tasks have a threshold below which they cannot really be performed at all: for example a Pre-A1 learner can hardly *address an audience* or *act as an intermediary* in an intercultural situation. Generally speaking though, tasks themselves do not have levels. It is the teacher who creates the level of the task, by the introduction of conditions, scaffolding and/or constraints, as discussed further in Section 4.2.3.

As we discussed in Section 2.3 above, competence is not the simple addition of different types of declarative knowledge (*savoir*), skills and know-how (*savoir-faire*), disposition, attitudes and comportment (*savoir-être*) or knowing where to find resources, manage people etc. etc., which is, as Richer (2017) points out, sadly the impression often given by reference works. Such long lists of different ways in which one should be perfect are more depressing than motivating.

Employing and acquiring competences is a dynamic process, in which both the response to any exigence and the further development of the competence are *individual and situated*. There is no 'right' or 'best' response (Richer, 2017: 7); there are diverse ways of resolving issues. Of course, good ways of responding are dependent on motivation. Without motivation, the mobilisation of competences is partial and inept. If a person does not want to act (*vouloir agir*), or is unable to act because of restrictions on their freedom of action (*pouvoir agir*), not a lot will happen. Motivation, as every teacher knows, is central. But part of the problem with motivation is that not all of the activities and tasks that teachers choose are particularly motivating. The action-oriented approach to developing communicative competence can help here. As Richer concludes:

> ... the influence of the conceptualisation of competence developed in the world of work is visible in the methodological proposition put forward by the CEFR, and this is achieved in such a way as to allow one to see in the CEFR a renewal of and improvement on the communicative approach, not 'the possibility to implement the communicative approach in its "advanced" version,' as suggested by Beacco (2007: 91), but rather the emergence of a new methodological paradigm. (Richer, 2017: 16, our translation)

Communicative language competence is not constructed in a vacuum. As will be explained in Section 3.9, the CEFR aligns with dynamic systems theory (De Bot *et al.*, 2007; Larsen-Freeman, 1997, 2011; Larsen-Freeman & Cameron, 2008) and stresses that each new acquisition changes the previous situation, the previous landscape, and the previous system. The CEFR insists on flexible notions with respect to unbalanced and changing competences. These are particularly highlighted when the 'plurilingual' and 'pluricultural' dimensions are discussed (Council of Europe, 2001: 133). For this reason, the CEFR introduces the notions of 'profile' and 'partial competences' (Council of Europe, 2001: 135; Council of Europe, 2018: 36–40) where each language modifies the other (or several others) as well as the mother tongue. As is the case with competences, the notion of plurilingualism is a dynamic one (Beacco & Byram, 2007a; Stratilaki, 2005).

However, before we discuss this new paradigm in detail, we will first present the various theories that have influenced language education and brought us to this point (Chapter 3), retrace their influence on the development of language teaching methodologies (Chapter 4) and properly introduce the CEFR itself (Chapter 5).

Notes

(1) At the time of writing the Key Competences are undergoing a review process.
(2) https://ec.europa.eu/education/initiatives/key-competences-framework-review-2017_en.

3 Towards an Action-oriented Approach: Theoretical Underpinnings

This chapter outlines the contributions of different research streams to an understanding of the action-oriented approach (AoA). There have been many advances in the conceptualisation of SLE, each informed by a core theoretical vision. Often, theories are presented as being in opposition, incompatible with one another. However, rather than seeing the different theories in this way, it is more fruitful to consider their various contributions to the development of second lanuage education (SLE). In the last couple of decades, a major impulse has come from sociocultural/socio-constructivist theories, according to which the individual (re)constructs for him/herself language and concepts through mediated social interactions. This view aligns with the AoA and contradicts traditional theories that explain language learning as a cognitive process happening at the level of the individual, later put into practice in a social context. However, the AoA does not solely embrace this theory, but draws its theoretical bases from a broader array of domains, including, as we saw in Chapter 2, a humanistic vision of competence as situated action. The non-linearity of the learning process is also underlined by complex and ecological models which explain the teaching and learning process in terms of the ways in which different elements, as well as the relationships between them, come into play. The key tenet of the AoA is the interdependence between the cognitive and the social in a principled and strategic process of learning, driven by the agency of the individual seen as a 'social agent', as proposed in the CEFR descriptive scheme.

3.1 In Search of a Theory of Language Education: The First Steps

Almost all human sciences have investigated the concept of language. Some have underlined the structural normative character of language, others its social, cultural and symbolic value. Yet others have emphasised the psychological aspects, the neurological, or the creative and artistic. However, it is only quite recently that both language itself and the language class have started to be seen as complex and adaptive systems (Larsen-Freeman, 1997), and that the contributions of different disciplines and perspectives have begun to be seen as interdependent. We propose extending Mitchell and Vidal's (2001) metaphor of a river to describe the influence that different theories have had on SLE: a river that is enriched by various streams whose waters interact with one another, and grows through this process. It is not an 'either-or' philosophy that we embrace here but rather a 'both … and' one. This is the perspective we follow in this book, as we will also see when we talk in Chapter 4 about the development of methodologies. In the present chapter we consider the different theoretical perspectives that have contributed to the development of the AoA, focusing on their complementarity.

The postmodern vision (Lyotard, 1979; Baumann, 1992), rejects the concepts of universal truths, objectivity and systematisation and shows the extreme difficulty of drawing clear demarcation lines between different theories. Despite the risks of relativism, this vision offers a wider lens than the rationalistic, Cartesian one that preceded it. This is the perspective that we adopt in this book as we investigate some of the major concepts that have contributed to theorising SLE and that have helped develop the concept of the AoA.

It is interesting to recapitulate the way SLE theorisation has developed over time in order to understand why certain ideas persist or even dominate and what challenges one faces in moving towards a broader conceptualisation that encompasses and goes beyond the specific field of language education to investigate the contributions of other human and social sciences.

3.2 From Mental Gym to Habit Formation: The Enduring Impact of Behaviourism

Traditionally, in the Western world until remarkably recently, education consisted largely of imitation and rote learning. In at least Europe, the approach was linked to much negative stimuli. New-fangled ideas that one should explain things to children and apprentices rather than beating knowledge into them started with Enlightenment educationalists like Pestalozzi and Rousseau, but took until the 1950s–60s to enter the educational mainstream. Meanwhile, the small intellectual elite learnt the grammar of Latin and Greek, and modern languages by accessing the classical texts, mainly through translation. The main scope of this type of learning was 'Bildung': the study of the language as an object alongside the study of classical literature was considered essential to a well-rounded education and the main springboard for the cultural and intellectual development of the individual. Aristocrats also supplemented their learning of foreign languages, with fencing, dancing, and playing a musical instrument, all mainly through imitation and practice with their preceptor (= personal tutor).

General theories of learning have been developed from the 17th century onwards by educational philosophers like Comenius, Locke, Hume and Rousseau. However, neither the practice of learning languages through the translation of the classics followed by rote memorisation of vocabulary and grammar rules, nor the tradition of conversation with a native speaker tutor, was based upon any theory of language learning in the modern sense of the word (Richards & Rodgers, 1986). Learning a language was considered as a way of 'shaping the mind' of the learner, fostering reasoning through the study and use of morphology and syntax, and as a tool for developing rhetorical skills by studying classical models.

So the appearance in the 1930s of a theory that viewed language learning as stimulus, association, repetition (Skinner, 1938, 1957), based on Ivan Pavlov's theory of conditioning (stimulus-response-reinforcement) was welcomed as a sound, scientifically-based approach. In behaviourism, learning is seen as an unconscious, automatic process that happens through exposure, reaction to a prompt and repetition. Explanation is considered less useful if not counterproductive. An efficient programmed learning system will present all relevant learners with the subject matter in bite-sized chunks in a logical order for repetitive practice. Technology is used where possible as a presentation aid in order to create a 'feedback loop' for further practice on mistakes – usually without any explanation.

One reason behaviourism became pervasive in the 1960s was the development of the related 'behavioural objectives' approach (Mager, 1962); the operationalisation of the two concepts became completely intertwined in 'mastery learning' (Bloom, 1968). Bloom's famous taxonomy (Bloom & Krathwohl, 1956) was related to this effort to systematise subject knowledge and to break it down logically into elements that could be presented discretely as objectives for presentation, practice and assessment of mastery. Usually assessment happened through multiple-choice test batteries, but the search for objectification also led to an avoidance of any judgement in marking by hiding behind arithmetic (Stern, 1992).

The guiding principle of behaviourism is control: control of the environment, control of the subject matter – including strict avoidance of any 'false stimuli' (like mistakes written unintentionally or intentionally on the whiteboard) – and control of the learners' behaviour. In a behaviourist method, essentially everything is scripted and the teacher follows the script. Technological advances allowed the development of teaching machines for programmed learning including, in our field, the language laboratory.

The effects of behaviourism and behavioural objectives echo down the years in our field, as discussed in Chapter 4, though it is difficult to separate these effects from those of structural linguistics, with which behaviourism became intertwined. This is not surprising, because in life in general we also learn by repetition and reinforcement. But turning this natural process into something mechanical and fully codified is counterproductive. Equally counterproductive is applying this theory extensively as if it could explain the entire learning process. Therefore, there is little, if anything, in common between behaviourism and the AoA. However, in the AoA, some repetition and controlled practice has its place at some stage, in anticipatory or remedial work, mainly at very low levels of proficiency. Repetition, the basis of almost all children's games, is, for example, well exploited in communication and grammar games. Besides, 'stimulus, response, feedback' still has a role in pronunciation work. But the relevance of behaviourism is limited to these stepping stones, inserted purposely by the teacher as little segments either before or after task performance.

3.3 The Cognitive Perspective

Language learning is not solely a question of imitation and rote learning. It inevitably and centrally involves cognition.

> Learning language involves determining structure from usage, and this, like learning about all other aspects of the world, involves the full scope of cognition: the remembering of utterances and episodes; the categorization of experience; the determination of patterns among and between stimuli; the generalization of conceptual schema and prototypes from exemplars; and the use of cognitive models, metaphors, analogies, and images in thinking. (Ellis, 2014: 397)

The reaction against behaviourism was a rejection of the dressage of learners that saw language as just another behaviour in which, starting from a *tabula rasa*, people could be drilled into automaticity. A cognitive perspective, by contrast, is interested in the thinking process behind the visible behaviour. Chomsky's (1965) controversial Language Acquisition Device (LAD) and accompanying concept of Universal Grammar, hard-wired in the human species is in many ways reflected in some recent cognitive approaches. Ellis (2006: 109) for example talks of the learner being a *tabla repleta*, endowed with:

> ... a general purpose cognitive apparatus, embodied within the general human form that filters, constraints, and determines our experience, for each of us to learn about our particular world. In the first few years of life, the human learning mechanism optimizes its representations of first language from the cumulative sample of first language

input. One result of this process is that the initial state for SLA is a tabula repleta; it is no longer a plastic system, it is one that is already tuned and committed to the L1. (Ellis, 2006: 109)

Learning a second language is not the same process as learning a first language. Ellis goes on to say that precisely this L1 predisposition interferes with the L2 learning process. Yet at the same time, L2 learners can exploit concepts they already possess. Ellis (2006) gives the example of adverbials – acquired relatively late in L1 but available right from the start in L2 for marking temporal relations before morphology is learnt. From a cognitive perspective, SLE is thus a conscious process that requires the adoption of learning strategies (Oxford, 1990) and some conscious focus on form (Spada, 1997) for learners to *notice* (Schmidt, 1990, 2001) relevant cues. SLE is more effective if there is *meaningful learning* (Ausubel *et al.*, 1978), in which new information is related to and built onto existing knowledge, as opposed to traditional rote learning, that echoes behaviourism.

With the increasing focus on cognition and meaningful learning, applied linguists began to give the ideas of Piaget 'the serious attention it deserved' (Rivers, 1983: 20). It was Piaget's (1950, 1969) work that first brought a more complex perspective to learning theories, with the view that the knowledge of an individual is based on the perception and interpretation of physical and social experiences. These experiences are interpreted by the mind: the learner is no longer seen as a passive vessel to be filled with knowledge, on the contrary he/she *assimilates* new knowledge brought by experience into the schema that he/she uses to understand that aspect of the world for as long as this is feasible. At a certain point, a new piece of knowledge no longer fits the relevant existing schema, which then, after a period of destabilisation, evolves in order to *accommodate* to the new knowledge, thus reshaping that particular schema, and hence the whole world view. In language learning this shift of the system to accommodate new knowledge is called *restructuring* and the destabilisation caused can lead to 'backsliding,' as forms previously used correctly are, at least for a time, used incorrectly (Lightbown, 1985).

A second cognitive perspective on language learning concerns information processing. Chomsky's early research on transformational grammar was conducted in the context of a machine translation (MT) project at MIT. Although he himself then and later expressed zero interest in MT and apparently never got involved in the translation project, his concepts of universal grammar and transformational grammar were of great interest to computational linguists trying to develop MT (Kibbee, 2010). In fact, Chomsky's aim in developing his transformational-generative grammar was actually to try and account for the way people could attribute meaning to any arbitrary sentence and produce an infinite number of meaningful sentences themselves. However, (a) the superficial similarity of his work to that of computational linguistics (who used rather ad hoc graph transformation grammars or transfer grammars for MT); (b) the common 1970s metaphor of a computer for the human brain, and (c) a common association of language use as information exchange across an information-gap led to the introduction of terms such as 'input', 'intake', 'output', 'feedback', etc. to the language teaching literature.

The information processing view of second language acquisition (SLA) is thus another cognitive perspective. Users/learners are seen as having limited processing capacity, meaning that they have to juggle with their free resources to fulfil the demands of the context. In an effort to safeguard fluency, the learner tends to switch performance styles. Ellis (1989, 1992) calls people at the two extremes of the continuum of performance styles 'error-avoiders' and 'communicators'. Foster and Skehan (1996) and Skehan (1998, 2001) demonstrate the way different types of text (e.g. narrative, discussion) result in different compromises between the complexity, accuracy and fluency of the language produced. Other research suggested that error is not a linear phenomenon (higher level = fewer errors): there seems indeed to be a *decrease* in accuracy at around B1 as the learner is trying to accomplish a broader range of more complex tasks and use the language more creatively to do so (see for German: Klein, 1986; for English: Fulcher, 1993, 1996; for French: Forsberg & Bartning, 2010; for Finnish: Martin *et al.*, 2010).

Such findings appear to confirm information-processing theories of second language acquisition (O'Malley *et al.*, 1987; McLaughlin & Harrington, 1989). In relation to an individual's L1, the result is thought to be a comprehensive network which acts *as if* it knew grammatical rules ('parallel distributed processing': Rummelhart & McClelland, 1986). As Ellis puts it, in explaining the associate-cognitive CREED,[1] 'an individual's creative linguistic competence emerges from the collaboration of the memories of all of the utterances in their entire history of language use and from the frequency-biased abstraction of regularities within them' (2006: 101). Ellis continues pointing out that memory of regularities and associations are 'fired' by cues in the context/co-text, with points that are frequently fired becoming 'primed' – needing less stimulation from co-/context to be fired subsequently. However, the extent to which L2 learners can realistically aspire to such a network unless they have very wide exposure to the language over a long period of time is at best uncertain. Skehan (1998) therefore argues that learners need access to rules as well as to their own more limited networks of *exemplars:* 'specific contextually coded items which may contain structure, but which are learnt as chunks' (Skehan, 1996: 42).

The replacement of the traditional representationist metaphor of cognitivism with new constructivist metaphors has allowed the reconceptualisation of cognition as 'a process of organizing and reorganizing one's own subjective world of experience, involving the simultaneous revision, reorganization, and reinterpretation of past, present and projected actions and conceptions' (Davis & Sumara, 1997: 109). This new broader, constructivist conceptualisation of cognition has represented a big leap forward. However, it still sees the individual as autonomous and separate from the context and from other individuals. Thus it adopts a monological view, which is divisive and implies the existence of fixed boundaries and of knowledge as a separate entity. As we will see later, the enactivist theory of cognition and the complex paradigm will go beyond this view and bring in a dialogical perspective that does not conceptualise individuals as being separated from each other and from the context.

The significance of the cognitive paradigm for the AoA is that:

- Learning takes place in a meaningful context.
- There is a need for plenty of interaction in the classroom, so that learners can develop the associations Ellis is discussing.
- Learners need to notice and understand linguistic phenomena in order to recognise them as 'cues' in the first place, so:
- There is a need for focus on form on top of focus on meaning, as well as the development of learning strategies.
- In addition to their developing creative repertoire, learners need – at least during the earlier stages – a collection of useful, functional 'chunks' that they can employ in a strategic way in order to maintain fluency and gain time to formulate original utterances.

3.4 Language as Meaning Potential

The work of Michael Halliday takes an alternative approach to the investigation of how humans acquire a network of language knowledge and skills. Halliday saw the ability to communicate in terms of what a speaker *can mean*, but crucially saw this potential as existing in the *context* and not – in some abstract way – in the person.

> Halliday sees language as *meaning potential*, a system of choices that lies before the speaker. The *context of culture* defines the meaning potential (in ecological terms we might say the semiotic potential or the affordances), the *context of situation* determines how this potential is realised through choices and in action. (van Lier, 2004: 74)

We will consider the concept of affordances, closely related to meaning potential, later in the chapter. Halliday himself said that his concept of meaning potential is 'not unlike Dell Hymes' notion "communicative competence" except that Hymes defines this in terms of "competence" in the Chomskyan sense of what the speaker knows, whereas we are talking of a potential' (Halliday, 1973: 54). Halliday is not interested in seeing language 'subjectively as the ability or competence of the speaker' (1978: 109). He sees this potential, what the speaker can mean, as defined by the range of options characteristic of a specific situation type.

Halliday presents a functional grammar organised in three macrofunctions: ideational, interpersonal and textual. He proposes a 'basic distinction between an ideational (representational, referential, cognitive) and an interpersonal (expressive-conative, social, evocative) function of language' (1975: 52). He underlines the fundamental binary distinction between an idea of language as representation of thought on the one hand and as a communication tool on the other (Piccardo, 2005a), with the interpersonal function defined as embodying 'all use of language to express social and personal relations' (Halliday, 1973: 41) including 'the expression of our own personalities and personal feelings on the one hand, and forms of interaction and social play with other participants in the communication situation on the other hand' (Halliday, 1973: 66). Halliday considered that the language system employed by adults was based on a wide range of functions, which could all be defined as being either ideational or interpersonal. The ideational function is then itself divided into two elements: (a) experiential (giving information, recounting experiences) and (b) logical (Halliday, 1978: 187). Halliday's third macrofunction, the *textual* aspect 'enables the speaker to organise what he is saying in such a way that it makes sense in the context and fulfils its function as a message' (1973: 66), since 'ideational content and personal interaction are woven together with and by means of the textual structure to form a coherent whole' (1973: 109).

It is interesting to note that Halliday did not see himself as a pure linguist but was more interested in the practical aspects of language learning. He identifies the learning of a language as essentially being the learning of a semantic system, adding 'that this process is already well under way before the child has any words at all' (1975: 9). He suggests a list of seven functions, shown below with early exponents of them (1975: 37). The first six are acquired in Phase I of development, between six and seventeen/eighteen months:

Instrumental	"I want"
Regulatory	"do as I tell you"
Interactional	"me and you"
Personal	"here I come"
Heuristic	"tell me why"
Imaginative	"let's pretend"
Informative	"I've got something to tell you"

Whilst the informative, transactional function dominates professional and academic life, it appears late in the child's development, in Phase 2, after the other six functions. The imaginative function, on the other hand is acquired in Phase 1, well before informational language use, and thus appears to be intrinsic to language (Piccardo, 2005a). Halliday defines it as follows:

> Finally we have the imaginative function, which is the function of language whereby the child creates an environment of his own. As well as moving into, taking over and exploring the universe which he finds around him, the child also uses language for creating a universe of his own, a world initially of pure sound, but which gradually turns into one of story and make-believe and let's pretend, and ultimately into the realm of poetry and imaginative writing. This we may call the 'let's pretend' function of language. (Halliday, 1975: 20)

It is interesting that this imaginative function is acquired before the child could put it into a text, since the textual macrofunction is acquired later. The imaginative function appears in the form of 'let's pretend' and singing but remains relatively unchanged during Phase 2 until the acquisition of the textual macrofunction during Phase 3 (after the second birthday). The process is summarised in Figure 3.1.

Halliday's interest in the textual aspect led him to emphasise the tendency in linguistics – and language teaching – to exaggerate the ephemeral 'imperfection' of spoken language as opposed to a 'perfection' in written form:

> The idea that spoken language is formless, confined to short bursts, full of false starts, lacking in logical structure etc. is a myth – and a pernicious one at that, since it prevents us from recognising its critical role in learning. It arises because in writing people only ever analyse the finished product, which is a highly idealised version of the writing process; whereas in speech they analyse, – indeed get quite obsessed with – the bits that get crossed out, the insertions, pauses, the self-interruptions, and so on. (Halliday, 1989: 89–90)

Halliday goes on to say that 'If we persist in treating speech as a caricature of itself, while putting writing (like an inscription) on a pedestal, then there is no way we will ever come to understand how it is that a human child is able to learn' (1989: 101). He suggests that the spoken and written language are quite different in nature:

> ... the written language presents a SYNOPTIC view. It defines its universe as product rather than as process ... as a **thing** that **exists**, ... the

spoken language presents a DYNAMIC view. It defines its universe primarily as process, encoding it not as a structure but as constructing – or demolishing. In the spoken language phenomena do not exist; they **happen.** (Halliday, 1989: 97)

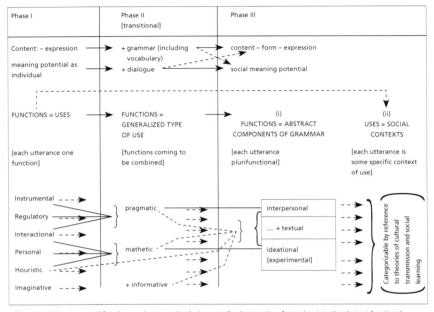

The original developmental functions evolve at one level. via generalized categories of meaning. into the abstract functional components of the linguistic system; and, at another level. into the social contexts of linguistic interaction.

Figure 3.1 Halliday's functions in the phases of child development
Source: Piccardo, 2005a: 23.

This concept of spoken language as a dynamic process of construction and demolition brings us to the study of language in action in speech communities, the study of language as communication. We turn to this dimension in the next section, but before that let us remind ourselves why Halliday's theories are important to understand some of the key tenets of the AoA:

- Halliday's distinctions between interpersonal, informational, and logical use of language had a very strong influence on the scheme adopted to structure communicative activities and their descriptor scales in the CEFR (North, 1994, 1997, 2000; Council of Europe, 2018 – see Table 5.1: Macro-functional basis of CEFR categories for communicative language activities).
- The idea of what a person can mean in a particular type of situation but might not actually perform – for any one of a variety of reasons –

is attractive and comes close to what is intended by the use of 'can do' descriptors in the AoA, which imply that a person can, in the sense of having the potential, act in a certain way in a certain communicative situation.

- In the four skills split between speaking and writing, speaking is essentially treated as a product rather than as a dynamic process, even when it is done impromptu or is the product of an exchange between two people. So all the messy traces of this process are expected to be invisible. In the four modes of communication proposed by the CEFR and AoA, on the contrary, the messy nature of spoken interaction – with the kinds of short bursts, false starts, pauses and self-interruptions etc. to which Halliday refers – is fully recognised. But at the same time, recognition is given to the fact that speech, as well as writing, can, on the other hand, take the form of sustained, logical production, as for instance when putting a case or addressing an audience (for which there are CEFR scales).

- Finally, the AoA approach to working with tasks, which is discussed in Chapters 4 and 7, emphasises the difference between language as mediating *process* and language as final *product* that Halliday makes. Action-oriented tasks have a product, which will presumably be in the target language(s), will almost certainly be the result of an iterative process of drafting or rehearsal, and will be assessed in relation to quality criteria. However, it is during the *process* of developing the product, that the learners mobilise all of their resources – including their L1 or other languages if desired – and that the learner acquires the language as a semiotic code.

Halliday's ideas also had a considerable influence on van Lier's ecological approach and on theories of situated cognition, which we consider later in the chapter.

3.5 Language as Communication

Different conceptualisations have contributed to the move towards considering language as communication. Austin and Searle's work paved the way for this move with their speech act theory. Whereas Halliday saw meaning potential as located in the speech situation, speech act theories saw meaning more in terms of speaker intention. According to Levinson (1983), speech act theories consider meaning to be the product of the addressor, picked up by the addressee by attributing 'illocutionary force' (= functional intention) to the prop-ositional meaning of the words through a process of idiom recog-nition, inference in relation to behavioural and situational cues, or recognition of conversational implicature (= things that can be logically 'read between the lines' in the situation: see Grice, 1975). There were two main approaches to speech act theory, associated with the two philosophers of language Austin (1962) and Searle (1969) respectively. Speech act theory in general and the work of Austin in particular was crucial in the study of communication. In his 1977 *Introduction to Discourse Analysis*, Coulthard commented:

> ... the influence of Austin in particular is evident in all aspects of research into spoken discourse. Workers in a whole range of disciplines – anthropology, sociology, linguistics, psycholinguistics, applied linguistics – have adopted the concept of a speech act in their search for adequate analytical categories ... virtually everyone acknowledges some debt to speech act philosophy. (Coulthard, 1977: 27)

Austin's work, though inspirational, was unfinished at his death. His famous book *How to do Things with Words* (Austin, 1962) consists of a series of lectures given in 1955 at Harvard, the notes for which were later edited into a book by others. Austin focused on the way all utterances perform an action: in this respect Sbisà talks of the 'conceptions of action and agency underlying Austin's speech act theory (2007: 471). Austin defined three types of such acts: locutionary acts (factual statements); illocutionary acts (with illocutionary/functional force, e.g. ask, suggest, advise); and perlocutionary acts (achieving an effect, e.g. convince, persuade), though he emphasised that these distinctions were abstractions Searle further developed Austin's ideas in a systematic attempt to develop a theoretical framework for and comprehensive classification of speech acts. Searle posited that illocutionary force is a rule-governed semantic notion located in the expression. He outlined a procedure that reconstructs the logical process a person goes through (presumably subconsciously) to deduce the intention of an indirect (as opposed to a direct) speech act (Searle, 1975: 63).

In SLE, it is Searle's approach that has greatly influenced the development of taxonomies of speech acts (commonly called functions) such as in Wilkins (1976) notional syllabuses, van Ek's (1975) *The Threshold Level*, and its subsequent update in specifications for different levels (van Ek & Trim, 2001a, 2001b, 2001c) (see appendix to Green, 2012 for functions at all levels). No one seems completely happy with the precise details of the taxonomies which have since resulted, because arriving at a definitive classification even for a single language is difficult. Austin (1962: 150) suggested that there were thousands of English verbs with illocutionary force (i.e. speech acts), whereas Searle (1976) considered that many of these verbs concerned different degrees of force in relation to the same act (e.g. different degrees of intensity in *suggest* and *insist)* and came up with a far shorter list. Even more problematic than a definitive list and/or classification is the question of sample exponents for specific functions. The selection of language examples for functions in works like that of Wilkins and van Ek (and more recently North, Ortega & Sheehan, 2010 for English; Eaquals & CIEP, 2015 for French) is often criticised on the grounds that there is no such direct relationship between form and function in the use of language. As Spolsky (1989: 79) pointed out, functional and structural views of proficiency are complementary and cannot actually be mapped in one-to-one relationships. Learners, it is therefore claimed, should not be presented with connections that are exaggerated.

Despite these problems of classification and form-function relationships, speech act taxonomies with suggested example exponents for different acts (following Wilkins and van Ek), have been hugely beneficial in advancing SLE. They have been influential points of reference for the development of generations of communicative course books and so, indirectly, helped teachers to move beyond just seeing the language as a formal grammatical system. However, such a speech act focus, like a grammatical focus, in teaching as in linguistics, still focuses at the level of an isolated sentence. Meaning is still seen to lie in the sentence. This is not what Austin intended.

Austin's position with regard to the location of meaning was considerably more flexible and action-based than Searle's. He considered that the illocutionary force was located in the whole speech situation – not just in the expression used by the speaker. (At least) two people are involved and they need (1) to share sociocultural conventions and references and (2) to understand one another and agree. Austin, unlike Searle and other speech act theorists who followed him, did not reduce language to the sentence and the speaker's intention in uttering such a sentence. On the contrary, he emphasised the importance of total speech situation saying that 'the total speech-act in the total speech-situation is the *only actual* phenomenon which, in the last resort, we are engaged in elucidating' (Austin, 1962: 148, original emphasis).

Austin considered language as a part of action. He considered that it is the discourse (linguistic and paralinguistic) in the speech situation which determines meaning in context. That is, for Austin, unlike Searle, meaning is co-constructed and situated. However, since speech act theory came from philosophy, it studied artificial sentences and tended to ignore context, particularly culture, discussing sociolinguistic differences between languages at best tangentially: 'All major speech act theorists have ignored cultural diversity' (Allan, 1997: 465). Many researchers therefore moved on from speech act theory to the question of the relationship between and sequencing of the acts, and in particular to the contexts in which the acts occurred: the settings, speech/cultural communities, speech situations and the discourse itself. Here we turn to the work of scholars like Hymes, Goffman and

Schegloff, among others. They took what would become known as an ethnographic or sociolinguistic perspective.

Dell Hymes, one of the fathers of sociolinguistics and ethnography of communication, was an anthropologist with a deep interest in the cultures and plight of indigenous Americans. As Johnstone and Marcello (2010: 1) put it, he was 'fundamentally concerned with linguistic diversity, and so ... he demanded that language study be grounded in ethnographic observation rather than introspective theorizing' (2010: 2) seeing language based in its sociocultural context. He wanted linguistics to start with diversity and study 'the poetic, aesthetic, reflexive aspects of discourse through which cultural knowledge is circulated' (2010: 1). A 'speech community' uses 'means of speech' in a 'speech economy.' A speech community is 'a community sharing rules for the conduct and interpretation of speech, and rules for the interpretation of at least one linguistic variety' (Hymes, 1972b: 54). This view emphasises the contextualised, relational nature of communication and the role of the community in judging appropriateness, in which grammatical correctness would play but a small part. Performance is central. 'For Hymes, only fully-performed speech is fully poetic. The poetic features of performance ... are thus designed to put tradition (linguistic and cultural) on display, to present it rather than just to describe it' (Johnstone & Marcello, 2010: 10). Gumperz also underlined the situated, cultural nature of communication and the consequent need for schematic knowledge and appreciation of contextual conventions, built up through experience of previous talk. He saw culture as 'an integral component of what discourse analysts call schematic knowledge. Although we customarily think of schemata as ways of organising factual information in terms of basic conceptual structures, conversational analysis shows that assumptions about norms, interpersonal relationships and interactive or communicative goals are also involved' (1984: 11–12).

Hymes first presented the notion of communicative competence, which we discussed in Chapter 2, at a conference on language development among disadvantaged children (1966), in which he focused on the importance for children to grow up in a linguistically rich environment since:

> ... a normal child acquires knowledge of sentences not only as grammatical, but also as appropriate. He or she acquires competence as to when to speak, when not, and as to what to talk about with whom, when, where, in what manner. In short, a child becomes able to accomplish a repertoire of speech acts, to take part in speech events, and to evaluate their accomplishment by others. (Hymes, 1972a: 277)

Furthermore, communicative competence 'is integral with attitudes values and motivations concerning the language, its features and uses, and integral with competence for, and attitude towards, the interrelation of language with the other codes of communicative conduct [for this last point Hymes refers to Goffman's work of 1956, 1963 and 1964] (Hymes, 1972a: 277–278).

Erwin Goffman came at conversational analysis from a more prosaic angle. He was a sociologist who studied the social interaction of American everyday life and interactions that were 'framed' – like theatre. Goffman saw much face-to-face communication as unplanned, cooperative, social interaction within a social frame in which 'everyone is accorded the right to talk as well as to listen and without reference to a fixed schedule' with all contributions 'encouraged and treated with respect' (Goffman, 1976: 264). This type of casual conversation is fundamentally phatic communication: 'a type of speech in which ties of union are created by a mere exchange of words' (Malinowski, 1946: 315 cited in Ventola, 1979: 278) of which the aim is 'to create a friendly atmosphere, to establish contact, to forge new social relationships and maintain old ones' (Ventola, 1979: 278). Goffman (1963) describes this as happening in an 'eye-to-eye ecological huddle [which] tends to be carefully maintained' (1963, cited in Gosling, 1981: 168). Conversation is a cooperative venture in which participants collaborate to behave consistently and to protect each other's face: 'A person's performance of face-work, extended by his tacit agreement to help others to perform theirs, represents his willingness to abide by the ground rules of social interaction' (Goffman, 1972: 336).

Schegloff took a broad definition of the setting for conversation analysis to include 'chats as well as service contacts, therapy sessions as well as asking for and getting the time of day, press conferences as well as exchanged whispers and "sweet nothings"' (1972: 375). With Harvey Sacks he took more interest in so-called 'adjacency pairs', the moves and responses to them that are made in conversation, particularly the openings and closings of conversations and turn-taking conventions in general (Schegloff & Sacks, 1973).

The work of scholars such as Hymes, Goffman, Schegloff, together with the work of others that we did not even mention would deserve a far deeper treatment than the limited space of this section allows. They profoundly changed the boundaries of applied linguistics and facilitated the birth of a branch of discourse analysis that concerned itself directly with the educational value of classroom talk (e.g. Sinclair & Coulthard, 1975; Sinclair & Brazil, 1982). This concern with (a) the features of natural conversation and (b) the quality of classroom discourse coincided with the development of the communicative approach to language teaching, inspired by the concept of communicative competence that was introduced in Chapter 2 and that will be further discussed in Chapter 4 in relation to second language methodologies.

In addition to contributing directly to the communicative approach, there are certain points in the developments described in this section that are particularly relevant to the AoA:

- David Wilkins and John Trim were delegates at the first Council of Europe intergovernmental symposium on language learning in 1971, called to discuss the possibility of developing a European unit/credit scheme for adult language learners. It was there that they proposed to base such a scheme on semantic notions and the speech acts (functions) to express them, rather than on the grammatically and situationally based approaches of the time. In retrospect, one can say that their decision was the first step towards the CEFR and the AoA.
- Austin's starting point was language as situated action. Unlike other speech act theorists, he saw this action in the discourse taking place in the context of situation. For Austin, meaning was co-constructed as the speech situation involved at least two people, and an act was not enacted unless there was what he called 'uptake' by the other person.
- These various developments in applied linguistics, but particularly the work of Austin and Hymes, led to an increased attention being given to the quality of discourse in classrooms, starting with the studies by John Sinclair and others at Birmingham, already referred to, plus the pioneering work of Douglas Barnes (Barnes & Todd, 1977) and Gill Brown (Brown *et al.*, 1984) on discourse in small groups. In addition, in SLE, various schemes for classroom observation of teacher and learner behaviour appeared, launching discussions about their respective roles.
- The same developments also led to a greater focus on interaction between learners in the language classroom, with the introduction of collaborative communicative tasks (e.g. simulations, case studies, problem-solving tasks, research and production tasks) carried out in small groups (e.g. Candlin, 1987; North, 1986; Nunan, 1989; van Lier, 1988; Willis, 1996), a move that itself contributed directly to the development of the AoA.
- These last two complementary points informed the vision of interaction in the AoA, for example with descriptor scales already included in the CEFR in 2001 for *Goal-oriented cooperation* and *Informal discussion (with friends)*, as well as for interaction strategies (Tarone, 1980, 1983) like *Turntaking*, *Cooperating* and *Asking for clarification.*)

These last points, concerning work in groups, also relate to the shift from constructivism to the socio-constructivist theories to which we now turn.

3.6 Language as Socialisation: Sociocultural/Socio-constructivist Theories

As we saw in the previous section, the social dimension came to the forefront in relation to SLE. Greater importance started to be given to social aspects with an emphasis on the discourse in which speech acts occur, on interaction and the negotiation of meaning, rather than just production of utterances, on collaborative work in small groups on top of teacher-student interaction in the classroom. In general the social dimension of language started to get centre stage, with all that this implies. This development reflects, and is accompanied by, deep changes in the way psychologists conceptualise learning in general and language learning in particular. Different attempts were made to provide a theory able to explain the development of language in the child, and, as is often the case, these attempts happened in parallel. The two names that stand out are Piaget and Vygotsky. Piaget, the father of constructivism, whose work we discussed in Section 3.3, saw overall development as intrinsic, from the inside outwards. His ideas were further developed in an increasingly socially-oriented direction by his followers (Willem Doise and Anne Marie Perret-Clermont among others) which enabled the move from constructivism into socio-constructivism (Doise & Mugny, 1997), placing the emphasis on learning through social interaction and the environment where the process takes place.

At the time that Piaget was developing his theories in the 1920s and 30s, the Russian psychologist Lev Semenovich Vygotsky was also working on theories that would prove to be extremely important for understanding the development of higher cognitive functions, especially language. Vygotsky's early death together with the political development of the Soviet Union prevented his work from becoming widely known in the West before the publication in English of a collection of his writing under the title *Mind in Society* (Vygotsky, 1978).

Both Piaget and Vygotsky considered that language and thought develop through a process of construction in relation to the social environment. However, while for Piaget the child's language moves from an internal function of the child (egocentric speech) towards a social function (socialised speech) – i.e. development is from the inside outwards, the social phase not being the prominent one, for Vygotsky language is a complex mental function that develops thanks to the cultural mediation and co-construction of meaning in interpersonal communication, before later being internalised and used to regulate cognitive processes and behaviour – i.e. development from outside in, the social dimension being the core one. Thus, Vygotsky rejects cognitive theories according to which the development of concepts occurs first at the individual level to be then transferred to the social level. On the contrary, social activity – and with it the different forms of social and cultural mediation – precedes the emergence of concepts (Lantolf, 2000). The individual reconstructs for him/herself the mediated social interactions that he or she has experienced: 'The true development of thinking is not from the individual to the social, but from the social to the individual' (Vygotsky, 1986: 36).

Furthermore, Vygotsky rejected the linear vision of learning that characterised Piaget's theories. Lantolf *et al.* (2016) explain that 'Vygotsky argued that the process was not universal and monotonic but was instead context-dependent and non-linear and was especially impacted by the quality of instruction provided through formally organized education' (Lantolf *et al.*, 2016: 4). In fact, Piaget had envisaged a series of steps in the cognitive development of children that unfold more or less in the same way, i.e. at approximately the same age children develop different types of learning readiness that allow them to move further. This perspective greatly influenced educational theories in general and SLA research in particular, but was also accused of misleading them (Egan, 2002) and of being 'the likely source of the assumption that language development unfolds in essentially the same way, including under instructional intervention' (Lantolf *et al.*, 2016: 4).

> Vygotsky eschewed naturalistic explanations, unlike Piaget, who specified universal biologically mandated stages of child development. Humans created culture, their own artificial environment, which modified evolutionary determinism. (Marginson & Dang, 2017: 120)

Both socio-constructivism and sociocultural theory (SCT) stress the crucial importance of interaction and collaboration in the learning process. Both perspectives in fact are operationalised in activities with a focus on process. There is a strong emphasis on the use of tasks in collaborative group work, on discovery learning, and collective problem-solving and, in the case of the sociocultural perspective, on the culturally situated nature of all human phenomena, including language. In this section, we only consider SCT, because of its specific relevance to SLE. Furthermore, the conceptualisation of the role of culture in SCT provides a frame for both the relationship between language and thought and for the shift of emphasis in applied linguistics, discussed in the previous section, from grammaticality and speech acts in sentences to the sociolinguistic, sociocultural context of discourse, and Halliday's socio-semiotic view of language stressing the process of learning how to mean. Finally, SCT has interesting links with other theories, especially that of 'affordances' and the ecological perspective in language education (van Lier, 2002, 2004) that we discuss in the next section.

The most fundamental theoretical postulate of SCT is *mediation* of human thinking, where 'instruction, development, and assessment are inseparable processes dialectically unified in the Zone of Proximal Development (ZPD)' (Lantolf, 2007: 693), which Vygotsky defines as: 'the distance between the actual developmental level as determined by independent problem-solving and the level of potential development as determined through problem-solving under adult guidance or in collaboration with more capable peers' (Vygotsky, 1978: 86). For Vygotsky, all learning is *mediated*, so to learn, the learner needs other people. As Lantolf puts it:

> Vygotsky argued that the fundamental dialectical process that gives rise to human thinking (i.e., consciousness) is the interpenetration of two different forms of matter: the human brain, which is subject to the laws of biological evolution, and human social activity, including social relationships shaped by institutions such as family, politics, economy, education, religion, leisure time, and so forth as well as the artefacts that humans create as they participate in the various institutional activities at the core of human life. He argued that consciousness is the consequence of social activity reflected in the human brain. (Lantolf, 2014: 371)

Lantolf uses the term 'dialectic' is in its philosophical sense. For Hegel, thought was a mediation process, an abstract operation through which knowledge was acquired, a view to which Marx and Engels added a social dimension in which mediation was a form of relation between opposing domains and forces in the society. This shows an early consideration of the twofold nature of mediation. Vygotsky then facilitated the crucial transition to psychology and education by explaining how social interaction plays a fundamental role in the development of cognition.

According to Vygotsky, it is the process of mediation which allows one to break out of the dichotomy between the individual and the social dimension, thus overcoming the Cartesian thinking that separates the individual from culture and society (Engeström, 1999), and to see individual processes as completely embedded in (and determined and structured by) social and cultural processes. 'Indeed to become a person is to act with mediational means' (Lantolf & Poehner, 2014: 81).

> Vygotsky repeatedly emphasized the role of mediation in the development of reflexive self-determining human agency, or 'active adaptation' (Vygotsky, 1981, pp. 151–152). Humans internalized their own evolution while securing change in their environment, remaking both their conditions of existence and themselves. (Marginson & Dang, 2017: 119)

The action of mankind with the environment is always mediated by tools that are socially constructed and culturally connotated, and evolve over time as a result of the experience of successive generations. We exploit our environment as 'agents-operating-with-mediational-means' (Wertsch, 1998: 24). All human behaviour is organised and controlled by material (i.e. concrete) and symbolic (i.e. semiotic) artefacts (Swain *et al.*, 2015). And in mental activity the sign as a symbolic tool replaces the material tool. It is with symbolic tools that we construct ourselves and others: whereas the material tool acts on nature, the sign acts on oneself and on other individuals. Language stems from social interaction and it is not until later that it becomes the object of a reflection, in which the learner can reconstruct and internalise processes like thought or learning. We can say that such mediation is at the core of knowledge (co)construction. Indeed, the whole language acquisition process can be defined as 'socialization into communities of practice through the mediation of material signs' (Kramsch, 2002: 6). Internalising another mediational system has a powerful impact on the way people communicate with others, the way they think and eventually on the identity construction process (Pavlenko & Lantolf, 2000). Mediation is itself a complex phenomenon that has been classified in different ways. Lantolf and Poehner (2014) agree with Miller (2011) who identifies three orders of mediation: (a) first order – metacognitive – originating in interpersonal communication and having a regulatory function, (b) second order – cognitive – that has to do with culturally constructed tools that help construct concepts and knowledge, and (c) the third order that concerns the macro-level of institutions and society which influence both first and second order mediation.

In this vision, language takes a vital role as the principal vehicle for mediation, and is used to structure learning both at the individual and social levels. Language as a phenomenon manifests itself through different varieties and is the individual's main accompaniment in his/her search for meaning. The relationship to language becomes even more complex since language is at the same time a working tool, an object of learning, a vehicle for knowledge and a support for reflection and the construction of meaning. The notion of *languaging* 'a dynamic, never-ending process of using language to make meaning' (Swain, 2006: 96), which has developed in SCT, describes the way thought is articulated in order to mediate meaning. This can serve a social goal when a group approach a task (*collaborative dialogue*) and a private one when an individual thinks aloud to mediate the development of an idea (*private speech*) (Swain *et al.*, 2015). These two aspects can also be related: when one person articulates an idea aloud, it helps others to follow the thinking and further develop the concept in question. Language fully plays its role as a semiotic tool to facilitate both thought (private speech) and co-construction of meaning and concepts (collaborative dialogue).

This dynamic and radically innovative view of learning, and in particular the contribution of SCT to our understanding of the process of language learning, greatly contributed to the conceptualisation of mediation in the CEFR Companion Volume. The shift towards the four modes of communication that the CEFR had proposed alongside the idea of social agent was a first step towards a more socially-oriented view of language learning. However it was the fertile scholarly discussion around language learning and teaching that characterised these last decades that enabled the operationalisation of these concepts in the CEFR Companion Volume. The concept of mediation, which is one that had been neglected in mainstream SLE, is crucial to the paradigm change represented by the AoA. Language learning does not occur through studying a code, but by using language as a means to make sense of the immediate environment and as a vehicle to co-construct meaning with others. In mediation activities, the user/learner is not primarily concerned with simple everyday functional goals, but with constructing new knowledge, relationships, identities, and with assisting other people to do so, as we discuss further in Section 6.4.

Vygotsky's theories and SCT are crucial for the AoA, and have many implications, among which are the following:

- This view completely contradicts traditional theories, which explain language learning as a cognitive process that happens at the level of the individual, later put into practice in a social context. Language is no longer seen as a thing apart, separate from both the individual and the social context.
- The consideration of the learner in a social context in which they interact with one or more communities, the increased importance given to the role of others in language learning, to collaboration and exchange and to the support of the community, allows the move beyond a focus on functional exchanges as in the communicative approach to a perspective involving collaboration in the construction of new knowledge.
- Articulating thoughts through the process of expressing them (*languaging*) – and acquiring new knowledge by doing so – is at the heart of collaborative learning, which encourages learners to build upon each other's contributions in action-oriented project work.
- The open vision of mediation proposed by SCT relies upon learners exploiting *all* of their resources, including their L1(s) during collaborative dialogue or private speech, so that they can 'mediate their understanding and generation of complex ideas

(languaging) before they produce an end product (oral or written) in the target language' (Swain & Lapkin, 2013: 122–123). This is further enhanced by a process of *plurilanguaging* (Piccardo, 2018), i.e. exploiting different linguistic and semiotic resources to communicate and (co)construct meaning.

- Even though it is 'an overarching principle' (Lantolf & Poehner, 2014: 57), mediation is not a monolithic concept. It is on the contrary modulated according to the function(s) it performs and the types of elements involved (human and non-human). In all these forms language plays a key role.
- Finally Vygotsky's perspective is a liberating one when it comes to the adoption of theoretical and methodological frameworks. He himself was no purist when it came to theories of learning and methods. He in fact provided concepts that would lay the foundation for subsequent developments of theories of learning. As Marginson and Dang underline:

Vygotsky did not employ a single theory of learning. He saw 'all teaching and learning as conditional and contingent' (Daniels, 2001: 1). These were 'collaborative activities' with 'no uniform methods' (Daniels, 2001: 1). Learning was responsive to social conditions and social conditions were constantly changing. This again creates space for global plurality. (Marginson & Dang, 2017: 124)

This is core to the AoA in which making strategic and reasoned methodological choices for different purposes is a key tenet, as we will see in Chapter 4.

3.7 Expanding the Field: Emotions, Plurilingualism and Creativity

The move towards a socially-oriented perspective, including the use of all semiotic and cultural resources in a process of collaborative co-construction broadens considerably the scope of SLE. Therefore it is not surprising that the theorisation of SLE is currently reaching out to theories developed in other domains, such as psychology (study of emotions and creativity), neurosciences (study of the functioning of the brain), and to other theoretical conceptualisations like complexity theories (study of the functioning of complex systems). These are currently enriching our understanding of what it means to use and to learn a language, and they are essential to theorise the AoA. We start considering these wider issues by discussing emotions, plurilingualism and creativity.

Until very recently, the interest in emotions in SLE was very limited and still under the influence of Krashen's (1981) idea of the 'affective filter,' that might interfere with learning. Emotions for cognitive theories pertain to the individual, localised in the mind (Arnold, 1999), in the brain (Schumann, 1997, 1999) or in general as psychological states (Ehrmann, 1999; Horowitz, 2001). They are seen as emerging from inside the individual, in a process of *inside-out* (Ahmed, 2004; Benesch, 2012: 21). The social dimension is limited to the reaction of the individual when faced with another language and culture (Arnold & Brown, 1999) and the subsequent effect on motivation. By and large, the traditional position of emotion in SLE has been at the margins (Aden, 2010; Piccardo, 2013b).

It is only quite recently that a greater role for the emotions in SLE has been recognised (Pavlenko, 2006). Emotions begin to be regarded not solely as properties of an individual but within the social sphere. The interaction is no longer seen as confrontation but rather as a structuring collaboration: emotions work *'outside-in'* (Ahmed, 2004: 8), being generated in the social interaction and then internalised by the individual. Nevertheless, the place of emotions is often not sufficiently theorised, even in the sociocultural perspective where 'a shared understanding of emotions is assumed' (Benesch, 2012: 26). In fact, although the emergence of emotions in social relations as well as their inextricable link with cognition and the context are emphasised in the sociocultural approach, Benesch pleads for 'a more embodied and dynamic approach to emotions' (2012: 35) and calls for an 'affective turn' (2012: 36). In fact, neurological research makes it clearer and clearer that there is no separation between body and mind: cognition involves the whole body (Damasio, 1994, 1999, 2003). This is not a new idea: already Spinoza rejected the Cartesian idea of a mind/body dichotomy. For him the emotions acted as modifiers to the body, increasing or decreasing its capacity to act (Spinoza's Ethics: 1677/1981). In recent times, a fluid vision of a being capable of modifying others ('affecter') and of being modified ('être affectée') has been proposed (Deleuze & Guattari, 1987). For Oatley and Jenkins (1996) the term 'affect' refers not just to emotions but to a wide range of phenomena linked to emotions, such as moods, aptitudes and preferences, Arnold and Brown (1999) go further still and include everything not included under the term cognitive under the term 'affect,' in order to underline the complementarity between the two. More recently scholars using SCT as their theoretical framework highlight the close interconnection of the cognitive and emotional dimension, that makes it quasi impossible to conceptualise let alone analyse them separately (Swain, 2013; Poehner & Swain, 2016).

In addition, emotions, the 'affect', are heavily influenced by our physical state. We are anchored to our emotions, which determine how we see the world – almost cartographically. Everybody who learns a new language has to somehow (re)create such cartography in order to navigate the unfamiliar linguistic and cultural territory (Kramsch,

2009). Psychologically, the ego has to be redesigned because concrete and symbolic reference points all need to be (re)created. 'The sense of continuity of the self comes from being firmly grounded in the body and its neurological processes. It is precisely this continuity that foreign language learners lack' (Kramsch, 2009: 69). This is because 'what the body remembers are not facts, persons, and events, but neural patterns associated with these phenomena. These neural patterns form the basis of meaning-making practices that are symbolic' (Kramsch, 2009: 70). The symbolic value of language is very strong: one does not learn a language in the way one learns other subjects because language steers our relationships together with our affective, symbolic anchoring, which in turn influences our imagination and values (Coïaniz, 2001). One does not just see the (same) world from a different perspective. Through a new language one redesigns the world (Kramsch, 2009).

The dynamic and social nature of meaning making that we discussed earlier, paired with the implication of both the cognitive and emotional dimensions in the process of learning a language, aligns with the new vision of personal trajectories and linguistic repertoires of the AoA. A person shapes him/herself through exposure to and contact with different languages and cultures throughout life. Understanding that learning another language cannot be seen in a linear, additive manner, but rather in a complex, unbalanced way (Larsen-Freeman, 1997, 2002, 2011; Piccardo, 2005b, 2015; Piccardo & Puozzo, 2015; van Lier, 1997, 2000, 2002, 2004) is at the basis of the concept of plurilingualism (Coste et al., 1997; Council of Europe, 1996, 2001; Lüdi & Py, 2009; Piccardo, 2013a, 2018) that aptly complements the new, open and socially embedded view of language learning that we have outlined. In a plurilingual perspective the process of learning languages has a profound impact on the different dimensions that make up our personalities – e.g. cognition, emotions, culture, identity, body as well as mind.

Far from considering the brain as a sort of vessel with limited capacity where languages would be in competition for space, a new vision of the brain has also emerged, where connections and neuroplasticity (Doidge, 2007) are at the forefront and have brought a radical change (Li & Grant, 2016). 'The idea that the brain is like a muscle that grows with exercise is not just a metaphor' (Doidge, 2007: 43). In addition, there is increasing understanding that 'the plasticity of the mind is embedded and inextricably enfolded with the plasticity of culture' (Malafouris, 2015: 351). The mind/body dichotomy is less and less accepted and the brain is seen as interacting actively with the environment in a dynamic process of reciprocal co-evolution over time.

The brain of bilinguals and plurilinguals, in particular, is no longer seen as a sum of monolingual brains, but rather as a unique, complex system (Bialystock, 2001; Perani et al., 2003). Until very late in the

20th century, the view that 'a facility in two languages reduces the amount of room or power available for other intellectual pursuits' (Baker, 1988: 10) was still common, despite Peal and Lambert's (1962) finding that bilingualism promoted mental flexibility, abstract thinking and superiority in concept formation, favouring development of verbal IQ (Baker, 1988: 17). However, a recent body of research shows that, as the presence of different languages requires activation of the executive control mechanism, bi/plurilinguals enjoy a cognitive advantage (e.g. Abutalebi & Green, 2007; Adesope *et al.*, 2010; Alladi *et al.*, 2013; Bak *et al.*, 2014; Bialystok, 2009; Bialystok *et al.*, 2007, 2008; Thierry & Wu, 2007). This body of research reporting such advantage for both early and late bilinguals (the latter learning languages after infancy) is impressive and growing (Bak *et al.*, 2014). Adesope *et al.*'s meta-analysis of 63 studies showed that 'bilingualism is reliably associated with several cognitive outcomes, including increased attentional control, working memory, metalinguistic awareness, and abstract and symbolic representation skills' (Adesope *et al.*, 2010: 207).

A study undertaken for the European Commission (2009) aligns well with these conclusions. This survey of research over the previous 30 years reported evidence which suggests that knowing more than one language can lead to mental flexibility (the flexible mind); ability to cope with difficulties (the problem-solving mind); enhanced metalinguistic ability (the metalinguistic mind); better ability to learn (the learning mind); increased capacity of interpersonal communication (the interpersonal mind); and a reduction of age-related mental diminishment (the ageing mind). Another article published in the same year came to similar conclusions, stating that 'given high-level plurilinguals' increased perceptual awareness, they are likely to gain new insights, create new analogies and experience creative moments in any domain where perception is at work' (Furlong, 2009: 365).

It is precisely this potential that a new broad conceptualisation of language learning in general and plurilingualism in particular brings to the fore that helps us see further connections with advances in other scientific fields. This is the case of psychology, where the study of creativity has come to conceptualisations that can greatly help us to better understand what is happening in the process of learning languages and to see further connections with advances in other scientific fields.

In the same way as there has been a move away from linear, content-oriented, balanced views of language learning, where languages were considered as discrete entities and learners as depersonalised disembodied and emotion-free individuals, there has also been a parallel move in the conceptualisation of creativity in general. The last few decades have seen a move away from positivistic, person-centred, and unidimensional conceptualisation of creativity toward socially-oriented, dynamic conceptions and systems-oriented research models (Friedman & Rogers, 1998; Glăvenau, 2013, referring to John-Steiner, 1992; Jones, 2009; Montuori & Purser, 1997; Sawyer, 2012). Creativity is increasingly seen as 'an emergent process that involves a social group of individuals engaged in complex, unpredictable inter-action' (Sawyer, 2003: 19).

> Also, in the last few years, a broader sociocultural perspective has appeared, which is characterized by a growing interest in the creativ-ity of different communities and is nurtured through contributions from sociology and anthropology as well as cultural and sociocul-tural psychology (Montuori and Purser, 1997; Tajfel and Turner, 2001; Jones, 2009; Glăvenau, 2010; Sawyer, 2012; Mouchiroud and Zenasni, 2013). (Piccardo, 2017: 6)

Newer models of creativity proposed have a tendency to stress either creativity's multidimensionality (Kharkhurin, 2014), or the necessity to change the lenses through which we study creative acts (Glăvenau, 2013). Glăvenau stresses the social, systemic, ecological, and cultural dimensions and proposes 'a five As framework with the following elements: actor, action, artefact, audience, and affordances' (2013: 70). The relationship between these is shown in Figure 3.2.

The model sees 'creativity as a simultaneously psychological, social, and cultural process and [adds] to it a material dimension repre-sented here by the creative use of affordances' (Glăvenau, 2013: 71). We discuss affordances in the following section: briefly they are perceived invitations to action. For Glăvenau, 'creative action emerges out of actor–audience relations that both produce and are mediated

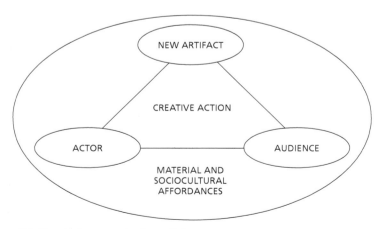

Figure 3.2 Five As framework of creativity
Source: L. Glăvenau, 2013: 72.

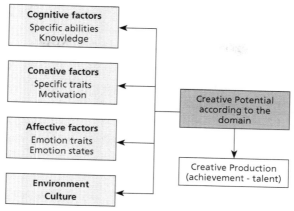

Figure 3.3 Multivariate model of creativity
Source: After Lubart, 2003, revised 2017 by the author, personal communication.

by the generation and use of new artefacts (objects, signs, symbols, etc.) within a physical, social, and cultural environment. In the end, this environment and its affordances are also gradually transformed by creative action' (2013: 71–72).

A second model considers the dynamic interrelationship between a multiplicity of factors: cognitive, conative, affective and environmental. This is the multivariate approach (Lubart, 2003; Sternberg & Lubart, 1995), shown in Figure 3.3.

In addition, Csikszentmihalyi presents creativity as the result of the dynamic functioning of 'a system composed of three elements: a culture that contains symbolic rules, a person who brings novelty into the domain, and a field of experts who recognize and validate the innovation' (Csikszentmihalyi, 1996: 6). Csikszentmihalyi sees a parallel between creativity and the process of genetic modifications responsible for biologic evolution.

Taken together, these three models help us to conceptualise creativity in a way that aligns with the AoA. With these three models together, we can analyse at the individual, social and environmental levels at the same time. All three stress the interdependence of the different elements, actors and factors that come into play. Glăvenau's five A's framework focuses on the interdependence of actor, affordances available to them, and audience, plus the way that artefacts only exist within a social and material environment and embody specific cultural traditions. Lubart's multivariate model sees an individual as a complex system, in which cognitive, conative, and emotional elements interact, nested in a broader system, the environment, with which they interact. In relation to this interaction at the various levels, Csikszentmihalyi's (1996, 2015) systems model shows an emergentist vision in which each element is necessary for creativity, but is not sufficient by itself to produce innovation.

Such a holistic view of creativity is essential if we want to overcome the still very linear perspective of research on the impact of bi/multilingualism on cognition and creativity and capture the rich potential of plurilingualism. Taken together, these three models also conceptualise creativity in a way that aligns with complexity theories, to which we turn in Section 3.9.

The AoA thus broadens the scope of language education by giving personal and collective creativity a central role and by embracing a plurilingual vision.

- The AoA requires an active participation on the part of the learners. This means that they need to be emotionally engaged if they are to be motivated to create artefacts.
- In the AoA, the task is not a more or less authentic activity that is really just an excuse for practice of certain language. The learners are engaged in a co-creation process and in stretching their capabilities to attain a goal in a secure, non-judgemental environment. Hence, apart from being more strongly motivated whilst undertaking the task itself, they have stronger personal, emotional and mental associations with the language used, which will help them remember it better.
- The autonomous (re)construction of concepts and facts, in free association and disassociation, that can be generated by action-oriented tasks within a framework of play and pleasure with free use of all linguistic and non-linguistic resources, can unleash creativity (Piccardo, 2005a) and memorable learning experiences – and people retain better learning associated with pleasurable memories.
- A plurilingual approach, allowing and encouraging learners to use all of their linguistic repertoire and to code switch and experiment with different languages, will help them overcome any monolingual disposition and feel free to further experiment and see connections, common roots, etc. This can be done from a very low level of proficiency.
- Being real-life oriented, action-oriented tasks tend to be open to linguistic and cultural diversity, thus, the AoA encourages learners to be naturally curious about diversity and to consider it as an ordinary characteristic of human nature and everyday life and language.

3.8 Beyond Language Education: Other Theories

The non-linearity of the language learning process that we have highlighted so far and the innovative nature of the AoA calls for the contribution of other theories and concepts that have not been developed specifically for language education. It also calls for a complex ecological perspective (Kramsch, 2002, 2008; van Lier, 2000, 2002, 2004) capable of framing the entire analysis of the paradigm shift that the AoA represents in SLE. In particular, the concepts of agency, communities of practice, collective intelligence and situated cognition cast light on the teaching and learning process in general and present a great potential for the understanding of the innovative conceptualisation of language education that the AoA is fostering. These concepts, together with theories of action, will complete the colourful picture of the AoA theoretical framework. Such a colourful picture calls for an all embracing theory and an ecological perspective capable of bringing all the elements into a coherent and meaningful whole. As we shall see in the final section of the chapter, complexity theory can fulfil that function and act as the meta-theory that provides overall coherence to the AoA.

Agency

As we mention many times in this book, the language user/learner is seen in the AoA as a social agent, i.e. a person who exercises *agency*. 'To be an agent is to intentionally make things happen by one's actions' (Bandura, 2001: 2), in fact, 'the core features of agency enable people to play a part in their self-development, adaptation, and self-renewal with changing times' (Bandura, 2001: 2). Agency is a concept increasingly discussed in education, reflecting the shift away from viewing children/learners as empty vessels to be filled towards the cognitive, constructivist and socio-constructivist/sociocultural views of learning discussed above in this chapter, as well as the dynamic, humanistic view of competence discussed in Chapter 2: 'The human mind is generative, creative, proactive, and reflective, not just reactive' (Bandura, 2001: 4). The concept of agency comes from socio-cognitive theory that 'subscribes to a model of emergent interactive agency' (Bandura, 1989: 1175). This theory rejects determinism (the idea that the environment alone determines what actions a person can take), proposing instead that:

> In acting as agents over their environments, people draw on their knowledge and cognitive and behavioral skills to produce desired results. In acting as agents over themselves, people monitor their actions and enlist cognitive guides and self-incentives to produce desired personal changes. (Bandura, 1989: 1181)

It might be helpful to distinguish clearly between the concepts of actor and agency at this point. Ahearn (2001) cites Karp's (1986) distinction in which an actor is a person who acts in a rule-governed or rule-oriented way whereas an agent is a person who exercises the power to bring effects and to (re)constitute the world. The two terms represent ways of looking at a person's action from different perspectives. Ahearn defines agency as 'the socioculturally mediated capacity to act. According to this bare bones definition, all action is socioculturally mediated, both in its production and in its interpretation' (2001: 112).

Agency occurs in three modes: personal agency, proxy agency (when someone acts for one) and collective agency, which is socially coordinated. Agency has four core characteristics:

- *Intentionality*: centred on plans of action, with 'initial partial intentions ... filled in and adjusted, revised, refined or even reconsidered in the face of new information during execution of an intention' (Bandura, 2001: 6–7).
- *Forethought*: involving likely consequences, anticipation of future events, expectations of outcomes, and the selection of actions. People draw on their knowledge to generate hypotheses about what will happen, weight and integrate relevant factors into composite 'rules' to test their hypotheses against outcomes, remembering which notions they had tested previously, and how well they had worked.
- *Self-Reactiveness*: 'multifaceted self-directedness operates through self-regulatory processes that link thought to action' (Bandura, 2001: 8). These self-regulatory processes serve motivation and include goal-setting and moral judgements about one's conduct – related to personal standards. 'Action is motivated and directed by cognized goals rather than drawn by remote aims' (Bandura, 1989: 1179).
- *Self-Reflectiveness*: reflection on the soundness of thoughts, judged against the outcomes of actions, on motivation.

Furthermore, crucial to Bandura's theory of agency is the concept of 'self-efficacy'. Bandura says that unless people believe that they can achieve a desired result and avoid a bad one, they lack motivation to cope with the unforeseen and overcome difficulties in order to reach the goal. Belief in self-efficacy is enhanced through the following means: cognitive (think positive), motivational (believing motivation can influence the outcome), affective (learning to cope with setbacks), decisional (creating opportunities through careful choices). This all relates closely to Richer's (2017) and Le Boterf's (2010) requirements of *pouvoir agir* and *vouloir agir* for the development of competence, as discussed in Section 2.3.4. In collaborative work, this is particularly important. A group will only function well if people contribute fully, for which they need a belief in self-efficacy: 'If people are to pool their resources and work together successfully, the members of a group have to perform their roles and coordinated activities with a high sense of efficacy' (Bandura, 2001: 16).

In this short section we have given an overview of the concept of agency. Agency is studied in many disciplines and although Ahearn's definition 'Agency refers to the socioculturally mediated capacity to act' (2001: 112) succinctly gels with the CEFR's concept of the learner as social agent, it leaves many questions open, for example: 'Must agency be human, individual, collective, intentional, or conscious? Some studies of agency reinforce received notions about western atomic individualism, while others deny agency to individuals, attributing it instead only to discourses or social forces' (2001: 130). Agency is clearly central to the sociocultural theory discussed in Section 3.6, which, whilst it focuses on the individual, sees the directionality of all learning as being from the outside in (i.e. from the community and its culture). We return to this focus on the individual's interaction with their environment when discussing affordances, ecological approaches and complexity theories in Section 3.9.

Agency theory has several direct implications for the AoA:

- In relation to the goal-setting where 'cognised goals' work better than 'remote aims', hence concrete goals (such as those offered by descriptors selected in relation to specific tasks) work better than vague long term aims or even vaguely formulated short term aims.
- The motivating belief that one can be successful (self-efficacy) is strengthened by experiences of previous success, the chance to compare one's performance with those of others and verbal encouragement.
- Learners operate by an iterative process of feedback and feedforward in relation to challenges: 'motivation is self-regulated through the joint influence of proactive and feedback mechanisms' (Bandura, 1989: 1180). With the proactive control, learners set themselves a target, a standard to reach. They then gauge what they lack to achieve these goals by undertaking an 'anticipatory estimation of what it would take to accomplish them' (Bandura, 1989: 1180), with feedback control after the performance then leading to adjustments in order to reach the desired result. 'The adoption of further challenges creates new motivating discrepancies to be mastered' (Bandura, 1989: 1180).
- In relation to the actual task performances: while learners have problems with tasks that are too difficult for them, especially less self-confident learners, they will undertake challenging ones provided that the work proceeds in an iterative fashion and they thus have the opportunity to be imperfect in their first try, and are not constantly expected to produce a linguistically perfect performance. This suggests an iterative approach to

task performance. As Bandura puts it: 'Conceptions are rarely transformed into masterful performance on the first attempt. Monitored enactments serve as the vehicle for transforming knowledge into skilled action' (1989: 1181).

Action

Austin's theory of language as action (*How to do Things with Words*), which we discussed in Section 3.5 above, started a process that would bear many fruits in linguistics, in particular in the study of the nature and significance of discourse. However, more recent studies have taken Austin and Searle's perspective, focused exclusively on language, to another level focused on action as a broader concept, and particularly on situated action, as we will explain further.

As Filliettaz and Bronckart (2005) aptly point out, in spite of important epistemological differences, the disciplines that study discourse in different academic traditions 'have fundamentally adopted a set of convergent principles: the study of solid empirical data, the consideration for the contexts in which discourse is produced, the importance of individual and collective resources in the regulation of discursive processes, as well as the fundamental role of interactional relations in elaborating semiotic units' (2005: 7, our translation). They talk of a reorientation of the field (2005: 7), or an actional turn (*virage actionnel*) (Vernant, 1997; Filliettaz, 2004), which they see as being rooted in the work of Russian scholars (Leontiev, 1979; Vygotsky, 1999; Bakhtine, 1984), who investigated the issue of activity/action. Filliettaz and Bronckart stress how this constitutes a major shift in applied linguistics, which brings applied linguistics closer to disciplines focusing on the analysis of work. Thus, they identify: (a) the *situation* as the meeting point for researchers and practitioners, (b) *action* as a core issue in social sciences and as a unit of analysis of individuals in workplaces; and (c) *discourse* as both mediation process and tool for planning, evaluation or reconfiguration of actions in a situation (Filliettaz & Bronckart, 2005). It is evident that this goes beyond pragmatics as the study of actual use of language and becomes 'a real general theory of action, in both its linguistic and non-linguistic dimensions' (Vernant, 1997: 20, our translation). The researchers who espouse this theory – based in Geneva – clearly distinguish actions from events, and human action from behaviour, the former of the two in each case stressing agency and the intelligent role of the agent. They also underline the intentionality of every action, highlighting that the goal is not necessarily practical or transactional, but may be aimed either to act on the environment (for instance solving a problem or obtaining something) or to act on oneself (for instance presenting oneself or talking about own experience). In this respect, Denyer (2009) says that during a complex task both types can coexist (she mentions for instance a visit to the doctor), or that, according to the situation, they can be more of the first type (assembling a piece of furniture) or more of the second type (a romantic meeting).

As Richer (2009) reminds us, actional linguistics (where he considers the CEFR is firmly anchored) draws on this theory of action, which is both constituted by action characterised by plans, pre-existing frames and schemas and also situated, i.e. planned and constantly reframed under the influence of repeated evaluation of the context. This allows us to overcome a strictly linguistic vision of discourse and to adopt what Lacoste (1995, as cited in Richer, 2009) calls 'la parole d'action' where the linguistic dimension can only work in relation to structures of action, which go beyond and guide language, but which at the same time are constructed at least partially through language.

The actional shift shows very clearly the importance of praxeology (i.e. the deductive study of human action), and at the same time points out that the praxeologic dimension is rooted in culturally connotated schemas and roles (Filliettaz, 2002). Thus, as Richer (2009) reminds us, these schemas and roles cannot be taken for granted, one cannot assume that the learner has acquired them through their L1 or other languages, as they are not culturally transparent. As Richer (2009) says, the AoA is grounded in these concepts, so there are several implications here:

- Action – exerting agency – is not the same as behaviour: it involves taking the initiative. In the AoA, the learner is expected to act – not just behave properly. That also means the structure of the course and the classroom itself, the nature of the task must all allow the learner room to manoeuvre and so to take the initiative.
- Discourse is seen as both (a) mediation process (constructing knowledge and facilitating that process) and (b) a meta-cognitive tool for planning, evaluation, reconfiguration/revision: these are the two fundamental processes occurring in collaborative group work, which we discuss further in Chapter 6.
- The CEFR and AoA draw on this theory of situated action, with its emphasis on the learner as an agent acting strategically by planning, checking the hypotheses of pre-existing frames and schemas for the context concerned, and reframing these based on experience in a cyclical manner. The expressions used in CEFR Section 4.4 are planning, execution, evaluation, and repair.
- Goals are often not practical or transactional and may primarily involve acting on the self (presenting oneself or talking about own experience).
- In a complex task, also in the classroom, both types of goals, transactional and (inter)personal can usually be accommodated – recalling Halliday's distinction between the ideational and

interpersonal macrofunctions – always bound together in text. Schemas and roles about when to act, how to act, what actions/gestures accompany speech – the entire praxeologic dimension – is culturally-dependent. In the CEFR, this is one of the three aspects of pragmatic competence: called 'design competence:' interaction schemata for how things are done (routes through situations) in the language and culture concerned (Council of Europe, 2001: 126-128). It also relates to socio-pragmatic issues like proximity, body space, whether or not any physical contact is appropriate (touching an arm, shaking hands, kisses as greeting, etc.). This is all part of *savoir être* as well. In the AoA they are learned alongside the language in a conscious, reflective process that precisely develops both communicative language competences *and* general competences.

- In a complex task, also in the classroom, both types of goals, transactional and (inter)personal can usually be accommodated in the same task. This recalls Halliday's point that the ideational (= transactional + logical) and interpersonal macrofunctions of language are always bound together in his third category – text – in any communicative situation.

Communities of practice

Community of practice (CoP) is, as Wenger (1998, 2006) says, a new term for an age old practice. CoPs are 'groups of people who share a concern or a passion for something they do and learn how to do it better as they interact regularly' (2006: 1). The community shares an interest in a particular domain, but members do not necessarily need to work together or even meet often. CoPs are typically organised around a core group, with an inner circle of active members and a wider circle of less active or less frequent participants, who may only provide feedback. Wenger cites the Impressionists as an example: they met regularly but not frequently. The community has more than just interest in common: they take collective responsibility and develop 'a shared repertoire of resources: experiences, stories, tools, ways of addressing recurring problems – in short a shared practice. This takes time and sustained interaction' (Wenger, 2006: 2). The CoP has an informal structure, but a clear facilitator, and needs motivation from its members in relation to a clearly defined mandate. Wenger coined the term with Jean Lave (Lave & Wenger, 1991) in relation to apprenticeships since they noticed that junior apprentices actually learn a lot more from other, usually more senior, apprentices, than they do from the instructor directly.

In our field, we think of CoPs mainly in relation to the continuous professional development of teachers through informal networking, but the concept has a wider potential application, including in the classroom itself. In relation to education, Wenger poses three questions which are also central to the AoA:

Internally: How to organize educational experiences that ground school learning in practice through participation in communities around subject matters?

Externally: How to connect the experience of students to actual practice through peripheral forms of participation in broader communities beyond the walls of the school?

Over the lifetime of students: How to serve the lifelong learning needs of students by organizing communities of practice focused on topics of continuing interest to students beyond the initial schooling period? (2006: 5)

Whilst CoPs can be cultivated, they cannot be 'set-up' or externally imposed, follow preordained processes and strategies; there needs to be a degree of spontaneity, ownership and investment of identity for CoPs to succeed (Pyrko *et al.*, 2017). 'CoPs come to life from the transpersonal process of thinking together' (Pyrko *et al.*, 2017: 390) rather than from external setup. Some of the key points in ensuring the success of communities of practice are to support them appropriately with coaching and logistics, to integrate them into the relevant formal structure in order to give them recognition, and to encourage them by publicising successes.

According to Wenger (2010) a CoP can be seen as a simple social system, whilst a complex social systems can be considered to be a set of interrelated CoPs (like a number of small groups in a class). CoPs demonstrate characteristics of (complex) systems such as emergent structure, complex relationships, self-organisation, dynamic boundaries, and ongoing negotiation of identity and cultural meaning (Wenger, 2010), which we investigate in Section 3.9. In discussing CoPs from a more ecological perspective, Pyrko *et al.* (2017) refer to the concept of *indwelling* (Polanyi, 1962, 1966), 'which is an aspect of the knowing processes that accounts for learning. The process of indwelling captures the relationship of a knower's body with the external world that they learn about as the experience of everyday life' (Pyrko *et al.*, 2017: 393). In other words, indwelling posits fully embodied, situated cognition – rejecting a Cartesian mind/body dichotomy. The more a person dwells in a knowledge area, the more their body fuses with that knowledge area. They go on to talk of thinking together (a term popular with their practitioners) as 'interlocked indwelling' (Pyrko *et al.*, 2017: 394) in which there is personal engagement of identity, development of partnerships and a sense of community.

There are several clear implications from CoPs for the AoA:

- For the classroom, CoPs suggest collaborative tasks and projects in small groups that are oriented towards learners' interests, related to everyday experience that may involve an element of fieldwork outside school.
- A collaborative project can connect the experience of students to actual practice, and possibly even contact in the language concerned with other people beyond the walls of the school.
- Project work does not function automatically: there has to be a 'clear mandate' and the teacher needs to facilitate the task when necessary: just getting them talking is not enough.
- 'Thinking together' comes from personal engagement of identity, partnerships and a sense of community: a group needs this to function.
- Learners can learn a lot from each other as well as from the teacher.
- Giving recognition and publishing success can be documented through a portfolio element; there should be recognition of the effort made in both the process of collaboration and in the artefact produced.

Collective intelligence

The CoP is based upon an assumption of collective intelligence: the group as a whole is stronger than the sum of its parts, bringing a multiplier effect to group problem-solving. Collective intelligence as a term comes from cybernetics: the foundation of the world wide web was inspired by a vision of future collective intelligence. Wikipedia and Google are sometimes cited as examples of collective intelligence – Google answers questions we ask, based on input from previous web users – and artificial intelligence makes steady advances by the incorporation of the expertise of relevant experts. However, the concept is well known in relation to the animal world – the problem-solving behaviour of ants being a commonly known example.

Levy (2010: 71) defines collective intelligence (CI) as 'the capacity of human collectives to engage in intellectual cooperation in order to create, innovate and invent', saying that it can be applied on any scale, from a small group to our entire species. Levy also posits that six major streams of expertise contribute to CI: ethical, practical, biophysical, social, cultural, and epistemic. He sees a reciprocal relationship between CI and human development: 'CI can be seen as a driving force of human development and within this conceptual framework, conversely, human development provides CI with an environment for growth' (Levy, 2010: 71). Collective memory, media and symbolic systems each help the shaping of personal and collective cognitive abilities. The process is closely linked to the development of technology and new symbolic systems: the invention of the alphabet, for example, with around 30 signs rather than hundreds, 'led to the social extension of writing and reading abilities and fostered the development of abstract conceptual thinking' (Levy, 2010: 71).

Attempts have been made to empirically demonstrate the existence of CI, in both traditional groups (e.g. Woolley *et al.*, 2010) and in competitive virtual gaming (e.g. Kim *et al.*, 2017) through factor analysis. What is interesting in this research in relation to our current discussion is a statistically significant correlation between (a) the factor identified as CI and (b) individuals' social sensitivity and reasoning about the mental state of others (e.g. shame, guilt, curiosity, desire) (Woolley *et al.*, 2010). This finding was then replicated for both face-to-face and online groups in a follow-up study (Engel *et al.*, 2014). In this second study, the proportion of variance accounted for by the first factor (identified as CI) was very large, accounting for 49% and 41% for face-to-face and online groups respectively. In addition, the results from a test, which the researchers consider evidence of one aspect of emotional intelligence (Theory of Mind), correlated to the factor identified as CI ($r = 0.53$ and 0.55 for the face-to-face and the online groups respectively). Accordingly, the researchers suggest that the Theory of Mind of individuals (the ability to imagine what other people are feeling) is a predictor of collective intelligence and effective work in groups (Engel *et al.*, 2014).

There are echoes here of Halliday's (1975) distinction between ideational (conceptual) and interpersonal (managing relationships) discussed in Section 3.4; of Goffman's (1963) and Hymes (1972a) view of communication as social cooperation in a cultural context; and of the situated nature of communication and cooperation.

Implications for AoA include:

- CI theory suggests, in line with SCT, that effective co-construction of meaning is dependent on and intrinsically related to the social dimension. Each group is different: so the degree of success in the communication, or learning, or task completion is situated, unique to that group.
- In a group that functions, the whole is greater than the parts: there is a multiplier effect on group problem-solving. Cooperation leads to creating, innovating and inventing.
- Management of the personal relationships in the group is essential to its success: social sensitivity is a predictor of success. This aligns with conclusions of early research on classroom groups (Barnes & Todd, 1977).

Situated cognition

As Gallagher (2009) points out, the mind, body and environment (i.e. culture) make up a complex dynamic system. In fact, one learns to understand other people's behaviour and intentions (and to develop

Theory of Mind) 'through the acquisition of culturally-contextualised narrative scripts in childhood' (Gallagher & Hutto, 2008: 34). We learn to understand the range of human feelings and behaviour, and dangers associated with them, through stories: commonly culturally situated legends and/or fairy stories. The interface between cognition, language and culture is in fact the object of an increasing interest. As Orman says: 'there are no linguistic facts prior to any communicational episode. Communication is the co-construction of meaning in context – not the transfer of information across a gap.' (2013: 91). 'There is no mechanical transference or "faxing" of thoughts and concepts from one mind to another' (Orman, 2013: 94). Orman continues as follows: 'any piece of discourse may be subject to open-ended creative interpretation, the exact nature of which will be a product of its unique contextualisation by whichever individual is doing the interpreting' (2013: 98). The point being made here, about communication being the co-construction of meaning in context, goes way beyond the context of the situation to the context of the language itself: to its culture(s). This relates to perhaps the most pervasive fallacy in relation to language and language learning: the 'language myth – a belief that language is a finite set of rules generating an infinite set of pairs, in which material forms are combined with meanings; it is used to exchange thoughts in accordance with a prearranged plan determined by those rules (Harris, 2001). In keeping with this belief, the function of languages is to express (encode) thoughts and transfer them from one head to another' (Kravchenko, 2016: 108). Coming from the perspective of ecolinguistics, Kravchenko goes on to say that 'the fixed-code fallacy, institutionalized in an education system, accounts for the publicly shared illusion that language is a kind of tool for the transfer of thought' (Kravchenko, 2016: 108).

In fact, researchers into linguistic relativity have shown that the relationship between language, culture and thought is far deeper than is usually admitted (Kramsch, 2004; Niemeier & Dirven, 2000). As anticipated by the Sapir-Whorf hypothesis (Athanasopoulos *et al.*, 2016; Hoijer, 1954), the structure of a language affects the ways in which speakers of that language conceptualise the world, i.e. their '*Weltanschauung*', and both the language and worldview are naturally influenced by the culture concerned. Needless to say, 'culture' is being interpreted in the broadest sense, including for example, an institutional culture, the culture associated with a particular academic/professional discipline or any other social (sub) group. The AoA recognises this connection: the concept of plurilingual and pluricultural competence appears in the CEFR as a single competence.

Echoing Gallagher, Brewer (2018) points out that any *enaction* unites person (mind), action (body), and situation (world) into one global structure. He cites Masciotra, who posits that human functioning emerges from the 'situating/situated dialectic' (Masciotra *et al.*,

2007: 4). An enactive perspective on learning considers that conscious human activity is therefore not something that the mind achieves on its own. Learning needs to be rooted in *dynamic learning situations*. Masciotra and Morel (2011) propose making such enaction, which they call *situated experience*, the central concept in pedagogy, since the person, his/her action and the situation (here: in the classroom) are inseparable in the user/learner's experience. Therefore they talk of developing competent ways of acting (*agir compétent*) by integrating in their experience *action* (A) in a *situation* (S), *knowledge*, (*connaissance*: C), *attitude* (A) and the material and social *resources* (R) on which the person can draw in order to accomplish a real world task, proposing as a result an experiential educational approach they call ASCAR. Parallel to the above, the enactivist position reconceptualises teaching as follows: 'Teaching, like any other collectively situated experience, occurs in wholly embodied contexts that in some way must cohere' (Davis & Sumara, 1997: 113). As they point out: 'the enactivist claim is that cognition does not occur in minds or brains, but in the possibility for shared action' (1997: 117).

In a different educational context, Brown *et al.* (1989) too see all cognition and learning as situated. In addition, they state that conceptual knowledge constitutes a set of tools. They point out that because 'tools and the way they are used reflect the particular accumulated insights of communities, it is not possible to use a tool appropriately without understanding the community or culture in which it is used' (1989: 33). They emphasise the need for learners to engage in authentic activity for any learning to be effective, defining authentic as 'the ordinary practices of the culture' (1989: 34). For instance, if one wants to become a tailor, one has to engage in the ordinary practices of a tailor. They propose a form of *cognitive apprenticeship* and *collaborative learning*, which is described as *situated learning* by Lave and Wenger (1991). The initiatives of Brown *et al.* and Lave and Wenger reflect the move towards competence-based vocational training, and the common factor is a move towards practice-related tasks in a specific profession-related, complex situation.

There is a clear link between these various conceptualisations of situated learning and the concept of competence as situated action that was discussed in Section 2.3.2. In the professional world, competence came to be seen during the 1990s as always situated in action, involving improvisation in the face of unexpected developments (Richer, 2012) and management of complex unstable situations (Le Boterf, 2010). Training at a high level in public institutions (US Government, European Commission) is informed by *action learning* (Kramer, 2007) in identifying problems, reflection plus question formulation, followed by problem solving. This is not unlike *action research* in teacher education (Edge, 2001).

The main implications of situated learning for the AoA are the following:

- Situated experience is a central concept in the AoA. The teacher needs to provide *dynamic learning situations.*
- Authentic activity is necessary for any learning to be effective; decontextualised activity is not authentic and will not lead to efficient learning. Tasks should reflect the kinds of activity that would occur in real life.
- Language is always associated with a (sub) culture, which has a domain of use, a register and a style associated with it. AoA tasks should be situated in this sense, so that learners learn to adopt different genre styles in artefacts they produce, or – if the task involves a performance – that the brief makes clear what register and tone is appropriate.
- The fact that we are used to learning through 'culturally-contextualised narrative scripts' (often fairy stories that have a message) can be exploited in a creative way in tasks related to identity, compilation of experiences – or text products in familiar genre (perhaps of this type)
- An information-gap view of language has been criticised since the early 1980s (e.g. Alderson, 1983; Smith, 1985). Texts do not have the same meaning for every reader; concepts cannot be transferred one-to-one across languages. These two facts have implications for how learners approach tasks – they need to be made aware of this.

During the 1980s there was also a recognition in SLE of the need for organising language teaching and learning around broader, complex, situated tasks (e.g. Debyser, 1986; Jones, 1982; Nunan, 1989) and a new vision of giving learners more autonomy (Holec, 1981) in using all of their language resources in such tasks (Candlin, 1987; North, 1986; Willis, 1983). In applied linguistics the theoretical underpinnings of such moves came from research fields that studied language as a situated phenomenon (ethnography, pragmatics and conversational analysis: see Section 3.5; sociocultural/constructivism: see Section 3.6). But the ideas are also closely related to Halliday's concept of the situated meaning potential (Section 3.4) and the related notion of affordances, to which we now turn.

3.9 Affordances, Ecological Models and Complexity Theory

As we have seen in this chapter, many different theories have, in one way or another, contributed to broadening the vision of SLE over the last thirty years, stressing its situated and collaborative nature. These theories have contributed to understanding what happens in

SLE at the various levels, from the individual learner to the social level of the group and/or class, providing lenses from which one can analyse from both the learning perspective and the teaching perspective. As we have seen, so many layers and dimensions are involved in the act of teaching/learning a language: linguistic, psychological, cognitive, sociological, collaborative, environmental, among others. It is time to try and see these influences together, rather than viewing them separately in a linear way and deploying one or the other, or one after another, in an eclectic manner. It is in fact crucial to understand the way in which all these various factors interrelate, if we wish to have a pedagogy in which teachers have a rationale for their practice and can share this with learners. This calls for a broad theoretical framework, one that allows us to see the connections and to encompass theoretical contributions at the different levels. This requires the adoption of ecological and complex models, the only ones that are able to act as metatheories and provide us the key to interpreting phenomena, help us to see the interrelation of different elements, human and environmental, and to understand the way in which, through this interrelation, they all influence each other and change over time.

From an ecological perspective of SLE (Kramsch, 2002, 2008; van Lier 2000, 2002, 2004), complexity theory helps us to study the systems that are involved at different levels, modelling the way these systems work and further develop over time. 'Systems theory, being process-oriented and content-based, offers specific suggestions on how to research complex processes such as language learning in ecological ways' (van Lier, 2004: 214). Within this ecology, the notion of affordances provides a precious key that helps to better understand the concept of agency and its role in a systemic perspective. This ecology is what we are going to discuss in this section.

As van Lier already noted 20 years ago:

> An ecological perspective on language learning offers an alternative way of looking at the context in which language use and language learning are situated. ... The concept of ecology embraces not only the context of classroom learning but, more fundamentally, the very definitions of language, of development, and of mind. It proposes to be a radical alternative to Cartesian rationalism, body-mind dualism, and the anthropocentric world promoted for several centuries. It replaces these views with a conception of the learning environment as a complex adaptive system, of the mind as the totality of relationships between a developing person and the surrounding world, and of learning as the result of meaningful activity in an accessible environment. (1997: 783)

In the same article, van Lier says that an ecology is a complex network of interacting organisms and therefore that an ecological perspective requires an approach to theory that 'learns from complexity science and chaos theory [Larsen-Freeman, 1997]' (van Lier 1997: 786). Larsen-Freeman herself at the time says that 'The study of complex nonlinear systems and the study of language have much in common' (1997: 147) particularly in the sense that both language and second language acquisition are dynamic, variable processes – not well captured by models of that time – and in the sense that they are subject to growth and change with language 'grow[ing] and organiz[ing] itself from the bottom up in an organic way, as do other complex nonlinear systems' (1997: 148).

It is no coincidence that van Lier (2004) points out many parallels between Halliday's systemic view of language, which we discussed in Section 3.4, and the ecological perspective. For Halliday, meaning potential is embedded in the situation as choices that are offered to the language user. As we pointed out in Section 3.4 it is culture that determines the meaning potential, which van Lier says could be seen as 'the semiotic potential or the affordances' (2004: 74) and it is the situation that determines 'how this potential is realised through choices and in action' (2004: 74). In other words, van Lier equates meaning potential with affordances, a concept which is key in the ecological perspective. In this respect he proposes the expression 'action potential' (2004: 92).

Affordances are 'opportunities for action in the environment' (Käufer & Chemero, 2015: 166). Gibson (1986), in introducing affordances, stressed three principles (a) perception is direct and not inferential; (b) perception is related interdependently to action, and (c) the environment provides sufficient information for both perception and action. Subsequent researchers (e.g. Cole, 1996; Valsiner & Rosa, 2007) refined Gibson's view of affordances in a way that is particularly relevant for education. Rietveld and Kiverstein (2014), for example, stress how '[a]ffordances are relations between aspects of a material environment and abilities available in a form of life' (2014: 335). There are endless affordances at any given moment, even though only some of them are perceived as invitations to action. Käufer and Chemero suggest that a human or animal engaged in a task 'is only sensitive to the affordances that are relevant ... Only those relevant affordances ... are experienced as invitations' (2015: 203). The way we engage with the environment, including the ability to perceive affordances is determined by culture (Glăvenau, 2012). The world is structured by cognition and action, and appears as an *affordance space* (Brinker, 2014; Gallagher, 2015), determined by individual characteristics and experiences, including the stage of physical and mental development, plus sociocultural constraints.

In relation to language, Cowley and Gahrn-Andersen (2018) talk of a 'united view of language and agency' and state that: 'Turning from input–output metaphors, people act as they perceive and, inseparably, perceive as they act. Language is part of what, echoing Berthoz, we call *perçaction*' (2018: 3). As van Lier puts it in discussing an action-oriented, ecological approach: 'From an ecological perspective, language *learning-as-agency* involves learning to perceive affordances (relationships of possibility) within multimodal communicative events. Every subject and every topic is an 'affordance network' that is accessed through collaborative activity' (2007: 53, our emphasis). Kramsch and Whiteside (2008) talk of the ecological approach's 'notion of activity, grounded in physical, social, and symbolic affordances, among which language plays an important part as 'a system of relations' (van Lier 2004: 5)' (2008: 657–8).

Chomsky's idea of the language acquisition device (LAD) that we discussed in Sections 2.2 and 3.3, was based upon the assumption that the environment does not provide enough experiential information about the rule-governed, generative nature of language and that therefore a child, in order to acquire language, must have access to a non-experiential (i.e. internal) source: the LAD. In outlining an ecological interpretation of child development, Reed (1995), by contrast, claims that: 'The ability to use language generatively develops out of the uniquely human action skill of prediction, which itself develops out of a suite of perceptual, cognitive and action skills, including the ability to indicate, categorise and understand objects and events in the surrounding world' (1995: 2). Almost every toddler 'finds him or herself in the midst of at least one quite active linguistic community manifested in the persons of the toddler's caretakers, family and friends' and the child's explorations of their capacity to communicate occur in a 'richly structured environment of daily routines, abounding with gestures and vocalizations' (1995: 2) in which cognitive developments such as 'the increased comprehension of ecological relationships such as possession, causality and intentional action' (1995: 2) and their possible transformations, are modelled and remodelled for the child on a daily basis with routines, interactive games, songs, etc. 'Far from being a receiver of stimulus inputs, who must somehow hypothesise the structure of the language around her, the human infant is a very active agent' (Reed, 1995: 10). For example, the learning of syntactic patterns 'comes about not through a specifically linguistic process, but through a combination of perceptual, actional, and interactional learning' (1995: 16). Reed concludes that 'the elements of language development are truly ecological, being the relationships that exist between the child and the world she encounters, and her growing appreciation of those relationships. ... The inherent tensions between the very young child's skill at using words and the complex patterns required by caretakers and others to fully understand what the child is doing with those words ... lead to a strong motivation for the child to develop mastery of a number of aspects of linguistic variation' (1995: 24).

This theory supports the idea that one is involved in a dynamic, creative process whilst learning a language. According to Glăvenau, 'creativity can be defined as a process of perceiving, exploiting, and "generating" novel affordances during socially and materially situated activities' (2012: 196). He proposes a tripartite model to theorise creative acts that comprises the intentionality of the actor and the normativity of any cultural context, underlining the importance of making visible affordances that are as he put it, uninvented, unperceived and/or unexploited. A major issue is the relation to the norm. Glăvenau associates creative expression with the exploration of a *terra incognita* (Piccardo, 2017), i.e. of the full *landscape of affordances* (Gallagher *et al.*, 2017; Rietveld & Kiverstein, 2014) offered, not just following the usual, well-trodden track. He uses a case study concerning traditional Easter egg-decoration to show how stretching and transgressing the norm, without violating it, can have a creative force since it makes more affordances visible, and therefore available, and permits the adaptation, or even breaking of, existing rules and conventions, whilst remaining true to the overall tradition. This is the basis of an ecological, action-oriented perspective. Education is a process of learning 'to selectively pick up some aspects of the environment while ignoring others' (Rietvel & Kieverstein, 2014: 335) and this process can either be a restrictive or empowering one, depending on how it is itself experienced by the learner, and on the rigidity of norms. This recalls the distinction made between an 'actor' and an 'agent' when discussing the theory of agency in the previous section. Less restrictive pedagogic norms allow agency.

Affordances are acted on by individuals when they exercise their agency by accepting invitations that they perceive in the environment. But individuals do not act in a vacuum. The result of their actions in the environment and their use of the resources, interacts with the actions of others and the environment itself in complex ways, leading to the emergence of new phenomena and states. The result of all these interactions in an ecology is change – often unpredictable – over time. Complexity theories study precisely complex systems changing over time (Le Moigne, 1994/2006, 1996, 2003, 2012). For this reason, they are essential in casting light on an ecological perspective on language learning and teaching (de Bot *et al.*, 2007; Davis & Sumara, 2005; Larsen Freeman, 1997, 2002, 2011; Larsen Freeman & Cameron, 2008; Piccardo, 2015). However, complexity theories are themselves a galaxy, as they developed in different scientific fields and were nurtured by diverse contributions. In a sense, they also emerged over time. Therefore, we dedicate a little space to help the reader come to terms with this galaxy before explaining their crucial contribution to SLE and the AoA.

The plural term 'complexity theories' encompasses studies on complexity, general system theory, dynamic systems theory, fractals, and what is generally known as 'the butterfly effect'. Many different disciplines have researched complexity and contributed to our understanding. It would be beyond the scope of this book to discuss the differences between these contributions. After a brief overview of the overall development, we will focus on the core message that complexity theories convey, in particular the use of the concept of Complex Adaptive Systems (CAS) to investigate phenomena difficult to study from a classical, linear perspective. We will draw upon both Chaos/Complexity theory (C/CT) and Dynamic Systems Theory (DST), offered by scholars working on the two sides of the Atlantic, in particular Larsen-Freeman in the US and De Bot, Lowie and Verspoor in the Netherlands, as we agree with Larsen-Freeman that C/CT and DST are complementary and insightful when it comes to studying second language acquisition (Larsen-Freeman, 2007). We will also draw upon the French-speaking tradition, where the preferred terms are '*théorie de la complexité*' and '*théorie du système* or *systémique*', a choice that is also preferred in other continental contexts. Thus, our terminological choice is 'complexity theories' (CTs) in the plural form to try and capture theses multiple perspectives.

A complex phenomena is very different from a complicated one, although both concepts share a common etymological root. In Latin, '*complexus*' (participle of complector) is made up of '*cum*' and '*plecto*' (Greek πλεκο: to fold and to weave, from Indo-European plek: part, fold, intertwining). Complicated things (from Latin *cum-plicare* > *complicatus*) can be chunked down or unfolded into their components, as for instance with a motorbike; complex things (from Latin *cum-plectere* > *complexus*) cannot, because they consist of elements linked to and interdependent on each other, so any attempt to go back to their simple components destroys the entire fabric (Alhadeff-Jones, 2008). For instance in a recipe, ingredients – like the oil and egg in mayonnaise – are no longer separate components, they cannot be retrieved in their initial state. This important distinction, which recalls the main statement of Gestalt philosophy that the whole is more than the sum of its parts, is at the core of complexity theories. CTs are incompatible with the second Cartesian principle that states that if we want to understand a phenomenon, we must subdivide it into its components so that we can analyse them one after another. Cartesian vision is linear; it conflicts with a complex vision. In a complex phenomenon or situation, a certain lack of simplicity is inevitable and rather than seeking to reduce things to a simple level, the appropriate response is to engage with and try to understand the complexity (Ardoino, 2000).

Gaston Bachelard (1934/2003) pioneered this idea already in the 1930s when he pointed out that an apparent lack of order is an intrinsic characteristic of natural phenomena. Warren Weaver, in the article *Science and complexity* then provided the foundation for complexity theories in 1948 with the vision that complexity is not a casual assemblage of elements, but rather refers to organised – but non causal – relationships between different elements that create a model or pattern. Von Bertalanffy's *General System Theory* (1950, 1968) provided the conceptual tools necessary to investigate systems characterised by a high number of interrelated and mutually interactive elements (= complex systems). Scientists analysed the way in which the elements in a system, through their interaction, spontaneously and autonomously developed collective characteristics and patterns (Nicolis, 1995). In the 1970s and the 1980s, chaos theory then underlined the unpredictability and evolution of systems (Gleick, 1987), which were understood to be able to generate by themselves (Maturana & Varela, 1980; Mingers, 2001; Varela *et al.*, 1974, 1991). Fractal theory (Mandelbrot, 1983) highlighted the recurrence of geometric patterns, nested in each other at different scales. De Bot (2016: 126) points out that: 'Dynamic systems are typically nested: large systems consist of sub-systems and these in turn consist of sub-sub-systems and so on.' Van Geert (1994) defined dynamic systems as 'set[s] of variables that mutually affect each other's changes over time' (1994: 50). DST is particularly interested in this aspect. In general though, all CTs are concerned with the study of complex systems and their changing over time.

The development of complexity theories was not the exclusive realm of the natural sciences. Social sciences have also greatly contributed to the complexity turn. The philosopher and sociologist Edgar Morin (1977, 1990/2005, 2001, 2004; Morin & Le Moigne, 1999), one of the major theoreticians in this field, took a comprehensive, interdisciplinary approach encompassing ethical and political dimensions of complexity. Together with Jean-Louis Le Moigne, who came more from the engineering and business management side, he is one of the leading figures in the European programme MCX *Modélisation de la complexité* (www.mcxapc.org). In general, complexity-informed research in social sciences also encompasses epistemological questions concerning the nature of knowledge, how it takes certain forms and how these forms are accepted and validated by the relevant communities and cultural contexts. Thus, one should stress that the conceptualisation of complexity is the result of work in many natural and social sciences. Therefore, instead of seeking a unified theory, it makes more sense to recognise the kaleidoscopic nature of the complex vision in order to investigate phenomena from different viewpoints.

For Le Moigne (2006) systemic theory is a meta-theory which enables *modelisation* of reality as opposed to (Cartesian) analysis: '*La science des systèmes s'entend comme la science de la modélisation systémique*' [The science of systems is understood as the science of systemic modelling] (2006: VII). Larsen-Freeman and Cameron also consider C/CT as a meta or supratheory (2008). The dynamic, evolving pluralistic nature of societies, cultures and language varieties, both at the social and at the individual level, is well captured by CTs, which have at their core 'the understanding of the behaviour and organization of living organisms as dynamic systems' (Herdina & Jessner, 2002: 77). CTs provide powerful metaphors that facilitate describing, modelling and predicting development over time, which play a major role in all scientific work (Herdina & Jessner, 2002). CTs have thus proved effective in a re-conceptualisation of language and language education (de Bot *et al.*, 2007; Larsen Freeman, 2011, 2017; Larsen-Freeman & Cameron, 2008; Piccardo, 2010a, 2015, 2016b; van Geert, 2008; Verspoor *et al.*, 2010). Larsen-Freeman summarises the potential as follows: 'complexity theory seeks to explain complex, dynamic, open, adaptive, self-organizing, nonlinear systems. It focuses on the close interplay between the emergence of structure on one hand and process or change on the other. Language, its use, its evolution, its development, its learning, and its teaching are arguably complex systems' (2011: 52).

CTs can thus be particularly suitable for the study of the inter-relationships between phenomena like situated learning, collaboration, creativity, socialisation, plurilingualism, particularly since, as we have seen in this chapter, such concepts include multiple aspects, and overlap with each other. In CTs, systems are increasingly investigated as Complex Adaptive Systems (CAS), with elements generating patterns and collective properties through their spontaneous interactions. CAS have a number of essential features, of which the following are the most central:

- *Dynamism*: elements interact dynamically, physically or through information exchange.
- *Openness*: in constant contact with their environment, dependent on both internal and external resources and a constant flow of energy.
- *Sensitive dependence on initial conditions*: a small disturbance can lead to very different effects, small differences in the initial conditions may or may not have an impact.
- *Self-organisation*: aiming to reach a state of balance called homeostasis through an internal regulatory process – yet constantly transforming and so any balance is only transient.
- *Adaptability and development*: either as a whole or through the interacting elements, they develop over time in an iterative, interrelated way.
- *Self-similarity*: the same (or a similar) shape is found at whatever scale one observes the system. This is the core of fractal theory and explains the nested nature of CAS.

CAS evolve constantly, independently of initial conditions, towards particular conditions or ensembles called *attractors*: over time 'a dynamic system will move from one attractor state to the next, but what the next attractor state will be is unpredictable ... and the same system with identical initial conditions may show different attractor states' (de Bot, 2016: 128). Attractors can be just simple recurring equilibrium states, or growing and changing patterns, representing regions of connected order at the edge of chaos. The attractors can also be chaotic, in which case we talk of 'strange' attractors.

Fundamentally, *phenomena of emergence* characterise CAS. That is to say, CAS experience the spontaneous development of new properties or structures. The term *emergent properties* is used to refer to a property of the whole system which emerges from the interaction between its component elements; the term *emergent process* is similarly used to describe a process that affects the whole system, without affecting any of the system's elementary processes, which emerges from the interactions and combinations of those elementary processes. Emergence happens when simple elements or organisms self (re)organise to form more complex systems which are able to adapt to new conditions. 'Emergence is the appearance in a complex system of a new state at a level of organization higher than the previous one. The emergent behaviour or phenomenon has some recognizable "wholeness"' (Larsen-Freeman & Cameron, 2008: 59).

> Emergence presupposes a non-reductive change, from a lower-level phenomenon to a higher level phenomenon, from individual ants to an ant colony, from a bunch of houses to an organized city, from perception to thought, from pointing to language, etc. *Non reductive* means that the lower-level elements (things, behaviours, skills) cannot explain the higher-level ones, thus they are qualitatively different, yet the higher level is clearly in some way based on, derived from, or built up from, the lower level. (van Lier, 2004: 82)

Emergence is a core notion in CTs, stressing the capacity of CAS to self-organise and change over time – as opposed to following a pre-existing form of plan or external order. Thus, CTs are particularly suitable for the analysis of the role of languages and cultures within our increasingly linguistically and culturally diverse societies which include multiple elements, can be approached from different perspectives, and develop over time. If one adopts complexity as a theoretical framework, a plurilingual vision of linguistic exchanges captures all these characteristics. Such an exchange can be considered a CAS that evolves towards specific conditions, which can also be chaotic. CTs are equally important to investigate the complex phenomena happening in the class, where each individual is a CAS, a collaborative group is a CAS, and both of these CAS are nested in a broader even more complex adaptive system, the class (which is itself, by the way, nested in the school, the education system and society). All these CASs interact with each other and are modified by these interactions. This process takes them through periods of chaos, to new phases of homeostasis (balance), which are themselves temporary and transitory. In all these interactions new phenomena emerge, new learning takes place. Larsen-Freeman and Cameron point out that: 'Emergence in learning occurs when new ideas fall into place' (2008: 60) and that 'learning a language is not a single process of emergence but a succession of cycles of emergence' (2008: 61). Larsen-Freeman points out that the usage-based and emergentist perspectives on first language acquisition (such as Ellis's views discussed at the beginning of Section 3.3 and by Ellis & Larsen-Freeman, 2006), which hold that 'humans are sensitive to frequency of perceptually salient and semantically transparent linguistic features in the language to which they are exposed' align well with complexity theory (2011: 55). However, she continues that frequent exposure is not sufficient to trigger development: as suggested by affordance theory, the salience must actually be noticed and the transparency (relationship of the cue to meaning) must be clear.

Larsen-Freeman and Cameron add that a language itself 'emerges from the multiple interactions of its speakers'. In fact, language, like culture, is not an entity existing independently of the users of that language, it is precisely an entity that emerges from the use of that language by all the individuals concerned. This is why it undergoes a never-ending process of change, and any form of stabilisation is only transitory and context-related. Not only does language emerge, but cognition too 'exists in the *interstices* of a complex ecology of organismic relationality' (Davis & Sumara, 1997: 110), thus understanding can be theorised by adopting the same perspective that Gadamer (1990) adopted to discuss conversation, seen as distinct from other modes of interaction. The topic of conversation and the way it unfolds emerge in the very process of conversing: 'the conversation is not subject to predetermined goals, but unfolds within the reciprocal, codetermined actions of the persons involved' (Davis & Sumara, 1997: 110), a phenomenon that the authors link to Merleau-Ponty's concept of 'coupling' (1962) and more recently Varela *et al.*'s concept of 'co-emerge' or 'mutual specification' (1991). Thus, they highlight, using both emergence and co-emergence in an enactivist perspective, we can explain the complex behaviour of a system, such as a student or the teacher (through emergence), and the emergence of larger systems, such as the class or society (through co-emergence). This double perspective allows us to completely overcome the separation of the individual and the collective, and thus adopt a complex, ecological perspective.

One point that needs to be made is to emphasise that with the concept of emergence, CTs do not imply determinism or deny agency: 'complexity theory provides a nondeterministic logic, suggesting that complex dynamic systems are free to develop along alternative trajectories' (Larsen-Freeman, 2011: 59). Larsen-Freeman goes on to say: 'it is not contradictory that, at the same time as individuals are operating in intentional ways in the moment [i.e. are exerting their agency in relation to affordances in the context], their personal language resources and those of their speech communities are being transformed beyond their conscious intentions' [as the CAS at each level – individual/community – further evolves through the process of emergence] (2011: 59).

CTs thus not only offer a new vision of scientific knowledge, they provide an apparatus for interdisciplinary teams to investigate complex systems in the social sciences, including applied linguistics. In this field, it is particularly interesting to apply CTs both to the language itself that can be seen as a CAS (Ellis & Larsen-Freeman, 2009; Larsen-Freeman, 1997, 2011; Larsen-Freeman & Cameron, 2008) and to the class and the teaching/learning process (Davis, 2008; Davis & Sumara, 2005; Larsen-Freeman & Cameron, 2008; Piccardo, 2005b, 2010a, 2015). In fact: 'Taking a complexity theory perspective on the language classrooms places the focus on action: communicative and speech action, teaching action, language-using, thinking, task action, physical action' (Larsen-Freeman & Cameron, 2008: 197). Stressing the dynamic nature of the language, the interconnection of all elements in the classroom system, the co-adaptation that characterises change within the system as well as the role of the teacher in managing the dynamics of the learning process, Larsen-Freeman and Cameron (2008) show the potential of adopting CTs to make sense of all these forms of action. We certainly agree with this and we stress the potential of CTs for providing a general framework, a meta-theory able to help researchers and practitioners in conceptualising the development of language education at all levels, including the fostering of creativity (Piccardo, 2016b) and plurilingualism (Piccardo, 2018).

> [L]earning (and, similarly, teaching) cannot be understood in monological terms: there is no direct, causal, linear, fixable relationship among the various components of any community of practice. Rather, all the contributing factors in any teaching/learning situations are intricately, ecologically, and complexly related. Both the cognizant agent and everything with which it is associated are in constant flux, each adapting to the other in the same way that the environment evolves simultaneously with the species that inhabit it. In simplest terms, ecological thinking understands that the boundaries we perceive between different objects and different events are mere heuristic conveniences. Everything is inextricably intertwined with everything else. (Davis & Sumara, 1997: 111)

Thus a complex, ecological perspective offers a great potential as an overarching framework for SLE, as we have seen in this final section of the chapter. Some of the most significant points in relation to the AoA are summarised briefly below:

- Language growth occurs at the border between order and chaos: 'life at the edge of chaos' is a chapter title in Waldrop (1992: 198). Learning a language operates in a similar way: learning occurs at the edge of learner's comfort zone.
- Meaningful activity in the classroom entails a dynamic rather than linear approach; the CAS (or CASs) that the class represents is to some extent self-organising and can develop through shared goals and experiences into a Community of Practice.
- The move towards complexity is a move away from the linear, computer metaphor of language learning that implied 'input', some processing and an 'output'. This viewed language as a ready-made product (= code) to be consumed. In a complex ecological view, language emerges in action and interaction; it is constructed while it is used and thus is never exactly the same as on previous occasions (van Lier, 2004).
- From a complexity perspective, language is seen as 'a dynamic set of patterns emerging from use ... with grammar seen not as the source of understanding and communication, but rather a by-product of communication' (Larsen-Freeman, 2011: 52).
- Rather than providing 'inputs' to learners one should therefore expose them to a rich landscape of affordances. This will foster emergence of language. Language emerges in the relationship between the availability – and perception – of affordances, the intentionality of the actor, and the normativity of any cultural context. CTs help us to make sense of the delicate relationship between what a learner should do (norm) what a learner could do (affordance) and what a learner would do (intentionality) (Glăvenau, 2012). It does that not by providing a causal explanation but by enabling modelling of recurrent patterns.
- Language is learnt in a social context '... by affording possibilities for co-adaptation between interlocutors. As a learner interacts with another individual, their language resources are dynamically altered, as each adapts to the other – a mimetic process. ... Co-adaptation is an iterative process; indeed, language development itself can be described as an iterative process, with learners visiting the same or similar territory repeatedly' (Larsen-Freeman, 2001: 54).
- The curriculum should not therefore consist of lists of 'content' to be 'covered,' but should take the (real life) activities, needs and emergent purposes of the learner as the starting point. The teacher then provides, scenarios, tasks and resources relevant to these

activities, needs and purposes and guides the learner's perception and action towards arrays of affordances that can further his or her goals (van Lier, 2007, paraphrased). This will naturally provide the context for the iterative process of co-adaption to occur.

- Emergence implies that lower level elements are qualitatively different from higher level elements. In a language class, a complex task is a higher level element than an exercise or game focusing on form. There is no direct link or transfer from the lower to the higher level. This helps explain learners 'failure' to transfer as expected by the teacher. It is only through reaching for new, more complex language during the course of completing a task that genuine learning will occur – fixed in place by a necessary, subsequent reflection phase.

- Larsen-Freeman cites Thelen and Smith's (1994) concept of 'soft assembly' to refer to the process of the mobilisation of competences and strategies in order to complete a specific task. She says that 'the assembly is said to be "soft" because the elements being assembled, as well as the specific ways they are assembled, can change at any point during the task or from one task to another' (2011: 54). One cannot therefore expect user/learner to automatically transfer tactics and particular use of language from one (part of a) task to another.

- CTs can account for change over time, including phenomena familiar to teachers such as 'vocabulary bursts' and the 'U-shaped learning curves' (Larsen-Freeman & Cameron, 2008: 129) in which learners make errors they did not previously show. This is a good example of the way in which instability during the process of moving towards a new state of balance is inevitable in language learning, with see-sawing personal trajectories that are quite discomforting to the teacher, despite incremental growth in the average overall progress of the class.

- 'Stability is possible only through constant change' (as when making little adjustments to the way one is standing in order to stay standing erect): 'the system changes every time a form is used, if only to increase the probability of the form's use in the future' (Larsen-Freeman, 2011: 53). This helps to explain language loss and reflects the adage 'use it or lose it.' 'From repeated soft-assemblies in co-adapted interactions, stable language-using patterns emerge' (2011: 54). However, Larsen-Freeman emphasises the importance of an iterative approach (e.g. a series of tasks designed to a similar template) to achieve this, rather than traditional repetition. This creates a 'cumulative, though selective, record of one's linguistic experience' (2011: 55) with repeated use of particular patterns leading them to become 'entrenched in the user's mind' (2011: 55).

In this chapter we have aimed to explain the development of the AoA from a theoretical point of view. In particular we have shown how an innovative approach such as the AoA does not happen in a vacuum, but rather emerges when the time is ripe for it, i.e. when the discussion around the ideas that inform it solidifies into coherent conceptual and theoretical frames, able to provide keys for explaining cognitive, educational and sociocultural phenomena as well as their relationship. We have also outlined how previous theories – that would be obsolete nowadays if applied in their integral form – contributed some elements to the development of the AoA that also need to be taken into consideration. We presented, albeit within the limited space of this chapter, the essence of those theories and concepts, coming both from the tradition of language education or education in general, and from other scientific fields of inquiry, and we summarised for each of them the salient contributions that we consider they have made to the AoA. Finally, we discussed how a complex ecological perspective has the potential to embrace the multifaceted theoretical underpinnings of the AoA by situating them within a broader perspective able to show the synergies that their different contributions bring to our understanding of the multiple implications and dimensions of language learning and teaching.

In general, we can say that both scientific and philosophical investigation is looking for new models able to deal with increasing diversity since 'the traditional methods of science and analytical philosophy are not sensitive enough to the dynamics of complex systems' (Cilliers, 1998: 141). This does not mean embracing pure relativism by saying that anything goes, but rather trying to look for a shared core understanding of phenomena and to build on the different contributions and perspectives that the different theoretical lenses can bring. This search for a common multiple understanding of what language is and what it means to learn (and to teach) a language has been at the basis of a seminal article in the field (The Douglas Fir Group, 2016). A number of scholars working in the field of language education and coming from different theoretical perspectives produced this paper that aimed to capture the effects of the epistemological expansion in the field, which started in the late 1980s. All the authors agreed that the different perspectives they came from shared a number of principles when it comes to conceptualising language and language learning:

> All the authors came to see our ontologies and with them our theories of language and learning as broadly compatible in important ways, despite their different optics. When explaining what language is, our various theoretical understandings emphasize three attributes as central: meaning, embodiment, and self-adaptive local emergence of patterning. Further, when it comes to explaining what learning is, at least conceptually and often empirically, our various theories stipulate the mutual entailment of the cognitive, the social, and the emotional. (The Douglas Fir Group, 2016: 21)

Thus, they made a bid for interdisciplinarity that they fleshed out by proposing 'a transdisciplinary framework that assumes the embedding, at all levels, of social, sociocultural, sociocognitive, sociomaterial, ecosocial, ideological, and emotional dimensions' (The Douglas Fir Group, 2016: 24). This framework articulates ten fundamental inter-connected themes, in turn organised into three levels (micro level of social activity, meso level of sociocultural institutions and communities, and macro level of ideological structures), which they offer for 'their potential as affordances [Gibson, 1979], that is, their potential to offer action possibilities that can be appropriated, negotiated, transformed, and made into means or constraints for L2 researching, learning, and teaching' (The Douglas Fir Group, 2016: 26).

The bid for transdisciplinarity that the authors of the article made only a few years ago is in a sense already overtaken by reality: trans-disciplinarity is actually an essential condition, a *sine qua non* for the understanding of the AoA. As we explained throughout the chapter, the AoA has shaped itself on the basis of diverse theoretical contribu-tions, certainly in a relatively unstructured way, but not without an internal and external logic. The former logic responds to the idea of a post method era (Kumaravadivelu, 2001, 2003) that corresponds to postmodern epistemologies (Lyotard, 1979). As we said, this involves the awareness of the limits of previous methods, and of the concept of method itself, even in the new open form of 'approach' that CLT represented. Thus, it is the understanding that one theory alone cannot provide all the answers needed in order to understand the nature of language and of the complex process of language learning (and teaching). The latter logic is a response to a new societal development in which cultural and linguistic diversity in individual trajectories and social constructions is becoming the norm and where information and communication technologies have completely broken down the classical units of time, space and action. The theoretical diversity and density that we have presented in this chapter needs to be considered as a sort of palimpsest: new theories have built themselves in relation to the existing ones, in parallel or in synergy. The AoA benefits from this rich tapestry, informed by an ecological, complex perspective.

In Chapter 4, we now turn to the main methodologies and approaches in SLE that developed as a result of these theories and consider the contribution that they make to the AoA.

Note

(1)   CREED: Construction-based, Rational, Exemplar-driven, Emergent, Dialectic.

4 Preparing the AoA: Developments in Language Teaching Methodology

Over the past century a number of methodologies have cast light on our understanding of SLE. Each of these different methodologies has been rooted in a specific view of what a language is, and what it means to use – and learn – a language. This process has sometimes happened in a very explicit way with methodologies openly claiming their affiliation to a specific theory, and sometimes in a more subtle or even hidden way, with reconstructions – and hypotheses – of what theory(ies) might have informed specific methodologies made *a posteriori*. Thus, there is not a clear, shared history of second language methodologies that receives full consensus. This is true not only across geographical and cultural areas and countries but also within the same country, since different languages developed separate educational traditions linked to specific theoretical developments and culturally bound epistemologies.

Tracing back all these different developments would be beyond the scope of this book, besides not bringing a real added value to the theorisation of the AoA. However, a discussion of the main tendencies that are clearly identifiable within the journey that characterises the development of methodologies is of relevance, as it helps to identify what some French researchers have called '*ruptures épistémologiques*' [epistemological breaks] (Bourguignon, 2006; Puren, 2009a, 2009b) and some Italian researchers '*destrutturazioni*' [destructuring] (Serra Borneto, 1998).

It is evident that seeing language learning as an intellectual exercise, as habit formation, or as communication implies a totally different attitude towards what teaching and learning a language means and requires. These visions each brought a great contribution to our conceptualisation of SLE and research has increasingly shown how complex and multi-layered the language learning and teaching process is, and how reductionist it may be to adopt a single perspective in the analysis of what are both social and natural phenomena. Such complexity calls for a more flexible and principled methodology capable of articulating the different elements of the process of teaching and learning languages into a coherent whole, in order for learners to become engaged, more autonomous – and hence more successful. Awareness of this complexity has increasingly informed reflection on SLE and has led to a wealth of important and complementary conceptualisations of the process of teaching and learning languages. This chapter will discuss these advances in our understanding of the tenets of SLE and will explain the extent to which they prepare the ground for the AoA, which represents a new vision that encompasses and goes beyond the previous approaches. The new view of the responsibility of the teacher as a strategic actor, who not only understands the rationales behind the different methodologies, and the compatibilities and tensions between them, but is also able to employ different approaches and techniques in a targeted manner within specific constraints, is presented. A characteristic of the AoA is in fact the triangulation between the definition of learning objectives, the methodological choices, and an integrated view of assessment.

4.1 Evolution of Methodologies: From a Pendulum to a River

Language methodologies can be seen as having a very long history, 5000 years if we count, as Germain (1993) does, the teaching of the Sumerian language to Akkadians in the ancient city of Sumer, near present day Baghdad. However, this history has been very patchy, with a considerable shift due to the change in the role of Latin, from living to 'dead' language and consequently with a shift in teaching towards a grammar-translation method which would *de facto* become the model for the teaching of modern languages. Precursors of different forms of innovation in language education existed already during the 16th and 17th century, with the work of philosophers Michel de Montaigne and John Locke, who discussed the role of second language preceptors (= personal tutors) and teaching modalities, and Jan Amos Komenský, better known as Comenius, who is considered to be the father of language education as a specific discipline (Germain, 1993). However, it was not until the late 19th century that a reaction against the dominant grammar-translation method started and reforms were envisaged that foregrounded the beginning of the more scientifically-based development of SLE that characterised the 20th century.

SLE has developed through a difficult process, informed by many disciplines and theories as we saw in Chapter 3, sometimes swinging between opposite viewpoints in a way that, as mentioned, has often been described as a pendulum. As Germain (1993) noted, there is a strong tendency to group advances in approaches to SLE into macro-categories, usually identified with particularly periods (Celce-Murcia, 1991; Puren, 2004). Although such categorisation is helpful in understanding fundamental concepts informing different approaches, dividing an evolutionary process into little boxes tends to limit reflection, dialogue and cross-fertilisation. Multidimensional metaphors, such as a broad river resulting from the confluence of different streams (Mitchell & Vidal, 2001) or a multiple-sided polygon (Porcelli, 2005) prove more effective in conceptualising the range of disciplines involved and the methodological options available, and in overcoming the quixotic quest after the methodological Holy Grail. Like medicine, language education can be considered as being at the same time a theoretic and a practical field, which aims to find solutions in a contextually effective manner (Porcelli, 2005), the different sciences informing targeted and situated pedagogical action and providing the necessary rationale to allow for principled choices (Borg, 2006). SLE is therefore increasingly seen as a complex endeavour, in which practitioners play a strategic role (Piccardo, 2010a) that needs to be grounded in a comprehensive and dynamic conceptual framework.

In order to capture the essence of the different visions that informed the meandering development of SL teaching methodologies we will focus on the different ways language learning – and consequently teaching – has been seen over time. To build on Mitchell and Vidal's metaphor of 'a major river, constantly flowing, fed by many sources of water – rivers, streams, springs in remote territories, all fed by rain on wide expanses of land' (2001: 27), what we are aiming at is to provide a good sense of those different sources, and of their specific characteristics, so that someone who were to analyse the resulting water at the river estuary would be able to recognise the different elements they found.

The idea of a post-method era (Kumaravadivelu, 2001, 2003) that marked the end of the 20th century was instrumental in the shift towards a more holistic conceptualisation of SLE, meaning that teachers needed to put on field researchers' hats and become 'strategists of complexity' (Piccardo, 2010a), decision makers aware of underpinning principles, the rationale(s) for their teaching, and the consequences of their actions. This is a crucial feature of the AoA as we will see later in the book.

4.1.1 Language learning as an intellectual exercise (the grammar-translation method)

The grammar-translation method (GTM) developed mainly in the German-speaking areas of Europe during the 19th century to teach modern foreign languages, mainly French and English, taking as a model the methodology used to teach classical languages, i.e.

Latin and ancient Greek, which had evolved during the 17th and 18th centuries. Latin had long been the dominant 'international' language in the Western world, in as different areas as religion, philosophy, education, government and commerce, and was therefore the most widely studied foreign language (Richards & Rodgers, 1986; Trim, 2012). However, it started to see its position challenged in the course of the 16th century by other languages, especially Italian and the emerging French, English and Spanish languages. Study of these last three languages grew rapidly thanks to their increasing political and economic importance. Latin as a result slowly ceased to be a vehicle of communication, being displaced to other roles, mainly linked to education and culture. Latin started to be seen as a noble discipline, indispensable for a solid education, a powerful 'mental gymnastic' on the one hand (Titone, 1968) and the main way to access the literature essential for any cultivated person. The Latin language, and especially its grammar, started to be studied as an object, a vehicle to develop the intellectual faculties of the learner as well as to broaden their cultural horizon, rather than as a means of communication.

The idea of education was until well into the 20th century an elitist one, with only a small minority continuing to secondary school. The main goal was the overall education ('*Geistesbildung*') of the learners through reasoning and intellectual discipline, focusing mainly on mathematics, philosophy and language (normally Latin and ancient Greek). When modern languages started to be taught, they had to compete with Latin and ancient Greek in the curriculum. 'It was thus natural that their teaching reproduced the same method. The language was treated at the level of the sentence only ... there was little if any consideration of the spoken language [and] accuracy was considered to be a necessity' (Harmer, 2001: 63). Even though one of the broader aims was to bring learners to read the classics, longer texts were only introduced at later stages. For quite a while, learners were just given abstract explanations of grammar rules followed by sentences that exemplified those rules. Learners were then asked to translate sentences from the target language (L2) into their first language (L1) and from L1 into L2.

A number of features of the GTM made it a very unbalanced method for the general teaching of modern languages: (a) the presentation and meticulous study of comprehensive grammar rules in isolation; (b) the long lists of vocabulary with their translation into the L1, to be learnt by heart; (c) the development of reading and writing at the expense of oral skills, and (d) the focus on the sentence level, which was an attempt to make things easier for learners, but which negated the very idea of bringing learners closer to literary masterpieces, the ultimate goal of the method.

Despite these weaknesses, the GTM is still used, and not only in situations where the primary focus is understanding literary texts. One reason for this is that it is not very demanding for teachers, who, once they master the target language and its grammar well enough, can rely on structured material, use a lecture-like, teacher-centred style, which assures a good control of the class, and feel they are following a well-designed curriculum for a humanistic education. The position of the teacher as the source of knowledge and the undisputed authority (Serra Borneto, 1998) is another major factor responsible for the success and durability of the method. Some languages are still mainly taught using GTM or an adaptation of it, depending on the context and the pedagogic and cultural traditions.

What is particularly problematic in the GTM, though, is the position of the L1. In the GTM in fact: 'The first language is maintained as the reference system in the acquisition of the second language' (Stern, 1983: 455). One of the pillars of the GTM was the assumption that all learners in the classroom shared the same L1, because the ability to operate constant comparisons between the L1 and L2 in translation was essential, as was the ability to understand explanations of the L2 grammar given in the L1. This duality is fully unrealistic in a large proportion of present day classrooms, which are increasingly multilingual and culturally and socially diverse, so this prerequisite of the GTM is now lacking. The second weakness was the study of languages as static codified objects, as if they were dead languages. As Harmer (2001) reminds us, it is precisely the place of the students' first language in the classroom, alongside the attitude to languages that have mainly characterised the methodological debate until the present time.

All histories of language methodologies underline the problems with the GTM, and heavily criticise some of its characteristics. The issues generally underlined include aspects such as: (a) its being removed from reality and not really tackling communication, thus creating frustrations among learners who felt they were unable to function in the L2, and (b) its extreme focus on accuracy, which is linked to the idea that mastering the grammar and vocabulary of a language automatically means mastering the language. In general the GTM has been the object of extended criticism in spite of being still very widely used, albeit not openly. The harshest criticism came from Richards and Rogers who went as far as to say that the GTM had no theoretical justification or relation to issues in linguistics, psychology, or educational theory (1986: 5). While it is very easy to attack the GTM, and we are certainly not here to defend it, it would be more useful to try and see what its merits are and the reasons why so many students did manage to learn the language effectively with such a method, as several anecdotal examples from individuals living in geographically or politically secluded areas (e.g. the former USSR) have proved. Let us look now at some of these positive aspects.

The first was the idea of setting the language in a context. To be sure, the context was remote as it was provided by literary texts that usually did not have any link to everyday reality. However, the need for embedding the learning process in a wider cultural framework was at least perceived, if not explicitly stated. One of the criticisms of the GTM is that the sentences proposed for translation were very odd and artificial, being driven only by the grammatical structure they aimed to exercise. However, this was the case only for the translation from the L1 into the L2, while the translation from the L2 into the L1 was usually done from literary texts, which provided a form of authenticity. The second positive aspect was the focus on the conscious mastery of the language as a system, which implied the ability for learners to cope with difficulties and come up with plausible solutions, thus engaging in a decision-making process. Furthermore, this process was always conducted in a comparative way, since one of the principles of the GTM was the constant back and forth between L1 and L2. Deducing the meaning of unknown words from context was also a particular feature. Finally, the use of classic authentic texts from a different culture had a general educational value (*Geistesbildung*), as well as introducing learners to the fact that each culture conveys a particular worldview (*Weltanschauung*).

In fact, the GTM did have some conceptual underpinnings:

- Pedagogical justification: language learning was not just seen as a formal educational process but also a one in which personality was shaped in the daily 'meeting' with and reflection on the target culture.
- Linguistic justification: the language was described through the filter of formal categories that derived from Latin, and seen as a sort of construction set, where the single elements could be assembled to form the final – linguistic – building.
- Cognitive-learning theories: learning a language was seen as an educational process of developing individuals' thinking capacity and of training the mind.

The problems with the GTM were of a different nature. Firstly, they were sociological as the GTM embraced an elitist vision of education in monolingual schools and societies. Secondly, the GTM had other crucial weaknesses that had already been explained perfectly in the late 19th century (Vietör, 1882). The first one was the idea of describing – and thus fixating – a living language through the rules of a 'dead' language, forgetting that a modern language is what the speakers make of it, how they use it, and that it is constantly changing and evolving. The second weakness was the idea that one could deconstruct a language into a series of stand-alone rules of grammar or words, forgetting that each language is a holistic entity. This type of criticism is much more useful as it points to something that would be understood much later, and that is core to the AoA.

What we can retain from this discussion is firstly the need not to forget the few, positive aspects of the GTM for a possible targeted use at certain moments of the class, and secondly the lesson that can be learnt from what it lacks: namely the idea of the language as a complex, flexible and ever-changing system and tool.

The criticism of the GTM resulted in two alternative methods, one which appeared very early on, at the end of the 19th century (the direct method, also called the reform method or natural method: Morris, 1966) and the audio-lingual method, which appeared alongside the audio-visual method in the mid-20th century. Although these methods were developed in different times and geographical contexts, they all share one important aspect: the total rejection of the principles of the GTM in order to embrace a new vision of the language, that of habit formation. This is why we will be discussing them together in the next section, again with the aim of highlighting both their strengths and weaknesses and what they have contributed to language education.

4.1.2 Language learning as habit formation (direct/audio-lingual/ audio-visual methods)

The opposition to the GTM gave rise to what would later be called the reform movement in SLE, which started in the 1880s. Fundamentally, this movement 'led to the so-called direct method, which – historically speaking – replaced the GTM and prepared the ground for the world famous audio-lingual method' (Neuner & Hunfeld, 1993: 33, our translation). As the name suggests, the direct method saw the learning and teaching of the target language as direct, that is, without the burden of the mother tongue and its interfering presence, which was banned from the classroom. Also, in radical opposition to the GTM, the direct method fully prioritised the spoken language over the written form.

The main idea, the one which has remained the strongest all the way through the decades up until the present, was that by eliminating the L1 from the classroom, learners would end up by thinking in the L2 and constructing a fully new language system, completely independent from their mother tongue and/or other languages they might know. The complete turn in methodology that the direct method fostered had several underlying reasons: firstly, the GTM was perceived as rather ineffective. Secondly, the idea of treating all languages in the same way, i.e. by organising them through the lens of grammatical categories borrowed from Latin, appeared inappropriate. In fact, linguistics increasingly showed how each language has its own structure and nature. Furthermore, research in phonology contributed to creating awareness of the totally different nature of written and spoken language. The final reason, but probably the most important one, was related to the socio-economic changes that characterised the world in the final decades of the 19th century. Languages ceased to be just an intellectual pursuit and became a practical tool for an increasingly mobile world. People needed to be able to use languages, not just to master the system or to access and study – and possibly admire – literary pieces of art.

On top of all that, the emerging science of psychology started to be interested in the way languages were learned and started to have its say. The learning of second/foreign languages was seen as modelled on the learning of the mother tongue, even though there was awareness that the conditions were very different. Thus, a lot of importance was given to learning in a natural way, in order to foster associations and to create a sense of the language (*Sprachgefühl*): 'When we learn our own language we associate words and sentences with thoughts, ideas, actions, events' (Sweet, 1899/1964: 102; cited in Stern, 1983: 317). In fact, the main idea was to abandon a deductive method, like the GTM, which fostered a conscious insight, and embrace a method that encouraged the use of language without too much reflection and thinking.

As is understandable, the need to move towards an increased use of the language, a spontaneous, natural use in everyday situations, and above all the idea that language learning is equivalent to acquiring a *habitus,* became particularly strong during the mid-20th century. This led to the appearance of new methods on the two sides of the Atlantic that both aligned with the vision of the direct method, even though with their own specific characteristics. The first was the audio-lingual method developed in the US (the so-called 'Army method', as it was developed for soldiers during the Second World War). The second was the SGAV (*Méthode structuro-globale audio-visuelle,* normally referred to in English as the audio-visual method), conceived by P. Guberina between 1954 and 1956 and popularised through the textbook *Voix et images de France [Voices and Images of France]:* Rivenc & Boudot (1962), published by the French CREDIF (*Centre de Recherche et d'Études pour la Diffusion du Français*). As the two names reveal, the former was more focussed on the audio-lingual aspects – i.e. listening and repeating was at the core of the learning process, the form of the words (and consequent correct reproduction) was prioritised over meaning – while the latter gave great importance to the use of visual input alongside aural input, so that the two together would enable learners to grasp the meaning, which would be later explained and further repeated.

In all the methods that saw learning languages as habit formation, listening and repeating was crucial and this process should not be blocked by conscious thoughts. Vocabulary was mainly taught through visuals and explanations in the target language. Like the GTM, the main problem with these methods was their focus on isolated words or sentences. Here the atomisation was extreme as model sentences were used for pattern drilling, which was the main activity in the lesson. Rote memorisation of these model sentences was fostered through endless repetition with minimal variations. This vision was clearly a very partial one, the pendulum had moved away from the meticulous, detailed study of the 'object' language that characterised the GTM to fully ignoring the characteristics of the language as a system, assuming that a language can be acquired by absorption through repetition and recasting. As is understandable, neither extremes of the pendulum captures the complexity of the process of learning a language, which we will be addressing later. However, reflecting upon the characteristics of old methods helps us to identify certain aspects that contributed some insight into the whole process of teaching and learning.

The idea of language learning as habit formation was also the object of severe criticism. However, even more than in the case of the GTM, the impact of these methods is still very considerable in today's language classes. Some aspects have proved particularly difficult to eradicate. The first is the misleading idea that the learners' L1 needs to be banned from the L2 class as it is an impediment and a source of errors. The second is the idea that, the longer the speaking time of the learner in the target language the better, independently from the quality of that speaking and the awareness of the meaning by the learners. Finally, from these methods comes the idea that the analysis of the structure of the language provides a sufficient basis for the curriculum, thus implying a progression based solely on the linguistic complexity of the target language.

These weaknesses have certainly proved extremely powerful stumbling blocks on the way towards effective language teaching. However, not everything was negative and, as we did for the GTM, what we would like to stress here is the contribution that methods focusing on language as habit formation have made to the advancement of language pedagogy in a broader sense. The audio-lingual/audio-visual methods have contributed some interesting elements that would prove useful in informing later developments.

Firstly, the use of visual supports and the idea of communicating from the very beginning in the target language brought to the fore the need for learners to acquire informal language, the language used in everyday situations. Secondly, the priority given to spoken language helped contribute more balance to the lesson, helping to identify different language skills, first listening, followed by speaking –

albeit mainly in the form of repetition – then reading and finally writing. Thirdly, the focus was no longer on the knowledge of the language, but rather on what one can do in the language ('*Ziel ist das Sprachkönnen, nicht das Sprachwissen wie in der GÜM* [The aim is being able to use the language not just knowing the language like in the GTM]' Neuner & Hunfeld, 1993: 61). This last point is linked to the previous one and explains the priority given to oral skills. Fourthly, one must remember that both the audio-lingual and audio-visual methods were developed in a conscious attempt to develop mass language education with which the majority of the population, remaining longer in school after the Second World War, could profit from the opportunity to learn a language. The audio-lingual and audio-visual methods were serious attempts at inclusive, quality education. A final positive aspect of these methods has been the use of technologies, which, even though it was rather mechanical and repetitive, represented a first step towards a technologically enhanced practice in language education.

4.1.3 Language learning as a conscious process

The success of both the audio-lingual and audio-visual methods was mainly due to their being rooted in a powerful theory of language: structural linguistics, and in an equally powerful theory of learning: behaviourism, which had been developed by a prominent school of American psychology and which 'claimed to have tapped the secrets of all human learning, including language learning' (Richards & Rodgers, 1986: 50). However, very soon structuralism appeared to be a rather rigid theory of language and behaviourism a rather narrow theory of learning. Neither of them in fact captured the complexity of the language phenomenon nor of the act of learning, especially learning such a living and ever-changing thing as a language. Furthermore, the practical results of the audio-lingual/audio-visual methods fell short in terms of learners' proficiency, a major problem being the move from repetition to authentic production.

The first powerful attack that would open a new phase in second language education came from Chomsky, who fully rejected the structuralist view of languages and behaviourism as a theory of learning. By claiming that neither language nor its learning are based on habit but are rather a creative process based on underlying rules, and that human beings possess innate structures of the mind through which they can process their experience linguistically, producing original utterances, Chomsky was crucial in shifting the focus away from a static view of language and a reductive idea of learning as a simple stimulus-response-reinforcement process into a more conscious, individually meaningful endeavour. For Chomsky behaviourism-inspired learning practices would produce behaviours in language, not real learning, or, as he would say, not real competence.

The consideration of the learner as a thinking being, with a network of existing knowledge and skills that could be enriched and further developed, was a turning point. The cognitive dimension considers the process taking place in the mind of each individual who acquires information. 'Cognitive theories view learning as involving the acquisition or reorganisation of the cognitive structures through which humans process and store information' (Good & Brophy, 1990: 187). Taking into account cognitive dimensions (again) brought great benefits to the development of SLE. Concepts like language awareness, autonomy and self-direction, and reflective learning that emerged as a result in the following decades would change perspectives in research, in the classroom and in the learner's vision of how to learn (Hawkins, 1984; Hawkins, 1999).

Although the storm provoked by Chomskyan positions did not translate into a developed and structured method, it helped to bring back attention to the cognitive aspects related to language learning. It also had the merit of stressing the creative process related to language learning and use. As a matter of fact, learning a language cannot be equated with any other type of learning, the language being at the same time the object to be learned and the means through which individuals express themselves and learn. But if cognitivism brought depth to the consideration of the learner, it continued, like behaviourism, to focus on an individual isolated from the social context.

Chomsky's idea of a clear cut between competence and performance would prove rather problematic, especially as the former was presented as an internal characteristic and measured against an ideal – and actually idealised – native speaker. Also, since competence was seen as the ability of an ideal native speaker/listener living in a homogeneous speech community to produce correct sentences (Chomsky, 1965), the product, the linguistic form, was still at the very core. As Canale and Swain pointed out 'a theory of competence is equivalent to a theory of grammar and is concerned with the linguistic rules that can generate and describe the grammatical (as opposed to ungrammatical) sentences of a language' (1980: 3). Thus, in a sense, knowing a language was reduced to knowing its grammar, and in fact accuracy and conscious knowledge of the rules remained a priority throughout the 1960s and early 1970s as communicating was equated to applying rules.

As we saw in Chapter 2, the notion of competence is a challenging and elusive one. Not only was the debate around it extended beyond linguistics or language pedagogy, but within applied linguistics, it also saw a harsh debate around the very possibility of distinguishing between competence and performance. Some scholars, particularly those following sociocultural theory, consider that there is no abstract competence: everything is situated, and meaning and learning only occur in the context of a 'social' exchange. So in a sense, for these scholars, we can only talk about performance, as the internal cognitive dimension cannot be taken in isolation. As we will see in the following paragraph, the lack of consideration of social aspects and the 'purified' vision of the language that characterised Chomsky's position became the object of great criticism from the very early 1970s, especially after the famous article by Dell Hymes (1972a) 'On Communicative Competence'. And it is certainly true that severe limitations characterise Chomsky's idea of competence and, in particular, of the idealised language of the 'native speaker', and that the focus on accuracy can be very problematic for language learners – all of which may explain why Chomsky's theories never translated into any specific second language methodology. However, as we did in the previous sections of this chapter, we should consider the way in which certain aspects of his theories contributed to the advancement of reflection in second language pedagogy.

The main impact of Chomsky's work was that of swiping away the idea that language learning was a simple question of habit formation, of *dressage*. In addition, he made clear that language learning did not equate to any other learning, but had a very specific and unique nature that needed to be taken into consideration. Finally, a major contribution was that of stressing the creative nature of language and language production. 'Chomsky had demonstrated that the current standard structural theories of language were incapable of accounting for the fundamental characteristic of language – the creativity and uniqueness of individual sentences' (Richards & Rodgers, 1986: 64). Chomsky's position opened the door to taking into consideration the cognitive aspects of language learning and in a sense it led the way to a very rich debate that would inform SLE in recent decades: that of the role and respective place of focus on form and focus on meaning, as we will see in the following section.

4.2 From Methods to Approaches and Beyond

Until the end of the 1960s, the idea of method in SLE was still dominant. As we saw, each period had produced a structured, well-organised system for teaching and learning languages. This does not mean that each of these methods was used in its pure form. Actually, various mixes could be found in the day-to-day practice of language teaching, in relation to different target learners or different preferences of the teachers. Even an explicit example of a thorough attempt to mix the GTM with the audio-lingual method was what the Germans called a '*Vermittelnde Methode*' [Facilitating/mediating method].

The main example of this was the textbook '*Deutsche Sprachlehre für Ausländer*' [German Language Course for Foreigners] (Schulz & Griesbach, 1955), where alongside a rigid grammatical progression, elements of the audio-lingual method coexisted, namely the idea of focusing on the oral, on everyday situations and of using the target language in teaching the lesson. In the British context, 'Situational language teaching', where basic structures were practised through situation-based activities, particularly dialogues, was very widespread during the 1960s and informed a great number of textbooks. Furthermore, alongside the methods discussed above, several other methods appeared during the 1970s, which were not informed by linguistic or second language education theories, such as 'The Silent Way', 'Counselling-Learning' or 'Total Physical Response,' to name but a few. Although these methods never made it through to mainstream education, some of their core principles contributed to the advancement of SLE (Piccardo, 2005a; Stevick, 1980).

As discussed in the previous section, Chomsky's theory had shaken the very basis of the vision of language learning as habit formation. However, this had been just the first big change in reconsidering language and language learning. Two crucial concepts would completely change our perspective on language education: the concept of communicative competence (Hymes, 1972a), and the concept of language needs (Nation & Macalister, 2010; Richterich & Chancerel, 1980).

> Communicative competence emphasizes that language is communication first and foremost, and the goal is precisely to prepare learners to be able to communicate. The notion of language needs contends that language teaching must be closely linked to the learner for whom it is intended and to the context in which it is delivered. (Piccardo, 2014a: 9)

As we saw in Chapters 2 and 3, the notion of communicative competence was rooted in Dell Hymes' work of the early 1970s (Hymes, 1972a) and developed throughout the decade both in Europe (Moirand, 1982; Widdowson, 1978) and in North America (Canale & Swain, 1980; Savignon, 1972, 1983). What we are interested in here is to show how the perspective has become broader since the 1970s with increasing consideration given to the complexity of language learning and teaching This enabled the shift from the idea of 'method' to that of 'approach'.

The notion of method is a rigid one: 'methods are "turnkey" products that teachers are required to apply in the classroom' (Piccardo, 2014a: 9), and the focus of methods is on language as an object rather than on the individual learning the language. Approaches, on the other hand, are far less structured and 'give the teacher far greater latitude. The teacher is no longer someone who simply follows and applies a set of strict rules designed by experts; he or she is expected to draw on principles and techniques to prepare activities and design learning that is adapted to the needs of learners' (Piccardo, 2014a: 9). Contrary to ways in which the distinction between approaches and methods has often been conceptualised (Anthony, 1963; Richards & Rodgers, 1986), there is no hierarchical relationship between approaches and methods, neither in the sense that methods are based on an approach (Anthony, 1963), or vice versa – as Richard and Rodgers (1986: 28) claim – that approaches are one of the three elements of a method, alongside design and procedure.

In fact, the shift from method to approach is a substantial one, as an approach refers to the theories that describe the language and language learning. Because it describes how people use and acquire a language and makes statements about the conditions which promote successful language learning, an approach provides principles that inform language teaching (Harmer, 2001). By taking this stance, an approach implies that teachers are called on to play a multiplicity of roles, such as decision-makers, planners, evaluators, but also coach, and in general 'significant other' in a strategic way. In the case of methods, on the contrary, all decisions have already been made about types of activities, procedures, roles of teachers and learners, materials, and program organisation.

As we will see in the next section, with the communicative approach, the focus of teaching moves away from a narrow grammatical or lexical competence towards the broader and more articulated communicative competence. It is not by chance that the term 'method' was replaced by 'approach' at this point: the rigidity of a method would have been fully inadequate to describe pedagogical practices that aimed to develop effective communicative competence among learners with different needs and backgrounds and to cater for the new roles of the teachers and learners and a new vision of language teaching.

4.2.1 Language learning as communication (the communicative approach)

As is the case in all social sciences, development in the conceptualisation of language education does not happen in a vacuum. We have already seen how the audio-lingual method was influenced by advances in psychology and how Chomsky's theories were not completely unrelated to computational linguistics (see Chapter 3). We want to point out here how the limitations of Chomsky's view of:

... an ideal speaker-listener, in a completely homogeneous speech community, who knows its language perfectly and is unaffected by such grammatically irrelevant conditions as memory limitations, distractions, shifts of attention and interest, and errors (random or characteristic) in applying his knowledge of the language in actual performance (1965: 3)

stood out as completely at odds with a new, more complex and situated view of language. This view translated in linguistics into an interest in ethnographic studies, in the radically new perspectives brought about in the philosophy of language by the studies of Austin and Searle, in the birth of sociolinguistics and pragmatics, in conversation and discourse analysis (see Section 3.5) and, in general, in western societies experiencing political and socio-economic shifts, in steps towards a more inclusive society. The turn of the decade at end of the 1960s and beginning of the 1970s marked a shift to seeing communication as the main purpose of language and therefore in equating learning a language with learning to communicate in that language. And clearly communication happens in a social context and is influenced by sociocultural factors. Precisely the lack of consideration of sociocultural factors was the main shortcoming of Chomsky's theory. As we saw in Chapter 3, the main voice pointing out this lack was that of the linguist and anthropologist Dell Hymes, who coined the term 'communicative competence' in the first place as a way of overcoming the abstract notion of competence proposed by Chomsky and the rigid and artificial distinction between competence and performance. Hymes took a political as well as linguistic stance, with the clear intention of moving away from Chomsky's elitist view and from the deficiency perspective that his view of performance suggested. Instead, Hymes focused precisely on real use, on real people using the language and on their needs. Hymes pointed out that the simple knowledge of the rules of a language is not sufficient for communicating effectively: as he says, 'there are rules of use without which the rules of grammar would be useless' (1972a: 278).

In speaking of competence, 'it is especially important not to separate cognitive from affective and volitive factors' (Hymes, 1972a: 283). Communicative competence is a very complex endeavour as it implies that a speaker has the capacity to understand when to speak and when not, what to talk about and with whom, in what way, where and when. It is evident that the focus is now the communicative event, which is characterised by different elements, namely the situation where the event takes place, the participants in the event, the scope of communication, the content of the message, the code, the channel and the register used. We are in a perspective of 'ethnography of communication' a term invented by Hymes himself together with John Gumperz, at the intersection of anthropology and linguistics (Cazden, 2018).

By introducing the term communicative competence and by explaining its characteristics in his different publications Hymes was key in fostering a fundamental renewal in language pedagogy and *a fortiori* in language education. However, once again, he was not alone. As we saw in Chapter 3, this shift can be fully understood only by considering the synergy between, and complementarity of: Hymes' (1972a) concept of communicative competence and Halliday's (1973, 1975) theory of the functions of language and meaning potential; Austin (1962) and Searle's (1969) speech act theory which focuses on the performative function of utterances in language and communication, and Widdowson's call to attention for discourse and language use (1978, 1979), particularly the communicative acts related to different purposes.

An increasing awareness of the complexity of language and of communicative competence showed itself in the idea that language:

- serves different purposes;
- performs different functions;
- allows one to 'do' different things and to perform different acts to which, as we saw, different contextual, social and affective dimensions contribute,
- and that all this happens in a two way cyclical process of use and learning.

It is not surprising, therefore, that this entirely new perspective sparked the publication of different analyses and models of communicative competence in seminal works published in the years immediately afterwards, as discussed in Section 2.2.3 and shown in Table 2.1, for example:

- Grammatical, sociolinguistic, and strategic (Canale & Swain, 1980).
- Linguistic, discursive, referential, and sociocultural (Moirand, 1982).
- Grammatical, sociolinguistic, strategic, and discursive (Canale, 1983).
- Linguistic, referential, sociocultural, sociolinguistic, and strategic (Bergeron *et al.*, 1984).

Alongside this innovative theoretical reflection, another important impetus to radically change language education came from the work that the Council of Europe began in the 1970s within an intergovernmental symposium that recommended the development of a Europe-wide unit-credit system for adult language learning. At that symposium, John Trim and David Wilkins developed the concept of a notional-functional approach. As mentioned in Section 3.5, notional-functional syllabuses (Wilkins, 1976) were developed, pairing notions such as time, quantity, frequency etc. with functions such as requests, orders etc. (Scalzo, 1998). The approach was first realised in the specification of *The Threshold Level* (van Ek, 1975; van Ek &

Trim, 2001b) and its equivalent for French (Coste *et al.*, 1976). This work had a profound influence on the development of the communicative approach in Europe with the first communicative textbooks being published soon afterwards (the late 1970s BBC multimedia course *'Follow Me'* by John Trim and Tony Fitzpatrick (see Trim, 1995: 12, 2007); *Deutsch Aktiv* [Active German] by Neuner *et al.*, 1979; *Strategies* by Abbs *et al.*, 1975 and its follow up series; *Sans frontières* [Without Borders] by Verdelhan-Bourgade *et al.*, 1982; *Cartes sur table* [Cards on the Table] by Richterich & Suter, 1981).

> With the publication of *Threshold Level* by the Council of Europe, for the first time, language was divided not into grammatical structures, but into a list of concepts and functions defined according to minimum needs. *Language functions* or *communicative intentions* made it possible to use the target language effectively in situations that involved communication. Introducing oneself, asking for directions, ordering a meal, and purchasing a train ticket are typical examples found in textbooks. These functions take place within notions such as time, space, social relations, and so forth. (Piccardo, 2014a: 11)

The communicative approach (or communicative language teaching: CLT) was the product of the cultural effervescence and innovation that characterised the 1970s and spread well into the 1980s. It was not confined to Europe: Savignon's (1983) *Communicative Competence: Theory and Classroom Practice* was very influential, as was her research that learners following a communicative course could equal the test scores achieved through grammatically-based courses and in addition displayed communicative competence in unrehearsed communicative tasks that 'significantly surpassed that of learners who had had no such practice' when assessed with criteria like fluency, comprehensibility, effort and amount of communication (Savignon, 2002: 3). CLT tried to provide a response to the changes that were profoundly marking different societies. Considering it the first substantial destructuring in language education as does Serra Borneto in his *C'era una volta il metodo* [Once Upon a Time There was The Method] of 1998 is not an exaggeration. It is in fact a good way to underline that the time of a 'method' as a fixed, all-embracing teaching package gave way to something much more open and flexible. However, perhaps because of this flexibility, the approach is also more demanding for teachers and learners alike, who are faced with different options and called upon to make choices. The very fact that the attention shifts from learning a language as a *system* to being able to *do* something in that language implies flexibility, since communicative functions can be performed at different levels and in different contexts at a greater or lesser linguistic difficulty. Serra Borneto lists other factors that would complexify the view of language learners

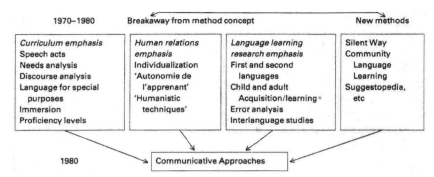

Figure 4.1 Change and innovation in language teaching: last section: 1970–1980
Source: Stern (1983: 113).

after the shift initiated by the communicative approach. These factors are: the centrality of the learner; the idea of learners' autonomy; self-directed learning; the consideration of the individuality of the learner, including cultural (and intercultural) aspects, and, in particular, the psychological dimension, which had been brought to the fore by the humanistic approaches we have mentioned earlier.

This view aligns with Stern's (1983) idea of considering the decade between 1970 and 1980 as a 'breakaway from the method concepts', towards communication approaches. His illustration of this is shown in Figure 4.1.

This idea of considering the learner as a person and focusing research on the nature of the learning process brings as a consequence the idea of learner-centred lessons, where the teacher's role is that of facilitator of the learning process, which in turn implies a shift from the product (the language to be learned) to the process (the learning of the language). In this perspective, it is clear that the concept of learners' needs (Richterich & Chancerel, 1980) becomes crucial alongside that of curriculum and syllabus, the planning process, and the idea of setting realistic objectives that will help and guide the learner and steer the learning process.

To summarise, the main aspects of the communicative approach, or communicative language teaching (CLT) as it was often called in the English-speaking world, are the following:

(a) *Communication is the main goal of teaching and learning*: language is studied to be capable of communicating messages either orally or in writing. Communication involves much more than just exchanging information. It also means expressing emotion, articulating thoughts, and eliciting a reaction from the interlocutor.

(b) *Learner needs* are central to effective teaching. Both initial and ongoing needs analysis are essential to select the language that needs to be taught and to plan the teaching process.

(c) Language learning is organised around *four skills* (two oral: listening, speaking; and two written: reading and writing)

(d) Learning is a pathway *from the known to the unknown*, from the simple to the complex, and from the general to the specific.

(e) *The language syllabus is organised around a series of communicative intentions* which enable effective use of the target language in situations that involve communication. Different functions such as, asking for directions, describing experiences, discussing plans are used, at least partially, to organise the syllabus. Speech acts are accomplished by speakers who act upon interlocutors through their words. Each speech act, like for example asking, instructing, or affirming, can be expressed differently depending on the context, and the situation.

(f) Students must *use the target language in meaningful ways*. The class must facilitate the ability of the learner to communicate in the language, exchanging information and accomplishing speech acts.

(g) Speaking activities involve *interaction between learners* and give opportunities for interpretation, expression of opinions and negotiation of meaning, in addition to information transfer or regurgitation.

(h) In order to communicate effectively, one must know not only how a language works (grammar), but also *what parts of the language to use and when*, depending on the situation, the context, the interlocutor and the communication intention.

(i) Form-focused practice and meaning-focused experience – *accuracy and fluency* – are both given importance.

(j) Teaching/learning is organised around real-life situations. Situations are suggested that make it possible to use language to transmit information, implying choices of what needs to be said and how to say it.

(k) Priority is given to such *authentic materials* selected from real-life sources (newspaper articles, radio programs, advertising, excerpts from books, video clips, and so forth), above all to reflect the meaning and themes being covered.

(l) *Vocabulary is taught in context* rather than through memorisation of lists of words. Vocabulary is introduced not in a rigid progression, but rather following a spiral approach as authentic documents are studied.

(m) The learner becomes a communicator engaged in the negotiation of meaning and also takes responsibility. The teacher alternates as a 'model,' a 'facilitator,' an 'organiser,' an 'advisor,' a 'co-communicator,' etc.

(n) *Pair and group work* become important. The teacher fosters, encourages, and orchestrates the work of the learners. Learning is now described as 'learner-centred' and 'learner-focused'.

(o) *Teachers are given responsibility* to adopt approaches and techniques that suit their learners: no 'method' is prescribed.

(p) CLT thus involves a *broader array of content and activities* than earlier approaches (e.g. authentic materials, realistic situations, language presented in context, meaningful practice in all four skills, interaction in pairs and small groups). Lessons no longer all follow the same pattern but will have different weighting. Lessons are grouped into larger, *holistic 'teaching units' of maybe 3–7 lessons*, which offer *balanced coverage* of all of these aspects, with *lessons linked together* by topic themes and language themes.

All but one of the points in the list above have remained core aspects of CLT – though the attention paid to point (b), needs analysis, is sometimes more lip service than real. The odd man out is point (e): communicative intentions or 'functions' as an organising principle, originally the quintessence of the approach, which was an early casualty. Already by 1981, Brumfit proposed a functional 'snake' around a syllabus based primarily on grammatical progression, with the very influential 1984 *Cambridge English Course* proposing a multistrand approach. As Thornbury (2016) documents, the appearance in 1986 of the 'unapologetically grammar-based' (2016: 228) *Headway*, or rather its immediate and resounding commercial success, killed off the attempt to move beyond a linear conception of syllabus based on grammatical progression. 'The reversion to the grammar syllabus in the mid-1980s ... helped to cement [an] accuracy-to-fluency approach, and most published materials ever since have perpetuated it' (Thornbury, 2016: 229) with just 'the grafting of a communicative "veneer" onto what has remained basically language-focused stock' (Waters, 2011: 321, cited in Thornbury, 2016: 233).

But the other points on the list proved enduring in many contexts. A key element of the communicative approach is the very final point, which reflects the significantly increased importance of the curriculum – or to be more precise of the syllabus. The syllabus provides a summary of the themes and content taught and the activities provided in a particular context/class, translating the overall content of the institutional curriculum into a sequenced programme of teaching units for a specific group. The shift that this represents brings together the two avenues that helped to translate the ideas of communicative competence into the practice of communicative language teaching (CLT): On the one hand, there was the conceptualisation of communicative competence (Hymes, 1972a) with its declination into different models listing similar components (see Table 2.1), together with the Halliday's language functions, and

Austin and Searle's speech acts (see Sections 3.4 & 3.5). On the other hand, the analysis of the learners' needs enabled the definition of Threshold Levels in the different European languages, i.e. specifications of the language required to function in a relatively autonomous way in everyday situations.

It is the idea of syllabus that will inform one of the main developments of CLT, namely task-based learning (TBL) more often called task-based language teaching (TBLT), and, more generally, the first conceptualisation of *task* as an element capable of providing a meaningful context for the language learning process.

The theoretical reflection that has informed TLBT has also tried to overcome the intrinsic limitation of CLT that Brumfit pointed out in 2001. According to Brumfit, the different models developed to describe communicative competence are very static, and they seem 'to see the language learner/user as a passive victim of the inherited rule system of the past' (2001: 52), but – he asks – 'what happens if we suggest that users construct their own responses to rule systems – that probabilities in language are only there because of tacit agreement by language users, including language learners?' (2001: 52). Brumfit (2001) himself answers this question as follows:

- grammatical competence is a set of conventions to be negotiated according to the capacity of the language to express the learner's needs;
- appropriacy and sociolinguistic competence become more problematic and negotiable than what is usually admitted, as it is cultures not languages that determine appropriacy and rules;
- discourse and strategic competence are subject to cultural variation.

If the concept of communicative competence is to be applied to language teaching, it must centre on learners, for they are the sole justification for language teaching as a profession. If it centres on learners, it must become a far more dynamic concept than it often appears to be. (Brumfit, 2001: 53)

This implies a series of fundamental questions which Brumfit goes on to discuss, concerning the situated nature of any language teaching intervention; learners' freedom of choice in language use and in the use of all their linguistic resources to express themselves as naturally, freely and fluently as they can; the type of language and cultural models that they are exposed to, and what their position towards them is, plus the decision-making process concerning the choice of languages. As one can imagine, these are still – and will probably remain – open questions, but they certainly contribute to advancing reflection and discussion in the field. Certainly, the centrality of the learner together with the freedom and responsibility that are granted to them is a core feature of TBLT.

4.2.2 Approaches to task based language teaching (TBLT)

Task based language teaching is, as Larsen Freeman and Andersen point out, an example of 'the "strong version" of the communicative approach, where language is acquired through use. In other words, students acquire the language they need when they need it in order to accomplish the task that has been set before them' (2011: 150).

Ellis's scheme for distinguishing between tasks and exercises, shown in Table 4.1, provides a good idea of the link between TBLT and the communicative approach with the move away from non-communicative exercises to communicative tasks:

Table 4.1 Distinguishing exercise and task

	Exercise	Task
Orientation	Linguistic skills seen as prerequisite for learning communicative abilities	Linguistic skills are developed through engaging in communicative activity
Focus	Linguistic form and semantic meaning ('focus on form')	Propositional content and pragmatic communicative meaning ('focus on meaning')
Goal	Manifestation of code knowledge	Achievement of a communicative goal
Outcome-evaluation	Performance evaluated in terms of conformity to the code	Performance evaluated in terms of whether the communicative goal has been achieved
Real world relationship	Internalisation of linguistic skills serves as an investment for future use	There is a direct and obvious relationship between the activity that arises from the task and natural communicative activity

Source: Ellis 2009: 112.

The debate on the difference between exercise and task, between controlled and free use of language and between language practice and naturalistic communicative action has informed reflection on tasks and TBLT and has produced different interpretations of tasks and their role in the curriculum.

Nunan (2004) reminds us that already in the early 1980s Littlewood 'draws a distinction between a strong and a weak inter-pretation of CLT. The strong interpretation eschews a focus on form, while a weak interpretation acknowledges the need for such a focus' (Nunan, 2004: 9). Nunan himself takes a balanced position, stressing that 'the curriculum needs to take account of both means and ends, and must, in consequence, incorporate both content and process' (2004: 10) and underlining that 'the development of CLT has had a profound effect on both methodology and syllabus design, and has greatly enhanced the status of the concept of "task" within the curriculum' (2004: 10). When it comes to the distinction between CLT and TBLT, Nunan says that CLT is 'a broad philosophical approach to the language curriculum that draws on theory and research in linguistics, anthropology, psychology and sociology ... [and] task-based language teaching represents a realization of this philosophy at the level of syllabus design and methodology' (2004: 10).

For these reasons, the benefit of considering TBLT as the 'strong version' of the communicative approach, in line with Howatt (1984) as well as Larsen-Freeman and Andersen (2011), is that of highlighting the potential of the communicative approach and, at the same time, its peculiar destiny, i.e. that of having been misunderstood or at least under-estimated in its capacity for innovation. A major issue with CLT has been its actual implementation. Great misunderstandings and misuse were observed as well as great variations between its interpretation in different contexts. This is a possible consequence of the broad, diverse and somewhat fuzzy theoretical conceptualisation, and certainly a sign of the difficulty practitioners found in making the radical shift that CLT required and in performing the difficult role they were called to as early as in the 1970s. This resulted in a strange phenomenon where all the textbooks claimed to be communicative even though their interpretation of the communicative approach was extremely variable. It also caused a contradiction between a widespread idea among practitioners that CLT equated to an exclusive focus on meaning and the fact that many textbooks were still organised around a grammatical progression, albeit disguised in functions. All this fuzziness diminished the impact that the communicative approach could have had in advancing SLE practice.

As van den Branden *et al.* point out:

> ... the emergence of TBLT, placing communication at the heart of teaching procedures, was then a logical development [from CLT] in various ways. For one thing it cohered with much of the major think-ing within CLT. But in addition it offered a response to the partial incorporation of communication work within the field of language education. Furthermore ... its emergence was consonant both with parallel evolutions in other domains of education and with empirical research on how language acquisition occurs. Hence the introduction of 'task-based language teaching' articulated with modern views on the learning of complex functional abilities and catered for a model of second language education that was systematically conceptualized along holistic meaning-focused, learner-driven lines. (2009: 5)

One of the main criticisms of communicative language teaching was, echoing some of Brumfit's comments we mentioned above, that learners were still rarely given the opportunity to express themselves using their full range of linguistic resources in activities that were meaning-focused rather than form-focused. A series of 'naturalness' studies at the University of Birmingham attempted to address this issue, following the ideas of Sinclair (1983). In one of these studies, for example, Willis (1983) developed her first concept of TBLT. In another, North (1986) proposed a model distinguishing between different forms of pair and group work. The scheme suggests a continuum from teacher-led through form-focused and then meaning-focused activities to natural communication in tasks. North proposed that, from the points of view of both learning and assessment, *all* these types of discourse – from controlled to natural – had their role in the communicative classroom, but that it was essential to include meaning-focused tasks that gave learners the autonomy to mobilise *all* their communicative and linguistic resources in the language.

From a TBLT perspective, 'people not only learn language *in order to* make functional use of it, but also *by* making functional use of it (van den Branden & van Avermaet, 1995)' (van den Branden, 2006: 6). But in order to do so, they need to be given the autonomy to use all the resources in their communicative repertoire. In other words, as North (2014) points out, in TBLT 'The focus is on "natural communicative activity", which presupposes an approximation to types of natural discourse, as opposed to the task being a target "real world task"' (North, 2014: 148–9). Simulation of a real world situation does not necessarily guarantee 'natural' communicative behaviour; sometimes (e.g. simulating a purchase) it can degenerate into a roleplay in which students just use a narrow range of fixed artificial language, rather than communicating naturally. As van den Branden puts it:

> Tasks are supposed to elicit the kinds of communicative behaviour (such as the negotiation for meaning) that *naturally* arises from per-forming real-life language tasks, because these are believed to foster language acquisition. (2006: 9, our emphasis)

Using tasks in the classroom does not necessarily imply any one specific model of task-based learning (e.g. that of Willis, 1996). There are different interpretations – Bygate *et al.* (2001) and van den Branden *et al.* (2009) offer a range of views – and definitions given often contradict each other (see van den Branden, 2006: 3–10). After reviewing the rich literature and discussion on task definition, van den Branden summarises the definitions of tasks as follows: 'A task is an activity in which a person engages in order to attain an objective, and which necessitates the use of language' (2006: 4). He underlines how, in this view, using language is a means to an end and defining learning goals is a way of describing the tasks that a learner is expected to accomplish and the language use required to perform the tasks. However, he continues, a more difficult endeavour appears to be the definition of the way learners can be supported in developing the functional language proficiency necessary to perform tasks. The key prerequisites on which there seems to be some agreement are summarised by North (2014):

- Goal: The action is purposeful, motivated by a clear reason, possibly role.
- Context: The action takes place in a relevant context, with conditions and constraints.
- Meaning: There is a focus on personal meaning – not regurgitation.
- Interaction: There is collaborative work, exchanging ideas and suggestions.
- Cognition: Processes like framing the work, planning, taking stock are encouraged.
- Outcome: There is a concrete result, a product or an evaluation – plus reflection.

In TBLT, tasks are strongly oriented towards teaching, in the sense that the teacher provides the necessary scaffolding to take learners towards a specific content and results (Ellis, 2003). Even though some authors seem to suggest a broader definition of tasks, saying that tasks can expand to the point of sharing several characteristics with project work (Bygate *et al.*, 2001), there is a general consensus on the fundamental feature of tasks in TBLT: In communicative language use 'the user's attention is focused on meaning rather than on form' (Nunan, 2004) even though it is also underlined that form remains important, albeit not specified in advance. In fact, as Willis and Willis (2007) point out, learners can use different forms to reach the task outcome, as opposed to what is required in exercises.

Spada reminds us that 'explicit focus on form may be particularly effective in L2 classrooms which are communicatively based and/or where the L2 is learned via subject matter instruction' (1997: 82). There seems to be quite a consensus on the need for both focus on meaning and focus on form for effective language education. For instance on the basis of a meta-analysis of 49 studies, Norris and Ortega (2000) concluded that explicit L2 instruction and conscious learning has a positive effect on proficiency. Swan (2005) counters claims that (a) the task itself can lead learners to generate and acquire new or more complex and accurate language and (b) that it is sufficient to provide input and practice on language form just in real time during the task. He considers that systematic presentation and practice of language form are essential (alongside other course strands like communicative tasks), particularly for lower level learners in secondary schools:

The fact that systematic practice is associated with 'discredited' behaviourist theory, and with a short-lived fashion for exclusively mechanical structure-drilling which perhaps only achieved 'false automatization' (R. Ellis 2003: 105), has led many scholars to dismiss its use as irrelevant to acquisition (e.g. J. Willis 1996: 135). But if practice aids learning, it aids learning. A fact is not invalidated by the place it has been given in an outdated theory – in the words of the biologist Jean Rostand, 'Theories pass, the frog remains'. (Swan, 2005: 383)

The distinction between a weak version of CLT and a strong version of CLT (as TBLT) that we mentioned above also aligns with the crucial distinction 'between curricula/syllabuses that formulate lower-level goals in terms of linguistic content (i.e. elements of the linguistic system to be acquired) and curricula/syllabuses that formulate lower-level goals in terms of language use (i.e. the specific kinds of things that people will need be able to do with the target language)' (van den Branden, 2006: 3). Task-based syllabuses belong to this second category. The former, van den Branden explains, are based on elements of the linguistic system (sounds, morphemes, grammar rules, words and collocations, notions, functions), which means that the language, subdivided into preselected parts, is taught in a predetermined order, and language acquisition is regarded as a process of gradual accumulation of small pieces. The drawbacks and limitations of such a vision are numerous (see Long & Crookes, 1992, 1993) as this way of organising the syllabus – and of teaching – is at odds with the results of research. In particular we cannot equate input with intake. Nor is learning a linear process of accumulation but rather a complex endeavour, a cyclical back and forth between meaning and form, form and sociolinguistic and sociocultural use of the language. The latter, curricula/syllabuses that formulate lower-level goals in terms of language use – i.e. task-based syllabuses – 'do not chop up language into small pieces, but take holistic, functional and communicative "tasks", rather than any specific linguistic item, as the basic unit for the design of educational activity' (van den Branden, 2006: 5). Unfortunately, even if this distinction seems well-established now, in practice the use of tasks is often integrated into the former types of syllabus and the tasks are, as a result, still often reduced in their scope and potential.

Since the seminal writings of Long (1985) and Prabhu (1984, 1987), who pointed out the need for educators to provide students with meaning-focused functional tasks that allow them to use the language for real-world, non-linguistic purposes, work on TBLT has produced volumes that summarise the state-of-the-art concerning TBLT, especially from the theoretical point of view with research focusing on the role of tasks in second language acquisition (Bygate *et al.*, 2001; Ellis, 2003, 2018; Nunan, 2004, 2005; among others). Other publications have taken into account both the theory and the practical applications of TBLT (van den Branden, 2006; van den Branden *et al.*, 2009;

among others). In general, reflection on tasks, their nature and their role, and importance in curriculum, instruction and teacher education has boomed and has promoted a broader view of the nature and role that tasks and TBLT can play in innovating SLE and adopting a holistic view (Nunn, 2006).

Many working in task-based approaches would also say that tasks should reflect what learners would do in the real world (e.g. Long & Crookes, 1991; Skehan, 1996; van Avermaet & Gysen, 2006). However, the real-life orientation of tasks is somehow a two-edged sword at least in the way it has generally been conceived in TBLT. The idea of designing tasks based on specific content matter, so that the exchange of information would also relate to that content-matter (van Lier, 1988), inevitably neglects non-transactional aspects of communication. In general: 'Transforming target or real-world tasks into pedagogical tasks' (Nunan, 2004: 37) appears to be a major preoccupation of TBLT. And so is the need for developing the instructional sequence of a task according to a series of defined principles (scaffolding, task dependency, recycling, active learning, integration, reproduction to creation, reflection) (Nunan, 2004: 35–38). The clear definition of the type of language the learner is expected to use and produce in the real world situation (van den Branden, 2006) – and necessarily to rehearse and learn within and through the task – is a core point of TLBT.

However, as we discussed in Chapter 3 and as van Lier aptly reminds us, 'much of our day-to-day communication is not aimed at transmitting information or discussing content-matter problems, but rather at developing and maintaining social relationships and at self-expression' (van Lier, 1988: 228). Language use is a very complex endeavour: not only do both the interactional and transactional aspects of language and language use (Brown & Yule, 1983) need to be taken into consideration, but also more elusive dimensions such as ludic and aesthetic ones. As Halliday explained (1978), individuals use language for imaginative purposes right from the very first stages of acquisition (Piccardo, 2005a). Language is used for pleasure, creativity and imagination in real life and this is very relevant to language education as well (CEFR, 2001: 47 – see the French version for an expanded presentation). A broader and more holistic view of language and language use, plus the view of what a real-life task is, are central to the distinction between TBLT and the AoA, and further between the learner (as envisaged in TBLT) and the social agent (as envisaged in the AoA).

4.2.3 From TBLT to AoA: A broader and strategic vision

This development from TBLT to the AoA is to a considerable extent echoed in ecological approaches to language learning (Kramsch, 2002, 2008; Tudor, 2001, 2003; van Lier, 2000, 2002, 2004, 2010;

see Section 3.9). In his 2003 article, *Learning to live with complexity: Towards an ecological perspective on language teaching*, Tudor states that:

> The ecological perspective on language teaching focuses attention on the subjective reality which various aspects of the teaching–learning process assume for participants, and on the dynamic interaction between methodology and context. It thus confronts us with the complex and multifaceted nature of teaching and learning as they are actually lived out in specific settings. (Tudor, 2003: 1)

He talks of: 'Exploring the ethnographic underpinnings of the methodological options which are available at a given point in time' (2003: 9), of the uniqueness of each learning context and of a 'focus on the *dynamics* of teaching–learning situations' (original emphasis) in the light of complexity theories (2003: 9). Van Lier talks of situated cycles of action, perception and understanding, as discussed in Section 3.9: 'From an ecological perspective, language learning-as-agency involves learning to perceive affordances (relationships of possibility) within multimodal communicative events. Every subject and every topic is an "affordance network" that is accessed through collaborative activity' (van Lier, 2007: 53).

Van Lier develops his ecological perspective into what he calls 'action-based teaching' (AB). Like the AoA with its concept of learner as social agent, van Lier's AB puts agency (see Section 3.8), and in particular situated agency, at the heart of the approach:

> An action-based approach is related to other approaches, such as content-based, project-based and task-based teaching and learning. However, it makes agency, rather than the particular curricular organisation, the defining construct. (van Lier, 2007: 46)

Van Lier's ecological, action-based approach to language learning is very similar to the AoA. Both can be characterised by (a) a recognition of the complex nature of the learning process and the fact that classes, and sub-groups in classes, constitute CASs as discussed in Section 3.9; (b) the adoption of 'a "local" approach' to pedagogical decision-making (Tudor, 2003: 1) that is sensitive to the learners' sociocultural identities and needs, rather than the import of a 'method' or technological/technocratic solution developed in a different context far away, and (c) a focus on personally meaningful, situated activity in tasks and projects that provide affordances and the 'promotion of emergent understandings and growing autonomy of the learner' (van Lier, 2007: 62).

In the AoA, tasks are driven by action, as language itself is generated by action, and in turn it calls for an action (Richer, 2003).

'While acts of speech occur within language activities, these activities form part of a wider social context, which alone is able to give them their full meaning' (Council of Europe, 2001: 9). The association of learning with action goes back at least to Pestalozzi (1746–1827) whose 'Head, Heart and Hand' philosophy is reflected in educational approaches and contexts and is very coherent with other educational philosophies (inspired by the work of Maria Montessori and Rudolf Steiner) that also aim to develop the individual holistically. Van Lier (2007) also refers to these European antecedents, talking of the need for 'a holistic, whole-person, whole-language and embodied approach' (2007: 62). In addition, more recent research in embodied cognition suggests that learning in at least children is more effective if it is associated with action (Glenberg *et al.*, 2004; Glenberg & Goldberg, 2011; Glenberg & Kaschak, 2002; Tellier, 2008).

As we will see in more detail in Chapter 7, action-oriented tasks are equivalent to projects. Learners are no longer (more or less passive) recipients of the pedagogical action, but both actors and agents, since they take ownership of what needs to be done to reach the goal and what they have at their disposal to build on. They act strategically, in order to be constantly in control of the process of completing the task. Viewing learners as language users and social agents does not deny the need for those users/learners to accomplish a range of speech acts, to use the language in various ways – some of which might end up by being inevitably rather mechanical and decontextualised in the course of a learning sequence – but rather embeds those speech acts and those usages in a socially and culturally realistic context through real-life tasks. This makes those speech acts and usages meaningful and pedagogically purposeful as propaedeutic to communication and action.

The whole point of the AoA is to equip users/learners for real-life language use and part of that process must involve experience of tasks that are as authentic as possible. However here, as Bachman and Palmer (1996) and Weir (2005) have pointed out, there are two ways of looking at authenticity: situational authenticity (contexts like the target situations identified through needs analysis) and interactional authenticity (conditions and constraints that generate use of the competences and strategies that would be required in the target situations). As we said above, the user/learner acts and accomplishes tasks in order to learn; he or she does not learn in order to accomplish tasks. It is by engaging in tasks which will require an activation of relevant competences that learners/users build up those competences. To enable this process, tasks should be designed in a way that allows for both situational and interactional authenticity. If this is not the case, the task may be only situationally authentic, and generate only simplistic discourse that does not develop competences. Often what is presented as tasks are either simple role plays, or very structured activities where learners are only called on to choose from a list of options provided. For instance, Nunan (2004: 20–21) uses a very restricted example of this type to introduce the concept of task, contrasting it to an 'exercise' or a mere 'communicative activity'. This is exactly the issue that Di Pietro (1987) already pointed out in his book, *Strategic interaction*, where he analysed why simple role plays are not generally conducive to language development. If the whole point of tasks is for learners to activate existing competences and strategies and develop relevant new ones, then the task must be sufficiently demanding to require this: an action-oriented task must have interactional validity as well as situational validity (Weir, 2005).

As the CEFR points out a 'task may be linguistically demanding but cognitively simple or vice versa' (Council of Europe, 2001: 162). The particular type and design of a task has an effect on the kind of language that is generated. This may be more accurate, more complex, or more fluent (see Foster & Skehan, 1996; Malicka & Levkina, 2012; Robinson, 2001, 2007; Skehan, 1998; Skehan & Foster, 1995, 2001). A balance of different types is therefore to be recommended. But it is by no means just linguistic competence that should be practised and developed in tasks, even though this tends to be the aspect focused on in research. Apart from the obvious functional competence, there are two other crucial aspects of pragmatic competence: discourse competence: the way in which text and interaction are 'organised, structured and arranged' (Council of Europe, 2001: 123) and design competence: familiarity with the way in which interactions are 'sequenced according to interactional and transactional schemata' (Council of Europe, 2001: 123). Discourse organisation varies with text genre as does the sequencing and possible routes that the user/learner may take in interactions. A good way of operationalising this strategic aspect in interaction, and at the same time focussing on the user/learner's own experience, is the concept of scenarios. Users/learners have schemata and scripts for scenarios that they are already familiar with, such as a first evening with someone's parents, planning a trip with friends, participating in an online forum, etc. These schemata draw not just on linguistic, or even pragmatic, competences but also what the CEFR calls general competences (e.g. knowledge of the world, sociocultural knowledge, experiential competence – *savoir être*, etc.).

Reasoning in terms of scenarios rather than in terms of simple tasks is in fact what helps to understand the nature of, and the stakes involved in, action-oriented, real-life tasks. Di Pietro (1987) defined a scenario in the classroom as 'a strategic interplay of roles functioning to fulfil personal agendas within a shared context' (Di Pietro, 1987: 41). In Di Pietro's scenarios, students improvise when playing themselves in an imagined, real world situation with a specific goal and defined conditions and restraints. He suggested that scenarios can be a way of ensuring that syllabuses are related to learners' experience. The term 'scenarios' itself has two main connotations. Firstly it suggests a mental framework, the scripts or schemata for familiar situations that we mentioned above. Secondly the term suggests a real-life context rather than language exercises or pedagogic tasks, with a simulation in which learners as social agents are real people acting as themselves in realistic contexts. They play themselves 'within the framework of the role' (Di Pietro, 1987: 67), they do not adopt artificial roles as other people. The distinction between standard roleplays and roles in scenarios is explained by Di Pietro, as shown in Table 4.2.

A similar view of the role of the learner is at the core of *simulations globales* [global simulations] a concept and technique developed in French as a foreign language (Caré & Debyser, 1995; Debyser, 1986/96; Yaiche, 1996), which were mentioned as an example of complex situated tasks in Section 3.9. In these global simulations, learners invent an entire universe, including their identities in this universe, then sketch various situations and problems that would realistically occur in this closed universe, and finally act them out and produce the relevant artefacts as a consequence. Debyser defines the global simulation as follows:

> A global simulation is a protocol or a scenario-frame which enables a group of students – up to an entire class of 30 or so – to create a 'universe of reference' – a building, a village, an island, a circus, a hotel – to together bring to life the characters and to simulate all the language functions that this frame, which is both a place/theme and discourse world, is likely to require. (Debyser 1986/96: preface, our translation)

Table 4.2 The difference between scenario roles and standard role plays

Role Play	Scenario Role
1. Student is given a 'part'; student portrays someone other than self.	1. Student plays self within the framework of the role.
2. Student is often told what to do or think (e.g., you want to go to the movies but your partner doesn't).	2. Student is given a situation but not told what to think or do.
3. The target language is used to practice previously presented items, thereby reinforcing the syllabus.	3. Aspects of the target language are taken from the interaction and determine the linguistic syllabus.
4. Usually all the players know what the others will say and do.	4. The interaction contains a greater element of uncertainty and dramatic tension.

Source: Di Pietro (1987: 67).

Global simulations are still very much used, especially but not exclusively in the teaching of languages for specific purposes. This is because they offer a realistic context for acting out situations and dealing with problems that could well occur in the professional domain concerned (e.g. simulating an international conference, for future diplomats). There are many similarities to the approach taken in role-enacting simulations in English as a foreign language (Jones, 1982), but in the French version, learners have far more autonomy to create the communicative situations and the roles that they will play in them. Contrary to Puren (2009b: 157), we consider that global simulations should not be equated with roleplaying (a typical activity in CLT), and the term 'role-enacting simulation' is sometimes used precisely to emphasise the difference. In terms of Di Pietro's distinction given in Table 4.2, learners play themselves, within the framework of the role. For example, in relation to a role-enacting simulation concerning town planning, the 'townspeople' themselves decide which of the planned developments they support, taking account of the information they are given, and develop arguments to justify the position they have decided to take, in order to defend their own, personal point of view in, for example, a town hall meeting.

A scenario provides more than just a meaningful context for simulated yet realistic language use by the learner. In a scenario, tasks are realistic and include particular situations that occur in relevant domains of everyday life. However, more fundamentally, a scenario turns a task into a *project*. One of the fundamental, historical problems with language learning, particularly in a school context, is the difficulty learners may have with motivation when they are learning a language as an object. A needs-based, 'learner-centred' approach, such as advocated in CLT, only marginally changes this situation. Texts, practice tasks and communicative tasks may be more relevant, more realistic – but there is still little room for personal engagement and creativity; it is all external to the learner. As Bourguignon puts it:

> It is essential that the learner realises that language is not an inert object that one manipulates to get a good grade! It is essential that he/she realises that the manipulation of language is necessary in order to arrive at a goal that is to be accomplished, and that he/she is the actor/agent in this strategy.

> In this way, carrying a project through to completion means being engaged in an action for which he/she needs language can and should lead to a desire to know even more: thus the action becomes the facilitator of learning. (Bourguignon, 2006: 66, our translation)

Van Lier, in advocating his action-based teaching, also criticises the way that the treatment of language as an inert object in conventional language teaching only produces 'inert knowledge' (2007: 56), pointing out that this has been decried in education since at least 1929. Projects have long been recognised as a way of addressing motivational problems and achieving what Bourguignon and van Lier propose, 'because it is necessary to define a goal that will motivate communication. One does not communicate without a reason!' (Bourguignon, 2006: 67). Projects have been exploited in this way in language learning since at least the early 1980s. Legutke and Thiel (1982), for example, proposed preparing low level learners to interview travellers at the local airport; Brumfit (1984: 84) suggested groups of learners with responsibilities for different areas preparing a radio broadcast about their country. Willis and Willis (2007) also give field interviews and preparing a radio programme alongside web research as examples of 'task-based projects' (Willis & Willis, 2007: 99–105), which they define as 'a sequence of tasks based around one specific topic, each task with its own outcome or purpose, which culminate in a specified end-product that can be shown to others, displayed or made public in some way, for others to appreciate' (2007: 99).

This may seem similar to the concept of an *action-oriented scenario*. However, as we discuss in Chapter 7, there is a fundamental difference of perspective between CLT and the AoA. First of all, for Willis and Willis, as an example of TBLT as the 'strong' form of CLT (Howatt, 1984; Larsen-Freeman, 2011), '[p]rojects and creative tasks: class newspaper, poster, survey, fantasy, etc.' are just one of the seven task types in their 'task generator,' the others being: listing; ordering and sequencing; matching; comparing; sharing personal experience, and problem-solving (Willis & Willis, 2007: 108). Of these, only the last category, problem-solving, would have even the potential, alongside projects and creative tasks, to become (part of) an action-oriented scenario. Secondly, the role of the teachers and learners in the two approaches is fundamentally different. In the examples of projects given by Willis and Willis, teachers orchestrate the tasks in the project with precise instructions e.g. 'The students work in groups and choose the five best questions ... and answer them from the documentary' (2007: 102). In action-oriented scenarios, it is the learners who take responsibility and design what they are doing; the teacher asks about progress at intervals (of maybe a week) – as in real professional or academic life. Finally, though these are excellent communicative activities, we are still in the (1980s) communicative paradigm of finding nice, motivating ways for learners to use the language, and often to use specific language. The focus is on the language and on the learner as a *future* language user, rather than the user/learner acting as a social agent engaged in the process of co-construction in a project that they design and control, within given conditions and constraints, as in real life.

Puren cites the CEFR definition of task to illustrate this difference:

> A *task* is defined as any purposeful action considered by an individual as necessary in order to achieve a given result in the context of a problem to be solved, an obligation to fulfil or an objective to be achieved. This definition would cover a wide range of actions such as moving a wardrobe, writing a book, obtaining certain conditions in the negotiation of a contract, playing a game of cards, ordering a meal in a restaurant, translating a foreign language text or preparing a class newspaper through group work. (Council of Europe, 2001: 10).

The selection of examples deliberately mixes real world and classroom tasks. However, the focus is on action, not language use, which is not even mentioned. It is worth citing in full what Puren deduces from this definition:

> This emergence of the concept of social agent and its recognition both in the classroom and in society is a direct consequence of the way things have evolved economically, socially and politically during the course of the current process of European integration. It is no longer a question of educating learners, like at the beginning of the 1970s, to establish contact with and communicate with foreigners passing by. It is rather a question of educating the citizens of multicultural and multilingual societies capable of living together in harmony, ... as well as students and professionals capable of working together over an extended period of time in a foreign language/culture. (Puren, 2009a: 124, our translation)

The key expressions here are 'living together' and 'working together.' It is not so much a question of interaction as 'co-action' (Puren, 2002) or 'communic-action' (Bourguignon, 2006: 64), co-operation, exploiting full agency together to achieve something new in the social context concerned. Here we touch on the *communities of practice* and *collective intelligence* together with concepts like *cognitive apprenticeship, collaborative learning*, or *situated learning* (Lave & Wenger, 1991) coming from professional training, all discussed in Section 3.8. Educational theories are moving towards a situated, real-world related task/scenario-based approach. This move aligns with the new vision of competence discussed in Section 2.3 as the development and mobilisation of capabilities through situated, collaborative action.

Di Pietro, like proponents of collaborative, situated learning, pioneered the idea that scenarios are an ideal way of sequencing a syllabus:

> I wish to suggest that a well-executed sequence of scenarios can serve as the main organizing principle of the subject matter. All other aspects

(grammar, vocabulary, functions and notions) can be introduced naturally as the scenarios are prepared, performed, and discussed throughout the semester. (Di Pietro, 1987: 25)

Action-oriented scenarios are also a good way of implementing a 'backward design' approach (working backwards from objectives: North *et al.*, 2018; Richards, 2013) as well as the situated learning approach proposed by Lave and Wenger (1991). An approach such as this can produce action-oriented tasks in which learners mobilise all their competences and develop strategies to achieve a realistic goal. It is not surprising, therefore, that scenarios have recently started to be used more widely in SLE, particularly, but not exclusively, in relation to the linguistic integration of adult migrants (LIAM). The CEFR reference specifications for French at Level A1.1 (intended for immigrants) contain scenarios (Beacco *et al.*, 2006). Both the FIDE project in Switzerland (www.fide-info.ch, Schleiss & Hagenow-Caprez, 2017) and the Durham project in Canada (Durham Immigration Portal, 2016; Piccardo & Hunter, 2017; Hunter *et al.*, 2017) are entirely scenario-based. In addition, the CEFR core inventories produced by Eaquals for English and French (North *et al.*, 2010; Eaquals & CIEP, 2014) include an example scenario for each CEFR level and scholars at Michigan State University have been working with learning scenarios in relation to the US *Standards for Foreign Language Learning in the 21st century* (National Standards in Foreign Language Education Project, 1999; Nerenz & Spinelli, 2003), in which it is also the case that each scenario 'concludes with one or more culminating authentic assessments in the form of a student-created product, a presentation, or a project on a high-interest and age-appropriate topic of their choice' (Spinelli & Nerenz, 2004: 1). At the same time a school associated with James Purpura at Columbia University's Teaching College is currently exploring the potential of scenario-based assessment (Beltrán & Lin, 2017; Carroll, 2017).

Explanations of the way scenarios can be exploited are provided by Bourguignon (2010) and Piccardo (2014a) and are outlined in Chapter 7, together with examples of action-oriented scenarios from the LINCDIRE project (Cho *et al.*, 2018; Piccardo *et al.*, 2018).

4.2.4 Putting it all together

As we said at the beginning of this chapter, in discussing the development of SLE, we prefer Mitchell and Vidal's (2001) metaphor of a river nourished by various streams to the more commonly used metaphor of a pendulum. Some of the insights brought by the GTM, direct method and audio-lingual method should not necessarily be thrown overboard, but rather elements of them can usefully be deployed in a purposeful way in the class. There may well be occasions when, with a particular type of group for a specific learning purpose, the teacher may employ techniques that can be traced directly back to earlier approaches. However, the main development is the move away from the view of the teacher as an operative, implementing 'a method', towards viewing him/her as an educational professional making informed, purposeful and strategic choices and also giving the user/learner the opportunity to contribute to the decision-making process and to exercise agency.

In terms of development of second language methodologies, as we saw throughout this chapter, the AoA situates itself in a particular position as it really encompasses and goes beyond the advances of the previous methodological conceptualisations. As we have seen, both societal transformations and conceptual advances in different theoretical fields have brought to the surface the need to abandon a linear view of social phenomena and related domains, including education. As we saw in Chapter 3, scholars from different schools of thought have contributed to highlighting different aspects of this epistemological shift and have offered multiple lenses, which together help us grasp the breadth and depth of this shift. The metaphor of the river proposed over 15 years ago proved to be a forward-looking one that contributed to stepping out of an either-or logic. Nowadays, we need to build on that metaphor and broaden it to stress the iterative, bidirectional and cyclical nature of the teaching/learning process. The crisis of linear models has stressed the need for holistic, complex and ecological models based upon the idea that all elements are interrelated in a network and cannot be considered separately without losing their nature. Thus, ecologic metaphors like that of a pond, where all elements – water, plants, animals and soil – are interconnected and interdependent, or that of a forest, would be more appropriate to help us envisage the multiplicity of elements composing the system and the effect of actions on all these elements.

Piccardo (2014a: 4) provides a first attempt to capture the different elements that characterise the AoA without denying some of the methodological thought that marked previous conceptualisations. We propose here (Figure 4.2) this diagram to help readers capture some of this complexity.

The first of the three concentric circles surrounding the core LL – language learning – is subdivided into three segments, each showing one of the main perspectives which have marked the evolution of second language methodologies: GTM, the direct method as well as

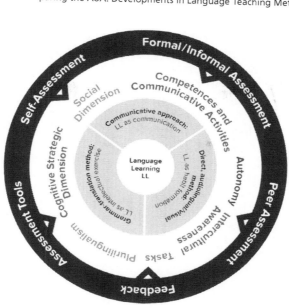

Figure 4.2 The action-oriented approach
Source: Piccardo (2014a: 4).

the audio-lingual/audio-visual, and the communicative approach –
CLT. Each of these segments shows the underlying vision informing
the methods, i.e. how language learning was seen by them. The
second concentric circle synthesises the key aspects that characterise
the AoA. Finally the outer, darker circle, focuses on assessment
(including roles, forms, purpose and tools). The little triangular
shapes pointing towards the previous circle recall the overall
function of assessment by reminding us that it has an effect on all the
different dimensions of the AoA, as we explain through the concept
of backward design and in the sections dedicated to assessment in
Chapters 5 and 7.

Whilst it is misleading to identify precise links, aspects of the
GTM, for instance, can be considered as a forerunner of cognitive
approaches. From CLT, the AoA most obviously takes the social
context, language as communication and the concept of a distinction
between communicative activities and competence (reflected in the
CEFR descriptive scheme shown in Figure 5.2). In the same way, the
idea of embedding assessment in teaching, by using it as a guiding
force and an engine for the iterative learning process that the AoA
advocates, is further highlighted by its position on the diagram, both
at the end and at the beginning, depending on the perspective adopted,
inside out or outside in.

We discuss further these issues in Chapter 7 where we present the tenets of the AoA and its practical implications. However, a full appreciation of the AoA is not feasible without considering the language policy document that proposes it. The AoA translates the philosophy of the *Common European Framework of Reference for Languages: Learning, Teaching, Assessment* (CEFR), into pedagogy. Thus, we need first to explore the key aspects of the CEFR for teaching and learning, to which we now turn in Chapter 5.

5 The Common European Framework of Reference and its Companion Volume: A Paradigm Shift

The CEFR is not only a language policy instrument. Its philosophy and descriptive scheme lay the groundwork for the AoA. The focus of this chapter will be on the innovation potential of the CEFR for classroom teaching through the AoA. The most visible aspect of the CEFR, the 'can do' descriptors, supports the setting of both educational and quality standards. It also provides a dynamic vision of learner-centred, intercultural, plurilingual, lifelong learning through the promotion of learner partnership and autonomy. Setting goals in relation to 'can do' descriptors emphasises meaningful action in the target language in the classroom. The centrality in the CEFR model of the co-construction of discourse in collaborative, interactive, real-life tasks, and a new, positive, interpretation of communication strategies by a language user fulfilling a mission in a realistic context, forms the foundation for the AoA. In this respect, the significance of the notion of agency, the user/learner as a social agent introduced by the CEFR, cannot be overestimated. With the introduction of the concept of mediation, the CEFR also moves the focus in language learning in an AoA beyond expressing one's own meaning to the understanding and development of concepts and the explanation of them to others. With the introduction of plurilingual/pluricultural competences, it moves beyond the borders of the isolated language classroom.

5.1 The CEFR as a Policy Document

The CEFR has had a considerable influence on language education, not only in the European context for which it was intended, but, as for example Piccardo *et al.* (2011a), Byram and Parmenter (2012) and O'Dwyer *et al.* (2017) show, also around the world. Porto (2012: 136) points out that the CEFR helped educators to provide the transparent, coherent goals for practical language proficiency that policy makers were increasingly demanding, but at the same time supported their efforts to include pluralistic and broader educational aims (such as social and cultural democratisation, intercultural competences, protection of local languages) in those goals. As North (2008a) describes in some detail, there is no contradiction between a pan-national, neutral reference document used as a common framework on the one hand and the freedom to produce locally appropriate standards and curricula on the other. In fact, rather than 'giv[ing] authorities a ready-made instrument to apply simplistically in language policy', the CEFR 'empowers institutions and associations by providing the means to develop differentiated, local standards and assessments appropriate to context, yet linked to international standards. Thus it helps avoid a takeover by multi-national high-stakes testing agencies' (North, 2014: 43).

Byram and Parmenter's (2012) informants confirm that the CEFR focus on communication and orality is having a considerable impact in initial teacher training (2012: 100) and that teachers of different languages are far more networked than previously (2012: 43, 205). The ongoing role of the CEFR as a reference document across Europe and beyond, and the importance that the descriptors in particular have taken in helping to orient curricula, led to requests from member states to update the CEFR illustrative descriptors and extend them to areas not provided with descriptors in the original edition (Council of Europe, 2001), namely mediation, online interaction, literature and plurilingual/pluricultural competences. As a consequence, the CEFR has been supplemented by a CEFR Companion Volume (Council of Europe, 2018), which contains both the previous descriptors and newly developed ones, in addition to an overview of key aspects of the CEFR for teaching and learning. (See North & Panthier, 2016 for background and North & Piccardo, 2016a, 2016b for the new development).

As might be expected, and is frequently the case with a complex document which spans several functions, the CEFR has been the object of quite a lot of, often unjustified, criticism. The CEFR has often been viewed in a reductive manner as if it:

- were just another proficiency scale like the ILR (Interagency Language Roundtable, n.d.; Lowe, 1985), ACTFL, (American Council on the Teaching of Foreign Languages, 2012; Liskin-Gasparro, 2003), and IELTS (Clapham, 1996; www.ieltsessentials.com/global/results/ielts9bandscale) the purpose of which is assessment;
- had a static view of competence as a list of components – rather than a conceptualisation of language learning and use;
- had descriptors that lack validation;
- were embracing a monolingual paradigm, and – most incredibly,

- were the product of a neoliberal ideology or superstate – rather than in fact being part of an ongoing (since 1964) fully non-binding promotion of inclusive quality education by one of the world's leading human rights organisations, particularly concerned with the protection of migrants and linguistic minorities: the Council of Europe (so often still confused with the European Union!).

Such preconceived, unsubstantiated criticisms (e.g. Fulcher, 2004; Leung & Scarino, 2016; MacNamara, 2011; MacNamara & Roever, 2006; Quetz & Vogt, 2009) fail to acknowledge the ethical context and theoretical conceptualisation that informed the CEFR, or the empirical research validating its descriptors (see North, 2014).

5.1.1 Origins, vision and mission

The CEFR is a continuation of the Council of Europe's work in language education which started in the 1960s. The Council of Europe is a broader institution than the European Union, and was founded in 1949 in order to protect human rights and avoid future war. 'As an intergovernmental organisation, it has no directive powers and works mainly by consensus, but its Committee of Ministers can make Recommendations to member states and its work can lead to European Conventions' (Trim, 2012: 21). With 47 member states today, the Council of Europe's mission is to promote democracy, human rights and the rule of law. The European Court of Human Rights has jurisdiction over all 47 member states. The Council also promotes international understanding (e.g. through the learning of the languages, history and cultures of other countries), and the protection of the rights of minorities and migrants. Today the Council's main focus in the language field is on the right to quality inclusive education for all, plurilingual and intercultural education, and the promotion of competences for democratic citizenship.

The CEFR had a slow germination. The main recommendation from the Council of Europe's 1964–73 major project concerning modern languages was a European-wide unit/credit scheme for adult learners. An intergovernmental symposium held in Switzerland in 1971 launched a series of projects in this direction, including:

- conceptualisation of needs analysis as a process of consultation with stakeholders, including learners, both before and during a course on an ongoing basis (Richterich & Chancerel, 1980);
- the specification of the language that an immigrant would need to live in a foreign country, first for English (*The Threshold Level*: van Ek, 1975; van Ek & Trim, 2001b) and French (*Niveau seuil* [A Threshold Level], Coste *et al.*, 1976) and later for over 30 other languages;

- experimentation with 'can do' descriptors for self-assessment (Oscarson, 1979, 1984);
- studies in learner self-regulation and autonomy (Holec, 1981).

However, the idea of a European unit-credit scheme was rejected at a second symposium held in 1977. From the early 1980s, therefore, the focus of the Council's work moved to the promotion of CLT in the school sector. With the reunification of Europe, the climate became more favourable again for a European framework, so a Common European Framework of Reference was recommended at a third intergovernmental symposium held in Switzerland in 1991 and subsequently approved by the Council of Ministers. The CEFR was then developed during the 1990s by a group of experts from different countries and languages appointed by the Council of Europe to respond to this expressed need for increased transparency and coherence in language learning, teaching and assessing at all levels within and across the countries of the Council of Europe. The brief included the requirement that the CEFR should be 'comprehensive' in the sense that all professional users should be able to relate to it and find in it the approach that they applied. Hence, the authors took pains to maintain a certain neutrality of tone, underlining that they were 'raising questions not answering them' (Council of Europe, 2001: xi) and that it was not the function of the CEFR 'to lay down the objectives that users should pursue or the methods they should employ' (2001: xi). In addition, the many descriptor scales try to use categories that are familiar to teachers and curriculum developers (e.g. conversation, information exchange, grammatical accuracy, spoken fluency) rather than 'a theoretically sound but operationally very difficult set of categories [since such] an approach would be very likely to be dismissed by teachers as "theoretical, academic or airy-fairy"' (North, 2000: 35). This, plus the fact that in a language policy document presented as a compendium, detailed academic references are not given, has led many applied linguists to underestimate the theoretical basis of the CEFR in its three strands: learning, teaching and assessment.

After development between 1993 and 1996, partly on the basis of a National Research Foundation project in Switzerland (North, 2000; Schneider & North, 2000) the CEFR was piloted in draft versions before being published in English and French in 2001. It was then also recommended by the European Union and is now available in 40 languages. It is important to understand that the CEFR is neither a standardisation nor a language testing project. There is no body monitoring or even coordinating its use. The CEFR provides a common metalanguage, descriptive categories and levels with which to talk about language education, plus innovative concepts like interaction, mediation and plurilingualism. The aim in doing this is twofold. The first aim is to provide common reference points for the elaboration of language syllabuses, curriculum guidelines, examinations and textbooks across Europe. The second aim is, through the resulting networking, to act as a stimulus for reflection on current practice in order to encourage reform and improve the efficiency of language learning in schools. The main function of the CEFR is thus to facilitate reflection, networking and innovation. Trim puts this as follows:

> It was also agreed that the Framework should be flexible, open, dynamic and non-dogmatic, since the aim was not to prescribe how languages should be learnt, taught and assessed, but to raise awareness, stimulate reflection and improve communication among practitioners of all kinds and persuasions as to what they actually do. (Trim, 2012: 29–30)

It was very clear at an intergovernmental Language Policy Forum in 2007 that governments are much more interested in the second aim (stimulus to reform) than they are in the first (coordination through common reference points). The way the two aims are linked in the shared European space (Goullier, 2007b) that the CEFR is creating was recognised as being dependent on responsible collaboration through voluntary international projects, meetings and networks such as the ECML (www.ecml.at), ALTE (www.alte.org), Eaquals (www.eaquals.org) CercleS (www.cercles.org) and EALTA (www.ealta.eu.org). The result hoped for is an inclusive quality education for all and a Europe of open-minded, plurilingual citizens.

5.1.2 The need for transparency: The levels

As suggested above, the aspect of the CEFR that is still best known among professionals and lay people is the set of proficiency levels going from A1 to C2. The need for transparency within educational systems in Europe was very urgent and it became even stronger with socio-political evolutions of the 1990s. With greater personal mobility, it was more and more important that achievement could be articulated in relation to a set of common reference points. With the involvement of learners in self-assessment and the process of learning, it was increasingly important that these reference points should be defined in a transparent way. With growing recognition that language education should produce practical results, it was clear that both learning aims and learner achievements should be defined in relation to the continuum of real-world ability in the language. This is in fact the original and true meaning of the expression 'criterion-referenced assessment' (Glaser, 1963, 1994a, 1994b).

It is, however, important to remember that the CEFR levels are reference levels; it is specifically stated that: 'Establishing cut-off points between levels is always a subjective procedure; some institutions prefer broad levels, others prefer narrow ones' (Council of Europe, 2001: 32) and a series of examples are given of ways in which they might be adapted to suit different contexts or in which the levels used in a particular context might be related to the common levels. In the CEFR itself 'a distinction is made between the 'criterion levels' (e.g. A2 or A2.1) and the 'plus levels' (e.g. A2+ or A2.2) (2001: 32). In the CEFR Companion Volume, the current authors use the image of the colour spectrum in the rainbow (Council of Europe, 2018: 34) in order to make the point that, whilst the levels describe a continuum, some bands on that continuum usually appear more salient than others. All the boundaries on the rainbow are conventional, appear fuzzy, and are not always perceived in exactly the same places by different viewers. Yet, that does not stop us communicating about colours. Orange is a 'plus level' between red and yellow; scarlet is between red and orange, etc.

However, one must bear in mind that the descriptors are only 'illustrative' in two senses. Firstly they only provide examples of aspects that are new and salient at the level concerned; they do not attempt to describe everything relevant in a comprehensive, systematic manner. Secondly, they are presented '... as recommendations and are not in any way mandatory, as a basis for reflection, discussion and further action. ... The aim of the examples is to open new possibilities, not to pre-empt decisions' (Council of Europe, 2001: xiii-xiv). Second language acquisition research that has been undertaken to further validate the progression proposed in the CEFR descriptors (after suggestions from Alderson, 2007 and Hulstijn, 2007) has tended to support the conceptualisation in the descriptor scales (see North, 2014 for discussion).

The CEFR illustrative descriptor scales have become so popular precisely because they offer a visible, practical way to link the two main CEFR aims (coordination and networking; reflection and reform). The descriptors are presented in scales, with each descriptor being a stand-alone criterion statement describing an aspect of language proficiency at the level in question. The validity claim for the descriptors, both the originals in the 2001 edition of the CEFR and the expanded version in the 2018 CEFR Companion Volume, as stated in those two works, is that they:

- draw, in their formulation, on the experience of many institutions active in the field of defining levels of proficiency;
- have been developed in tandem with the descriptive scheme presented in CEFR Chapters 4 and 5 through an interaction between (a) the theoretical work of the Authoring Group; (b) the analysis of existing scales of proficiency; and (c) the practical workshops with teachers;

- have been matched to the set of Common Reference Levels A1, A2, B1, B2, C1 and C2;
- meet the criteria outlined in CEFR Appendix A for effective descriptors in that each is brief (up to 25 words), clear and transparent, positively formulated, describes something definite, and has independent, stand-alone integrity, not relying on the formulation of other descriptors for its interpretation;
- have been found transparent, useful and relevant by groups of non-native and native-speaker teachers from a variety of educational sectors with very different profiles in terms of linguistic training and teaching experience;
- are relevant to the description of actual learner achievement in lower and upper secondary, vocational and adult education, and could thus represent realistic objectives;
- have been 'objectively calibrated' to a common scale. This means that the position of the vast majority of the descriptors on the scale is the product of how they have been interpreted to assess the achievement of learners, rather than just the opinion of the authors;
- provide a bank of criterion statements about the continuum of foreign language proficiency that can be exploited flexibly for the development of criterion-referenced assessment. They can be matched to existing local systems, elaborated by local experience and/or used to develop new sets of objectives (Council of Europe, 2001: 30; 2018: 41–2).

First and foremost the illustrative descriptors offer a way to create lateral coherence across courses for different languages and the training of the teachers for them, thus helping to end the isolation of the pedagogic cultures associated with different languages, promote transversal competences and (cross-)language awareness. Even more fundamentally, they offer a tool to link curriculum development and quality management, as evidenced by the quality management schemes of organisations like Eaquals (www.eaquals.org) and UNIcert (www.uni-cert.eu) and recognised by writers outside Europe (e.g. Graves, 2008; Richards, 2013).

5.1.3 The construct of the CEFR: Interdependence of teaching, learning and assessment

The CEFR aims to facilitate transparency and coherence between curriculum, teaching and assessment *within* an institution plus transparency and coherence *between* institutions, educational sectors, regions and countries. In the CEFR these alignment aims are stated as follows:

- promote and facilitate co-operation among educational institutions in different countries;

- provide a sound basis for the mutual recognition of language qualifications;
- assist learners, teachers, course designers, examining bodies and educational administrators to situate and co-ordinate their efforts. (Council of Europe, 2001: 5)

Arbitrariness in defining educational standards has long been recognised as a problem in education. Before the CEFR, aims in language curricula were often vaguely formulated and gave the impression of having been 'plucked out of the air on the basis of intuition, which is frequently shown on closer examination to be wrongly conceived' (Clark, 1987: 44). Course materials often then had only an indirect link to the (vague) aims and assessment grades were often awarded on the basis of simplistic notions like counting errors rather than any transparent criteria connected with language use. The lack of well-constructed criteria is still unfortunately a major problem. In a language teaching programme, a validated reference framework like the CEFR can be a source for the formulation of locally appropriate standards. It provides descriptors in differing degrees of detail and with different emphases that facilitate transparent, coherent alignment between the overall curriculum aims, the detailed objectives teachers use to implement the curriculum, and the assessment of achievement in relation to them (= constructive alignment: Biggs, 2003; Biggs & Tang, 2011). Descriptors can also ensure lateral coherence in these aspects of the courses for different languages.

One of the main issues in SLE continues to be that assessment tends to be seen as something separate and independent from planning and teaching. Rather than having transparently defined, relevant objectives that are used to inform planning, teaching and assessment, assessment is often operationalised by using tests from the coursebook and offering students external public examinations. Planning, classroom enactment and assessment of progress should influence each other in a dynamic system, in a cycle of improvement. 'Planning, implementation and evaluation decisions should be consistent and interdependent rather than undertaken in a lockstep or piecemeal approach' (Graves, 2008: 148). As Graves suggests, curriculum needs to be considered as a dynamic system (Figure 5.1) and the structure of the CEFR is designed to help this conceptualisation.

In an action-oriented approach, classroom experience should feed back into definition of aims in a continuous process of ongoing needs analysis. Assessment should focus on the main aims and should reflect the types of classroom activities. Assessment should also inform the balance of activities in the programme in order to maximise success, as well as to provide feedback. The CEFR descriptors offer a way of

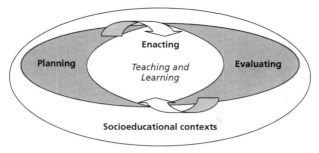

Figure 5.1 Curriculum as a Dynamic System
Source: Graves, 2008: 152.

facilitating this interactive, enactivist approach through a process that Richards (2013) calls backward design. Richards outlines a historical development from *forward design* (from content through methodology to assessment), through a *central design* (concentrating on the teaching and learning, classroom process) to *backward design* (from defined learner outcomes to an analysis of necessary course content). The central point in backward design is to see the learner as a *user*. This concept of the learner as a user is crucial in the development of SLE as we have seen in Chapter 4 on methodologies and will discuss further in Chapter 7 on the AoA. Backward design involves the definition of curriculum objectives in terms of 'can-do' descriptors. An innovation in the language field with the CEFR, this is now becoming standard across the curriculum in several European countries. Because of its broad coverage and scientifically validated descriptors, 'the CEFR is the most sophisticated framework currently available and currently the most widely used tool for backward design in language education' (Richards, 2013: 26)

The can-do descriptors also help to establish a link between the real world tasks that are the 'end-objectives' and the competences that are necessary to perform those tasks effectively: the 'enabling objectives.' Here the CEFR descriptive scheme offers a clearly articulated vision that can help to inform curriculum development.

5.1.4 The conceptual density of the CEFR: The hidden part of the iceberg

Because the CEFR is far more than just an alignment project, its second aim is to stimulate educational reform by encouraging users to consider different aspects of language, language learning and the organisation of the provision of language education, evaluating their current practice in that process and reflecting on options that the CEFR presents.

As mentioned in Section 1.3.1, the CEFR offers:

- a sophisticated model of language use;
- a rich, structured hierarchy of descriptor scales (50 in 2001; 80 in 2018);
- a discussion of the organisation of language learning and teaching, the role of tasks;
- an educational philosophy promoting flexible curricula for plurilingual and intercultural education.

A sophisticated model of language use

The CEFR approach (CEFR Chapter 2) sees the collaborative co-construction of meaning to accomplish a given task under the prevalent conditions and constraints, mobilising competences (both personal and linguistic) and strategies to do so. Thus, competences and strategies are mobilised in accomplishing tasks – and in turn further developed through that experience. A detailed descriptive scheme covers different aspects of both language use (CEFR Chapter 4) and the user/learner's competences (CEFR Chapter 5) – see Figure 5.2. The CEFR situates itself in an ecological paradigm and emphasises the two key notions of co-construction of meaning in interaction and constant movement between the individual and social level in language learning, mainly through its vision of the user/learner as a social agent (Piccardo, 2012a).

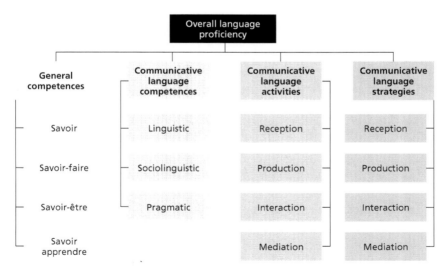

Figure 5.2 The structure of the CEFR descriptive scheme
Source: Piccardo *et al.*, 2011b: 55, reproduced in Council of Europe 2018: 30.

A rich, structured hierarchy of descriptor scales

Scales are offered for different communicative language activities and communicative language strategies (CEFR Chapter 4) and for aspects of communicative language competences (CEFR Chapter 5) plus plurilingual and pluricultural competences (in the CEFR Companion Volume: Council of Europe, 2018). The descriptors on the scales reflect the CEFR principle of the positive formulation of educational aims and outcomes at all levels. The categorisation for the descriptor scales for communicative language activities (North, 1994, 1997) is an open-ended list of discourse types/target situations, each of which would have its own socio-pragmatic and discourse conventions, organised in the four modes of communication (reception, production, interaction, mediation).

A discussion of the organisation of language learning and teaching and of the role of tasks

CEFR Chapter 6 follows a discussion of language learning objectives and the roles of different actors in the teaching and learning process with a survey of aspects involved in different language teaching methodologies. The CEFR aims for inclusivity and avoids being prescriptive right from the beginning:

> One thing should be made clear right away. We have NOT set out to tell practitioners what to do, or how to do it. We are raising questions, not answering them. It is not the function of the Common European Framework to lay down the objectives that users should pursue or the methods they should employ. (CEFR: Notes to the User, xi)

But methodological neutrality is impossible. CEFR Chapter 6 suggests that 'formulating objectives in terms of tasks has the advantage, for the learner too, of identifying in practical terms what the expected results are, and can also play a short-term motivating role throughout the learning process' (Council of Europe, 2001: 138). For this reason, the CEFR includes a chapter on tasks (CEFR Chapter 7).

An educational philosophy promoting flexible curricula for plurilingual and intercultural education

Much of the discussion of objectives in CEFR Chapter 6 and the whole of CEFR Chapter 8 is devoted to outlining the CEFR vision for language education, again as a series of options for discussion rather than as a prescription. The notion of plurilingualism as a dynamically developing, unbalanced, partial competence that should be a major educational aim is introduced to language education in these chapters. This is in keeping with the CEFR positive educational philosophy that is also reflected in the 'can do' descriptors.

The points above are elaborated in more detail in the CEFR Companion Volume, whose primary purpose is to make clearer to practitioners the innovative aspects introduced in the CEFR, but not always explained. These concepts in fact provide the basis for a substantial development in second language pedagogy, as we will see.

5.1.5 Supporting curriculum reform

It is widely recognised that the CEFR is a heuristic to stimulate curriculum development and reform. In her state-of-the-art article on the language curriculum, Graves, for example, acknowledges that the CEFR is: '[o]ne of the most important curriculum publications in the last decade' (2008: 148). It is important to emphasise the term 'heuristic'. As mentioned above, the CEFR makes clear from the outset that it is setting out options and is a reference tool for reflection, not a panacea to be 'applied'.

The CEFR descriptors, for example, are illustrative. They are intended are an aid to curriculum design, as emphasised in the CEFR Companion Volume:

> The aim of the descriptors is to provide input for curriculum development. The descriptors are presented in levels for ease of use. Descriptors for the same level from several scales tend to be exploited in adapted form on checklists of descriptors for curriculum or module aims and for self-assessment. (Council of Europe, 2018: 40)

In a formal survey of Council of Europe member states (Martyniuk & Nojons, 2007), 79% of the respondents reported 'high' or 'very high' use of the CEFR for defining learning outcomes with proficiency levels and descriptors adapted to the age, interests and needs of learners. This reflects the fact that the levels (75%) and in particular the descriptors (83%) were the dimensions of the CEFR most highly referred to in official documents and implemented in practice. In addition, 75% reported that the CEFR has been highly helpful or very highly helpful in promoting a learner-centred, action-oriented, task-based approach to learning, teaching, and assessment. When asked specifically about how helpful the CEFR was with (a) curriculum design, (b) course book design and (c) design of assessment, tests and certificates, the respondents reported 71% highly or very highly helpful for the first two and 79% for designing assessments etc. Interestingly, these proportions are reversed in a recent survey of CEFR-related projects in 23 member states (Piccardo et al., 2019a). Here, the aggregated data show that 50% of the projects mentioned concerned curriculum and/

or objectives whereas only 30% concerned assessment and testing. This suggests that the CEFR is increasingly having an impact on curriculum, rather than just on levels and examinations, which were member states' initial focus.

The CEFR promotes a *proficiency* perspective to curriculum development guided by 'can do' descriptors rather than a *deficiency* perspective focusing on what the learners have not yet acquired. Planning backwards from 'can do' descriptors offers an effective way to move from planning based on a linear progression through language structures towards syllabuses based on needs analysis and oriented towards real-life tasks. Following such an approach, language is taught for a purpose, not just because it exists or follows on nicely from what was just taught.

CEFR Chapters 4 and 5 provide a basis for the transparent definition of curriculum aims and of standards and criteria for assessment. The descriptors in CEFR Chapter 4 focus on language activities ('the WHAT') and those in Chapter 5 focus on competences ('the HOW'). Of course, this is only a starting point. Other, broader educational aims and learning experiences will need to be incorporated as discussed in CEFR Chapter 8 on curriculum options. But the definition of outcomes is one of the main steps in curriculum design, and the descriptors for language use (CEFR Chapter 4) and for different kinds of competences (CEFR Chapter 5) provide a concrete basis for development. Since the CEFR itself is not a set of specifications for any particular language, further resources are needed to provide suggestions for content specifications, sample tasks and performance examples at different levels. Some of these can be found for certain languages on the CEFR website (www.coe.int/en/web/common-european-framework-reference-languages/home).

5.1.6 An open-ended and evolving tool

The CEFR makes clear that it is intended to be 'open and flexible, so that it can be applied, with such adaptations as prove necessary, to particular situations' (Council of Europe, 2001: 7): '*open*: capable of further extension and refinement ... and ... *dynamic*: in continuous evolution in response to experience in its use' (2001: 8). Users are constantly reminded that it is they who need to make choices and adapt to context. In particular, it is stated that: 'the taxonomic scheme presented in Chapters 4 and 5 of the Framework is not seen as a closed system, but one which is open to further development in the light of experience' (Council of Europe, 2001: xiii). The descriptors, are described as a 'bank' of 'illustrative descriptors' (Council of Europe, 2001: 25, 30, 37) with the idea that a descriptor bank, like an item bank, is designed to be extended. Such extension has been carried out in different ways:

- in adaptations for ELPs, which were required to trace their descriptors back to the CEFR originals; a 'bank' of such ELP descriptors (Lenz & Schneider, 2004) is available on the Council of Europe's website, with a version for young learners (Szabo & Goodier, 2016);
- in projects that calibrated descriptors to the CEFR scale using methodologies similar to those used in the original research, for example Lenz and Studer (2007) and Negishi *et al.* (2013) for lower secondary school learners, Green (2012) for C-level learners, and de Jong *et al.* (2016) for general and different specific purposes in English;
- in the 2014–17 Council of Europe project to fill gaps on the original scales and extend the set to new areas, notably mediation, online interaction and plurilingual/pluricultural competence (North & Piccardo, 2016a, 2016b), which resulted in the publication of the CEFR Companion Volume (Council of Europe, 2018).

The CEFR is supported by a number of policy documents such as a *Guide for Users* (Trim, 2001), a *Guide for the Development of Language Education Policies in Europe – From Linguistic Diversity to Plurilingual Education* (Beacco & Byram, 2007a), a manual *for Relating Language Examinations to the Common European Framework of Reference for Languages* (Council of Europe, 2009), and a *Guide for the Development and Implementation of Curricula for Plurilingual and Intercultural Education* (Beacco *et al.*, 2015). There are also a series of CEFR-based detailed specifications for different languages in publications called Reference Level Descriptions (RLDs): e.g. for German: Glaboniat *et al.* (2005); for French: Beacco *et al.* (2004, 2005, 2007, 2008); for Spanish: Instituto Cervantes (2007); for Italian: Parizzi and Spinelli (2009), and for English: English Profile: www.englishprofile.org, Salamoura and Saville (2011); Hawkins and Filipovic (2012). Then there are video samples of performance at different CEFR levels, with documentation and scientific reports on the calibration seminars, sample test tasks, supplementary descriptors, and further material related to tests and examinations – all accessible on the Council's CEFR website. Finally, there is a separate website devoted to the European Language Portfolio (ELP) (www.coe.int/en/web/portfolio) with many useful materials including guides.

In addition to the resources from the Council's Educational Policy Division mentioned above, there are also materials that have been developed in projects coordinated by the European Centre for Modern Languages (ECML: www.ecml.at). There have been several CEFR-related projects at the ECML, which are all accessible through the ECML website. These include the ECEP project (a mine of teacher training materials), FREPA/CARAP (descriptors and materials for pluralistic approaches), PRO-Sign (with CEFR descriptors in sign language), QualityMatrix (a quality management tool for CEFR implementation) and RELEX (a simplified version of the manual for relating tests to the CEFR). Finally, Eaquals (www.eaquals.org) has developed a 'Core Inventory' of key content at different CEFR levels for English (North *et al.*, 2010) and French (Eaquals & CIEP, 2015) and has other useful CEFR-related documents on its website.

5.2 The Innovation Potential of the CEFR in Language Education: From the CEFR to the CEFR Companion Volume

As mentioned above, the primary purpose of the CEFR is to contribute to reform, innovation and networking in order to improve the efficiency of language learning in the school system. The CEFR introduced many innovative aspects based on a series of studies that fed into its development. The CEFR descriptive scheme of general competences, including intercultural competences (Byram *et al.*, 1996) and the definition of communicative language activities, strategies and competences (North, 1994), marks a significant advance on the then reigning communicative language competence/proficiency models (e.g. Bachman, 1990; Canale & Swain, 1980). The emphasis on the co-construction of discourse in interaction and the distinction between interaction and production (see Section 5.1.4) has had a considerable effect on teaching, course materials and examinations. This impact shows promising signs of being repeated with the publication of the CEFR Companion Volume, with its descriptors for mediation and plurilingual/pluricultural competences. These concepts offer a dynamic way of viewing the needs of language education far more suitable to the superdiverse contexts of today's classrooms than the static, traditional, monolingual systems of yesterday. The educational philosophy of the CEFR takes into account linguistic diversification, partial competences, plurilingualism and pluriculturalism, differentiated learning objectives and lifelong language learning, and has been further developed in the guides referred to in the previous section (Beacco & Byram, 2007a, 2007b; Beacco *et al.*, 2015).

With these innovations, the CEFR not only moves on from the traditional focus in language education on learning the language as an objectified system, but it also brings to the fore the complete interdependence of individual linguistic expression and social co-construction of meaning, concepts and communication.

5.2.1 A new model of language activity

The traditional focus in language teaching since the early 1960s (Lado, 1961) has been the four skills: reception and production, each divided into spoken and written. The focus with the four skills approach is on the use of the language as a code by the individual learner acting as speaker/writer or listener/reader. The qualitative aspects traditionally associated with this view, the 'elements' in Lado's model, are (accurate use of) grammar, vocabulary and phonology/graphology, with the native speaker as the model. The CEFR and the AoA go beyond this historical vision of language as code and learner as individual novice following a pre-set path; instead they put the emphasis on the co-constructed, social nature of language, with the learner seen as a language *user* who acts as a *social agent*. The CEFR/AoA model defines reception and production (i.e. the four skills) as only two of the four modes of communicative activity, the other two modes being inter-action and mediation, which represent the social dimension of the use of language: the co-construction of meaning and the creation of discourse.

Look again at the diagram of the descriptive scheme in Figure 5.2. As can be seen, the same categories – reception, production, inter-action, mediation – are used for both communicative language activities and communicative language strategies. The CEFR Companion Volume sets out the advantages of replacing the four skills with a scheme of this type, that had been put forward by North (1994, 1997) in one of the background studies that led up to the CEFR. This shift was crucial in shaping the CEFR descriptive scheme and in informing the further development that led to the CEFR Companion Volume. The points are cited in the CEFR Companion Volume as follows:

- the proposed categories (Reception, Production, Interaction, Mediation) make sense not just for insiders but also for users: such categories reflect more the way people actually use the language than do the four skills;
- since these are the types of categories used in language training for the world of work, a link between general purpose language and language for specific purposes (LSP) would be facilitated;
- pedagogic tasks involving collaborative interaction in small groups, project work, pen friend correspondence, language examination interviews, would be easier to situate with this model;
- organisation in terms of transparent activities in specific contexts of use would facilitate the recording and profiling of the 'slices of life' which make up the language learner's experience;
- such an approach based on genre, encourages the activation of content schemata and acquisition of the formal schemata (discourse organisation) appropriate to the genre;

- categories which highlight the interpersonal *and* sustained self-expression are central by A2 and may help to counterbalance the pervasive transmission metaphor which sees language as information transfer;
- a move away from the matrix of four skills and three elements (grammatical structure, vocabulary, phonology/graphology) may promote communicative criteria for quality of performance;
- the distinction Reception, Interaction, Production recalls classifications used for learning and performance strategies and may well facilitate a broader concept of strategic competence;
- the distinction Reception, Interaction, Production, Mediation actually marks a progression of difficulty and so might aid the development of the concept of partial qualifications;
- such relatively concrete contexts of use (tending towards supra-genres/speech events rather than abstract skills or functions) makes the link to realistic assessment tasks in examinations easier to establish, and should help facilitate the provision of more concrete descriptors. (Council of Europe, 2018: 31, based on North, 1994)

The separation of spoken interaction from spoken production, pointing out that interaction is far more than merely the sum of reception and production, provided practitioners with a rationale that fitted well with the focus on the negotiation of meaning in CLT, and on the interaction in groups that is a feature of TBLT. The move reflected developments in applied linguistics during the 1980s, for example Breen and Candlin (1980: 92), who had talked of three underlying abilities: 'interpretation, negotiation and expression'; Brumfit (1984: 69–70), who had made a distinction between conversation/discussion and extended speaking/writing; Alderson and Urquhart (1984: 227), who had distinguished dialogue (like in conversation and in correspondence) from monologue, and Brown *et al.* (1984: 15) had researched short turns and long turns. Finally Swales (1990: 58–61) had argued that all communicative interaction on the one hand and literacy on the other is developed from chat (= interaction) and storytelling (= sustained spoken production) respectively, with storytelling creating the reciprocal activity of sustained listening (= reception).

The CEFR Companion Volume presents the scheme for communicative language activities in Table 5.1.

Communication happens for a purpose, which generally is related to one of the three major macrofunctional uses of language: creative/interpersonal, transactional and evaluative/problem-solving. This distinction goes back to Halliday's (1973, 1975) theories discussed in Section 3.4, the latter two categories reflecting his subdivisions of the ideational use of language. As North (1994, 1997) discussed, in real

Table 5.1 Macro-functional basis of CEFR categories for communicative language activities

	Reception	Production	Interaction	Mediation
Creative, Interpersonal Language Use	e.g. Reading as a leisure activity	e.g. Sustained monologue: Describing experience	e.g. Conversation	Mediating communication
Transactional Language Use	e.g. Reading for information and argument	e.g. Sustained monologue: Giving information	e.g. Obtaining goods and services Information exchange	Mediating a text
Evaluative, Problem-solving Language Use	*(Merged with reading for information and argument)*	e.g. Sustained monologue: Presenting a case	e.g. Discussion	Mediating concepts

Source: Council of Europe, 2018: 31.

life, of course, the different communicative activities are combined in different ways (e.g. *information exchange* or *sustained monologue: describing experience*, are often embedded within the context of a *conversation*) so there is no firm line between the categories, they shade into each other.

The aim of including scales for different types of target situation/ genre, grouped under the three macrofunctions, is to encourage a more differentiated pedagogical approach, since each of these different situation/genres has very different culturally determined discourse conventions. The hope is also to inspire teachers to exploit a variety of tasks to reflect the range of types of interaction that occur in real life.

5.2.2 A new dynamic vision of learner-centred, intercultural, plurilingual lifelong learning

As is apparent from the previous discussion, the CEFR and AoA do not see language as a (school) subject to be learnt for a qualification, reflecting the shift in the conceptualisation of competence and the resulting change in the aims of education and training that was discussed in Chapter 2. Language learning is seen in the CEFR as a dynamic, lifelong process from the home and kindergarten, through primary and secondary, possibly tertiary, and finally adult education as well as leisure pursuits. Learners undertake a trajectory in the course of which they add and change linguistic and cultural environments (e.g. schools, groups of friends, neighbourhoods, cities, countries, academic disciplines, professional domains, clubs and associations). With today's levels of diversity, as discussed in Chapter 1, these trajectories become more complex, involving wider spaces, different cultures, more linguistic varieties. Therefore, plurilingual and intercultural competence become increasingly crucial.

Few would debate the fact that mastery of one's most commonly used language(s) – which may or maybe not the L1 – is improved with maturity and experience. With time one normally acquires more registers for different domains, more schemata for different genres/situations, more skills for effective reading, more sophisticated expression, wider vocabulary, etc. With second language learning, the situation is more complicated. In relation to cognitive and neurological aspects of language learning, there has long been a debate about the best age to learn a second language. The conclusion reached is that there is no evidence for any specific 'critical period' but that it is true that learners who start later in life tend not to reach as high a proficiency level as those who start sooner. Muñoz and Singleton (2011) caution against jumping to conclusions about the reasons for this, saying that 'given the high degree of interrelation of the factors that influence L2 acquisition, it seems reasonable to hypothesize that the effects observed may result from the interplay of a range of variables (including age of acquisition) rather than the decline of any specific faculty' (2011: 11). One can, in fact, start learning a language at almost any age: learners at different ages have different advantages and disadvantages. Some of the many factors involved, as Muñoz and Singleton (2011) go on to outline, are psychological and social, to do with satisfaction with one's (e.g. phonological) profile in the second language, whether one *wants to* sound like a native speaker, attitudes towards the target language culture, opportunities to use the language, etc.

If language learning is a lifelong process, then the most important aspect of competence is what Delamare le Diest and Winterton (2005: 40) called 'meta-competence' (see Sections 2.3.4-5) which the CEFR describes as 'ability to learn' (Council of Europe, 2001: 106; see Section 2.3.4). This connects with the focus on conscious learning in a cognitive approach discussed in Chapters 3 and 4. Learning strategies (Oxford, 1990) are essential as the learner takes steps towards self-direction (Dickinson, 1987), becoming an autonomous learner (Holec, 1981; Little *et al.*, 2017), who can expand his/her plurilingual/cultural repertoire, eventually without the need for scaffolding from a teacher. The result of this process of development is inevitably dynamic rather than static and uneven rather than balanced. In the same way that certain areas of the brain become more developed in relation to experience and use, certain areas of language activity become more familiar and routine as a result of experience and regular use in certain languages, varieties and/or registers. If one often reads Spanish but rarely speaks it, if one often speaks German but rarely writes it, if one sometimes participates in formal meetings or gives presentations in French but never watches films or

TV in French, this will all affect the shape of the proficiency profile in each of the languages or varieties concerned. Plurilingual profiles are thus expected to be uneven and dynamic. It is precisely to assist in preparing a plurilingual profile that the CEFR contains so many descriptor scales:

> The fact that the Framework does not confine itself to providing 'overview' scaling of communicative abilities, but breaks down global categories into their components and provides scaling for them, is of particular importance when considering the development of plurilingual and pluricultural competences. (Council of Europe, 2001: 133)

As Spolsky (2008) comments, frameworks of descriptor scales need to be able to describe the complex profiles of a wide range of different plurilingual proficiency profiles for different (types of) learners. With its wide range of descriptor scales (50 in 2001; 80 in 2018) this is precisely what the CEFR provides.

Earlier versions of the ELP encouraged learners to record their proficiency in all the communicative activities in each language one after another (see Figure 5.3).

However, more recently, plurilingual graphic profiles are starting to be used. For example, Figure 5.4 profiles listening across several languages. In an ELP, this would be followed by profiles for reading, spoken interaction, spoken production, etc. Such profiles can raise awareness of plurilingual competence.

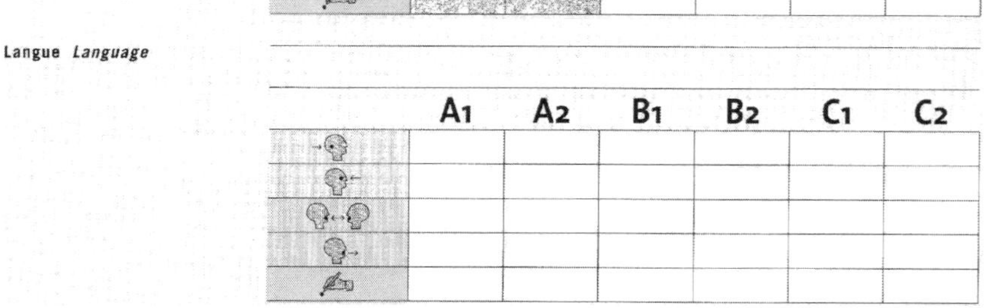

Figure 5.3 An ELP Language Passport profile
Source: Eaquals/ALTE, 2000.

LISTENING	Pre-A1	A1	A2	A2+	B1	B1+	B2	B2+	C1	C2	Above C2
English											
German											
French											
Spanish											
Italian											

Figure 5.4 A plurilingual proficiency profile: listening
Source: Council of Europe, 2018: 40.

The LINCDIRE project (Cho *et al.*, 2018; Piccardo *et al.*, 2018) has produced a different plurilingual profile, which gives an overview of proficiency in all the different languages with superimposed graphics. A diagram inspired by this development is included in the CEFR Companion Volume and shown in Figure 5.5.

This dynamic view of intersecting proficiency levels in different languages and different weighting for various types of activities is important not just for profiling existing proficiency, as discussed above, but also when it comes to setting priorities and goals for learning. This

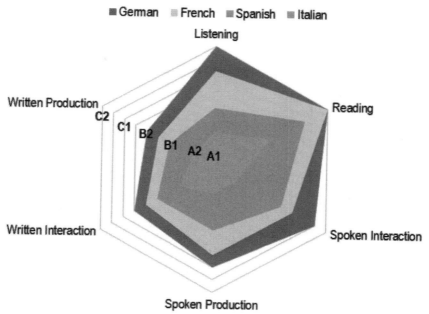

Figure 5.5 A plurilingual proficiency profile
Source: Council of Europe, 2018: 39.

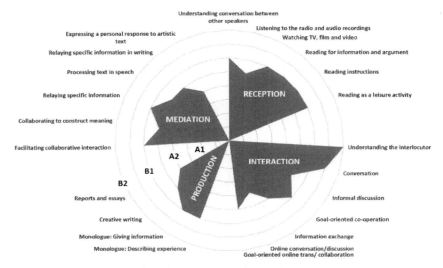

Figure 5.6 A fictional profile of needs in an additional language – lower secondary
Source: Council of Europe, 2018: 37.

relates to the concept of *needs profiles*. Figure 5.6 above, taken from the CEFR Companion Volume, gives an example of a needs profile. This is more complicated than the graphic profiles shown above, since it shows the appropriate level on all relevant descriptor scales for each of the four modes of communicative language activity: reception, production, interaction and mediation. Such a diagram could equally be used to summarise a self-assessment of current proficiency.

Let us now turn to the process of goal-setting in more detail.

5.2.3 Goal setting through 'can do' descriptors

'Transparency and coherence' was part of the title of the inter-governmental Symposium that recommended the CEFR back in 1991 (Council of Europe, 1992). In fact, descriptors facilitate relating curriculum aims to real world needs, thus giving a framework to action-oriented learning, providing transparent 'signposting' to learners, parents, sponsors, and relating assessment criteria both to the curriculum aims and to an external framework. Byram and Parmenter (2012) document the way in which the positiveness and clarity of the 'can do' valorisation of achievement and promotion of self-assessment represented a welcome change from the rather negative descriptions of learner ability that were prevalent before the CEFR. The CEFR proposes that the learners, their needs and experiences, their interests and ambitions, should be put at the centre of the planning process – which implies needs analysis and goal setting. These occur at two levels: at the level of the institution, with the establishment of the main needs profile(s), and at the level of the class with diagnosis of the particular needs of the individual learners concerned. 'Can do' descriptors are key tools at both levels.

At an institutional level, the rich 'menu' of language activities offered by the list of CEFR descriptor scales can be used to identify the language activities that are a priority, and possibly the target level in each activity. The CEFR Companion Volume outlines a procedure to define curriculum aims for a particular language in this way. The descriptors selected can then be analysed to see what language they imply:

Step 1: Select the *descriptor scales* that are relevant to the needs of the group of learners concerned. ... Clearly this is best undertaken in consultation with stakeholders, including teachers and, in the case of adult learners, the learners themselves. Stakeholders can also be asked what other communicative activities are relevant.

Step 2: Determine with the stakeholders, for each relevant descriptor scale, the level that the learners should reach.

Step 3: Collate the descriptors for the target level(s) from all the relevant scales into a list. This gives the very first draft of a set of communicative aims.

Step 4: Refine the list, possibly in discussion with the stakeholders.

An alternative approach is to:

Step 1: Determine a global target level for the course.

Step 2: Collate all the descriptors for that level.

Step 3: Identify the descriptors that are relevant, in consultation with stakeholders, and delete the rest. (Council of Europe, 2018: 42)

At the institutional level, a procedure like this can be carried out as the first step in developing a curriculum for any kind of course. As mentioned above, Figure 5.6 provides a (fictional) example from the CEFR Companion Volume of the type of needs profile that can result from the first procedure shown above, illustrating this point for a CLIL (Content and Language Integrated Learning) class. Whichever procedure is followed, the product in either case would be a list of communicative objectives, which can be analysed and discussed to determine what compe-tences (language competences and general competences) they imply.

At the class level, descriptors can be used to 'signpost' aims to learners, explaining syllabus choices and lesson relevance, as well as to assess achievement. With older learners, a 'can do' checklist can make a negotiated group syllabus a reality. Whether done on paper or digitally, a collation of the personal priorities of the class involves the learners in determining the group programme, plus individual needs to be met separately.

To summarise, descriptors can be used in needs analysis, curriculum aims, syllabuses, cross-referenced resources lists, module plans, lesson aims, informing learners about objectives, syllabus negotiation, personal goal-setting, recommending specific self-study activities, (self-)assessment checklists, documenting achievement, progress report cards, and reporting results to stakeholders.

'Signposting' in this way with descriptors helps both the teacher and the users/learners to be in control of the teaching/learning process. This entails a shift in the role of the learner, who needs not only to be informed about what is happening, but also to take account of the objectives and become more autonomous in his/her learning. In turn, this entails a complementary shift in the role of the teacher, who needs to both support the learner in this autonomisation process and release part of his/her responsibility.

5.2.4 Learner autonomy and responsibility

As van Lier (2007) points out, pedagogic scaffolding takes place at three levels and time scales:

- Macro: planning (a syllabus, a chain of tasks, a project, etc.) over a long term period.
- Meso: planning the steps of a particular activity or task.
- Micro: moment-to-moment interactional work. (van Lier, 2007: 60)

Involving learners in the planning/goal-setting process is a form of training towards self-direction and autonomy. When users/learners are informed and involved in this way, 'teacher and learners operate on three scales of awareness. They know where they are going, as a class or a group (or individually even), they know what the job of today or this hour is, and they know that they are interacting here and now to move towards the goal sets that are in place' (van Lier, 2007: 61).

Learners react very positively to their involvement in goal-setting implied by the kind of 'can do' approach discussed above. As mentioned in Section 5.1.1, self-assessment and learner autonomy were already two of the three main areas of the Council of Europe development in the 1970s. Furthermore, as a direct follow-up, they are also reflected in the CEFR-related ELPs. The ELP's Language Biography contains a checklist for each CEFR level of 'can do' descriptors for self-assessment and goal-setting. The first step towards setting goals as an autonomous learner is to have an idea of where you are starting from. This can come from self-assessment. Needless to say, such self-assessment will be more accurate if learners are trained to reflect on their progress with the help of descriptors.

The view of the user/learner as someone who exercises his/her agency, as a social agent, implies a strategic vision of learning. The learner should always be aware of what he or she is doing, what is happening in the classroom, the reasons why he or she does certain things, and the goals he or she sets. The learner takes charge of his or her own learning experiences. The teacher consults learners and creates conditions conducive to this learning by offering adapted tasks that create logical sequences of experiences that move the learner toward learning goals. The teacher acts as a resource, as a guide or mentor, and as an observer able to offer effective feedback, rather than as all-knowing font of wisdom. Finally, the teacher can use descriptors to prepare grids and/or checklists and share them with the learners to help them monitor and evaluate how they performed in the task.

To further enhance the development of autonomy, the grids/checklists can also include communicative strategies, since 'if one takes the view that [*strategies*] enable an individual to mobilise his or her own competences in order to implement and possibly improve or extend them, it is worthwhile ensuring that such strategies are indeed cultivated as an objective, even though they may not form an end in themselves' (Council of Europe, 2001: 137). Adding descriptors of strategies to curriculum aims in addition to descriptors of communicative activities makes it easier to focus on process, and not just on product. For example, in oral interaction, the aims (and related assessment criteria) will also deal with the process of how to conduct the interaction to ensure that it is effective. This involves, for example, being able to say that one didn't follow, being able to ask for a reformulation, being able to reformulate, and so forth. Explicit work on strategies is a valuable way to help the learner recognise strategies, use them more effectively, and transfer them in a process of lifelong learning. It also develops awareness and the ability to think and reflect. Becoming aware of one's own work methods, strengths, and weaknesses, along with what it takes to improve and make progress, stimulates a self-direction which will make the process of learning more efficient. Becoming aware of universal characteristics of language and communication, of the synergy between linguistic and non-linguistics competences in the completion of tasks, and understanding cultural similarities and differences, stimulates an interest in language and helps the learner to become a more pluricultural, plurilingual citizen.

5.2.5 Co-constructing meaning and discourse

One important aspect of the development of autonomy is giving learners the opportunity to co-construct meaning together in collaborative tasks, rather than seeing them only as individual speaker/ listeners. The move in the CEFR and CEFR Companion Volume, away from the four skills (reception and production each divided into spoken/written) to the four modes of communication (adding interaction and mediation) reflects this. The 'four skills view' sees the learner primarily as an individual speaker/listener or writer/reader. With production and reception, what is in focus is the expression of individual thought and its transmission to another person. Of course this involves negotiation of meaning, in the sense of getting onto the same wavelength so that the 'message' can pass from one person to another. CLT exploits this type of meaning negotiation through 'information-gap' activities (such as 'describe and draw'; comparing two maps/pictures, etc.).

However, the co-construction of meaning is not just a transmission of pre-existing meaning. 'Communication is the co-construction of meaning in context – not the transfer of information across a gap' (Orman, 2013: 91). There is no 'faxing' of thoughts from one mind to another. As pointed out in Section 3.8 while discussing situated cognition: discourse is 'subject to open-ended creative interpretation, the exact nature of which will be a product of its unique contextualisation by whichever individual is doing the interpreting' (2013: 98). The purpose of communication is very often not transactional at all, but interpersonal, and sometimes purely phatic, with no 'message' at all: 'Conversing as we all know is a cooperative activity that involves active participation and coordination of moves by two or more participants in the joint production of talk' (Gumperz, 1984: 1). The cooperation and co-construction is affected 'by conversational implicatures based on conventionalised co-occurrence expectations' (Gumperz, 1982: 131) and proceeds through the identification by participants of contextual cues – both verbal and non-verbal – which contribute to the negotiation of meaning. People use these cues to activate schemata they possess for the situation concerned, with their interpretation of meaning through the conversational implicatures (Grice, 1975). Although the linguistic and paralinguistic cues carry information, the meaning lies in the interactive process in context, in the discourse not in the linguistic forms. Every interaction requires adjustments on both sides to expectations and hypotheses about intentions and meaning: dialogue in the true sense of the term. This is particularly the case when the dialogue is a discussion of ideas and viewpoints. Dialogue (from the Greek 'dia-logos') means an acceptance, by two participants or more, that they will compare and contrast their respective arguments. 'Dialogue is not designed to lead to a definitive conclusion. It is a constantly-renewed means of re-initiating the thinking process, of questioning certainties, and of progressing from discovery to discovery' (UNESCO, 2009: 14). One moves towards the conversational partner(s), but at the same time seeks to retain perspective.

The inclusion of action-oriented interaction shifts the focus of attention from the individual to the social and from (just) the expression of personal meaning to the collaborative co-construction of meaning. Seeing users/learners as social agents who co-construct meaning in target situations/genres that are relevant to them implies the strategic mobilisation of competences that we discussed in Section 2.3 and 2.4. One needs to take into account the communicative strategies that are developed in communication and which then constitute a large part of communication ability (Holec, 1981). In Section 2.2.3, and especially in Table 2.1, we saw the way in which strategic competence was increasingly taken into account in applied linguists' models of communicative competence. The view of strategies also moved increasingly away from Canale and Swain's (1980) focus just on compensation strategies. Bachman gave strategic competence a central position as 'a general ability, which enables an individual to make the most effective use of available abilities in carrying out a given task, whether that task be related to communicative language use or to non-verbal tasks' (Bachman, 1990: 102, 106) and related his concept to the broad view of communication strategies first taken by Faerch and Kasper (1983).

In the CEFR, following the kind of approach taken by Faerch and Kasper, strategies are seen in terms of a cyclical process of planning, execution, evaluation and repair. Descriptor scales for reception, production, interaction and (in 2018) mediation strategies are provided. Interaction strategies were particularly influenced by views of turn-taking and topic management strategies (Sinclair, 1983; Kramsch, 1986), 'challenging' for clarification (Burton, 1980), cognitive strategies for framing ideas in discussion, formulating and evaluating hypotheses (Barnes & Todd, 1977), and the collaborative/cooperative strategies for eliciting, commenting on and referring to other contributions (Barnes & Todd, 1977; Wilkinson, 1992).

Mediation activities take this process of co-construction a step further. Mediation is discussed in more detail below in Section 5.2.9. The essence of mediation is that the user/learner is not just focused on personal expression (as in production), or with negotiating meaning in order to communicate with other people (as in interaction), though both of these language activities continue to be involved in mediation. As the CEFR Companion Volume and the project report behind it (North & Piccardo, 2016a) explain, mediation is primarily concerned with two things. Firstly it involves the mediation of concepts: the collaborative (co-)construction of new meaning, with the establishment of the conditions in which this (co)-construction can take place. Secondly, it involves the facilitation of the (co)-construction by others, together with facilitating the conditions for it to take place. This may mean mediating a text for other people so that they can understand concepts, or it may mean directly mediating between other individuals as an intermediary. The CEFR Companion Volume provides over 20 scales for different mediation activities, plus scales for mediation strategies.

The development described above echoes the move from CLT to TBLT that was discussed in Chapter 4, but goes further because in the AoA, the focus is on the user/learner as a social agent, collaborating with other people in a context or situation. The tasks involved are not trivial: they echo the theories of situated learning, collective intelligence, communities of practice and, underlying them, the socio-constructivist/sociocultural and ecological theories discussed in Chapter 3.

5.2.6 Learners as social agents engaged in real-life tasks

The CEFR 'views users and learners of a language primarily as "social agents", i.e. members of society who have tasks (not exclusively language-related) to accomplish in a given set of circumstances, in a specific environment and within a particular field of action. While acts of speech occur within language activities, these activities form part of a wider social context, which alone is able to give them their full meaning' (Council of Europe, 2001: 9).

The CEFR approach has several implications that are quite radical for language teachers. Firstly, it sees language activities, and speech acts that occur within them, as fully situated and contextualised in non-linguistic action; social actions always have a goal other than language. 'In reminding us that the learner is a social agent, the CEFR emphasises the contextual and situated nature of tasks and the importance of strategy and co-operation in the use of language and, *a fortiori*, in the learning of language' (Piccardo, 2014a: 18). One example used to introduce the concept of 'task' in CEFR Chapter 2 is moving a wardrobe. One cannot easily move a wardrobe alone and to do it some communication with another person is necessary, and there is even a 2001 CEFR scale to describe the language activity involved (*goal-oriented collaboration*). However, it is hardly a task focused on language; it could indeed conceivably, if necessary, be achieved with rather laborious communication through gestures, drawings and grunts. In other words, the task calls for 'contingent use of language' (Widdowson, 1984: 123) – but is not, *per se*, language focused.

Secondly, in the accomplishment of this specific task, as is the case with most real-world tasks, the social agent's general competences are going to be at least as important as language competences. Indeed, as regards this second point, the CEFR goes on to specify:

We speak of 'tasks' in so far as the actions are performed by one or more individuals strategically using their own specific competences to achieve a given result. The action-based approach therefore also takes into account the cognitive, emotional and volitional resources and the full range of abilities specific to and applied by the individual as a social agent. (Council of Europe, 2001: 9)

The notion of the social agent implies interaction between the individuals concerned but also between the individuals and the external context. Piccardo explains that:

> Each learner has experiences and has contact with an ever-widening number of other individuals, and this helps to define and shape his/her identity. The learner becomes aware of his/her own knowledge and competences, and uses them in and for social action. In turn, through this social action and this sharing of language, the learner receives feedback that helps him or her to keep building up knowledge and competence. In other words, the learner acts in order to learn; he or she does not learn in order to act. (Piccardo, 2014a: 19)

Talking about the relationship between the individual and the context Piccardo further stresses that it is not only the social context in which the user/learner acts that is important, the user/learner's own mental context is important as well:

> It filters and interprets the external context or situation. And the form that this interpretation or perception takes will depend on many different factors: physical, cultural, practical, cognitive, affective, emotional, etc. There is in fact a constant back-and-forth between the individual dimension and the social dimension and between the social context and the mental context. The user/learner's representations, capacities, and mental processes influence his or her social action and, therefore, his or her learning. In turn, this social action and learning influence the user/learner's representations, processes and capacities. (Piccardo, 2014a: 18)

Descriptors can be used to help to design action-oriented tasks and also to observe, and if desired, (self-)assess the language use of learners during the task. Clusters of the 'can-do' descriptors selected as aims can also inform the design of tasks integrating different communicative activities. Tasks with any degree of complexity may have phases of different types of language activities, involving reception activities (e.g. getting information from source texts), interaction activities (e.g. exchanging and discussing points found), mediation activities (e.g. processing a text for someone else; facilitating the work in the group) and production activities (e.g. addressing the class as an audience, writing a report, making a poster). For many such activities, descriptors describing such real-life activities suitable for the level of the learners can be found in the 80 scales of descriptors that the CEFR Companion Volume provides.

5.2.7 Teachers as strategic planners/professionals

One of the major parameter shifts fostered by the CEFR concerns the role of learners and teachers in the process of language learning, the teachers being professionals, decision-makers, mentors and mediators, the learners bearing responsibility for the learning process in and out of the institution.

As mentioned previously, the history of course design can be seen as a development from forward design (a fixed programme sequentially following the supposed complexity of concepts) through central design (focusing purely on the processes of teaching and learning) to backward design (North *et al.*, 2018; Richards, 2013). Backward design is renamed from the concept 'understanding by design' (Wiggins & McTighe, 2005), developed in mainstream education in response to teachers' natural tendency to plan from what they did today, rather than thinking in a strategic way, i.e. determining learning goals and then working backwards from those goals to plan the course. The competence-based approach, now being adopted across all school subjects in more and more countries, naturally implies defining such goals (usually with 'can do' descriptors) and working backwards from them. The shift from an educational programme of fixed content taught in the same order year after year to a more dynamic approach based on needs and competences mirrors the parallel shift in the view of professional competence. As we saw in Section 2.3, the 1980s saw a development from the traditional view of competence based on a one-off qualification to a dynamic process of continuous development, including involvement in the decision-making process and quality management.

Not all teachers welcome this shift. Dolz speaks for many when he says: 'The logic of competence comes to us [in education] from economic powers, it is part of a neoliberal deregulation project which it appears to us crucial to resist' (Dolz, 2002: 89, our translation). Actually, as we saw in Chapter 2, the dynamic view of competence comes from child development as well as the *sociologie du travail* and, as Richer (2017) explained, it represents a thoroughly humanistic perspective. This view of competence is equally relevant to learners and teachers and, recalling the many concepts related to competences discussed in Chapter 3 (e.g. situated cognition, collective intelligence, communities of practice – plus sociocultural and ecological theories), it explains the increasing prevalence of collaborative work in pedagogy, teacher education and the world of work (e.g. more workshops, projects, brainstorming meetings, (action) research, etc.). This has nothing whatsoever to do with neo-liberalism or deregulation. It has to do with a shift in the understanding of the nature of learning and of the nature of effective work, as well as the need for a strategic approach to both.

What is actually at stake in this type of opposition against competences, which is not uncommon, is the desire to stay with a simple, familiar paradigm, rather than accepting that language, learning and classrooms are each complex phenomena. Operating with a paradigm of simplicity within a programme presenting sequenced elements appears reassuring for both teachers and learners, but it gives only a false impression of control, because unfortunately, complexity is rarely capable of being effectively simplified in this way. As Tudor (2001) underlines, one can see a classroom in four ways: as a controlled learning environment, as a communicative classroom, as a school of autonomy and finally as socialisation: as a place in which participants have different social agendas. It is important to keep in mind the numerous interactions and overlaps between all these 'types' of classroom, which exist simultaneously in a complex dynamic system. 'As is the case with respect to the concepts of language and of learning, then, the classroom itself is by no means a simple or uncontroversial phenomenon' (Tudor, 2001: 130). As we discussed in Section 3.9, the user/learner can be viewed as a CAS (complex adaptive system), nested in a class, nested in the (pedagogic) society, in turn nested in the wider environment.

A shift to a complex perspective, as advocated by the AoA can help to achieve more effective language education. Here, Piccardo points to three needs: 'taking into account the complexity of the process of teaching/learning, preparing teachers to adopt a reflexive attitude and the capacity to manage this complexity, integrating research on SLE in both teacher education and practice' (Piccardo, 2010a: 93, our translation). In relation to the first point, the planned programme has its place, but cannot itself provide success in a complex context, because the interactions between different elements in the constellation of complexity that is a classroom will always throw up the unexpected. As Morin says:

> Complexity requires a strategy. Certainly, programmed segments are useful or necessary for sequences in which there is no randomness ... but the strategy becomes unavoidable as soon as something unexpected or uncertain occurs, that is to say as soon as an important problem appears. (Morin, 2005: 110–111, our translation)

In adopting a competence-based, backward planning curriculum design, one is setting clear overall goals based on (hopefully analysed) learner needs (macro level). Some of these goals, expressed as descriptors, may be selected as the objectives of the particular learning module/series of tasks (meso level). But there will also, of course, be enabling objectives, ongoing learner needs that have not been predicted and that only become apparent – to both teacher and learner –

during the course of the work (micro level). No two classes, and probably no two groups within the same class, will have precisely the same needs or take precisely the same amount of time on a task. As soon as learners are engaged in co-construction there are simply too many variables in play (e.g. their ambition in their version of the task; their pooled expertise and state of knowledge; the relevance of the resources available) to expect everything to fit by itself nicely and neatly into a fixed programme, as in a P-P-P (Present-Practice-Produce) lesson. In acting strategically at the micro level, monitoring the action and intervening if and when necessary, the teacher may have to adapt either their own, or even a group's plan. Plans give direction and when they are communicated to or developed with learners they increase motivation and engagement. But no plan should be fixed in stone. When one adopts an action-oriented, ecological, complex approach, there will always remain a creative tension between the planned and the unpredictable, which provides a dynamism to the teaching and learning process. Van Lier puts this point as follows:

> The dynamism (and tension) between the planned and predictable and the improvised and unpredictable is essential in the development of true AB [= *action-based*] pedagogy, and I would argue, in all pedagogy. There has to be enough predictability and security for learners not to feel lost and bewildered and, like every culture, the classroom needs its rituals but there must also be enough room to innovate and move in novel directions for learners to develop autonomy and fuel their intrinsic motivation. (van Lier, 2007: 53)

Taking account of complexity in the classroom involves adopting an appropriate strategy for the particular moment, selected from a repertoire of strategies relevant for the context concerned. Piccardo (2010a) refers to Lado's (1964) metaphor of doctors' practice and Tudor's (2001) metaphor of musicians' jam sessions to explain this point. A doctor has studied various sciences and aspects of medicine, but never applies them in isolation. Besides, he/she cannot 'apply' (parts of) this knowledge in an abstract sterile manner, since, to be effective, he/she must operate taking account of the conditions and constraints of the particular situation. As regards the jam session, the emphasis here is on flexibility, co-construction and adaptation during the course of the action. Contrary to what happens in pure improvisation, this involves reinvention, contextualisation and adaptation of classic themes, which then acquire a unique reinterpretation.

As regards teacher education, Piccardo (2010a) therefore suggests that, instead of working from simple to complex, thus reinforcing such an approach in teachers, one could imagine starting from an analysis of a complexity reflected upon and taken fully into consideration. Instead of trying to reassure trainee teachers by reducing complexity, one could imagine training based on the management of complex contexts, risk-taking and the development of trainee teachers' confidence and *savoir-être* in addition to *savoir* (knowledge) and *savoir-faire* (skills). Instead of encouraging teachers to search for universals (e.g. 'core grammar') one could focus on giving experience of different cases and contexts and so develop trainee teachers' ability to learn by generalising from their own experience. If one wants teachers themselves to adopt a complex paradigm in their teaching, then the training they receive should be coherent with this vision. If teachers are to offer action-oriented courses with transparent objectives expressed with descriptors in which users/learners co-construct meaning, then, for example, their course objectives should be equally transparent and the activities in the training course should involve collaborative co-construction of meaning. This type of training will be even more effective to the extent that the teacher educator then later explains this coherence between the principles being talked about and the principles on which the training course is constructed in order to introduce a metacognitive, a meta-professional dimension to the training itself.

Teachers need to be at ease in the face of the uncertainty that is a part of any complex context. The training they receive should cover several aspects at the same time, rather than keeping them neatly separated. They really need to be given the opportunity to develop strategies for dealing with complexity. This is what working on the *savoir être* of teachers really requires. It is not a question of 'attitudes;' it is a question of having resources and strategies to cope with uncertainty and make principled choices, to use materials and techniques in a selected, motivated manner according to the specific context: 'The interaction between methodology and context is a complex one. ... It is ... clear that methodology and context interact in a variety of ways, so that methodological choices cannot be made in abstraction of the context in which they are to be implemented' (Tudor, 2001: 155).

With its broad view of language, and of the intermeshing of general competences (intercultural, experiential, existential – *savoir être*) from language competences, and of language competences from language strategies, the CEFR offers teachers a broader, more strategic perspective. The AoA invites and requires learners to come out of their comfort zone and exercise their agency, taking some responsibility for their learning process. It demands the same of teachers. The CEFR Companion Volume contains rationales for all the descriptor scales because the aim is that teachers, as professionals, should understand why they do what they do. With the descriptors, language specifications and performance samples, the CEFR and CEFR Companion

Volume offer teachers the instruments with which to operationalise that perspective and plan professionally and transparently, informing and, if appropriate consulting, their learners in the process. Advice from different perspectives on how to do this in practice is given by North (2014), Piccardo (2014a), Beacco et al. (2015) and North et al. (2018).

5.2.8 Assessment: Feedback and feedforward

The CEFR and AoA also entail a more strategic view of assessment. As mentioned above, assessment was for a very long time viewed as a final phase that would be tackled once the teaching had taken place, in order to verify to what extent the planned learning had taken place. Measuring the outcomes of the learning process tended to be seen as separate from the teaching process. In SLE, until very recently, assessment has tended to be something that happens before the course (placement; gate-keeping exams) at fixed points like the end of term (progress testing) and afterwards (exit testing/final examinations). It is frequently seen as something totally external to the course, possibly even delegated to an external body. That does not mean that there is no place for the latter in providing language qualifications, in fact there is a manual to help examination providers relate their tests to the CEFR (Council of Europe, 2009) and a volume of case studies of doing so (Martyniuk, 2010). However, this is far from the whole story.

Views of assessment have changed in recent decades with the conceptualisation of the different functions of assessment (diagnostic, formative, summative initially, and then assessment for, as, and of learning), with the idea that assessment and teaching need to be considered as interdependent. This shift has occurred as much if not more outside SLE and language testing. The end of the 1980s saw increasing dissatisfaction with existing forms of assessment and the foundation of the Assessment Reform Group (ARG) in the UK. In language assessment, Brindley (1986, 1989) and North (1986, 1991) experimented with using descriptors for continuous assessment of performance in naturalistic, communicative tasks in the classroom. At the beginning of the 1990s in the US the expression 'alternative assessment' appeared (Herman et al., 1992). The importance of teacher assessment and of assessing what is happening in the classroom was reflected in titles like *Beyond Testing* (Gipps, 1994) and *Assessment for Learning: Beyond the Black Box* (ARG, 1999). By the end of the decade we also see a connection with educational standards with *Inside the Black Box: Raising Standards Through Classroom Assessment* (Black & Williams, 1998) and then *Aligning Teaching and Assessment to Curriculum Objectives: Imaginative Curriculum* (Biggs, 2003).

The CEFR thus is very much an example of this trend during the 1990s towards teacher-led 'assessment for learning' based on defined criteria linked to an external framework.

Although this shift can now be considered as integrated in most educational cultures, some aspects still remain very weak, in particular the last point – the coherence between the objectives/learning goals and the assessment criteria. Another crucial problem concerns these criteria: the modulation of degrees of proficiency in the rubrics/grids used as assessment tools. In fact, in many cases we still see that these are modulated on the basis of merely semantic distinctions made by alternating adverbials like 'consistently', 'usually', 'sometimes', 'occasionally' (e.g. the Achievement chart for the Ontario curricula: Ontario Ministry of Education, 2010, 2013; HKEAA, n.d.; IELTS, n.d.; Isaacs, 2016). This is despite the fact that such an approach had already been criticised for impeding rather than assisting valid assessment as long ago as 1941! (Champney, 1941; see also Alderson, 1991; North, 2000, 2008b). Thanks to the CEFR, the idea has started to spread that assessment plays a crucial role in the teaching and learning process, both when the teacher assesses learners and in the case of self-assessment, and consequently that transparency and coherence through well-constructed criterion-descriptors are of paramount importance.

Assessment should be mainly criterion-referenced (assessment in relation to the continuum of ability concerned: Glaser, 1963), rather than norm-referenced (assessment in relation to peers and to teacher expectation). Of course, one has to define that continuum of ability, and the thresholds between levels on it, as, for example, the CEFR descriptors and levels do. Criterion-referenced assessment also requires concrete definition of the performance standard expected, as one again finds in the CEFR illustrative descriptors and calibrated samples of performance. One of the key features of the CEFR is to provide clear stand-alone descriptors expressed through verbs of action (in the case of descriptors of communicative activities) that immediately make explicit what learners are expected to be able to do at a given level. Another key feature is to clearly decline, in form of transparent and stand-alone descriptors, the different competences (linguistic, sociolinguistic and pragmatic) that a learner is developing while engaging in communicative activities and performing actions. To these, descriptors for communication strategies are also provided. As mentioned earlier, the CEFR Companion Volume (Council of Europe, 2018) completed the CEFR with a range of descriptors for mediation, plurilingual and pluricultural competences as well as for mediation strategies. The wealth of descriptor scales provided by the CEFR recognises the multidimensional nature of second language ability and the need for a multidimensional approach to assessment.

In an action-oriented approach, as we will see further in Chapter 7, the focus is on 'competence put to use' (Council of Europe, 2001: 187) to achieve a goal or objective. This logic links assessment to the realistic mobilisation of competence and strategies, rather than to 'content' and 'inert knowledge' of the language (van Lier, 2007: 56).

CEFR Chapter 9, devoted to assessment, provides a tour around the myriad of possibilities in assessment, pointing out that modalities that are optimal for one context may well be inappropriate in another. These options are presented as dichotomies (e.g. self-assessment/ assessment by others; criterion-referenced assessment/norm-referenced assessment), and further glossed by Piccardo (2012b) and Piccardo *et al.* (2011b). CEFR Chapter 9 also explains the way descriptors can bring transparency and coherence to different forms of assessment, saying that it is important to distinguish between 'can do' descriptors of communicative activities (CEFR Chapter 4, describing WHAT the user/learner can do) and descriptors of aspects of language competences (CEFR Chapter 5, concerning the quality of the user/learner's language, HOW their performance is interpreted).

> The former are very suitable for teacher- or self-assessment with regard to real-world tasks. Such teacher- or self-assessments are made on the basis of a detailed picture of the learner's language ability built up during the course concerned. They are attractive because they can help to focus both learners and teachers on an action-oriented approach. (Council of Europe, 2001: 179–180)

Such assessments with 'can do' descriptors – by teacher, peer and/ or self-assessment – can be diagnostic (goal setting), formative and related to a particular lesson, assignment or project (micro level: with a very short list of relevant descriptors), a progress check at certain fixed reporting points like at the end of a unit, module or term (meso level: with a longer list), or summative at the end of a course (macro level: in relation to the core aims for the course). Assessment tools can be seen as a kind of roadmap for the learning journey. Both performance in tasks (process) as well as the outcome from them (product) can be assessed with descriptors from CEFR Chapter 4 and 5. Descriptors help to transfer mere impressions into considered judgements.

The creation of assessment profiling grids, in which the required level of performance is defined for various qualitative categories (e.g. range and complexity of language; accuracy; fluency; sociolinguistic/ cultural appropriateness) is an extremely useful exercise. The definition of such assessment criteria requires a great deal of attention and is central to the entire teaching/learning process. The CEFR does not offer 'off the shelf' assessment tools. It is up to users to select and adapt the material, creating assessment grids to reflect the context, teaching objectives, and institutional constraints concerned. Readers wishing to follow up in more detail practical ways in which descriptors can be used for assessment may wish to consult Piccardo et al.'s (2011b) rich collection of teacher training materials, North (2014), Piccardo (2014a) and North et al. (2018).

5.2.9 The concept of mediation: Moving forward

Mediation was introduced in Section 3.6 when discussing the legacy of Vygotsky and sociocultural theory. For Vygotsky it is through the mediation of symbolic tools, including acoustic, visual and linguistic signs, that we construct ourselves and others, and through which the individual reconstructs mediated social interactions that he or she has experienced. Language is experienced in social interaction before it becomes the object of reflection, in which the learner reconstructs and internalises new concepts.

As mentioned when introducing the CEFR descriptive scheme in Section 5.1.4, the CEFR pioneered the introduction of mediation, alongside interaction, to indicate communicative language activities, which are not covered by reception and production. The change in terminology from the 'four skills' (Lado, 1961) to four modes of communication: reception, interaction, production and mediation, highlights the collaborative co-construction of meaning to accomplish a given task, mobilising competences and strategies that are in themselves further developed through the experience of the task. This collaborative model recognises the centrality of the social dimension in language. Interaction is not seen as just the sum of reception and production, but introduces a new factor: the co-construction of meaning. Mediation takes this aspect a stage further. It includes reception, production and interaction, plus the process of developing or facilitating the understanding of concepts. Much of the time, when we use language, it is not just to express our own personal messages and opinions in spoken or written production, but rather to think something through by talking it through (= 'languaging': Swain, 2006; Swain et al., 2015): to facilitate someone else's access to new concepts, or to facilitate communication itself. In explaining the languaging (that tends to be central to mediation), Cowley and Gahrn-Andersen (2018) refer to the theories of Humberto Maturana, who 'replaces the received (or code) view of language by appeal to the achievement of communication and other joint activity. Crucially, languaging is both embodied activity and inter-individual coordination within which the relevant activity is embedded. It is argued that these two complementary aspects underlie all classes of phenomena in human communication' (2018: 2–3).

Mediation language activities, which 'occupy an important place in the normal linguistic functioning of our societies' (Council of Europe, 2001: 14) are introduced in the CEFR as follows:

> In **mediating activities**, the language user is not concerned to express his/her own meanings, but simply to act as an intermediary between interlocutors who are unable to understand each other directly, normally (but not exclusively) speakers of different languages. Examples of mediating activities include spoken interpretation and written translation as well as summarising and paraphrasing texts in the same language, when the language of the original text is not understandable to the intended recipient. (Council of Europe, 2001: 87)

The CEFR underlines that the external context will always be interpreted and filtered by the user/learner in relation to several characteristics:

> The mental context is ... not limited to reducing the information content of the immediately observable external context. Line of thought may be more powerfully influenced by memory, stored knowledge, imagination and other internal cognitive (and emotive) processes. In that case the language produced is only marginally related to the observable external context. (Piccardo *et al.*, 2011b: 20–21)

In other words, the CEFR reminds us that there is a form of interior mediation that takes place at the level of the individual, to which it adds the social dimension by speaking of the user as a social agent. The social agent and his/her interlocutor share the same situational context but may well maintain different perceptions and interpretations. The gap between these may be so great as to require some form of mediation, perhaps even by a third person. Thus, although the CEFR 2001 text does not develop the concept of mediation to its full potential, it emphasises, through its vision of the user/learner as a social agent, the two key notions of co-construction of meaning in interaction and constant movement between the individual and social level in language learning (Piccardo, 2012a), which are both key notions in the sociocultural approach: (Lantolf, 2000; Schneuwly, 2008).

In this way, although it is not stated explicitly, the CEFR descriptive scheme *de facto* gives mediation and agency key positions in the AoA, similar to the role that other scholars give them when they discuss the language learning process. In fact, as Piccardo (2012a) goes on to point out, the presentation of mediation in the CEFR, though scant, provides the key features for a further development of the concept. The full conceptualisation of mediation, both within and across languages and cultures, and the provision of descriptors for different types of mediation activities and strategies, was the main focus of the project that led to the CEFR Companion Volume (North & Piccardo, 2016a), as described in Section 6.4.

5.2.10 Plurilingual and pluricultural competences: Opening the classroom doors

Languages have traditionally tended to be taught in isolation: hermetically sealed from one another, even when taught by the same teacher, with scant regard for either the real world use of the language concerned or the existing (pluri)linguistic abilities of individual students in the class, the languages they speak at home, or with relatives. Seeing learners as plurilingual, pluricultural beings, on the other hand, means encouraging them: (a) to value their existing plurilingual profiles; (b) to learn other languages; (c) to exploit the metalinguistic awareness that even limited plurilingualism brings in order to see similarities and regularities between languages and cultures; (d) to regard their plurilingual repertoire as a rich resource that opens choices, possibilities and perspectives, and (e) to exploit all their competences and resources when undertaking tasks.

The concept of plurilingual and pluricultural competence is first introduced to SLE by the CEFR in its draft versions (Council of Europe, 1996, 1998) and an accompanying background study (Coste et al., 1997). The term plurilingualism itself has actually been used in linguistics since the 1950s (Orioles, 2004) being developed particularly by De Mauro (1977). In the English-speaking world, however, the concept is often ignored, subsumed into the concept of multilingualism. In fact there is a significant difference between the two terms. In the CEFR, plurilingualism is clearly distinguished from multilingualism, which is 'the knowledge of a number of languages, or the co-existence of different languages in a given society' (Council of Europe, 2001: 4). As we will see in the next chapter, plurilingualism is a much broader and more sophisticated concept than multilingualism, one that allows transcending boundaries between languages. We go into the phenomenon of plurilingualism and its relationship to other related terms in Section 6.3.

As the CEFR explains,

... experience of plurilingualism and pluriculturalism:

- exploits pre-existing sociolinguistic and pragmatic competences which in turn develops them further;

- leads to a better perception of what is general and what is specific concerning the linguistic organisation of different languages (form of metalinguistic, interlinguistic or so to speak 'hyperlinguistic' awareness);
- by its nature refines knowledge of how to learn and the capacity to enter into relations with others and new situations. (Council of Europe, 2001: 134)

For language education, therefore, plurilingual and pluricultural competence is both a means and an end. In addition to the societal advantages of open-minded citizens able to appreciate diversity, see problems from different perspectives and communicate across social, cultural and linguistic barriers, the development of plurilingual and pluricultural competence brings considerable educational value along the way, since the awareness that it brings can feed back into more effective language learning. As the Council of Europe's guide for the development of language education policies in Europe puts it:

> Language education policies in Europe should therefore enable individuals to be plurilingual either by maintaining and developing their existing plurilingualism or by helping them to develop from monolingualism (or, as is often the case for members of minorities, bilingualism) into plurilingualism. (Beacco & Byram, 2007b: 5)

In the 2001 edition of the CEFR (Council of Europe, 2001) no descriptors for plurilingual and pluricultural competence were provided, because conceptualisation of and research into these and related phenomena was in its infancy. Subsequently, inspired by the CEFR, projects like MIRIADI (Del Barrio, 2015), FREPA/CARAP (Candelier *et al.*, 2011), and MAGICC (Neuner-Anfindsen & Meima, 2016) have developed tools and instruments, including sets of descriptors, for intercomprehension, for pluralistic approaches and for plurilingual/pluricultural education respectively. The CEFR Companion Volume adds validated CEFR descriptors suitable for different levels for plurilingual comprehension, and for building on plurilingual and pluricultural repertoires respectively.

5.3 The AoA: A Paradigm Change in Methodology

As Richer (2009, 2012, 2017) and others (Puren, 2006) have pointed out, the CEFR generally suggests proposals for pedagogical change implicitly rather than explicitly. This has led some scholars to view the AoA as a continuation of the communicative approach or as a synonym for the task-based approach (see Chapter 4). There are several reasons for the rather indirect proposals. Firstly, as a language policy document for a group of 47 countries, the CEFR had a brief to be 'comprehensive' in the sense that it should be possible to locate within it the current approaches to language learning that were likely to be being used in the different pedagogic cultures of those countries. Secondly, the authors go out of their way to emphasise that the CEFR is not prescriptive and to provide at the end of each section what has come to be called a 'reflection box': a list of bullet points that users of the Framework might wish to consider in relation to the issues addressed in that section. Thirdly, the CEFR was the first synthesis of expertise in SLE from different educational, linguistic and cultural traditions, and therefore innovative pedagogical concepts and related terminology were presented with a degree of constructive ambiguity, both in order to maintain consensus across cultures and to spark reflection rather than rejection. This is in fact what happened: there was considerably more reflection than rejection.

However, the combination of these three points has sometimes led people to think that the CEFR is in some way pedagogically 'neutral.' In actual fact the CEFR is very upfront with its model of language learning and use in CEFR Chapter 2, in its promotion of an action-oriented approach and plurilingual/pluricultural competence, a centrality for tasks and in the provision of a plethora of different scales to describe the kind of actions that learners at different levels might find useful as learning objectives.

First and foremost, the concept of the learner as a social agent, rather than merely an individual recipient, is crucial, as we started to see at the end of Chapter 4 with reference to tasks. Promoting agency means providing learning and discourse environments in which learners can creatively access all their resources. Only through tasks in which they can exercise agency and judgement can learners mobilise and extend their competences and strategies. This implies giving learners a new role with a high degree of responsibility and consequently autonomy in the classroom. Furthermore, the CEFR emphasises that communicative language competences are *never* exercised separately from general competences. Any realistic action with language requires general competences (*savoir, savoir-faire, savoir-être*), aspects that language teachers often prefer to regard as 'personality factors' outside their remit. Learners should be free to combine and explore *all* their resources – be they linguistic or non-linguistic – in completing a task, as they would in reality. This means using all their (*pluri*)linguistic and general competences plus acquiring and deploying appropriate communication strategies (Faerch & Kasper, 1983). Examples of such strategies are given in the CEFR and CEFR Companion Volume for reception, production, interaction and mediation – with descriptor scales.

Secondly, such a focus on action, on tasks, on visible, practical outcomes ('can do') implies a fundamental shift away from prescribed 'content.' The CEFR is often criticised for not providing detailed lists of such functional and grammatical content, but this criticism is misconceived. First of all, it would be impossible to include such a specification for each and every language in the CEFR; this is the reason why this provision is delegated to the 'Reference Level Descriptions' for each language. Secondly, and most importantly, the CEFR does not propose such prescriptive lists of 'content' as this is fully at odds with the paradigm shift that the AoA requires. Not only should contents be determined in the learning context concerned on the basis of a needs analysis, but the logic of an action-oriented approach, based on action, on realistic tasks, is that there should be no such pre-existing list anyway. Linguistic objectives are just enabling objectives. It is the 'can do' descriptors, selected and adapted to context on the basis of a needs analysis, which might provide the end objectives (= real world objectives). An analysis of what 'content' needs to be taught is then fully context-dependent.

Finally, the AoA implies a change in the role of the teacher. In the communicative approach, the teacher accompanied the learner all the time towards the accomplishment of the task, guiding the whole process and providing all of the elements needed. In the action-oriented approach, the learner becomes an agent in his or her learning, understanding the end objectives and thus making choices and realising what knowledge and know-how will be required and what competences and strategies he or she will need to develop. The learner must therefore understand not only what the task is, but why he or she is doing certain things and how best to do them. The teacher facilitates this process, thus helping the learner to become more autonomous.

5.3.1 Action-oriented tasks as a locus of methodological innovation

As stated in Section 4.2.3, tasks are central to the AoA. It is made clear that the precise form that tasks in the classroom may take, and the dominance that they should have in the programme, is for the user to determine according to context. The place of classroom activities that are sometimes called pedagogic tasks (Nunan, 1989) is recognised in the CEFR (Council of Europe, 2001: 157–8), but it is with so-called 'real world' tasks that the AoA is more concerned. Action-oriented tasks try to break down the walls of the classroom and connect it with the outside world. In the communicative vision of the 1980s and 1990s, the task was seen as class work, involving comprehension, manipulation, production, and/or interaction in the target language, with an emphasis on content rather than form (Nunan, 2004). In the communicative approach, the goal was communication and the task served this goal. In the action-oriented approach, it is the reverse. Communication is one means at the learner's disposal for accomplishing the task, but not the only one. Strategy, reflection, and critical thinking also play an important role, with the aim being autonomous action:

> The task puts the learner into action; it places the learner in the action. The task must make the learner more autonomous as a user of the language. The task must enable the learner to line up needs and a goal to be achieved, by selecting relevant knowledge and useful skills. (Bourguignon, 2010: 19; our translation)

The main point of action-oriented tasks is to generate the strategic activation of specific competences. The learner/social agent chooses a goal, – one or more – objectives. In order to achieve these objectives, the learner must act strategically. In other words, he or she must make choices. The more the learner is aware of what he or she must do in order to perform the task, and what general competences and communicative language competences this will require, the more effective he or she will be.

Thus, action-oriented tasks are not designed around one or more language points that learners should practise, nor are they designed around a simple communication situation. Action-oriented tasks recreate what social agents do in everyday life, with communication coming into play when necessary to accomplish the tasks. As mentioned in Section 5.2.5, the task is not focused on language, though language is involved to varying degrees. The path is not clearly marked, the exact outcome is not really predictable and it is certainly not predetermined how the task needs to be completed.

Moving away from a focus on 'content' and exercises also opens the way for a more serious consideration of text as a vehicle for learning. Tasks and texts are closely linked and both play an important role in everyday life. In the CEFR, the concept of text is extensive, including oral texts of different types and written texts, such as business cards, bus tickets, newspaper articles, book excerpts, and wikis, to name just a few. Many tasks in real life involve some sort of text, and all texts have the purpose of performing (and enabling us to perform) tasks. Examples of everyday texts include transport timetables, city maps, bulletin boards, voice messages, announcements over a PA system, news items, lectures and pod/videocasts. Planning a task provides an opportunity to think about these different types of text and their linguistic and cultural characteristics. Instead of just presenting students with authentic materials for comprehension in order to give them a taste of the target culture as was the case in CLT, real texts are both the resources and models in order to accomplish real-life tasks.

5.3.2 AoA: Plan-do-check-reflect-act

As mentioned earlier in this chapter in Section 5.1.3, 'can do' descriptors can provide the means to create a quality cycle of planning, teaching, assessment and reflection/action. The four-point cycle plan-do-check-reflect/act was developed by the quality management specialist W. Edwards Deming (1986) during the post-war reconstruction of Japan. It is no coincidence that this same four-point cycle is also at the basis of the current concepts of curriculum design (Graves, 2008) and of action research by classroom teachers (Edge, 2001), as well as being operation-alised in several European quality assurance projects connected with language learning (Quality Guide: Lasnier *et al.*, 2003; LanQua: Kelly, 2009; QualiCEFR: Piccardo *et al.*, 2017, 2019a; CEFRMatrix: Piccardo *et al.*, 2019b) This cycle also inspired the approach to communication strategies taken by Faerch and Kasper (1983), which was adopted for the CEFR.

Perhaps the most fundamental point about the AoA is that it involves:

- planning backwards from the goal in mind;
- enacting what has been planned;
- checking whether things are going to plan and making – if necessary radical – adjustments and improvisations in the process;
- reflecting on the experience and noting things to do differently next time around.

In the AoA, this cycle can be said to operate, like a fractal in complexity theory, at three different levels: macro, meso and micro.

(1) The macro level here is what was discussed briefly in Section 5.1.3: the curriculum of the institution concerned. CEFR levels and descriptors offer a way of creating transparent and coherent, constructive alignment between the curriculum, teaching and assessment of parallel and/or consecutive programmes and classes, which are related to the identified real world needs of the learners. The operation at this macro level is described in detail, with examples, in North (2014) and North *et al.* (2018), among others.

(2) The meso level is that of the class teacher planning units or modules of linked lessons for teaching. At this level, the task is a

unifying tool, providing a common framework for the learners' work and the teacher's work, with descriptors being used for 'signposting'. Groups of descriptors that have been identified as relevant to the learners' proficiency level and needs can be used to give transparent objectives for the unit or module. At some point – probably towards the end – there will be a task that uses some sort of scenario to link holistically a series of phases in which the learners undertake the various language activities reflected in the descriptors that were selected as objectives. Those descriptors then form the basis for assessment. Classroom experience of the implementation of the objectives, of the assessment of the learners achievement in relation to them, should then feed back into a continuous process of (a) ongoing needs analysis in relation to the learners themselves, and (b) programme evaluation of the appropriateness of the objectives selected, the tasks used – noting adjustments to make for the following unit/module, and for any future use of this current unit/module with another group. This process is essentially the integration of an action-research mentality with teaching to objectives.

(3) The micro level is at the level of the small group who are carrying out the task and who need to act strategically to do so, mobilising all their resources. Acting effectively and autonomously together in a group requires a situation analysis as the first step in planning (judging the situation, issues to be resolved, resources available, resources lacking). This will then be followed by discussing how to go about the task and how to divide up work, by monitoring progress and deciding how to resolve outstanding issues, and then by finalising the product. The latter will also including checking to ensure it is complete. In a follow up, there will be a reflection on the experience, lessons learnt, things to work further on, etc.

In an AoA, assessment can be integrated into the plan-do-check-reflect/act cycle discussed in the previous section at the three levels of curriculum (institutional), teaching module (teacher), and task (learner).

- At the institutional/curriculum level, as discussed in Section 5.2.8, standardised ELP-style checklists of descriptors for the course level concerned can be used for both teacher assessment and self-assessment. In addition, 'can do' descriptors (WHAT: CEFR Chapter 4) can be used to design more formal assessment tasks, with suitable assessment criteria grids designed from descriptors related to aspects of competence (HOW: CEFR Chapter 5). Guidance and examples are provided, for example, in North (2014) and North et al. (2018).

- At the class/teacher level, the teacher can use the descriptors that were selected as the objectives for a unit or module to assess students' achievement in relation to them. This approach can be also used for self-/peer assessment, such as by making a short list of the 5–15 most important communicative objectives (descriptors), together with significant enabling objectives (e.g. discourse and sociolinguistic aspects, grammatical structures). Learners could, for example, be asked if they feel confident they have learnt this feature (3), if they would like some more practice with it (2), or if they have a problem with it (1). These priority aims could themselves be used for teacher observation of group work.
- At the micro level of a group of learners undertaking a task, self-assessment during the task itself is difficult because they are focused on the task. In addition, learners do not necessarily know how most effectively to engage in group work, and there is also the potential of non-participating or disruptive group members (Webb, 2009). This means that there is a range of aspects that could be the object of self-assessment and awareness-raising like the final artefacts, or the contribution to the group work, or the participation in discussions. We will return to this in more detail in Chapter 7.

6 Towards a Dynamic Vision of Language Education: Plurality and Creativity

This chapter focuses on the change in vision characterising the AoA: the idea that languages and cultures are not neatly separated 'objects' but rather phenomena evolving within a complex scenario that learners enter into a dynamic relationship with. In this process, several elements come into play:

(1) Change, unbalance and creativity. Unbalance is seen not as a negative aspect but as a precondition to creativity, an opportunity to see things from different perspectives, making new connections, expressing new combinations/fusions.
(2) A new vision of culture. Culture is seen as a dynamic personal mobility through a series of intercultural encounters, as one's pluricultural repertoire broadens, with culture(s) and language(s) interconnected and mutually dependent.
(3) Plurilingualism. Becoming plurilingual is seen not as multiple monolingualism but as a growing repertoire and trajectory: adding partial competences and language awareness, blending languages, using intercomprehension and translanguaging. Plurilingualism is a springboard to personal growth, self-awareness and professional competence.
(4) Mediation. The concept of mediation takes one from a static view of language as product to a dynamic vision of meaning being constructed and mediated in action; mediation creates the space for communication and creativity.

All these elements are inherent to the AoA and need to be seen in relation to one another in order to capture the extent of the paradigm shift that the AoA implies.

6.1 Change, Unbalance and Creativity

The fact that language is no longer seen as a codified entity to be studied – with 'core' grammar rules, functional exponents and vocabulary lists to be practised and learnt – is the essence of the paradigm shift that the AoA brings. Languages are, by their very nature, fluid entities within which each individual constructs their own holistic, plurilingual repertoire (or as Otheguy *et al.*, 2015, prefer to say: an 'idiolect'). We need as a result not only to embrace this fact but also see how we can employ this diversity in language pedagogy in such a way that the individual learner can understand the essential points of such codes and so function and meet the expectations of 'keepers' of such codes, as and when this is necessary – while at the same time exploring and developing their rich, diverse linguistic and cultural repertoire. If we wish to effect a real change in language education that takes account of this reality, we need to reflect on what change and imbalance imply in language education, and why they can be seen in a positive way, as driving forces for learners' creativity and personal development.

6.1.1 Testing hypotheses, reflecting and progressing

As we discussed in Chapter 4, the vision of language learning of the AoA involves a development in the roles of teachers and learners. In earlier approaches, the teacher essentially brought the learner to a body of knowledge and skills and mediated the process by which the learner, hopefully, mastered that content. Even in many forms of CLT, talking *in* the language is frequently what happens after presentation and practice of new content. In the AoA, on the other hand, acting in the language is not an accessory happening after such mediation by the teacher: it is the basis of the approach. Of course, insights about the structure of the language will be passed on, rather than constantly requiring learners to reinvent the wheel, but such an 'abstract' approach is peripheral in the AoA: the main focus is strategic. The view of the language learner as an active social agent implies a strategic view, in line with the change from the static focus on qualifications to the dynamic view of competence developed in the sociology of the world of work that was discussed in Section 2.3. This shift is reflected in the view of situated cognition and learning that came to language learning predominantly from professional training via 'language for specific purposes' (e.g. the *simulation globale*: Debyser & Yaiche, 1986; Yaiche, 1996). Also, as we saw in Section 3.7 when discussing the emotions and affect in relation to language learning, in learning a new language one has to reconstruct the 'cartography' which one uses to make sense of the world in order to navigate the unfamiliar linguistic and cultural territory (Kramsch, 2009). This again requires a strategic approach. From the methodological perspective, the move away from the 'weaker' version of CLT – learning a language to exchange with the 'other' – towards the stronger version represented by TBLT – a learner engaged in holistic, functional and communicative tasks that allow them to use the language – and from there to the AoA – where tasks are action-driven and language itself is both generated by action and calling for new action – is the proof of a shift towards a more strategic, socially engaged and self-reflecting process in language learning. In Section 5.2.5, we looked briefly at the way in which the CEFR descriptive scheme presents communication strategies as a process of planning, execution, evaluation and repair, providing descriptor scales for some of these aspects for reception, production, interaction and mediation. As we stated when discussing learner autonomy in Section 5.2.4, seeing the learner as a social agent – exercising that agency – implies a strategic vision of learning through hypotheses, reflection and evaluation. The learner must be at least fully aware of the goal-setting process, if not intimately involved in it, for which the provision of transparent descriptors is a prerequisite. The learner should be aware of what is happening and why: before, during and after, i.e. at the level of planning, enacting and evaluating. In terms of the theory of affordances, discussed in Section 3.9, the learner/agent is presented with a landscape of affordances (Gallagher *et al.*, 2017; Rietveld & Kiverstein, 2014); if they are aware of the goals, they will be increasingly able to perceive the totality of what is available, and which affordances are 'invitations' worth taking up.

One could talk of the way in which all these influences can shape a new kind of user/learner, whom we could call the 'individual 3.0'. In the same way that the web 3.0 analyses the information it receives, 'understands' it, makes logical connections between the different pieces of information and specifies a personalised pathway, the individual 3.0 is also able to gradually analyse, compare, and understand the other and the context, in order to construct their knowledge and their reactions. However, in contrast to the web 3.0, where the software only adapts to the user's input in order to deliver increasingly relevant content, the process that the individual 3.0 undergoes is not just a process of adapting to an interlocutor. He or she is part of a shared process of being affected while affecting the other, where he/she is both a part of the interaction, in which mind, body, emotions, languages, and cultures are involved. Thus, language education becomes a three-dimensional undertaking, articulating communication, cognition and socialisation in a harmonious process (Piccardo, 2013b). In fact, 'language learning involves an alignment of one's language resources to the needs of a situation' (Canagarajah, 2007: 94), alignment being 'the means by which human actors dynamically adapt to — that is, flexibly depend on, integrate with, and construct — the ever-changing mind-body-world environments posited by socio-cognitive theory' (Atkinson *et al.*, 2007: 171). In this perspective, learning languages becomes a conscious, dynamic process where learners (co)construct their learning by testing hypothesis, reflecting and thus progressing.

6.1.2 Embracing plurality: Seeing things from different perspectives and creating new connections

Education in general, and language education in particular, are called upon to attempt a challenging transformation: moving from the teaching and studying of a language as an isolated, codified object, to (co-)constructing a plurilingual and pluricultural trajectory. Bauman's (1992, 2000) view of our liquid modernity, which we touched on in Chapter 1, is very inspiring and is particularly relevant to the theory of plurilingualism and the practice of plurilingual education:

> ... the pluralism of modern civilized society is not just a 'brute fact' which can be disliked or even detested but (alas) not wished away, but a good thing and fortunate circumstance, as it offers benefits much in excess of the discomforts and inconveniences it brings, widens horizons for humanity and multiplies the chances of life altogether more prepossessing than the conditions any of its alternatives may deliver. We may say that, in a stark opposition to either the patriotic or the nationalistic faith, the most promising kind of unity is one which is achieved, and achieved daily anew, by confrontation, debate, negotiation and compromise between values, preferences and chosen ways of life and self-identifications of many and different, but always self-determining, members of the *polis*. (Bauman, 2000: 178)

Here Baumann is saying that the only effective response to this linguistically and culturally diverse world is to embrace the enrichment of perspective that it offers. Two of the key individual character traits for innovation and success in education or business are the ability to see an issue from different perspectives before jumping to a conclusion, and to tolerate the consequent ambiguity while doing so. This type of characteristic should be a core aim of programmes offering language learning and cultural exchange. At a societal level, Baumann is arguing that one must take the same, inclusive approach and that the only successful unity is that achieved through extensive contact and discussion. Yet unfortunately, in politics and societies, even in multicultural societies, the response is frequently different. Rather than contact and intermingling there is often the phenomenon of different cultural communities living alongside one another with little blending or even contact. Such *communautarisme*, as the phenomenon is called in France, implies a high risk of ghettoisation, of creating enclaves, both linguistic and cultural, which hardly communicate with each other beyond a basic, functional level.

As a matter of fact, it is impossible, besides being undesirable, to keep languages and cultures in hermetically sealed, separate compartments. As Byram comments: 'Not only are the boundaries between groups unclear, but minority cultures are themselves internally pluralistic, and the symbols and values of their various constituent groups are open to negotiation, contest and change. ... Thus, a multi-cultural society is not a patchwork of several fixed cultural identities, but a network of crosscutting networks and identifications which are situated, contested, dynamic and fluid, and heavily dependent on context' (2009: 4–5). Languages are not closed and homogeneous 'monosystems' either, but rather each is a unique, complex, flexible dynamic 'polysystem'. As Wandruska (1979) stressed, languages are composita: each language itself a conglomerate of language varieties that are constantly moving, overlapping both internally and also externally – reaching other languages. Thus, he asserted, languages, like archaeological sites show different cultures and their influences, superimposed or harmoniously integrated. However, unlike archae-ological sites, languages are neither static nor complete. They are dynamic, flexible, and in a continuous process of creation and modifi-cation, both through internal change and through contact with other languages.

This is true also at the level of the individual. Language learning is a constant work in progress. Even people who learn only one language learn several layers of that language – regional and social variations, as well as language for specific domains and disciplines that they will continue to expand later in life. Wandruska stressed the unique pluri-lingualism of each individual, saying: 'already in our mother tongue we are plurilingual in all the colours of the sociocultural spectrum. Therefore it is also difficult to say what exactly our own personal language is, what constitutes the individual use of language of each of us' (1979: 38, our translation).

Embracing a plural paradigm in this way fosters a more flexible attitude towards norms, as we saw in Section 3.9 when discussing affordances. Opening up to hybrid spaces and the crossing of bound-aries are both conducive to creativity (Maddux *et al.*, 2010; Saad *et al.*, 2013). As Furlong reminds us: 'Heightened perception of [these] boundaries and "in-between" spaces ... is crucial to enable the process of creativity' (2009: 356). A plural approach integrates the idea of imbalance, adopts a perspective of development and dynamism, and encourages risk-taking and creative use of the language. Plurilingualism stresses the role of the user/learner as a holistic being acting socially, whose personality develops through complex interaction of his/her own entire set of resources: cognitive, emotional, linguistic and cultural. In fact:

Language is not only a major aspect of culture, but also a means of access to cultural manifestations. ... [I]n a person's cultural compe-tence, the various cultures ... to which that person has gained access do not simply co-exist side by side; they are compared, contrasted and actively interact to produce an enriched, integrated pluricultural competence, of which plurilingual competence is one component, again interacting with other components. (Council of Europe, 2001: 6)

It is to this new, plural approach to culture to which we now turn.

6.2 A New Vision of Culture

Language has long been seen as closely related to culture, with learning about the culture of the target language being one of the objectives of language courses. A German textbook for English in upper secondary from the early 20th century (Lincke, 1912) for example, has units organised by cultural topics concerned with contemporary cultural behaviour plus key topics in English history (e.g. a ship at sea; an English home; St Paul's cathedral; Shakespeare). Even at that time, however, an attempt was made to include popular culture (small 'c') as well as high culture, literature etc. (capital 'C'). This type of approach to culture may still be found, called *Landeskunde* in Germany and *civilisation* in France. Indeed, this traditional view of culture is far from obsolete. As Kramsch reminds us:

> Language learners can only understand the situated choices made by interlocutors in conversations or by writers in texts if they understand how the 'subjectivity [of speakers] is locked into the historical experience of groups' (Freadman, 2014: 368), that is, their collective memories – in other words, if they understand what a text relies on but does not need to say. (Kramsch, 2014: 300)

More recently, however, following the work of communication researchers like Hymes, Gumperz, Goffman, etc. that we discussed in Section 3.5, the focus expanded to include societal norms and socio-pragmatic/socio-linguistic features such as attitudes to time, proximity, degrees of directness, etc. In the CEFR, such sociocultural knowledge is taken under declarative knowledge (CEFR 5.1.1: *savoir*) alongside knowledge of the world – but also intercultural awareness. Next to declarative knowledge, the CEFR places skills and know-how (5.1.2: *savoir-faire*), with practical skills and know-how in the social, living, professional and leisure domains now complemented by intercultural skills and know-how – defined as including:

- the ability to bring the culture of origin and the foreign culture into relation with each other;
- cultural sensitivity and the ability to identify and use a variety of strategies for contact with those from other cultures;
- the capacity to fulfil the role of cultural intermediary between one's own culture and the foreign culture and to deal effectively with intercultural misunderstanding and conflict situations;

- the ability to overcome stereotyped relationships. (Council of Europe, 2001: 104–5)

Existential competence (5.1.3: *savoir-être*) then also includes elements inseparable from culture, such as attitudes, motivations, values, beliefs, cognitive styles and personality factors. The way cultural issues are outlined in the CEFR illustrates the way in which the view of culture moved, in line with the view of language, from being seen as a static body of relevant knowledge to be transmitted, towards a dynamic process of development that includes an ability to take distance from one's own language/culture, an awareness of and respect for the fact that things are perceived in radically different ways from different perspectives, a capacity to be sensitive to contextual cues and cultural expectations, and a disposition to adopt an acceptably appropriate presence in another language/culture, in a constantly evolving appreciation of the complexity involved. Descriptors for many of these aspects are included in two of the new CEFR scales provided in the CEFR Companion Volume: *Facilitating pluricultural space* and *Building on pluricultural repertoire* (Council of Europe, 2018: 122, 158).

Proposals for such a wider view of culture and a focus on the language teacher as an intercultural mediator were already being made during the 1990s (e.g. Byram, 1997; Byram & Zarate, 1996; Byram *et al.*, 1996) with the 'intercultural speaker' instead of the 'native speaker' as the goal of language learning (Byram & Zarate, 1996: 241). The change was influenced by the developments in theories and concepts informing language education that were outlined in Chapters 2–4, but also more generally by the linguistic and cultural diversity brought about by migration.

6.2.1 Individual mobility and personal trajectories

As mentioned above, in today's diverse environments, personal mobility has increased exponentially. Mobility can be seen not just in the sense of migration, but as a personal progress outwards in a series of concentric circles, from the youngest age onwards with the expansion of environments from the home, through different schools, groups of friends towards different professional contexts and membership of various groups and networks in adult life. In discussing the complexity of contemporary societies and the consequent need to develop inter-cultural education, Byram (2009) puts the issue as follows:

Plurilingual individuals belong to and identify with complex group-ings, some of which are temporary, resembling interconnecting net-works more than the stable and named groups such as professions,

nationalities or minorities. Whereas the role of compulsory education may have previously been to confirm established groups and
introduce young people to identification with them, it is now wider
than this and includes familiarisation with the alterity of comparable
groups – other nationalities for example – and their perspectives on
the world, including their perceptions of one's own taken for granted
beliefs, values and behaviours. (Byram, 2009: 4)

The result of this dynamic process, in today's world, is the development of complex individual identities. An adult person may be, at
the same time '"a teacher", "a Real Madrid supporter", "a German",
"a Parisian" etc.' (Byram, 2006: 6) and they will tend to speak differently according to the situation, at work, in the family, in a conference,
when travelling, etc., since, as Byram (2006) goes on to say, speaking
in the 'right way' makes one an 'insider'. Furthermore, since written
language is standardised at school, no matter how complex an identity
a child may have, they are likely to be required to write in the 'right
way' in the national language of schooling, forgetting whatever other
identities they have.

Several educational tools have been developed to try and reverse
this trend by raising awareness of and giving value to the complexity
of learners' identities. One simple technique, first proposed by
Hans-Juergen Krumm (Krumm & Jenkins, 2001) and then further
developed by others (e.g. Prasad, 2014) is the drawing of a self-
portrait and colouring parts of the body with different colours representing different languages, and then explaining the thinking and
feelings behind these choices. Another tool is the concept of identity
texts proposed by Jim Cummins (Cummins & Early, 2010; Cummins
et al., 2015). These illustrated texts, generally written in two (or more)
languages, are the product of a project chosen by the child concerned.
They themselves decide how to carry out the project, encouraged to
use the full repertoire of their language and other competences to do
so. Most projects will be collaborative, with several students sharing a
similar background involved, and adult members of their community
will often become involved in helping them to write their story or
research a report in their heritage language, in addition to the help
with the language of schooling given by the class teacher.

In addition, two tools from the Council of Europe, which both
appear in versions for adults and for children, are designed to raise
learners' awareness of their cultural and linguistic trajectories. *The
Autobiography of Intercultural Encounters* (AIE: Byram *et al.*, 2009)
is a tool to help learners to think about, and learn from, intercultural
encounters that have been particularly significant for them. Learners
are guided to make sense of the concepts of culture and intercultural
experiences in the face of diversity and otherness. In addition, the AIE
aims to facilitate reflection on the role language plays in intercultural

encounters and the consequences of contacts with, and adjustments to, other languages and/or varieties within the same language. The second, more widely known, tool is the European Language Portfolio (ELP). This tool, of which there are over 100 different versions, contains three sections: a Language Passport (for recording one's pluri-lingual profile in terms of proficiency level in different communicative activities, a Language Biography (to describe aims and achievements) and a Dossier (to collect evidence of one's progress). All ELPs include materials to engage in a process of self-reflection conducive to lifelong learning. Several also integrate sections to help learners develop a metacognitive, metalinguistic, intercultural attitude and to apply it in a plurilingual, pluricultural perspective.

6.2.2 Language(s), culture(s) and intercultural encounters

In the teaching of modern languages, intercultural competence has rarely been dealt with sufficiently in practice, despite numerous theo-retical studies on the subject (e.g. Brown, 2007; Butjes & Byram, 1990; Byram, 2008; Levy & Zarate, 2003; Zarate et al., 2004) and practical, easily accessible guides for teachers (e.g. Byram et al., 2002). Already in 1990, Butjes and Byram present transnational communication as being both interlingual and intercultural, with motivation and acqui-sition as functions of the former, and information and mediation as functions of the later. A comprehensive definition of interculturality is offered in a concept paper for the AIE by Byram et al. (2009):

> Interculturality involves being open to, interested in, curious about and empathetic towards people from other cultures, and using this heightened awareness of otherness to evaluate one's own every-day patterns of perception, thought, feeling and behaviour in order to develop greater self-knowledge and self-understanding. Interculturality thus enables people to act as mediators among people of different cultures, to explain and interpret different per-spectives. It also enables people to function effectively and achieve interactional and transactional goals in situations where cultural otherness and difference are involved. Notice that, according to this definition, interculturality does not involve identifying with another cultural group or adopting the cultural practices of the other group. (Byram et al., 2009: 10)

Liddicoat and Scarino give a definition of intercultural competence specifically for languages learning as including at least:

- accepting that one's practices are influenced by the cultures in which one participates and so are those of one's interlocutors;
- accepting that there is no one right way to do things;

- valuing one's own culture and other cultures;
- using language to explore culture;
- finding personal ways of engaging in intercultural interaction;
- using one's existing knowledge of cultures as a resource for learning about new cultures;
- finding a personal intercultural style and identity. (Liddicoat & Scarino, 2013: 24)

Since Byram's ground-breaking work referred to earlier (Byram, 1997; Byram & Zarate, 1996; Byram *et al.*, 1996), there has been a tendency to classify intercultural communicative competence (ICC) into knowledge, skills, and attitudes, following the US competence 'KSA' model discussed in Section 2.3. This type of model has been criticised as an individually-oriented list model (Matsuo, 2012) that ignores relational and interactional aspects of communication. Matsuo considers that: 'These types of models do not optimally assist teachers because, essentially, all they allow is for a teacher to be alerted to the constituent elements of competences and then to determine whether the competences are present – or absent – in individual students (Matsuo, 2012: 363). Byram's model was operationalised in the INCA model (INCA Project, 2004), an attempt to develop an approach to assessing ICC in a business context. Other ICC projects have also followed the KSA model, notably the *Guidelines for Assessment of ICC* (Lussier *et al.*, 2007) and the *Framework of Reference for Pluralistic Approaches to Languages and Cultures*. (FREPA/CARAP: Candelier *et al.*, 2011). FREPA/CARAP is a sophisticated multi-layered system of hundreds of descriptors and sub-descriptors organised in a partially hierarchical structure in relation to knowledge, attitudes and skills, accompanied by awareness-raising classroom materials.

In an alternative vision, Auger and Louis (2009) propose that the development of intercultural competence might be best undertaken with an action-oriented, problem-solving perspective, rather than through taxonomies of elements of ICC. They point out that the fundamental 'problem' in intercultural encounters is misunderstandings. Learners need first and foremost to be sensitised to the potential pitfalls that may be caused by both apparent convergences and actual divergences between languages and cultures, even on a simple linguistic level. Then, more fundamentally there are the socio-linguistic and socio-pragmatic (proximity, body language etc.) realisations of different social rituals (e.g. greetings) in the target culture. Thus, they propose that learners should be made aware of potential problems and of the strategies that they already possess to face up to them. They point out that attitudes like openness and tolerance of ambiguity are requisite dispositions in any cognitive approach to learning, rather than being unique to ICC, and propose a practical, three-step strategic approach to solving such intercultural 'problems' by adapting abilities that learners already possess:

(1) *Take account of the fact* that there is a divergence between the cultures concerned and consider the nature of the precise divergence that could be the origin of the difficulty encountered.
(2) *Analyse* this divergence in terms of one's own initial, culturally determined, assumptions about one's own and the other culture, questioning the seemingly natural interpretation that one's own cultural filter 'imposes'.
(3) *Formulate and test a hypothesis* about how the other person may be interpreting the situation (slipping as best one can into the perspective of 'the other'), check out this hypothesis by consulting members of the culture or other available sources and, if it turns out to be correct, adjust strategies for the next occasion – and pass on the knowledge gained, thus acting, in a modest way, as an intercultural mediator.

This action-oriented perspective is in fact close to the approach that Byram (2008) proposes in his framework for intercultural citizenship, which is summarised in Table 6.1. In addition to the more traditional knowledge aspects (cognitive orientation) and attitudinal aspects (evaluative orientation) he adds a third – comparative orientation (skills of interpreting and relating) – that involves identifying ethnocentric perspectives in documents and events, identifying areas of misunderstanding and dysfunction, and mediating between conflicting interpretations of phenomena. Earlier, in discussing the comparative orientation, he emphasises 'becoming conscious of working with Others (of a different group and culture)' (Byram, 2008: 188) and of 'creating a community of action and communication that is supra-national and/or composed of people of different beliefs, values and behaviours which are potentially in conflict – without expecting conformity and easy, harmonious solutions' (2008: 189).

Byram's fourth category, 'action-orientation' (skills of discovery and interaction), like Auger and Louis' approach, emphasises the use *in real time* of a combination of knowledge, skills and attitudes – recalling the view of competence as action, as *savoir combiner*, discussed in Section 2.3. This action-oriented, mediating perspective is the approach taken in the formulation of descriptors for *Facilitating pluricultural space* and *Building on pluricultural repertoire* in the CEFR Companion Volume (Council of Europe, 2018).

Byram's framework summary shown in Table 6.1 mentions the expression 'mediation' as an aspect of interpretation, but the whole framework itself aims towards the education of intercultural mediators. He and Geneviève Zarate have long proposed that the reference

Table 6.1 Byram's framework for intercultural citizenship

Cognitive orientation		Evaluative orientation	
Language education: Knowledge	Political education: Contents	Language education: Attitudes	Political education: Affective/moral attitude
Historical and contemporary relationships between one's own and one's interlocutor's cultures; The national memory of one's own country and how its events are related to and seen from the perspective of other cultures; The national memory of one's interlocutor's country and the perspective on it from one's own culture; Institutions, and perceptions of them that impinge on daily life within one's own and one's interlocutor's culture and conduct and influence relationships between them.	*Lifeworld:* lifeworld... responsibility... family; tasks [...] of schooling; living in the community; other cultures. *Society:* Pluralism; civvil society; public life; social inequality. *Democracy:* basic values... creation of representative political will; the law in everyday life. *Globalisation:* all topics.	Willingness to seek out or take up opportunities to engage with otherness in a relation of equality... Interest in discovering other perspectives on interpretation of familiar and unfamiliar phenomena both in one's own and in other cultures and cultural practices. Willingness to question the values and presuppositions in cultural practices and products in one's own environment. *Language education: Critical cultural awareness* Respect for the value, the dignity and freedom of every individual person. Acceptance of the rule of law, search for justice, recognition of equality and equal treatment in a world full of differences. Recognition of pluralism in life and in society, respect for foreign cultures and their contribution to human development.	Make an evaluative analysis of the documents and events that refers to an explicit perspective and criteria. Interact and mediate in intercultural exchanges in accordance with explicit criteria, negotiating where necessary a degree of acceptance of those exchanges by drawing upon one's knowledge, skills and attitudes. Valorisation of mutuality, co-operation, trust and solidarity and the struggle against racism, prejudices and discrimination.

Source: Byram, 2008: 238–9.

Comparative orientation	Action orientation		Communicative orientation
Language education: Skills of interpreting and relating	Language education: Skills of discovery and interaction	Political education: Practical–instrumental competences	(Foreign) language education:
(a) Identify ethnocentric perspectives in a document or event and explain their origins. (b) Identify areas of misunderstanding and dysfunction in an interaction and explain them in terms of each of the cultural systems present. (c) Mediate between conflicting interpretations of phenomena.	(a) Elicit from an interlocutor the concepts and values of documents or events and develop an explanatory system susceptible of application to other phenomena. (b) Identify significant references within and across cultures and elicit their significance and connotations. (c) Identify similar and dissimilar processes of interaction, verbal and non-verbal, and negotiate an appropriate use of them in specific circumstances. (d) Use in real-time an appropriate combination of knowledge, skills and attitudes to interact with interlocutors from a different culture[84] taking into consideration the degree of one's existing familiarity with the culture (and where appropriate language) and the extent of difference between one's own and the other.	(1) Grasp and take seriously the opinions and arguments of others, accord personal recognition to people of other opinions, put oneself in the situation of others, accept criticism, listen. (2) Make one's own opinions (needs, interests, feelings, values) clear, speak coherently, give clear and transparent reasons. (5) Organise group work, co-operate in the distribution of work, accept tasks, demonstrate trustworthiness, tenacity, care and conciousness. (6) Tolerate variety, divergence, difference, recognise conflicts, find harmony where possible, regulate issues in socially acceptable fashion, accept mistakes and differences. (7) Find compromises, seek consensus, accept majority decisions, tolerate minorities, promote encouragement, weigh rights and responsibilities, and show trust and courage. (8) Emphasise group responsibility, develop fair norms and common interests and needs, promote common approaches to tasks.	(a) Linguistic competence; (b) Sociolinguistic competence; (c) Discourse competence.

point for modern language education should not be the native-speaker, but rather the intercultural mediator (Byram & Zarate, 1996). In the fuller version of the action-oriented section of his framework that appears earlier in his 2008 book, a final point is added: 'use in real time knowledge, skills and attitudes for mediation between interlocutors of one's own and a different culture' (Byram, 2008: 184).

In relation to such intercultural mediation Zarate (2003) proposed three complementary conceptions:

- mediation as an area for bringing together new partners. Mediators make intelligible to newcomers the cultural and linguistic contexts which the latter inaugurate;
- mediation in situations of conflict or tension, where languages and cultural references lead to exclusion and social violence. Different situations of re-mediation will be presented within a process which begins by specifying the object of the conflict, to go on to establishing a procedure for possible conflict settlement;
- mediation instilling specific dynamics into third areas as alternatives to linguistic and cultural confrontation. In this plural area difference is pinpointed, negotiated and adapted. (2003: 95)

These proposals of Zarate had a considerable influence on certain mediation descriptor scales in the CEFR Companion Volume (*Facilitating pluricultural space* and *Facilitating communication in delicate situations and disputes* respectively: Council of Europe, 2018: 123, 125). The former, reflecting Zarate's final point, builds on Kramsch's (1993) concept of 'third space' that we discuss in the next section. More recently, Liddicoat and Zarate (2017), reporting on a research network, talk of five key interlinking processes in inter- cultural mediation: reflexivity, re-establishing meaning, managing tensions, connecting and interpreting. The first and last ('reflexivity' and 'interpretation') operate more at the individual level and relate to the CEFR Companion Volume scale *Building on pluricultural reper- toire* (Council of Europe, 2018: 158–9). 'Re-establishing meaning' relates to the interpretations of mediation discussed in Section 6.4 below. 'Connecting' and 'managing tensions' relate again to the other two CEFR Companion Volume scales mentioned above in relation to Zarate (2003). These characteristics are very relevant to ICC, to the deployment of cultural mediation skills, and to the development of the pluricultural competence behind them. For that reason, they are very relevant to an action-oriented approach in our diverse classrooms.

A strategic, action-oriented approach to ICC is not limited to Europe. For example, the ATESL Curriculum Framework for English as a second language in Alberta, Canada has ICC as its seventh curriculum strand. The approach taken is to recognise culture as both product and process, to present ICC as a stance, or orientation, rather than body of content or method, and to offer strategies to help teachers to intentionally build ICC and foster more culturally responsive teaching and learning environments (ATESL 2005). The standards for ICC are adapted from a more conventional 'body of content' approach in Massachusetts.

The American Council on the Teaching of Foreign Languages (ACTFL) have also updated their proficiency guidelines to include 'can do' descriptors for intercultural competence, with (more global) proficiency benchmarks and performance indicators for 'investigate' (products, practices) and 'interact' (language, behaviour), plus lists of (more specific) paired 'I can' examples that link investigating and interacting in action. As Byram and Wagner (2018) state: 'The [NCSSFL-ACTFL] Can-Do statements ... help language learners as well as educators gauge what they can do to "use the language to investigate, explain, and reflect on the relationship between the practices or products and perspectives of cultures" (NCSSFL and ACTFL, 2017: 1) at different performance levels' (Byram & Wagner, 2018: 144). Like Byram (2008), Auger and Louis (2009) and the CEFR Companion Volume (Council of Europe, 2018), the NCSSFL-ACTFL guidelines take an action-oriented perspective, linking interculturality, language and action in context.

Byram and Wagner go on to introduce 'an action-oriented approach underpinned by citizenship education, to teach intercultural citizenship' (2018: 146), which is documented by Byram et al. (2017). Here a community of practice of teachers, linked by an internet platform, undertook intercultural projects, often paired with a class from another country, on subjects as diverse as historical problems (the Falklands/Las Malvinas war), environmental issues, mural art, and graffiti. In the Falklands/Las Malvinas project, a group of Argentinian future teachers and translators of English and a group of British undergraduates learning Spanish undertook dialogic and cooperative work online, mainly through Skype and a web conferencing program. Small groups including students from both countries jointly produced leaflets for reconciliation in relation to the conflict (Porto & Yulita, 2017). Development of criticality, a space from which to observe one's culture more objectively, played a major role in all of these projects and, as reported in relation to another of them concerning 11-13 year olds: 'Learners began to acquire the skills of criticality and then took action in their own communities as a consequence of their work in the classroom' (Byram et al., 2017: xxxi).

6.2.3 From third space to symbolic competence

In the plurilingual/pluricultural vision a space between languages/ cultures is opened, in which the user/learner can go back and forth, as many times as he/she wants, in order to learn something different each time and to make sense of the context. This idea of navigating in-between spaces is related to Kramsch's concepts of 'third space' (1993) and 'symbolic competence' (2009).

Kramsch developed her concept of 'third space' from theories of 'thirdness' that are used to break out of counterproductive dichotomies in semiotics, literary criticism, foreign language education (e.g. native speaker/non-native speaker) and literacy pedagogy. The concept of 'third space' is much used in postcolonial studies. For example the Chicana feminist historian Emma Pérez talks of 'mov[ing] beyond colonial history by implementing the decolonial imaginary with a third space feminist critique to arrive finally at a postcoloniality, where postnational identities may surface' (1999: 125). In discussing third space, Kramsch says: 'Understanding someone from another culture requires an effort of translation from one perspective to the other that manages to keep both in the same field of vision' (Kramsch, 2009: 237). She also made clear that: 'Thirdness does not propose to eliminate these dichotomies, but suggests focussing on the relation itself and on the heteroglossia within each of the poles. It is a symbolic place that is but no means unitary, stable, permanent and homogeneous' (Kramsch, 2009: 238). The focus is on the relations between the two poles, which echoes at least one definition of mediation (Coste & Cavalli, 2015: 12), that create 'in-between spaces' (Furlong, 2009: 356). To paraphrase Kramsch, the symbolic space between the two poles is made up of different elements in a relationship with each other, and is unstable, temporary and heterogeneous – all reflecting the definition of a CAS in complexity theory, which we discussed in Section 3.9. The third space is a 'heterogeneous, indeed contradictory and ambivalent space in which third perspectives can grow in the margins of dominant ways of seeing' (Kramsch, 2009: 238). It is a space in which a user/learner might take some distance from his/her cultural norms by 'reading against the grain' (Kramsch, 2009: 238) and become more aware of loaded connotations and biases. It should therefore be seen as a process, not a place (Kramsch, 2011).

'Reading against the grain' is very close to Byram's 'critical cultural awareness/political education: An ability to evaluate critically and on the basis of explicit criteria perspectives, practices and products in one's own and other cultures and countries' (Byram, 1997: 53 & 63). More recently Kramsch defined it as follows:

> It is the capacity to recognize the historical context of utterances and their intertextualities, to question established categories like German, American, man, woman, White, Black and place them in their historical and subjective contexts. But it is also the ability to resignify them, reframe them, re- and transcontextualize them and to play with the tension between text and context. (Kramsch, 2011: 359)

Acknowledging the complexification of our globalised society, Kramsch later proposes replacing her notion of third space with the notion of symbolic competence. This she defines as 'an ability that is both theoretical and practical, and that emerges from the need to find appropriate subject positions within and across the languages at hand' (Kramsch, 2009: 200) 'in the particularity of day-to-day language practices, in, through, and across various languages' (2009: 201). 'In this permeability between languages and cultures we can find aesthetic appreciation of the language, emotional involvement, exploration of both possible and invented meanings, play and creativity' (Piccardo, 2017: 8). The vision that emphasises only functional use of the language for practical, everyday communicative goals, and that words are but different labels for the same objects and concepts, is diametrically opposed to this idea of language as symbolic competence:

> Through symbolic competence, users and learners participate in communication, understood as the reciprocal exchange of meaning within and across languages and cultures, and come to understand the linguistic and cultural situatedness of all participants in any act of communication or act of learning. This situatedness is manifested in multiple interpretations of experiences and texts, representations, positionings, and meanings. (Leung & Scarino, 2016: 88)

In discussing symbolic competence, Kramsch emphasises that she is coming from 'an ecological perspective' (Kramsch, 2008: 402; Kramsch & Whiteside, 2008: 667). Through language and intercultural awareness learners seek meaning as embedded in, and dependent on, the context. They are helped to see beyond the conventional meanings of the monolingual vision of the world, to distinguish between glossodiversity and semiodiversity (Halliday, 2002), to understand that diversity of languages and diversity of meanings are not the same thing and are not interchangeable. 'To value semiodiversity is to protect language diversity and relativity' (Piccardo, 2014b: 201). However, occupying and using the in-between space is not a straightforward process. As Kramsch points out: 'making other people's words one's own while retaining their "otherness" requires distance, reflexivity, irony and a certain dose of humour' (Kramsch, 2009: 115). The ability to navigate linguistic trajectories and acquire the capacity of using different languages for creating different symbolic systems (Kramsch, 2009: 188) cannot be reached without the reflective involvement of the user/learner, without the development of a form of Socratic irony, able to help one remain both within and outside the new languages and cultures concerned. Kramsch and Whiteside (2008) therefore define symbolic competence as: 'the ability to shape the multilingual game in which one invests – the ability to manipulate the conventional categories and societal norms of truthfulness, legitimacy, seriousness, originality – and to reframe human thought and action' (2008: 667), as the ability 'to play with various linguistic codes and with the various spatial and temporal resonances of these codes' (2008: 664). Thus, as well as semiotic awareness, symbolic competence involves this 'ability to actively manipulate and shape one's environment on multiple scales of time and space' (Kramsch, 2008: 402; Kramsch & Whiteside, 2008: 667).

Linking directly to an ecological approach, Kramsch and Whiteside conclude by defining symbolic competence as:

> ... a mindset that can create 'relationships of possibility' or affordances (van Lier, 2004: 105), but only if the individual learns to see him/ herself through his/her own embodied history and subjectivity and through the history and subjectivity of others. Our symbolic survival is contingent on framing reality in the way required by the moment, and on being able to enter the game with both full involvement and full detachment. In this sense, the notion of symbolic competence is a late modern way of conceiving of both communicative and inter-cultural competence in multilingual settings. (Kramsch & Whiteside, 2008: 668)

Learning new languages inevitably involves engaging with their symbolic nature. Users/learners who become plurilingual have to come to term with a wealth of different symbolic systems and this symbolic dimension of the language is what constitutes the basis for identity construction. The different information and symbolic meanings that they accumulate through experiences of the mind and body constitute a kind of map which informs their world view and helps to structure their identity. What learners of a new language lack is precisely that map (Kramsch, 2009), something which can be puzzling, but also the chance for a new start, the possibility of exploring potential worlds and constructing a new plurilingual and pluricultural identity.

The plurilingual and pluricultural perspective captures the dynamic, situated and complex relationship between languages within individuals' linguistic and cultural trajectories and a proactive attitude towards linguistic and cultural plurality, with even inventions of meaning (Zarate et al., 2008). It opens the door to developing symbolic competence as it offers a wealth of possibilities to individuals who navigate between different languages and cultures.

We have mentioned plurilingualism many times; now it is time to consider it in a little more detail.

6.3 Plurilingualism

Plurilingualism has been a daily reality in many societies throughout history. It is endemic in the Indian subcontinent (Canagarajah, 2009; Canagarajah & Liyanage, 2012) and well-documented in Africa,

South America and Polynesia (Canagarajah, 2009). It was a feature of the Babylonian, Hittite, Assyrian, Persian, and more recently Austro-Hungarian empires, with the latter pursuing a consciously plurilingual language policy from the early 18th century (Dacrema, 2012; Piccardo, 2017). Europe has been plurilingual for most of its history (Krumm, 2003) with each village being able to understand their neighbouring villages (Wright, 2000, 2001). In addition, in many civilisations educated people have been expected to speak a couple of international languages on top of the language of the geographical neighbour. In the European context, cultured people were expected to know Latin and some ancient Greek in addition to French until the mid-20th century. Historically speaking, therefore, it is monolingualism that may be the exception, not plurilingualism.

Used in Italian linguistics since the 1950s as previously mentioned, the term plurilingualism emerged in language education in French by the 1990s (Berthoud, 1996; Coste & Hebrard, 1991), but was also used in English soon afterwards (Khubchandani, 1997). As mentioned in Section 5.2.10, plurilingualism was introduced to a wider audience in early drafts of the CEFR and background studies related to it (Coste *et al.*, 1997; Council of Europe, 1996). It is described in the CEFR Companion Volume as follows:

> Plurilingual competence as explained in the CEFR (Section 1.3) involves the ability to call flexibly upon an inter-related, uneven, plurilinguistic repertoire to:
> - switch from one language or dialect (or variety) to another;
> - express oneself in one language (or dialect, or variety) and understand a person speaking another;
> - call upon the knowledge of a number of languages (or dialects, or varieties) to make sense of a text;
> - recognise words from a common international store in a new guise;
> - mediate between individuals with no common language (or dialect, or variety), even with only a slight knowledge oneself;
> - bring the whole of one's linguistic equipment into play, experimenting with alternative forms of expression;
> - exploit paralinguistics (mime, gesture, facial expression, etc. (Council of Europe, 2018: 28)

Plurilingualism posits 'an uneven and changing competence, in which the user/learner's resources in one language or variety may be very different in nature to those in another' (Council of Europe, 2018: 28). In the plurilingual vision, developing language competence is seen as dynamic and unbalanced, which is why the CEFR stressed the concepts of 'partial competences' and profiles of different kinds (see Council of Europe, 2018: 36–40).

Every new language experience modifies the global language competence of individuals and shapes their linguistic repertoires. Errors are no longer seen as negative by-products of interference but also as a way of progressing; 'U-shaped' development is the norm as part of the phenomenon of emergence towards a new stable state. Pre-existing linguistic knowledge is taken into consideration, together with experience in language learning, task accomplishment, different aims, conditions, and constraints (Piccardo, 2010b). In this complex vision, learners are increasingly called upon to play an active role in the process of constructing their competence, enhanced by a reflective, autonomous attitude in which metacognitive and metalinguistic skills brought from previous language learning play an important role. Such a vision of developing language competence aligns completely with the complexity and ecological theories and concepts of situated action and learning that were discussed in Chapter 3 and the move to a nonlinear, more experiential conceptualisation of language learning outlined in Chapter 4. As Piccardo (2013a) puts it:

> The new and potentially revolutionary aspects of a plurilingual vision are supported in three theoretical domains, each representing lenses through which the phenomenon can be effectively explored:
> (a) The psycho-cognitive perspective, which studies language acquisition mechanisms. A new connectionist paradigm is increasingly predominant in describing the functioning of the brain (Bickes, 2004: 38), and the brain of bi/multilinguals is no longer seen as the sum of monolingual brains but rather considered as a complex and distinct system (Bialystok, 2001; Perani et al., 2003).
> (b) The sociocultural perspective, which posits that language acquisition occurs in the social sphere and is intrinsically linked to interaction and mediation between individuals, each possessing his or her own complex cultural system and all living within linguistically, culturally, and sociologically defined configurations (Lantolf, 2011).
> (c) The pedagogical perspective, a new complex vision of language teaching methodology, supported by the post-method movement (Bell, 2003; García, 2009; Kumaravadivelu, 2001). (Piccardo, 2013a: 603)

To summarise, then, what we have said in this section and earlier in the book, plurilingualism could be defined as follows:

Plurilingualism:

- is a dynamically developing, unbalanced, *partial* competence;
- particularly values *receptive competence* as a stepping stone to autonomous learning;

- encourages the development of the *executive control function* – suppressing all but one language/variety when it is appropriate, recognising that varieties have distinct features and grammars (see MacSwan, 2017) – with the benefits to cognition and creativity that this brings, as discussed in Chapter 3;
- is *outward looking* – *stimulating curiosity* about new languages and cultures, and an ability to see (and to look for) the links between languages, and between language and culture;
- is learning-oriented, *self-teaching*, in that it encourages one to deal with chaos;
- is *learning-oriented* in that it encourages exploitation of similarities: cognates, internationalisms, turns of phrase, expressions and metaphors;
- leads to an *increased awareness* of how languages – including one's own mother tongue(s) – operate, engendering a new feeling for the place and role of different registers and varieties;
- encourages *playful, creative stretching* of boundaries and norms – but at the same time encourages the appreciation of what those norms are – as in poetry;
- inevitably *involves mediation* of various kinds.

In the context of the superdiversity that was discussed above in Section 6.1, it is again time to consider plurilingualism as normal rather than out of the ordinary. Language diversity, contact and coexistence of different languages and cultures are not just linked to today's globalisation and mass migration, but have been present from the beginning of history.

Inevitably, the recognition of plurilingualism as a normality rather than an exception of interest only to specialists entails important consequences for theory and linguistic research. As Lüdi and Py (2009) argue:

> If plurilingualism is no longer considered a marginal phenomenon only of interest to specialists, but instead as a characteristic of the majority of human beings, there are various consequences for theory and linguistic research. In other words, a linguistics must be developed in which plurilingual linguistic repertoires are the norm, at both individual and social levels, a linguistics in which the choice of a language or an appropriate variety is necessarily part of a model of language in action, a linguistics which necessarily includes the management of plurilingualism – early as well as late – in all language-treating models. Stated otherwise, any theory of language would have – to be useful – to take account of plurilingual repertoires and the way in which plurilingual speakers exploit their resources in different forms of bilingual speech. (Lüdi & Py, 2009: 163)

6.3.1 Plurilingualism vs multilingualism

As mentioned in Section 5.2.10, the concept of plurilingualism has tended to be subsumed into that of multilingualism in the English-speaking academic world. This is despite the fact that there are very significant differences between the two notions. The term plurilingualism has transformed the existence of two different but similar prefixes – 'pluri-' and 'multi-' – into a lever for a crucial conceptual distinction. Multilingualism is defined in the CEFR as 'the knowledge of a number of languages (*note: by an individual*), or the coexistence of different languages in a given society' (Council of Europe, 2001: 4). The fundamental distinction between plurilingualism and multilingualism is parallel to the distinction between pluriculturalism and multiculturalism. The prefix 'multi' stresses the adding together of a series of elements like numbers in a multiplication, people in a multitude; the prefix 'pluri' on the other hand is holistic, with the idea of plurality, embedded difference. The distinction leverages the difference between the two opposing visions of linguistic and cultural diversity: otherness or empathy, living side by side or living together, tolerance or interest (Balboni, 2015).

The addition of languages that characterises multilingual contexts can also be observed in individuals. Some learners, particularly those who attempt to acquire a native-like persona in one additional language, see their languages as completely separate from one another. It is almost as if they pretend to be a different person in the other language, making a great effort to preserve purity and reach 'perfection', especially of pronunciation, at the expense of developing a flexible, open approach with a functional proficiency in several languages and an ability to see links between them. Plurilinguals, 'rather than being condemned to some original division against themselves, can draw strength from the flexibility and versatility afforded by their various languages' (Kramsch, 2009: 195).

In other words, it is possible to speak more than one language and not be plurilingual:

> A ... characteristic of plurilingual and pluricultural competence is that it does not consist of the simple addition of monolingual competences but permits combinations and alternations of different kinds. (Council of Europe, 2001: 134)

The distinction that the CEFR makes between multilingualism and plurilingualism goes well beyond a terminological one. The piling up of languages at the individual level, and the passive coexistence of languages and cultures alongside each other at the social level that multilingualism suggests, fully ignore the complex vision of language development. The concept of multilingualism puts the emphasis on separation, on boundaries. And it is such boundaries that are invented, not the languages/varieties themselves, as some have started to suggest (e.g. Makoni & Pennycook, 2007; Otheguy *et al.*, 2015). The phenomena of contact, hybridity and cross-fertilisation between languages are unavoidable. Historically, such mingling has influenced the evolution of languages. The super-diverse context in which we live accelerates such contacts and cross-fertilisation; plurilingualism provides a conceptual framework that helps us to come to terms with this acceleration. It is as a result unfortunate that the majority of applied linguists working in English, including Kramsch in the citation above, have continued for over 20 years to ignore the distinction between multilingualism and plurilingualism and the clear political and pedagogic philosophy associated with the latter[1].

This distinction between plurilingualism and multilingualism at an individual level, reflects the context in which the choices that lead to it occur. The linguistic and educational policies that countries adopt greatly contribute to the attitude towards language learning and use of their citizens, including in officially bi/multilingual contexts. In general an ideal of purism and separation informs language policies and curricula, thus exacerbating the quest for acquiring a 'perfect' level in the target language(s) among learners and creating an inevitable sense of frustration and inadequacy and consequent avoidance of the language – even in officially bilingual regions (e.g. Puozzo Capron, 2014). The situation of two linguistic communities living side by side in this way has been well described as the 'two solitudes' by Cummins (2008) in the context of French immersion in Canada. With a plurilingual vision, by contrast, the principle of the relationship and interaction between the languages concerned is fundamental:

> Plurilingualism differs from multilingualism (the simple addition of languages in societies – and/or individuals) in that it focuses on the relationships between the languages an individual speaks, the underlying linguistic mechanisms and cultural connotations, the personal linguistic and cultural trajectory as well as the person's attitude towards language diversity, stressing openness, curiosity and flexibility. (Piccardo, 2017: 2)

6.3.2 A developing repertoire and trajectory

Let us consider the fundamental characteristics of plurilingualism. It is an unbalanced and changing, dynamic competence, in which capacities in one language or variety may be very different to those in another, but make up *one holistic communicative repertoire*. This aspect reflects the concept of *multi-competence* (Cook, 1991; Cook & Wei, 2016) which challenged the notions of 'native speaker' and of separation of languages in the brain. This is because a person's plurilingual profile reflects their trajectory through life. As the CEFR puts it:

> An individual person's experience of language in its cultural contexts expands, from the language of the home to that of society at large and then to the languages of other peoples ... , he or she does not keep these languages and cultures in strictly separated mental compartments, but rather builds up a communicative competence to which all knowledge and experience of language contributes and in which languages interrelate and interact. (Council of Europe, 2001: 4)

Partial competences in different languages, the ability to function at a higher level in some activities or domains of use but at a lower level in others, is seen as being of great value as a stepping-stone to further development (Martin-Jones & Romaine, 1985; Skutnabb-Kangas, 1981). In short:

> The plurilingualism sought is not that of an exceptional polyglot but rather that of ordinary individuals with a varied linguistic capital in which partial competences have their place. What is expected is not maximum proficiency but a range of language skills and receptiveness to cultural diversity. (Coste, 2014: 22)

In this respect, it is worth remembering that competence in *all* languages, including the first language, is usually unbalanced. Above all, plurilingual competence is unbalanced, progressive, and decompartmentalised (Piccardo & Puozzo, 2012, 2015).

Plurilingualism is thus presented in the CEFR as the ability to call flexibly upon a holistic, integrated, interrelated, uneven, plurilingual repertoire in which all linguistic abilities have a place, and which the user/learner mobilises to blend, mix and translanguage as described in the next section. It is usually the case that plurilingual speakers develop a greater proficiency in one language than in the others, and that the profile of competence in each language is different (e.g. good reception in three languages, good interaction in two, but good written production in only one). The profile will reflect the individual's personal trajectory through life, his/her interests, relationships, educational exposure, occupational needs, etc. etc. The profile of pluricultural competence may be similarly unbalanced due to more exposure to the culture associated with one language, and the balance between pluricultural and plurilingual competence may itself be unbalanced (e.g. familiarity with Italian culture but not the language; familiarity with the English language but not the culture).

One way in which lack of balance and partial competences are exploited in a positive fashion is in the pedagogic practice *intercomprehension*, which encourages the acquisition of a receptive capacity in languages related to the language(s) in which one has an active competence. The concept turns the natural phenomena that, for example, Italians and Spaniards can often understand each other into a pedagogic philosophy. There have been several projects and studies experimenting with intercomprehension in secondary schools (e.g. Vetter, 2012), particularly among Romance languages (Carrasco-Perea, 2010; Degache, 2003). The MIRIADI project (www.miriadi. net), for example, has developed an extensive set of descriptors for learners and trainee teachers (del Barrio, 2015), which focus particularly on reception strategies.

Canagarajah highlights the fact that, generalising from his research, successful plurilinguals (translinguals in his terminology) display the following positive dispositions – meaning a set of tastes, values and skills in terms of language awareness, social values and learning strategies:

- Language awareness: (a) language norms as open to negotiation; (b) languages as mobile, semiotic resources; (c) a functional orientation to communication and meaning.
- Social values: (a) openness to diversity; (b) a sense of voice and a locus of enunciation; (c) a strong ethic of collaboration.
- Learning strategies: (a) learning from practice; (b) adaptive skills; (c) use of scaffolding. (Canagarajah, 2013: 181)

This plurilingual vision of dynamic, unbalanced, partial competences and developing language awareness and learning strategies reinforces the feasibility of lifelong language learning. Recent studies in fact suggest that there is no evidence for the idea of a critical period for language learning (Hakuta *et al.*, 2003; Marinova-Todd *et al.*, 2000). The advantage that older learners have is the potential of leverage from their previous language learning. In learning additional languages, one benefits from transversal competences and strategies developed previously in other languages: *savoir-apprendre* (learning to learn), building on successful experiences and techniques.

6.3.3 Language awareness

Apart from the enhanced ability to functionally communicate in a variety of diverse settings, the main advantage of a plurilingual approach is that it is a self-perpetuating, life-changing process: the more plurilingual you are the more plurilingual you become, with an enhanced metalinguistic awareness. The notion of language awareness is pivotal in plurilingualism. Language awareness is real openness to the 'other', a way of questioning one's own existing beliefs and frameworks. It is defined in the CEFR as follows:

> Sensitivity to language and language use [which] enables new experience to be assimilated into an ordered framework and welcomed as an enrichment. ... [T]he associated new language may then be more readily learnt and used, rather than resisted as a threat to the learner's already established linguistic system, which is often believed to be normal and 'natural'. (Council of Europe, 2001: 107)

Language awareness in a plurilingual perspective is not limited to awareness of linguistic forms of each language taken in isolation. It is awareness of similarities and differences between languages, cultures and the ways different languages express and symbolically represent a variety of cultures. Through awareness, both linguistic and cultural, the dominant linear vision of language learning – i.e. that learning a new language is putting new labels onto real world objects, events and ideas that exist independently from their linguistic denotation – is questioned. What is also questioned is the idea that the presence of at least one developed language system represented by the L1 (if not more in the case of an already plurilingual learner) may be irrelevant or even detrimental to the acquisition of a new language. In a plurilingual vision, the user/learner allows him/herself to venture along different paths which are not shaped around one centre but are polycentric and multidirectional. Awareness of languages represents Ariadne's thread that helps individuals navigate the labyrinth of paths. The study of different languages thus goes beyond the functional-communicative vision. Connotation becomes as strong as – if not stronger than – denotation as the learner/user comes to terms with the idea of embracing the new language on the one hand and maintaining the possibility of making a step back, of seeing things from a distance on the other.

Juxtaposition of dissimilar and deconceptualisation, two cognitive mechanisms studied in relation to creativity (Indurkhya, 2013), are core to plurilingualism: the former suggests juxtaposing linguistically and culturally dissimilar concepts or terms, thus potentially creating new meanings, insights and perspectives. The latter encourages moving away from existing conceptualisation of objects and ideas through estrangement, associations and metaphors, helping us to perceive differently and thus also potentially gaining new insights. In such a perspective, all aspects of the language acquire specific, well-defined, personal meaning and powerful connotations.

6.3.4 Blending, mixing and translanguaging

Currently there is an increasing interest in theorising translingual practices (e.g. Canagarajah, 2013; May, 2014; Otheguy *et al.*, 2015; Piccardo, 2017; Vogel & García, 2017) and describing (sub) phenomena of blending, mixing and transcending boundaries between languages and varieties which Marshall and Moore (2016) describe as 'lingualisms'.

Codeswitching (Gumperz, 1982; Lüdi & Py, 1986/2003; MacSwan, 2014) and *code alternation* (Androutsopoulos, 2006; Auer, 1995) are normally used to describe different ways of switching between languages within the same utterance. King and Chetty (2014) document how codeswitching is an everyday occurrence in Cape Town in media, in the street and by teachers. In the educational context, they and Creese and Blackledge (2010) document teachers following a statement or instructions in English with expansion, clarification and explanation in L1, with the final statement in English (2014: 47), echoing the first examples of *translanguaging* given by Williams (1996), while Lewis *et al.* (2012a) describe three different types of linguistic mediation being used as scaffolding techniques. Sometimes codeswitching is unconscious (e.g. King & Chetty's example) while sometimes it is conscious and 'responsible' (García, 2009) as a scaffolding technique that she calls 'co-languaging' (2009: 303). Creese and Blackledge (2010), also document codeswitching by the learners while carrying out the tasks, suggesting that the switching is primarily about 'which voices are engaged in identity performance' (Creese & Blackledge, 2010: 110), while Wei discusses similar use of codeswitching as a 'symbolic resource of contestation and struggle against institutional ideologies' (Wei, 2011: 381).

In addition to codeswitching, researchers use a wealth of expressions to describe the creativity, dynamism and shapelessness of plurilingual behaviour. Indeed, García and Wei (2014) now differentiate *translanguaging* from codeswitching:

> ... in that it refers not simply to a shift or a shuttle between two languages, but to the speakers' construction and use of original and complex interrelated discursive practices that cannot be easily assigned to one or another traditional definition of a language, but that make up the speakers' complete language repertoire. (García & Wei, 2014: 22)

However, translanguaging in an educational context does seem to involve 'responsible' codeswitching. For example, in translanguaging pedagogy in the Welsh context learners may choose together how to complete the task, for example, gathering information from the internet in English, discussing the content in English and Welsh, and completing the written work in Welsh. Alternately they might gather information in English, discuss the content in Welsh, and complete the written work in English (Lewis *et al.*, 2012a: 665). In a similar vein in another educational context García (2009) describes talking about a text in English in one's first language, web research in one's first language instead of or as well as in English, and drafting a piece in the first language to then later carefully produce it in English. García and Wei (2014: 64) cite Baker's (2001) list of the potential benefits of such a translanguaging pedagogic approach:

(1) It may promote a deeper and fuller understanding of the subject matter.
(2) It may help the development of the weaker language.
(3) It may facilitate home-school links and cooperation.
(4) It may help the integration of fluent speakers with early learners.

More recently, García and her colleagues have further developed the concept of translanguaging as part of the 'critical-pedagogy argument' (Bowes & Flinders, 1990: 239) in reaction to the way in which 'colonial and modernist-era language ideologies created and maintained linguistic, cultural, and racial hierarchies in society. It [translanguaging] challenges prevailing theories of bilingualism/multi-lingualism and bilingual development in order to disrupt the hierarchies that have delegitimized the language practices of those who are minoritized' (Vogel & García, 2017: 1). García *et al.* (2017) suggest the following strategic uses of translanguaging in education, which they say work together to advance social justice:

(1) Supporting students as they engage with and comprehend complex content and texts.
(2) Providing opportunities for students to develop linguistic practices for academic contexts.
(3) Making space for students' bilingualism and ways of knowing.
(4) Supporting students' bilingual identities and socioemotional development.

More generally, however, Otheguy *et al.* (2015) suggest that bilinguals have a linguistically integrated idiolect with which they *translanguage* as the whim takes them in a hetero-linguistic family or community. Translanguaging seeks to 'directly problematise the notion of "a language"' (Otheguy *et al.*, 2015: 282), considering that 'a named national language is the same kind of thing as a named national cuisine' (Otheguy *et al.*, 2015: 286). Translanguaging 'dismantles named language categories and takes up an internal perspective to describe the languaging of speakers who are said to be bilingual or multilingual' (Vogel & García, 2017: 5). García and her colleagues appear to agree with Makoni and Pennycook's view that 'languages do not exist as real entities in the world …; they are, by contrast, the inventions of social, cultural and political movements' (2007, 2).

This position has been criticised from both linguistic and educational perspectives. MacSwan reminds us that: 'Unpacking the ambiguity in the term language … helps us recognize the inherent socio-political nature of named languages, or E-languages, while still recognizing the linguistic reality of language diversity in the form of I-languages, or individual languages' (2017: 176). Although languages cannot be considered as entities that exist independently from their speakers, the convention of named languages helps the investigation of linguistic development and variability over time, shifts in language use, socio-political implications and the power dynamics of linguistic usage. Cummins, meanwhile, emphasises that for their speakers, languages are very real:

> García and Wei's (2014) dismissal of the construct of language/languages as illegitimate goes beyond the generally accepted claim that languages are socially constructed with fluid, permeable, and arbitrary boundaries. Although languages are certainly processed cognitively in dynamic and integrated ways, languages, as social constructions, *do exist* in the lives and experiences of teachers, students, governments, politicians, and countless agencies, and they generate an immense material and symbolic reality. (Cummins, 2017: 414, our emphasis.)

Perhaps as a response to such criticism, García and Lin (2016) have gone on to describe a 'strong' version of translanguaging (the position taken by Otheguey *et al.*, 2015 and Makoni & Pennycook, 2007) and a 'weak' version that pragmatically accepts the existence of named languages, exhorting bilingual programs to include both: 'For bilingual education programs to both offer a fairer and more just education to bilingual children and sustain minority language practices, it is important that they combine the weak and strong versions of translanguaging theory' (2016: 11). Vogel and García (2017) put the distinction more theoretically saying that: 'translanguaging theory draws a distinction between the way society labels and views an individual's use of two named languages (the external perspective), and the way a speaker actually appropriates and uses language features (the internal perspective) (Otheguy, García, & Reid, 2015)' (Vogel & García, 2017: 5).

While it has enjoyed great success, translanguaging is not the only other term developed to describe translingual practices. Other terms include *metrolingualism* to describe the linguistic behaviour of the globalised elite discussed by Otsuji and Pennycook (2010), the *polylanguaging* street talk described by Jørgensen *et al.* (2011), and the *code crossing* among youth from different migration backgrounds described by Rampton (1995). All these scholars describe creative language use that plays with the boundaries of named languages Meanwhile, Canagarajah (2011a) uses the term *code meshing* to describe using more than one language in a written academic text and prefers the expression *translingual practices* to translanguaging (2011b, 2013) as an umbrella term. Finally, *intercomprehension* is used to refer to the exploitation of similarities between languages (Carrasco Peres, 2010; Degache, 2003; Doyé, 2004, 2005; Pinho, 2015). Rehbein *et al.* (2012) state that *Lingua receptiva* is a further development of the concept of intercomprehension and there are currently attempts to extend its use (ten Thije *et al.*, 2017).

Let us look again at the way in which the concept of plurilingualism is introduced in CEFR Section 1.3 and the CEFR Companion Volume (Council of Europe, 2018: 28), as mentioned at the beginning of this Section 6.3, this time comparing the points made in the CEFR to these various new terms that we have been discussing:

"In different situations, a person can call flexibly upon different parts of this [plurilingual] competence to achieve effective communication with a particular interlocutor. For instance, partners may ..." (Council of Europe, 2001: 4):

(a) Switch from one language or dialect (or variety) to another;
(this relates to codeswitching, code alternation, flexible bilingualism and translanguaging).
(b) Express oneself in one language (or dialect, or variety) and understand a person speaking another;
(this relates to lingua receptiva and intercomprehension).
(c) Call upon the knowledge of a number of languages (or dialects, or varieties) to make sense of a text;
(this relates to translanguaging as pedagogic scaffolding in a language class, and intercomprehension).
(d) Recognise words from a common international store in a new guise;
(this relates to intercomprehension).
(e) Mediate between individuals with no common language (or dialect, or variety), even with only a slight knowledge oneself;
(this is acting as an intermediary in cross-linguistic mediation).
(f) Bring the whole of one's linguistic equipment into play, experimenting with alternative forms of expression in different languages or dialects, exploiting paralinguistics (mime, gesture, facial expression, etc.) and radically simplifying their use of language. (This relates to translanguaging, code crossing, code mixing, code meshing, polylingualism and metrolingualism).

At the same time as the scholars mentioned above have been inventing new terms, others have been modulating the traditional term 'multilingualism' with a variety of adjectives in order to try and capture the nature of creative, plurilingual behaviour. Herdina and Jessner (2002) present a *dynamic model of multilingualism*, Cenoz and Gorter (2011) propose a *holistic approach to multilingualism* in which 'multilinguals do not seem to be semilingual, but rather *hyperlingual*' (Cenoz, 2013: 11), their multilingualism dynamic as they use their whole linguistic repertoire. Cummins (2017) proposes *active multilingualism*, as an example of 'dynamic heteroglossic conceptions of bi/multilingualism' (Cummins, 2017: 420), stating that this is a core concept in, for example, Swedish and Icelandic educational policy. Finally, MacSwan, in rebutting Otheguy *et al.*'s (2015) suggestion that bilinguals possess a single grammar, proposes an *integrated multilingual model*, which 'posits that bilinguals have a single system with many shared grammatical resources but with some internal language-specific differentiation as well' (MacSwan, 2017: 179).

As Cenoz notes: 'The holistic view of multilingualism focusing on the multilingual speaker is sometimes referred to as plurilingualism (Canagarajah & Liyanage, 2012; Moore & Gajo, 2009)' (Cenoz, 2013: 12). One could in fact go a step further and say that all these translingual practices to be found in the literature align with the concept of plurilingualism and its attempt to capture the elusive, complex and multifaceted nature of the co-construction of meaning. Each of the terms discussed above – including the various extensions to the term 'multilingualism' – has contributed to deepening the reflection on and comprehension of linguistic diversity and its implications, at the different levels concerned, personal, societal and educational. However it is, to say the least, curious the way in which, as Marshall and Moore (2016) noted, scholars writing in English in the mainstream international academic culture tend to avoid using the term plurilingualism. There are even examples of people who previously embraced it (e.g. Canagarajah & Liyanage, 2012; García *et al.*, 2007) now avoiding it or dismissing it as synonymous with multilingualism (e.g. Vogel & García, 2017). Perhaps the fact that the term did not emerge in an English-speaking academic cenacle explains part of the resistance. Perhaps one of the obstacles is that plurilingualism represents a complex phenomenon that calls for a new, kaleidoscopic vision, in which terms like 'linguistic and cultural repertoire' and 'linguistic and cultural trajectory' act as conceptual guiding tools. Whatever the reason, the dominant English-medium academic culture appears to prefer possibly more straightforward notions, such as multilingualism and translanguaging.

6.3.5 Plurilanguaging

We discussed in Section 6.3.1 the difference between the terms plurilingualism and multilingualism, and in Section 6.3.4 above we discussed translanguaging and other terms to describe translingual practices. Here we introduce the term plurilanguaging. As mentioned in Section 3.7, various studies have shown distinct advantages for plurilingualism, including the fostering of characteristics associated with mental flexibility and creativity. As anticipated by the Sapir-Whorf hypothesis (Hoijer, 1954), the structure of a language affects the ways in which speakers of that language conceptualise the world, i.e. their '*Weltanschauung*', as researchers in linguistic relativity such as Niemeier and Dirven, (2000) or Athanasopoulos (2011, 2016) show. Bilinguals and plurilinguals thus have more than one perspective on any phenomenon. Encouraging such multiple perspectives calls for *plurilanguaging*, 'a dynamic, never-ending process to make meaning using different linguistic and semiotic resources' (Piccardo, 2018: 9).

The term plurilanguaging emerged in post-colonial, Latin American Studies. Arrizón (2006), for example, uses it in discussing the presentation of in-between identities in Anzaldúa's work *Borderlands/ La frontera: The New Mestiza*, of which Mignolo (2000: 227) had written: 'To read Borderlands is to read in three languages and three literatures, which is a new way of languaging' rejecting the monolingual worldview of the colonial heritage. Arrizón talks of the '"plurilanguaging system" that requires the historicization and politicization of subject formation and its relation to discourse practices' (Arrizón, 2006: 25). She relates it to the ability to navigate in 'in-between spaces', what Anzaldúa calls *la facultad*, saying that: 'Those who are pounced on the most have it the strongest – the females, the homosexuals of all races, the darkskinned, the outcast, the persecuted, the marginalized, the foreign' (Anzaldúa, 1999: 60). As Arrizón (2006) points out: 'In many instances, Anzaldúa describes *la facultad* not only in the many languages she speaks (Mignolo's analysis of plurilanguaging) but also in the embodiment of queerness and the coming together of opposites' (Arrizón, 2006: 27). In other words, the action of plurilanguaging tends to be embedded in pluricultural behaviour: the navigation of the 'in-between spaces' that the socially marginalised are only too familiar with.

More prosaically, the term is then picked up by Makoni and Makoni (2010) to describe 'the ongoing social process which involves a mobilization of diverse linguistic resources' (2010: 261) in the plurilingual practices of African taxi drivers. It is then used by Lüdi (2014) in a programme of research on the increasingly plurilingual nature of discourse occurring in everyday and professional contexts (Berthoud *et al.*, 2013; Lüdi *et al.*, 2016) to describe the negotiation of a ticket purchase between a Swiss clerk and a Brazilian traveller. In Lüdi's example, the ticket clerk speaks no Portuguese and the Brazilian speaks no German. The clerk improvises in a relaxed way with his limited French, Italian and Spanish and both sides exploit the intercomprehension possibilities of Romance languages and their common sociocultural script for a credit card transaction. At the end, referring to the rough and ready nature of the discourse, the clerk turns to the researcher and says in a Swiss dialect: '*es goht mit hand und füess aberes goht* (it works with hands and feet, but it works)' (Lüdi, 2014: 129). Pennycook (2017) describes a transaction between a Fijian customer and a Bangladeshi corner shop owner (conducted mainly in English) in which common food culture (frozen river fish in this case) provides the boundary-crossing commonality that the credit card transaction gave in the Lüdi example. Canagarajah (2018) discusses the way that a group of Chinese STEM (science, technology, engineering, and mathematics) scholars working in an English-speaking environment switch freely between verbal and graphic communication, and different languages, mobilising and combining all their semiotic resources, plus earlier texts they have produced and other artefacts in the environment, in a process of 'bricolage'.

These various examples describe the results of the empowering process of linguistic and cultural negotiation of meaning enabled by the exploitation of common scripts and awareness of possible synergies between different and partial linguistic resources used as building blocks. As Pennycook puts it: 'Repertoires are the product of social spaces as semiotic resources, objects and space interact' (2017: 277). Echoing Halliday's concept of meaning potential (determined in the situation) that was discussed in Section 3.4, Pennycook states: 'Neither agency nor language nor cognition is best understood as a property of the individual, as something located in the human mind or tied to personal action; rather it is a distributed effect of a range of interacting objects, people and places' (Pennycook, 2017: 277), describing the latter as 'semiotic assemblages'. Canagarajah (2018) also uses the expression 'assemblage' to describe this way in which collective verbal and non-verbal resources, plus artefacts in the environment, are combined and recombined in context to collaboratively create meaning. This of course also links to the ecological concept of the landscape of affordances discussed in Section 3.9.

However, in terms of the potential of plurilanguaging, these descriptions of everyday transactions show just the tip of the iceberg. In discussing ways of enabling possible synergies between plurilingualism and creativity, Piccardo (2017) describes the way in which plurilanguaging is:

- a cyclical process of exploring and constructing;
- an agentic process of selecting and (self)organizing;
- a process of dealing with chaos;
- an awareness-raising process that enhances perception, and an empowering process in relation to norms. (Piccardo, 2017: 5–10)

Exploring and constructing

Learning a new language is characterised by phases of emergence as individuals construct their learning in a recursive, complex way, acting on the environment as the environment is acting on them, with the two changing over time as two nested CAS. This process is enhanced by the variety of linguistic and cultural resources, with cognitive, emotional and environmental factors involved in the learning process (see Section 3.7). Secondly, the individual agent sees his/her new learning filtered, accepted or modified by the relevant speech community, comparable to the cyclical processes of divergent and convergent thinking, that has been identified as characteristic of creativity (Guildford, 1967; Kharkhurin, 2016). The phase of hypothesis making, decoding and meaning-making is divergent and the phase of filtering and adapting to the speech community's norms is convergent. In a plurilingual view, this alternation is purposefully sought: learners are encouraged and supported in a conscious process of divergent thinking and problem finding, and later they are guided towards awareness of the norm in a convergent thinking process.

Selecting and (self) organising

As we discussed in Section 3.9 when discussing affordances, an individual only experiences affordances as invitations if they are relevant to the task he/she is engaged in (Käufer & Chemero, 2015). Thus, when engaged in language learning and use, the social agent focuses on the affordances (linguistic, cultural, cognitive, emotional etc.) that are relevant to his/her learning process. As a consequence, the individual reaches a new state of balance: in DST terms, the entire nested system self-organises. However, with a plurilingual approach, the relevant affordances multiply, requiring both focused and lateral attention, and consequently more targeted decisions need to be made. The ambiguity connected with using multiple languages, in which the same idea may take different nuances in different languages, can bring an advantage in divergent thinking (Lubart, 1999).

Dealing with chaos

Dynamic systems undergo repeated cycles of order and disorder until they reach a new, temporary balance. It is only through positive acceptance of imbalance and awareness of the complex nature of language learning that individuals are able to negotiate in-between spaces, to construct, be inventive, and embrace change (Puozzo & Piccardo, 2014). 'A system at or near the edge of chaos changes adaptively to maintain stability, demonstrating a high level of flexibility and responsiveness' (Larsen-Freeman & Cameron, 2008: 58). For plurilinguals, dealing with chaos is a natural, positive state, where they feel free to make personal and creative use of all their linguistic and cultural resources. Research shows that plurilinguals have a higher degree of tolerance of ambiguity (Dewaele & Wei, 2013), a fundamental trait of creativity (Sternberg & Lubart, 1995; Vernon, 1970; Zenasni et al., 2008).

Enhancing perception

By embracing a plurilingual view, individuals experience a wealth of stimuli, because different languages encode concepts differently: 'a plurilingual's apprehension and perception of the world is likely to be expanded as a result of the multiple linguistic and pragmatic systems faced by him/her when engaging with interlocutors' (Furlong, 2009: 351). The concepts of embodied and situated cognition that align with DST and the theory of affordances help better conceptualise the functioning of the plurilingual brain. For Rietvel and Kieverstein: 'Skilled "higher" cognition can be understood in terms of selective engagement – in concrete situations – with the rich landscape of affordances' (2014: 326). Awareness is at the core of this process. Such engagement initiates change in the CAS and triggers further awareness of linguistic and cultural features, thus enhancing the entire learning process. Simple exposure to linguistic and cultural difference is not enough by itself to enhance creativity (Maddux et al., 2010).

Empowerment in relation to norms

Plurilinguals appear to have a greater facility in perceiving unusual analogies and associations and an increased capacity for metaphorical thinking (Kharkhurin, 2012), a key to creative processes. 'Where systems are stretched, where conventional rules are not upheld, where a point of criticality is reached, new forms emerge. ... New forms and patterns then become the resources of the community upon which members of the speech community can draw, exploit and reshape to populate with their own intentions and the affordances of the new context' (Larsen-Freeman & Cameron, 2008: 102). Embracing a plurilingual approach fosters a more flexible attitude towards norms, an opening to hybrid spaces and the crossing of boundaries, which are both conducive to creativity (Maddux et al., 2010; Saad et al., 2013). As Furlong reminds us: 'Heightened perception of [these] boundaries and 'in-between' spaces ... is crucial to enable the process of creativity' (2009: 356).

To summarise, 'to conceive of creativity in terms of affordances means to adopt a fundamentally *dynamic, relational,* and *action-oriented* approach to the phenomenon' (Glăvenau, 2012: 205, our emphasis). Embracing a plurilingual vision invites and enables individuals to perceive and exploit affordances that they would not normally notice. In turn exploration makes those affordances increasingly visible thus increasing the ability to perceive and explore further in a *dynamic circle*. Since learners are social agents, this process is *relational* because it engages individuals within the material and social world in a reciprocal way. Finally, these social agents need *to act* within their environment, they need to experiment with the linguistic and cultural resources at their disposal and drawing on these resources to engage with their physical and symbolic environment. This inevitably involves some form of mediation in order to be successful. Mediation aptly complements the dynamic vision of language learning and use that we have presented so far in this chapter.

Plurilinguals are constantly mediating: to (co)construct meaning, to enable communication across linguistic and cultural barriers, or to make sense of a text. They mediate across languages and within one language, one variety, since plurilingualism recognises variation of languages in a fractal configuration. Let us now therefore turn to this important notion, mediation, to explore further its tenets and potential in language education.

6.4 Mediation: From a Static View of Language to a Dynamic View of (Co)-Construction of Meaning

We have touched upon the concept of mediation in two ways so far in the course of the book. Firstly, we discussed it briefly in terms of its place in sociocultural theory (SCT) in Section 3.6. In SCT, mediation is seen at the individual and social levels in terms of the way in which the child or learner uses symbols and tools (including language) in order to mediate contact with the environment and make sense of the world, and also as a core feature of the process of socialisation and construction of knowledge when adults, siblings and peers interact with the child, providing scaffolding (Wood *et al.*, 1976). In SCT, mediation is central to the co-construction of knowledge.

We also met mediation in terms of the way in which it was introduced in the CEFR back in 2001 as an everyday activity in our society (Section 5.2.9), often – but not always – in a form of plurilingual behaviour when acting as an intermediary between individuals with no common language and/or when processing the content of a text for them. Mediation in this interpretation is being integrated into European language curricula and exams as a result. However, as the CEFR already recognised, language is not the only reason why people cannot understand one another. The difficulty may be caused by different perspectives, expectations – or interpretation of behaviour, of rights and obligations. Crosslinguistic mediation is therefore also a process of cultural mediation. However, as we saw in Section 5.2.9, the seed of mediation planted in the CEFR 2001 would develop slowly as in a sense, in order to germinate, it required precisely the shift in perspective that we have discussed in this chapter, together with the reflection that the SCT and the other theories mentioned brought to our understanding of language learning and use.

It is therefore not surprising that the notion of mediation has been pivotal in the recent revision of the CEFR, which has produced the CEFR Companion Volume (Council of Europe, 2018) with new descriptors for mediation activities, mediation strategies, plurilingual and pluricultural competences. The new, broader conceptualisation of mediation that has informed the CEFR Companion Volume provides fertile ground for reconceptualising languages around the notion of the social agent that the AoA requires. By developing mediation, the CEFR Companion Volume has completed the CEFR descriptive scheme, making explicit the move beyond the fours skills (reception and production) that we discussed in Section 5.2 to the full vision of situated social action and construction of meaning (interaction, mediation). The resulting four modes of communication (reception, production, interaction and mediation) provide the tools to translate the dynamic vision presented in this chapter into classroom practice.

The broader view of mediation taken in the project to develop the CEFR Companion Volume (North & Piccardo, 2016a, 2016b) was informed by many of the theories discussed in Chapter 3. In particular, sociocultural theory in which mediation was seen as being at the core of knowledge construction, the key to accessing meaning and enabling access to meaning, both at the social level, when mediating with or for others, and at the individual, cognitive level. In addition, the ecological perspective, the theory of affordances and above all the concept of agency, also discussed in Chapter 3, equally emphasise the interplay between the individual, social and environmental dimensions. From van Lier's ecological perspective, learning occurs through 'perception in action' (2004: 97) as the social agent's attention fixes on an affordance in the (perhaps linguistic) environment, something which he/she needs in order to do something else. In Bandura's socio-cognitive theory of agency, also operating at the social and individual level, social agents draw on their competences to produce results in their environment, and monitor their actions and mobilise resources in order to achieve personal development. Concepts of situated learning, communities of practice, collective intelligence also discussed in Section 3.8 are all related to the above. In each case, the individual is a CAS (complex adaptive system) nested in another CAS (group, class) and yet another CAS (environment) which all change over time from one state to a new – temporary – state of balance, which emerges after a period of instability, as discussed in Section 3.9. The creativity theories also mentioned in Chapter 3 show the way that creativity also involves an emergent process in complex interaction. Then again, other views of mediation – like cultural mediation discussed above in Section 6.2 –

led to the consideration of concepts like 'third' safe, pluricultural space and the management of tensions and disputes.

How can one capture this richness in a practical descriptive scheme that is easy to understand, without too much overlap between categories? Nowadays we understand that all categorisation in the social sciences, and even many in the natural sciences, are conventional rather than intrinsic (Broch, 2005; Piccardo, 2005b). Despite this fact, boundaries are useful and often necessary in order to discuss complex systems in any meaningful way (Cilliers, 2005; Larsen-Freeman, 2017). The Authoring Group[2] took as their starting point the interpretations of mediation in the academic literature in and beyond our field and in CEFR-related experimentation with the notion of mediation. The centrality of mediation in concept formation (cognitive or conceptual mediation: Halliday's ideational macrofunction), including acting as a facilitator/teacher (pedagogic mediation) was included from the start. So too was the management of personal relations in the provision of necessary conditions for communication and conceptual work (relational mediation: Halliday's interpersonal macrofunction). (Cross)-linguistic mediation of texts and spoken communication was obviously core to the CEFR vision and this could not be separated from cultural mediation, or from the avoidance of or handling of delicate situations, often described as social mediation. Then there were areas that were closely related to mediation, and possibly categories of it. In media studies the term mediation is used frequently; in online interaction (for which there had in any case been a demand for descriptors) the social agent appropriates and embeds texts, images etc. as tools to mediate meaning – and a collaborative group need to mediate their communication even more than in face-to-face communication. Texts that are being accessed, reacted to, cited and/or embedded – in face-to-face or virtual communication – in this process may be creative rather than informational texts (books, poems, songs, videos, films, graffiti etc.). And of course no mediation can be effective without taking account of emotions and affective factors. As a result of the consideration of all these different aspects, the diagram shown in Figure 6.1 was used as a heuristic during the development process.

The result of the long process of deliberation and consultation is the following broad categories:

- *Mediating texts* (broadly defined to include video, graphic etc. as well as verbal text).
- *Mediating communication* and reciprocal comprehension, establishing relationships across barriers, creating shared spaces that facilitate creativity, openness and mutual understanding and helping to avoid or solve critical situations or conflicts.

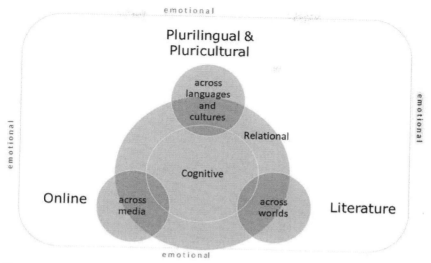

Figure 6.1 Aspects of mediation taken into account in the CEFR Companion Volume project

- *Mediating concepts* in a pedagogic context, firstly creating a suitable environment and conditions to enable learners to appropriate knowledge, and secondly by encouraging the kind of conceptual, dialogic talk (Alexander, 2008) and languaging (Swain, 2006) that will help them to do so.

In addition to these three categories, descriptors for mediation strategies were also developed. This development was intended to help teachers to show users/learners that mediation necessarily involves exercising agency, making choices, manipulating sources, etc. Scales were developed for simplifying a text, both for *Amplifying a dense text*, and for *Streamlining a text* that is badly organised. These scales are supplemented by three other scales for strategies that apply both to mediating a text and to mediating concepts and communication. These three other scales for strategies are: *Linking to previous knowledge*, *Adapting language*, and *Breaking down complicated information*. The development process is described in North and Piccardo (2016a, 2019). We consider below in the following sections the three overall categories that emerged, for each of which several descriptor scales were developed.

6.4.1 Mediating a text

Texts play an important role in classrooms. King and Chetty (2014) speak of explaining, summarising, clarifying and expanding a text from one language in another language more familiar to the learners, while Creese and Blackledge (2010) and Lewis *et al.* (2012) describe managing collaborative interaction or narrating a text flexibly in different languages in a multilingual classroom, to ensure that everyone is involved.

Mediating a text usually involves passing on to another person the content of a text to which they do not have access, often because of linguistic, cultural, semantic or technical barriers: 'mediation language activities, (re)processing an existing text, occupy an important place in the normal linguistic functioning of our societies' (Council of Europe, 2001: 14). In everyday personal and professional situations, users/learners quite often find themselves being asked to perform this function and, as Backus *et al.* (2013) confirm:

> ... people are often satisfied with much less than an exact rendering. In many cases, if you want to know what a phrase or text written in a foreign language means, just getting an idea of the gist is enough, and for expressing an idea in another language, it may suffice to just string words together in the form of a simple literal word-for-word translation. (Backus *et al.*, 2013: 203)

However, one should not overlook the fact that mediating a text can be intralinguistic as well as interlinguistic, the latter translating into pedagogic practices that require a movement between two or more language(s), the former implying the meaning-making process that always accompanies the decoding and/or relaying of a text in a given language. In the CEFR Companion Volume, scales are provided for *Relaying specific information* (picked from a text), for *Processing a text* (the entire text), for *Explaining data* (from graphs etc.) and for *Translating a written text*, with each practice broken down further into speech and writing. In each case, the mediation could be across language or within the same language, so each scale comes with a note pointing out that two different languages may be involved, two varieties of the same language, two registers of the same variety, or any combination of the above – or that the mediation may remain within the same language, variety and register. Often, in the process of mediating a text in this way, one needs to substantially manipulate and adapt the text and the way concepts are expressed in it, not just 'transfer' the content. This is one of the reasons descriptor scales for strategies were developed.

Mediation is also one way in which users/learners are encouraged to give a response to creative texts (including literature) in an educational setting. The CEFR Companion Volume offers two scales here: for *Expressing a personal response to creative texts* and the higher level *Analysis and criticism of creative texts*. Here the mediation is of a different kind, from the world of the imagination, reflecting the fact that in education and everyday life, reading a good book or seeing a good film tends to lead to talking about it. This emphasises the fact that the mediation of texts in the classroom does not need to be limited to texts used in class. Users/learners can be asked to read stories, read different versions of a common story (e.g. fairy story), research a topic on the web, and bring their findings to the class.

Recognition of the cultural and metalinguistic value of cross-linguistic textual mediation activities from an educational point of view has led to their introduction into the curricula of several European countries since the CEFR appeared in 2001, including Switzerland, Germany, Austria, Italy and Greece. In addition, mediation tasks are now being introduced into national examinations in some of these countries (Dendrinos, 2006, 2013; KMK, 2003, 2012 shown in Kolb, 2016; Piribauer *et al.*, 2015; Stathopoulou, 2013).

6.4.2 Mediating communication

The aim of mediating communication is to facilitate understanding, independently of sociocultural, or sociolinguistic or personal differences. The mediator tries to have a positive influence on aspects of the dynamic relationship between the participants. Understanding the other requires an effort of translation from one's own perspective to the other, keeping both perspectives in mind; sometimes people need a third person or a third space in order to achieve this. Sometimes there are delicate situations, tensions or even disagreements that need to be faced in order to create the conditions for any understanding and hence any communication. The skills involved are relevant to negotiation, pedagogy and dispute resolution, but also to everyday social and/ or workplace interactions. The CEFR Companion Volume provides two descriptor scales for this type of meditation: *Facilitating pluricultural space* and *Facilitating communication in delicate situations and disagreements*. The former relates to mobilisation of intercultural competences – the capacity to deal with 'otherness' to identify similarities and differences and to build on known and unknown cultural features, etc. – and symbolic competences (see Section 6.2.3 above) in order to provide a space in which people feel comfortable, to enable communication and collaboration. The latter concerns the type of mediation associated with professional mediators, arbitration, counselling etc. – but in an everyday sense. The user/learner may informally try to resolve a misunderstanding, delicate situation or disagreement between speakers. They are not concerned with their own viewpoint, but seek balance in the representation of the viewpoints of the other parties involved in the discussion, helping them to understand each other's positions.

In addition, mediating communication can involve acting as a linguistic intermediary between two parties who lack a common language. Here, Backus *et al.* point to extensive research that indicates that:

> ... lay interpreters can in fact achieve successful understanding in these situations, despite sometimes limited linguistic resources. They have been observed to apply, where necessary, the same productive communication strategies known from learner language research and also found in the use of the modes described above, including the creation of nonce words, borrowing and code-switching where possible, and by engaging in intensive negotiations of meaning with the other interlocutors. They have also been found to openly intervene in the course of the on-going interaction to prevent or solve disturbances and failures of communication and to help interlocutors achieve their goals. (Backus *et al.*, 2013: 203)

It is not difficult to imagine situations in today's diverse classrooms in which such lay interpretation becomes necessary. One can also imagine tasks which involve the L2 and L3 in situations in which two additional languages are being taught. Tasks reflecting this type of activity are already appearing in oral exams in Germany (between L1 and L2: KMK, 2003: 46, 49; KMK, 2012: 37, 118, shown in Kolb, 2016: 49–52) and Austria (between L2 and L3: Piribauer *et al.*, 2015).

6.4.3 Mediating concepts

Mediating concepts is more related to the co-construction of meaning and to mediation in a pedagogic sense, with particular relevance to the educational and professional domains. There are two types of mediation involved here, firstly social or relational mediation (establishing conditions) on the one hand and cognitive mediation (developing ideas) on the other. This distinction echoes Halliday's 'basic distinction between an ideational (representational, referential, cognitive) and an interpersonal (expressive-conative, social, evocative) function of language' (1975: 52) that embodies 'all use of language to express social and personal relations' (Halliday, 1973: 41), that were discussed in Section 3.4. As Halliday shows, these two aspects (cognitive, interpersonal) never appear in isolation: they are woven together in context through the third element of Halliday's scheme: text (Halliday, 1973).

In education or professional training, there are two contexts for this type of mediation: collaborative small groups on the one hand, and whole class/plenary on the other. The CEFR Companion Volume presents two pairs of scales for these four categories as shown in Table 6.2.

Collaboration in small groups is immediately relevant to the AoA since it increases learners' sources of mediation (van Lier, 2004; Walqui, 2006). Their first recourse is existing knowledge, internalised strategies and private speech, the second is being assisted by an expert

Table 6.2 Descriptor scales for mediating concepts

	Establishing conditions	Developing ideas
Collaborating in a group	Facilitating collaborative interaction with peers	Collaborating to construct meaning
Leading group work	Managing interaction	Encouraging conceptual talk

Source: Council of Europe, 2018: 118.

(e.g. parent or teacher, the classic scaffolding role), the third is collaborative interaction with equals, and the fourth is themselves mediating to a less capable peer. Mediating for another student 'is an opportunity to verbalise, clarify and extend their own knowledge of the subject matter' (Walqui, 2006: 168).

However, learners do not automatically know how to mediate. Indeed, mediation requires awareness-raising for both teachers and learners. In their pioneering research into discourse in small groups, Barnes and Todd (1977) found that the more successful groups were those who *facilitated the collaborative interaction with peers* and thought to 'bring in contributions from others' (Barnes & Todd, 1977: 43). As Webb (2009) discusses, students do not automatically know how to work well together, how to explain, reason, and engage in reciprocal questioning – that is how to *collaborate to construct meaning*. Teachers also do not automatically know how to prepare students for collaborative co-construction, how to assign to groups, and effectively *manage the interaction* in them. Webb cites examples of the fact that teachers who have received communication skills training 'asked more questions and carried out more mediated-learning activities (e.g. challenging students to provide reasons, highlighting inconsistencies in student thinking, prompting students to focus on particular issues, and asking tentative questions to suggest alternative perspectives' (Webb, 2009: 16). In turn the students of these teachers gave more elaborated explanations, themselves asked more questions, built on each other's contributions – that is *encouraged conceptual talk*.

Experience from piloting the descriptors during the development of the CEFR Companion Volume suggests that, given transparent descriptors, both learners and teachers can become more aware of mediation competences and strategies. One teacher wrote: 'We saw how the participants moved from needing to clarify and confirm mutual understanding to interacting more effortlessly by building upon each other's ideas and presenting one's own ideas to invoke discussion.' Another commented: 'The benefits gained from the activities were considerably beneficial to the students in organising collaborative work, exploiting a task, taking roles to perform it well and self-evaluating it. Basically, the role of the descriptors was to keep them on track, reminding them that they had to complete the task following certain strategies that would underpin the essential role of interaction. The use of the descriptors taught them that they should cooperate with their group members in order to take ideas further and develop them. The whole endeavour was a challenge for them that raised their awareness of collaborating with each other and co-developed ideas'.

6.4.4 The role of mediation in the AoA

Collaborative action, that allows one to make sense of things and structure learning through language, is accomplished through the mediation of the mental processes involved in the completion of a (complex) task (Piccardo, 2012a). However, in language education, it is clear that a vision of this type will collide with the traditional, static idea that a language is learnt through the memorisation of linguistic elements that may later be used to perform an activity. The classic orientation of language teaching, focused on the learning of grammatical and lexical knowledge, is not compatible with theories of learning based on the formation of concepts. In fact, grammar rules, the way they are usually explained in textbooks, are often not an effective vehicle for developing concepts. The alternative view is that 'language emerges from social and cultural activity and only later becomes an object of reflection' (Kramsch, 2000: 134). This corresponds to the AoA, where the user/learner is seen first and foremost as a social agent taking part in school life, buying things, participating in conversations, using all kinds of signs to mediate these activities, and later interiorising the signs in order to structure cognitive processes. Mediation is therefore crucial in the individual's psycho-cognitive development precisely because semiotic mediation is central to all aspects of knowledge (co)construction.

This view completely contradicts traditional theories of SLE, which explain language learning as a cognitive process that happens at the level of the individual, later put into practice in a social context. Such a vision relies upon a separation of language itself and language use: language is seen as a thing apart, separate from both the individual and the social context. 'Language can be studied *in* its social context, but language itself [in this traditional vision] is seen as a system of arbitrary signs or symbols that are given social existence through their reference to a context which is itself outside of language' (Kramsch, 2000: 133). Internalizing another 'mediational system' (Kramsch, 2000: 695) in turn has a powerful impact on the way people communicate with others, the way they think and eventually on the identity construction process (Lantolf & Pavlenko, 2000).

Introducing mediation descriptors in the curriculum supports a process of autonomous further development among teachers: a focus on mediation facilitates a dynamic vision of language learning that encourages freedom from barriers among and within languages through language integration, multiliteracies and multimodalities. In turn the awareness-raising process that these steps imply can enhance both cognitive mediation and social mediation. In class this means, for example, using resources in different languages as support for producing artefacts in a target language. It means students researching resources in a variety of languages and discussing them together in a collaborative group, before producing a report or display. That discussion and those reports/displays may take place in one or more than one languages. The process can be taken a stage further by introducing a plurilingual paper in school-leaving tests. This is the case with an (optional) new oral paper in the Austrian professional baccalaureate, through which learners can receive a certificate of plurilingualism (Piribauer *et al.*, 2015). In this oral, among other tasks, the user/learner relays information from L1 source texts in their L2 and L3 respectively, and then mediates a conversation between speakers of their L2 and L3. In the Greek national KPG examination (Dendrinos, 2006, 2013; Stathopoulou, 2013) users/learners take information from a source text in L1 in order to write a text in a different genre in the L2 (English) in order to fulfil a defined mission.

Mediation becomes an individual and social meaning-making, cognition-development process, which finds in the action-oriented approach its methodological realisation. It is to a more practical perspective that we now turn in our next chapter. Before we do, however, let us first consider the way in which the different aspects we have discussed in this chapter coalesce in a powerful argument for inclusive education to support social justice.

6.5 Mediation, Plurilingualism/Pluriculturalism and Inclusive Education for All

Mediation and plurilingualism/pluriculturalism combine in a plurilanguaging approach in the AoA and offer a new impulse to language policy, particularly in the form of education for democratic citizenship advocated by, for example Byram (2008) and Byram and Wagner (2017). The sources for many of the descriptors for mediation, especially for mediating communication, were associated with that theme. In talking about the action-oriented part of his framework for intercultural citizenship, Byram (2008) refers to an early version of what later became the Council of Europe's framework of competence for democratic culture (CDC) (Barrett, 2016), which defined some of the capacities for action as shown in the left hand column

Table 6.3 Capacity for action in relation to democratic citizenship

- The capacity to live with others, to cooperate, to construct and implement joint projects, to take responsibilities;	- *Facilitating pluricultural space* - *Facilitating collaborative interaction with peers* - *Collaborating to construct meaning* - *Encouraging conceptual talk* - *Goal-oriented cooperation* - *Cooperating* - *Sociolinguistic appropriateness*
- The capacity to resolve conflicts with the principles of democratic law, in particularly the two fundamental principles of calling upon a third person not involved in the conflict, and of open debate to hear the parties in dispute and try to arrive at the truth	- *Acting as intermediary in informal situations (with friends and colleagues)* - *Facilitating communication in delicatesituations and disagreements*
- The capacity to take part in public debate, to argue and choose in a real-life situation	- *Informal discussion (with friends)* - *Formal discussion (meetings)* - *Sustained monologue: Putting a case (e.g. in debate)*
(Audiger, 1998 cited in Byram, 2008: 184)	(Council of Europe, 2018)

Source: After Audiger, 1998/Byram, 2008: 184.

of Table 6.3. Relevant descriptor scales from the CEFR Companion Volume are shown on the right.

As mentioned in Chapter 2, the CDC Framework itself elaborates 20 competences listed under the four main headings: values, attitudes, skills, plus knowledge and critical understanding. Complementing these two developments are parallel projects concerning the language of schooling (Goullier *et al.*, 2016) and the linguistic integration of migrants (Beacco *et al.*, 2017).

It is not a coincidence that the Council of Europe projects to produce the CDC Framework and the CEFR Companion Volume both took place at more or less the same time. The massively increased linguistic and cultural diversity in our societies, the waning of traditional, fixed reference points and boundaries in favour of the liquid modernity we discussed in Section 1.2 and 6.1 represent at the same time a serious challenge – but also a great opportunity for a revitalisation of language education, and the connections between language education and the wider aims of education. This is at the forefront of a new paradigm that stresses interconnection, interdependence and creative thinking. As we commented in Sections 1.2.1 and 6.1.2 – and also in discussing the difference between the prefixes 'multi-' and 'pluri-' – the societal reaction to the profound social changes taking place situates itself along the continuum going from acceptance and interest to rejection and marginalisation, the latter often disguised as a 'live and let live'. As Balboni (2015) points out, there is a considerable difference between distrust of otherness and empathy, between living side by side in isolated siloes or living together, between tolerance – provided you are quiet – and interest (Balboni, 2015).The Council of

Europe's guide *From Linguistic Diversity to Plurilingual Education: Guide for the Development of Language Education Policies in Europe* puts the connection between plurilingual education and democratic citizenship as follows:

> The development of plurilingualism is not simply a functional necessity: it is also an essential component of democratic behaviour. Recognition of the diversity of speakers' plurilingual repertoires should lead to acceptance of linguistic differences: respect for the linguistic rights of individuals and groups in their relations with the state and linguistic majorities, respect for freedom of expression, respect for linguistic minorities, respect for the least commonly spoken and taught national languages, respect for language diversity in inter-regional and international communication. Language education policies are intimately connected with education in the values of democratic citizenship because their purposes are complementary: language teaching, the ideal *locus* for intercultural contact, is a sector in which education for democratic life in its intercultural dimensions can be included in education systems. (Beacco & Byram, 2007a: 36)

The executive version of the guide summarises the reasoning as follows:

- *language rights are part of human rights*: education policies should facilitate the use of all varieties of languages spoken by the citizens of Europe, and the recognition of other people's language rights by all; the resolution of social conflicts is in part dependent on recognition of language rights;
- *the exercise of democracy and social inclusion depends in part on language education policy*: the capacity and opportunity to use one's full linguistic repertoire is crucial to participation in democratic and social processes and therefore to policies of social inclusion;
- *economic or employment opportunities for the individual and the development of human capital in a society depend in part on language education policy*: individual mobility for economic purposes is facilitated by plurilingualism; the plurilingualism of a workforce is a crucial part of human capital in a multilingual marketplace, and a condition for the free circulation of goods, information and knowledge;
- *individual plurilingualism is a significant influence on the evolution of a European identity*: since Europe is a multilingual area in its entirety and in any given part, the sense of belonging to Europe and the acceptance of a European identity is dependent on the ability to interact and communicate with other Europeans using the full range of one's linguistic repertoire;

- *plurilingualism is plural*: because of the variation of multilingualism in different parts of Europe, the plurilingualism of individuals has to be appropriate to the area where they live; there is no preferred or recommended model of plurilingualism and the plurilingualism of the individual may change with mobility and throughout lifelong learning; plurilingualism is not only a matter of competence but also an attitude of interest in and openness towards languages and language varieties of all kinds;
- *plurilingualism is possible*: the potential for all individuals to become actually plurilingual is proven; the technical capacity for developing plurilingualism is available in language teaching methodology, and already realised in practice even though it is still not widespread; the Council of Europe's *Common European Framework of Reference for Languages*, its *European Language Portfolio* and other technical as well as legal instruments already provide the basis required; the opportunity to develop one's plurilingualism should and can be made available to citizens of European education systems and in the context of lifelong learning;
- *plurilingual education is practical*: education policies, curriculum patterns, teaching methods exist which permit the re-consideration of existing concepts of first, second, third etc. language, and the development of a plurilingual competence which enables individuals to acquire whatever language they need or are interested in at a given point in time;
- *a common discourse for the discussion and, where appropriate, co-ordination of language education policies is needed*: the purpose of this *Guide* is to provide the means of developing a common approach to language education policy development, but not a common policy since every situation needs its particular policy. (Beacco & Byram, 2007b: no page number.)

Plurilingual and pluricultural education is thus a major policy aim in Europe. The title of the conference that launched the CEFR Companion Volume was: *Building Inclusive Societies through Enriching Plurilingual and Pluricultural Education at a Grassroots Level: the Role of the CEFR Companion Volume*. The concern for inclusive societies and for inclusive, quality education for all connect with the issue of social justice and marginalised languages and cultures. As Byram & Wagner put this issue, citing other scholars in the USA, it is 'clear that [language education] has a role in education for social justice, as has been argued in the United States for some years. ... There are important parallels between fostering social justice and developing intercultural citizenship. Both concepts promote criticality in that educators enable students to reflect critically on language, discourse, and culture with regard to power and inequality' (Byram & Wagner, 2018: 147). In Section 6.2.2 we discussed Byram's (2008) framework for intercultural citizenship, and its operationalisation in a number of projects (Byram *et al.*, 2018) that demonstrate a link between language education and education for citizenship and between intercultural citizenship and the development of criticality.

Plurilingual and pluricultural education is an inclusive program in pursuit of social justice and openness. The aim of a such a holistic approach to language education is to integrate the approaches taken in the language of schooling, heritage languages, minority languages and modern foreign languages into one coherent policy that values and encourages users/learners to themselves value linguistic and cultural diversity as a source of enrichment and awareness and as a window on a wider world.

As the oldest and largest pan-European institution with 47 member states, the Council of Europe's mission is to uphold human rights, democracy and the rule of law in Europe. It has no power to make laws but, it does have the power to enforce international agreements that member states have reached on various topics. It is no surprise, thus, that at the heart of the Council of Europe stands the European Court of Human Rights, which enforces the European Convention on Human Rights. As we have suggested above, the aim of providing inclusive access to quality education to *all* children and of supporting *all* individuals to develop their potential and thrive is at the core of the Council's concerns. In this respect, the amount of engagement to this mission is extraordinary. One example is the work done to support marginalised communities and languages like the Romani with resources and guidance documents that help their language and culture to be valued and their community members to feel part of the European cultural space. To see the range of initiatives related to language policy and inclusive, quality education, the reader is invited to visit www.coe.int/en/web/language-policy.

Notes

(1) Kramsch states elsewhere that she is merely following convention since: 'While in the U.S. the adjective multilingual/multicultural applies both to individuals and to societies, in Europe it applies only to societies, and plurilingual/pluricultural is applied to individuals' (Kramsch, 2008: 390). We hope this section demonstrates that this description of the distinction is oversimplified.

(2) Brian North, Tim Goodier, Enrica Piccardo, Maria Stathopoulou.

7 The Action-oriented Approach

7.1 The AoA: An All Embracing Perspective

We started this book by underlining how the action-oriented approach (AoA) shaped itself through a bottom up process rather than being first theorised and then translated into practice as has often been the case in the development of second/foreign language methodologies. This process has proved very enriching as in a sense it has allowed for a spiralling of practical implementation and shaping of the approach on the one hand, and further deeper conceptualisation of the tenets of the AoA on the other. Going back to Kurt Lewin's famous aphorism, 'there is nothing more practical than a good theory' (1952: 169), we could say that there is nothing more theoretical than a good practice. The possibility of building on the sparse elements that were offered in the CEFR to shape the AoA in practice, and the reflective process necessary to refine and figure out its different aspects and implications, provided a solid basis for the collective intelligence that has since informed the development of the AoA itself. All this paved the way for the development of the CEFR Companion Volume which completed the CEFR descriptive scheme with a wealth of descriptors mainly for mediation and plurilingual/pluricultural competences, providing the AoA with crucial resources and guidance.

Throughout the previous chapters we have demonstrated how this iterative process, which has helped shape the AoA bottom-up, has been nurtured by advances in theoretical reflection around language education and how the AoA has in turn contributed to fleshing out some of these advances by anticipating issues related to innovation in language education at the classroom level. In this chapter we will bring the different concepts together and use them as a basis for explaining and discussing the methodological and pedagogic characteristics of the AoA. This in turn will help us move into the second half of the chapter where practical know-how and examples will be presented.

7.1.1 Centrality of the learner/user/individual: The learner as a social agent

The mantra that lessons need to be learner-centred has been repeated over and over again in the field of language education, from textbooks to conferences, from methodological discussion to development of technology-enhanced resources. However, in the best case, this 'learner' remained a very neutral, non-individualised being, with only very few voices highlighting the limitations and dangers of such a view (Coïaniz, 2001, being one of the first and clearest). In the worst case, this shift remained at the level of good intentions stated in the different documents and resources, without really changing the respective roles of learners and teachers, since the learner-centredness limited itself largely to increasing the frequency of pair and group work to make lessons more interactive.

The introduction of the social agent as the core feature of the AoA represents a real shift away both from this type of trivial learner-centredness and from a banal vision of the learner. As Puren (2009a) points out, by considering learners as social agents, the AoA chooses the semantic field of 'agir' (acting, doing) as made visible in the terms 'act', 'agent', 'to act' 'action' used repeatedly in the CEFR. Now, this is not without consequences: 'A new semantic network always covers a new conceptual reality and thus implies a new representation by the actors that experience this new reality. The new reality with which the teaching/learning of language-culture is faced is a complex reality' (Bourguignon, 2006: 61, our translation). There is a shift from 'learning' and 'learner' to 'use' and 'user,' and to 'agent in a social context', 'social agent'. This implies a movement away from the idea of bringing the outside reality into the class as with CLT – which implied preparation for a future reality – towards opening the class to the outside world, to the society. It is not just the learner, but the actual user, or, to be precise, the social agent that is targeted.

Seeing the language learner as a social agent implies a series of important consequences:

- The learner acts in a society, be it the class or outside (the barriers between the two are increasingly blurred).
- Action is what characterises learning in the same way as it characterises our everyday life in society.
- The class is an authentic social milieu where different individuals act together.
- Acting together is what we are increasingly doing when we are involved in projects. In the AoA project work is core since action-oriented tasks are indeed projects.

- Documents and artefacts produced by learners are authentic in the sense that they serve the purpose, respect conventions and genres and are the end product of the actions, exactly as happens in projects.
- Project work is by its very nature work in progress. Guidelines are helpful but what is crucial is the collective intelligence, the capacity to co-act and co-construct and the learning process that this entails.

As Puren points out 'for the first time learners are considered, in their learning activity and in the very space and time of their learning, as social actors in the full sense of the term' (2009a: 123, our translation) a reason why he suggests referring to the new action-oriented perspective as '*perspective de l'agir social* [social action perspective]' (2009a: 123, our translation). By being called to act in an authentic social milieu such as the classroom, to pursue authentic goals and produce authentic materials, individuals are automatically very far away from the neutral, unidentified 'learners' that characterised CLT. In the communicative approach, learners had a limited responsibility and an equally reduced range of choices. The point was to be able to function in everyday situations, performing speech acts that enabled communication. This characterises the communicative approach both in its weak 'classic' version and in its strong version, i.e. TBLT. Tasks in the AoA, on the other hand, are projects and as such they require real problem-solving and decision-making skills that enable actions here and now.

The role of the language changes in the AoA and consequently the way the language is learned changes too. This means taking distance from a language learning process organised around a spiralling progression of language functions (and relevant speech acts) and notions – let alone grammatical items – embedded within communicative situations or tasks, with the idea that performing those speech acts in communication would entail acquisition of the necessary language. In this vision, the adding of new communicative situations and tasks would generate the need to perform new speech acts and thus ensure expansion of proficiency in the language. But the AoA also involves taking a distance from the alternative – but fundamentally similar – entry point, the thematic organisation of contents, which is still currently proposed both in CLT and TBLT. In this case the theme, for instance 'At the restaurant', or 'The problem of pollution' is used as a frame to provide thematic coherence throughout the teaching unit. The different 'authentic' materials (very often not really authentic, but rather fake-authentic) are chosen within the same thematic area, but the logic is always that of helping students to perform increasingly demanding speech acts and, by doing that within communicative tasks, to learn the relevant language. The underlying vision of language education here is still rather linear: the progression through speech acts and new structures is the driving force of the pedagogic action and the process of increasing proficiency.

However, speech acts are only meaningful if they are accomplished within actions that are carried out in a social context. 'Each act of language use is set in the context of a particular situation within one of the domains (spheres of action or areas of concern) in which social life is organised' (Council of Europe, 2001: 45). With the AoA, learning is conceived as a form of *use* and the educational domain is listed among 'the broad sectors of social life in which social agents operate' (Council of Europe, 2001: 10). Finally tasks in which learners/users/ social agents are involved are authentic in the sense that they span life both within and outside the classroom as the examples given in the CEFR – for instance playing a game of cards, or preparing a class newspaper through group work (Council of Europe, 2001: 10) – show. It is no longer a question of preparation for the future, it is the idea of using the language *now* in a real-life scope, in real situations, with other real social agents. Furthermore, the world becoming increasingly globalised and interconnected, these other social agents may be very distant both geographically and in terms of language(s) and culture(s), so the users/learners/social agents need to be able to act with these other social agents as well. This explains why task-projects in the AoA should integrate a plurilingual/pluricultural perspective.

The perspective outlined above suggests an epistemological change not just an advance in relation to the previous methodologies, namely CLT in both its weak and strong versions. As Bourguignon underlines (2006), it is a move from the 'how?' to the 'why?' It is a total switch, from describing the object language and *how* it works (in linguistics and then in applied linguistics) and how it is used in practice, to reflecting on *why* the language is used, to reach what goals, for what purposes, and why precisely in those particular forms. CLT implies that learners acquire some knowledge in the class to use it later in real life, so 'action' in this case only serves to learn the language at the service of future Action with a capital A in the real world. It is usually a simplified, reduced version of the real thing and action happens within clearly defined paths. The AoA on the contrary *is* the real thing not just a mockup of future real life: the learner/user/social agent engages in actions which are authentic and real *here and now*. As Bourguignon says, referring to what the Italian philosopher Gianbattista Vico theorised at the beginning of the 18th century (1708), the individual thus finds again the possibility of giving a sense to their experiences of the '*monde de la vie* [world of life]', by making intelligible all the multiple interactions between knowledge and action, understanding and doing.

It is the reunification of the object and the method; it is, in a word, a complex perspective where the object of learning is not separated from the subject who is learning, as Morin aptly points out in his work (1990/2005). This dialogic perspective that Morin proposes throughout his work is particularly suitable to explain the perspective adopted by the AoA:

> The epistemological shift that accompanies the new perspective (the move from a positivist knowledge-based epistemology to an episte-mology of complexity) does not translate into a conceptual break, but rather into the implementation of conceptual 'dialogic' networks, to use E. Morin's expression, that is to say epistemologies which, even though they are opposed, do not exclude each other but rather complete and therefore enrich each other. (Bourguignon, 2006: 63, our translation)

In fact it is not a question of separating let alone opposing action and communication, or object of study and learner, or school tasks and real-life tasks, or competence and knowledge. It is, on the contrary, an integrated vision that gives the AoA its coherence. It is the respective roles and responsibilities of the learner/user/social agent and the teacher that prevents any disjunction or opposition.

7.1.2 Strategic and reflective role of the learner

As we have just seen, learning is constructed around action. Learners/users/social agents are called upon to act and this action implies strategic activation of competences in order to achieve a particular outcome. Now, by their nature, actions are contextualised and targeted to a goal, even in the case when this goal has no prac-tical or utilitarian function. Furthermore, actions have a goal other than language. We read in order to collect information, to under-stand a problem, to know how to prepare a cake, to be in contact with somebody we are close to, or simply for pleasure, in the case of reading as a leisure activity. We speak and write to inform or persuade somebody, to ask for help, to defend ourselves or others, and so on.

All these actions, and the pursuit of these goals imply more or less 'language' as we saw in Chapter 5, when we discussed the role of tasks in the CEFR. For instance, it is a very different endeavour, in terms of language use, to assembly an IKEA furniture as opposed to going out for lunch with a group of new colleagues and discussing a prospective project. Moreover, in both these cases things become more or less challenging according to the number of people involved and the conditions under which the action is situated, let alone the question of needing to function in one or more than one language. But whatever the variability, or precisely because of this variability, the language users/learners seen as social agents need to strategise their handling of the situation, estimate their resources and plan their action. This sometimes needs to be done under time pressure, but the process is basically always the same only very compressed; it even perhaps becomes automatic at some point. As the term *social* agent indicates, we are concerned with somebody who is interacting with others, who is part of a community. Now, not only is this something that certainly needs to be considered as part of the strategising process, it is also a key aspect of the AoA and of the new role of the user/learner.

In the short paragraph stating the approach adopted in the CEFR, users and learners of a language viewed as 'social agents' are described as 'members of society who have tasks (not exclusively language-related) to accomplish in a given set of circumstances, in a specific environment and within a particular field of action' (Council of Europe, 2001: 9). And the activities in which acts of speech occur 'form part of a wider social context, which alone is able to give them their full meaning' (Council of Europe, 2001: 9). As Puren (2009b) aptly reminds us, we move from speech acts that are forms of language action *on others*, to social action, which is a form of collective action done *with others*. And this action is done in the class, which implies considering the class as a society in its own right. The class, continues Puren (2009b) can be seen as an authentic learning enterprise:

> It is the case that a language-culture classroom is by nature an authentic 'learning enterprise', and that the collective learning of a foreign language-culture requires the strategic implementation of competences such as the ability to work in group, to take risks, and not only to admit one's own and others' errors but also to take advantage of it to the benefit of everybody, to face the unknown, the uncertainty and complexity, to reflect upon one's own activities (metacognition) and productions (conceptualization), to self-assess … : all competences which are precisely those that are now required from a collaborator who is not a simple 'employee', but a real actor within his/her enterprise. (Puren, 2009b: 156, our translation)

The expression 'taking risks' is key to understanding the new perspective that the AoA advocates. In a sense, one of the few common threads of the different methodologies has been that of avoiding learners taking too much risk. This was done either by having them repeat and somehow naturally acquire content, or vice versa by explaining exactly all details and elements of the language beforehand. These approaches aligned very well with a linear view of language learning. With the AoA, which embraces a complex view of language learning, the opposite position is taken: purposeful, measured risk-taking becomes pivotal for learners' success. Needless to say risk-taking and strategising go hand in hand. In project work just as in any real-life endeavour, learners/users/social agents (both individually and in groups) consider the expected outcome, evaluate and mobilise the different types of resources that they can draw upon, plan and strategise ahead, act, evaluate the results, if necessary adjust their action and finally evaluate the entire process in a reflection phase which is key for the learning process itself and for informing future actions. The process is a spiralling one.

The counterpoint of risk-taking is reflection. Reflecting is not just an add-on, it is the crucial element that completes the circle, besides being the real moment when new knowledge is assimilated: if learners/users/social agents are aware that there is a constructive reflection phase ahead, with an opportunity to revise and adjust design and content, including the appropriation of the language, they are less afraid of taking risks.

In this process, different elements and steps are involved, which sometimes may seem to take a divergent path. But in reality learners acting as social agents have a clear vision of the scope of all their actions, even those that to external viewers may seem unrelated, and of the way to get there. Learners are also aware of their strengths and weaknesses, know how to adapt to the situation and how to further adapt, if necessary, in order to be successful. This is what helps them withstand – and build on – the transitory phases of chaos and unbalance, which as complexity theory explains, are inevitable in order to get to a new phase of balance, which in turn is a transitory balance that is on the verge of starting a new process. Learning is thus precisely to be seen as change over time, as complexity theory (DST) reminds us.

This strategic vision is diametrically opposed to that of the learner as someone who is carried along passively and automatically trans-ferring unconscious learning to communication situations that require active use of the language. This vision represents a significant step towards learner autonomy. Responsibility is transferred from the teacher to the learner, who takes charge of his or her own learning experiences. It is clear that this new role of the learner/user/social agent calls for a deeply modified role of the teacher, however, it is one that is not diminished, quite the contrary, as we will see in the next section.

7.1.3 The informed reflective practitioner: The strategic role of the teacher

As we have just seen, the learner/user/social agent is called upon to mobilise their resources in order to act, and to maximise the chances of being successful in their actions. This is a delicate and challenging process that requires guidance, accompaniment and support. This apparent contradiction, i.e. that one does not become autonomous automatically but needs to be educated to autonomy, was already highlighted long ago (Holec, 1981). In the case of the AoA, it is even clearer that making sure that the learner/user/social agent is at ease with what is expected of them is crucial as it is precisely from this 'buy-in' that the success of task performance depends and *a fortiori* of the learning process itself. Thus, it is clear that the teacher is called to a new and more challenging – but also much more rewarding – role. The shift in the role of the learner that the AoA and the notion of social agent implies a corresponding, symmetrical shift in the role of the teacher. It is no longer a question of passing on knowledge or exercising skills. It is not even a question of being able to correctly plan teaching units based on a linguistic progression. Even less is it the idea of simply 'applying' or 'implementing' a curriculum or programme developed by someone else. The teacher is called upon to enact the curriculum (Graves, 2008): to create the conditions for the social agent to act effectively and be successful, and thus ensure that effective development and learning can take place. The role is quite similar to that of a coach of a sports team. That does not eliminate the need for many of the teaching procedures and techniques that teachers feel comfortable with and habitually use. What changes is the broader perspective and role that they have to adopt. Teachers too need to move towards a perspective of action, rather than of instruction.

Some of the verbs associated with this perspective are, for instance:

- to observe, analyse, orient, and rectify, the process of completing the tasks;
- to provide, make available or construct, according to circumstance, the tools which are necessary for this completion. (Denyer, 2009: 154, our translation)

It is for the teacher to create *learning situations* (Piccardo, 2015) by proposing, and encouraging project work, which is at the basis of real-life, action-oriented tasks, and to embrace the complexity that this type of work entails. If we conceive of language learning as a form of social action, we need to create the conditions for this to happen, so the social agent is engaged in a real project in an authentic environment, which is the class.

Puren schematises in an interesting way the possible intersection between the class and society outside the class, and his diagram is given as Figure 7.1. This shows not only the overlapping and intersection of the two but also the way in which the in-between space of the overlap constitutes the fertile ground for conception and realisation of actions/project work as well as the place for the teacher's scaffolding of the learner/user/social agent's learning process.

As a conclusion to this modelling, Puren reminds us of the core distinction between the conception of a project, which is the

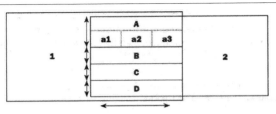

1. Society as the field for the completion of real life action (action in use)
2. The class as the field for the completion of tasks (action for learning)
A. The class as a context for scaffolding by the teacher, for the processes of learning linguistic, cultural and methodological knowledge, skills and know-how which are necessary for the student not only to complete the different actions (real and simulated) but also to draw maximum benefit in terms of learning. In relation to the completion of these actions, the scaffolding may take place before (a1: *preparation*), during (a2: support) or after (a3: exploitation) the completion of the action.
B. The class as a context for the *conception* of actions (real or simulated).
C. The class as a context for simulated actions.
D. The class as a context for real actions.

Figure 7.1 Intersections between class and society
Source: Puren, 2009a: 127, also in Puren, 2006.

responsibility of the learners/users/social agents themselves, and the preparation of the project, which is the responsibility of the teacher. Whilst the conception aims to plan the actions and in a recursive way refine and adjust if necessary the objects of the project itself, the preparation aims to identify (and make available) the different resources needed for the project. The teacher then needs to provide the necessary scaffolding during the project and guide and support the follow up reflection phase. In turn, accompanying and supporting this recursive process helps the teacher in their understanding of the learning process of the learner/user/social agent and of their progress, which then itself in turn makes him/her more at ease with and effective in the planning and scaffolding process. This is fully coherent with a complex vision of the class as a CAS where the different individuals involved (here learners and teacher) learn how to navigate necessary periods of chaos that bring them new learning (progress over time).

As we will see, this new vision does not require the teacher to throw away the set of techniques that constitute their 'tools of the trade', it is rather that they should use them purposefully and at the right moment. Finally, in the same way that the learner/user of a language is seen as a social agent working in a community, teachers are also increasingly seen as a community of practice, as interacting and collaborating with each other. This process is being greatly facilitated by support offered by the social nature of recent technological advances. Teachers increasingly constitute a 'learning community' based on the capacity of sharing, collaborating, self-assessing, reflecting and developing together in a recursive, lifelong process.

7.1.4 Project-oriented thinking and its implications

As we have discussed throughout the book, the AoA implies a paradigmatic and epistemological shift that is anchored in the new concept of the social agent and in 'action' as the core notion, the linchpin of the entire teaching and learning process. As we have just seen in the two previous sections, this shift requires a strategic attitude from both learners and teachers who are called upon to think ahead, specifically to think with the end goal in mind and plan backwards, identify and estimate their needs and available resources, and chunk down the work ahead into manageable, logically connected and incremental steps.

We saw in Chapter 4, when talking about the methodological dimension, that tasks in the AoA have a different, broader nature than tasks as they are usually interpreted in TBLT. We have also seen in Chapter 3 that different theories inform the AoA, which are broad in scope and which also go beyond the specific field of language education. Finally, we have just pointed out that in the AoA tasks need to be equated with projects and we will explain this further in Section 7.1.5. In relation to projects, we would like to stress with Puren that '[t]he idea of educating learners as social agents through the realisation by them of real social actions in a classroom that is conceived as an authentic mini-society is not new in general pedagogy: it is at the basis of what is called "project pedagogy"' (2009a: 126, our translation). He refers to Célestin Freinet as the most well-known representative of this type of pedagogy in France, but in other contexts the same type of tradition exists and has produced a precious body of knowledge from which SLE can take inspiration. This means that we can build on a solid tradition of knowledge and expertise, albeit developed in and for different disciplines.

The projects that learners are engaged in are rooted in reality, which gives to the project itself the three-dimensional nature that all real endeavours necessarily have. This means that the project management dimension is crucial for success. In particular the following elements need to be taken into consideration and applied in an iterative way:

- defining objectives and outcomes;
- planning within conditions and constraints;
- acting out what has been planned and reflecting on the actions;
- evaluating with clear success criteria at different phases of the project.

As we said, the final outcome, which involves some sort of product or artefact, is the key to setting the whole process in motion; it is the starting point of the backplanning process. Adopting this perspective is also the only way to ensure curriculum alignment, a core feature of the AoA, as we saw in Chapter 5.

Needless to say, one of the fundamental characteristics of social action is its dynamism and its adaptability to the context and situation. Thus, it is impossible for social agents to anticipate every contingency or to foresee the exact outcome of their actions, and indeed the ability to cope with the unforeseen is, as we saw in Section 2.3, a key aspect of a dynamic and humanistic definition of competence. Therefore, there is no contradiction between dealing with the unpredictability and the need for planning. Only, planning needs to be seen as a flexible and dynamic process, not as a straightjacket.

The main issue is to clearly define objectives and outcomes and then consider all the conditions and constraints within which learners as social agents are going to act. When it comes to defining objectives and outcomes, the descriptors of the CEFR and of the CEFR Companion Volume are particularly useful, not only because they are clearly organised by levels, which allows one to formulate objectives in a realistic way, within the range of possibilities that suit each learner, but above all because they are organised according the descriptive scheme, i.e. they provide a clear idea of:

- what a social agent is doing (descriptors of communicative activities of reception, production, interaction and mediation);
- how the social agent is performing activities (descriptors of linguistic, sociolinguistic and pragmatic competences), and
- which communication strategies the social agent relies/draws upon in performing the activities successfully (descriptors of reception, production, interaction and mediation strategies).

On top of this, the descriptive scheme helps one to keep in mind the general competences that are also mobilised during the action. Since, as the CEFR Companion Volume underlines, the general frame within which the social agent is operating is by nature plurilingual and pluricultural, he or she will acquire, in the course of the different actions, (further) plurilingual and pluricultural competences and thus modify his/her plurilingual/pluricultural profile.

The wealth of descriptors also allows for a modulation of objectives and sub-objectives. In fact getting to the end of a project is a challenging endeavour which is usually better broken down into steps or phases. These steps are also meant to pursue targeted objectives that are, in turn, functional to the main objectives of the final project. This process of breaking down a relatively long path necessary to successfully accomplish a complex project is essential for both the learner and the teacher, as it provides effective signposting of their respective actions and responsibilities.

The idea of dealing with conditions and constraints is also key to the project-oriented logic which the AoA calls for. Real life is always a

compromise between what one would like to accomplish and what it is possible to accomplish within a certain period of time, considering the different conditions and constraints that characterise the context where one has to work, as well as one's own strengths and weaknesses. Thus, the planning process is not only important as a way of signposting what will be done, but also as a moment of feed-forward reflection that anticipates issues and suitable solutions or adaptations. Again this way of proceeding is iterative, as adjustments and reorientations are typical of any project. Thus, the very process of accomplishing the project is a learning path which encompasses and goes beyond the dimension of language learning: it is educational in the broader sense of the term.

In addition to planning, the acting out of the different steps that will enable social agents to perform the culminating task and thus successfully complete the project, involve the symmetrical dimension to planning, that of reflecting. As we mentioned above, reflection is definitely not an add-on. Neither is it something happening exclusively at the very end of the project. It is, on the contrary, a recursive, awareness-raising, (self-)regulatory process that supports the social agent in his/her actions, risk-taking and learning processes. Exactly the same process applies to the teacher both in their guiding and/or accompanying role towards the learner/social agent, and in their own professional (self-)development over time. The reflection process does not always necessitate formal steps or formalised tools, it is very often an impromptu process done through personal, unstructured or even scribbled notes – or sometimes even just at the mental level. It is more the idea of creating a reflective habit that fosters self-regulation and other-regulation and self-confidence and eventually more effective autonomous learning. This does not mean that more formal end of project reflection is not useful, quite the contrary, this last type of reflection in fact further contributes to reinforcing and giving value to the reflective habit itself.

Finally, as we said, the idea is always that of planning with the end in mind and then proceeding backwards. This implies a circular relationship, a correspondence between objectives and outcomes. It also implies having clear in mind how one can say confidently enough that the objectives have been reached. For teachers this means establishing and clearly communicating success criteria very early in the process, something which helps learners/social agents to situate themselves in terms of competences and expectations and draw upon their strengths while, at the same time, working on their weaknesses. Again, the CEFR descriptors can help considerably with this process, especially as they are transparent, stand-alone criteria, which reduce to the minimum the inevitable subjectivity that any form of assessment implies, as we mentioned in Chapter 5. We will discuss this in further depth in Section 7.1.6, but before that let us turn to the action-oriented task to analyse some of its characteristics more closely.

7.1.5 Action-oriented real-life tasks/scenarios

Before we discuss tasks from a pedagogic point of view, let us go back to the passage of the CEFR which states the approach adopted, and the link between the AoA and tasks:

> The approach adopted here, generally speaking, is an action-oriented one in so far as *it views users and learners of a language primarily as 'social agents', i.e. members of society who have tasks* (not exclusively language-related) to accomplish in a given set of circumstances, in a specific environment and within a particular field of action. While acts of speech occur within language activities, these activities form part of a wider social context, which alone is able to give them their full meaning. *We speak of 'tasks' in so far as the actions are performed by one or more individuals strategically using their own specific competences to achieve a given result.* The action-based approach therefore also takes into account the cognitive, emotional and volitional resources and the full range of abilities specific to and applied by the individual as a social agent. (Council of Europe, 2001: 9, our emphasis)

The first part of the quotation stresses the social nature of the task, the second highlights the actions performed by the social agents seen as individuals and consequently the different aspects and resources that those individuals draw upon and at the same time develop while preparing for and performing tasks.

It is the interplay and the complementarity between the social action itself and the individual factors that the social agent involved in action mobilises that are key to the AoA. Both teachers and learners have to constantly bear in mind the need to operate at both levels – social and individual – simultaneously. In line with complexity theory we need to consider the two nested CAS (individual and class as community/society) and the interplay between them. Furthermore, we need to adopt the *both … and* position (Larsen-Freeman, 2017) that allows us to see at the same time two apparently contradictory poles as well as their interplay, something that Edgar Morin (1990/2005) considers essential to move towards an epistemology of complexity. Additionally, in line with sociocultural theory, we need to consider the different levels, starting with the level of immediate events, what Vygotsky calls the microgenetic domain, as this is where the mediated process of co-construction of meaning and concepts starts and unfolds.

The complex perspective that we need to adopt if we want to embrace the AoA is suggested by the CEFR when it talks about tasks:

> Task performance is a complex process, therefore, involving the strategic interplay of a range of learner competences and task-related factors. In responding to the demands of a task the language user or learner activates those general and communicative strategies which are most efficient for accomplishing the particular task. The user or learner naturally adapts, adjusts and filters task inputs, goals, conditions and constraints to fit his or her own resources, purposes and (in a language learning context) particular learning style. (Council of Europe, 2001: 159)

It is clear that the logic which informs the AoA is one that stresses, as a fundamental characteristic of social action, its dynamism and adaptability to ever-changing contexts and situations. This is at odds with the possibility for the social agent to anticipate every contingency or to foresee and plan the exact outcomes of his/her actions. Thus the task needs to be seen:

> As a tool for creating conditions conducive to social action ... the task is not a pretext for communication. Quite the opposite: effective communication is what enables social agents to be effective in completing a task and achieving a specific goal or goals. Communication plays such a central role that social agents will do whatever they can to communicate as effectively as possible. They will make choices, watch for reactions to these choices, and modulate their actions based on the reactions they observe. In fact, they will think before, during, and after the action. (Piccardo, 2014a: 38)

Needless to say, this is an ambitious educational goal and one which requires a high level of investment from the learner. Now, if this is what we want the learner as social agent to be willing to do, we need them to have an interest in investing in this. We need meaningful learning situations, some in which the learner can project themselves (Bourguignon, 2006: 67). While in the communicative logic the teacher constructed their action around a certain topic or text, based on their assumption of the learners' areas of interest, in the action-oriented logic, as Bourguignon (2006) points out, the learner is faced with a project, that implies realising what she calls 'a mission' which:

- *integrates* comprehension, interaction and production;
- *cannot be disconnected* from a context, from the interlocutors (speakers and co-speakers);
- *requires* taking a position. (2006: 67, emphasis by the author, our translation)

It is no longer the idea of putting the learner in a situation where he/she is faced with a topic – and possibly a related text – which will trigger some form of communication/language production. Within the project, in order to accomplish the mission, the learners/social agents will participate in exchanges following their assigned roles, in accordance with the goal of the communication concerned.

Working on a project, accomplishing a mission constitutes a complex endeavour, which necessarily needs to be subdivided into steps, and each of these steps will require performing some communicative activities (of reception, production, interaction or mediation, in any possible combination). But they all serve a more general aim: that of enabling the social agent to perform the action-oriented, culminating task.

The use of the term 'scenario' is very appropriate in the AoA, as it helps us keep in mind that, although the action-oriented task and its accomplishment is the end goal, this is only the last of a series of related steps, which together enable the social agent to be successful in his/her actions. The idea of adopting a scenario as the frame of action also facilitates embedding the different sub-tasks, which are less complex and more communicative in nature than the final culminating task, in a coherent meaningful sequence, so that each communicative activity, and even each and any moment where the needs occur for a short targeted preparation activity (what the CEFR refers to as pre-communicative pedagogic tasks), makes full sense. In fact, in a classroom learning situation, learners are not alone: the teacher is there to accompany them in this experience and to ensure that they have as many chances as possible to successfully complete the task. Thus, the teacher's role is not limited to proposing suitable, realistic tasks conducive to the learners' involvement and autonomy. The teacher must also anticipate which aspects of the task will pose difficulties, help the students to organise their work and choose resources, and even integrate brief periods of preparation and/or support when necessary, as well as some individualised work.

We can paraphrase the task definition of the CEFR (Council of Europe, 2001: 157), by saying that scenarios put learners/social agents in a situation which implies that they strategically activate specific knowledge and competences, with the aim of carrying out a series of purposeful targeted actions, which take place within a specific domain, and have a clearly defined goal and outcome. In this perspective, actions are really situated; not only do they make sense as they are not limited to rehearsing a linguistic structure within a more or less authentic context and manner with the aim of learning that structure, but also because they are logically chained together and learners can see – and contribute to – the goal of their actions, the learning path they are following.

Above all, the learners/social agents engage in a spiralling, recursive process in which they, on the one hand mobilise their competences (general and linguistic) and knowledge in actions – which in the sub-tasks or steps will often represent, as we said, the opportunity for the learner to engage in communicative language activities – and on the other hand they *develop* their competences and widen their knowledge in a bottom-up way starting precisely from the action, i.e. by doing. Needless to say, the language competences need to be seen in a broad perspective, including pragmatic and sociolinguistic/sociocultural competences. Thus, learners/social agents' cognitive and sociocultural capacities are put at the service of the action and in turn the situated action sparks learners' cognitive and sociocultural capacities.

We will see some examples of scenarios later in this chapter when we will exemplify possible ways of working practically in class with the AoA, but before that we need to analyse the role of assessment in this new perspective, and particularly how assessment is both influenced by the adoption of an action-oriented perspective on learning, and how it can contribute to making such a perspective more meaningful, coherent and effective.

7.1.6 Integrated view of assessment

As we mentioned in Sections 4.2.4 and 5.2.8, the position and function of assessment in the AoA has been profoundly modified. The change in perspective fostered by the AoA requires that:

> ... both the teacher and the learner have constant control over the teaching/learning process. The learner/social agent is able to set realistic objectives and pursue them. He or she is able to recognize his or her strengths and weaknesses; use the right strategies; and determine whether or not he or she has reached the level strived for. (Piccardo, 2014a: 43)

As we saw, this capacity needs to be built up through constant guidance from the teacher, as autonomy is not an innate characteristic of individuals but is rather acquired. It also needs to rely upon tools and support which can help signpost the path towards increased proficiency and autonomy in a clear, transparent and coherent way. This is where the CEFR and CEFR Companion Volume descriptors can help. Even though we need to remember that there are limits to the degree of structure, objectivity, and transparency in any form of assessment, the availability of a wide range of descriptors that can be used both to define objectives and to assess the learning outcomes is key in helping students know in advance what is expected from them and what is to be assessed. These descriptors can provide a valuable shared focus for developing understanding and communication and eventually enable a transparent assessment.

On top of transparency in assessment and awareness through the sharing of clear, appropriate and realistic objectives and criteria, there is an important aspect that needs to be highlighted. For the AoA, assessment is based on what the social agent is able to do in a real situation. Thus, teachers need to judge the way in which learners accomplish tasks in order to determine their level of competence. The teacher's task is to assess the social agent's performance and, based on this performance, to infer or deduce what competences and strategies were put to use and at what level. This assessment also fosters an understanding of the difference between knowing the structures of a language or the words in its vocabulary ('inert knowledge': van Lier, 2007: 56), and knowing how to use these appropriately in authentic situations in pursuit of an objective. While knowledge is necessary in order to perform tasks, having knowledge does not necessarily mean having the ability to apply it or, in the case of the social agent, having knowledge does not necessarily mean having the ability to accomplish tasks.

With this distinction firmly in mind, we move from a logic that states that assessment consists of monitoring acquisition and learning, to a logic of process or 'competence put to use' (Council of Europe, 2001: 187) in order to achieve a goal or objective. This logic links assessment to the use of competences, helping us to 'determine the extent to which each student has been able to mobilize and use his or her knowledge' (Bourguignon, 2010: 55; our translation).

The two core questions that the CEFR is concerned with when it comes to assessment are 'what is assessed' and 'how performance is interpreted' (Council of Europe, 2001: 178). In other words, the CEFR descriptors can be used:

- to define the content of a task, thus specifying *what* is being assessed, and
- to formulate the criteria that will allow teachers to draw conclusions on the basis of the way in which learners accomplish the task, or, as Bourguignon would put it, fulfil their mission (*how* performance is interpreted).

The decision in the CEFR to differentiate between descriptors of communicative activities (in CEFR Chapter 4) and descriptors of aspects of competences (in CEFR Chapter 5) is not trivial; it is crucial to both the new, CEFR vision of assessment and the AoA. In fact, 'Effective assessment implies the ability to describe what the learner can do and how he or she is able to do it' (Piccardo, 2014a: 44). This difference – and complementarity – is one of the most overlooked aspects in CEFR implementation. As this twofold task is certainly challenging for teachers, very often only the first type of descriptors has been used. The CEFR itself almost anticipated this risk when it depicted the attractiveness of this type of descriptors:

> The former [descriptors of communicative activities available in Chapter 4] are very suitable for teacher- or self-assessment with regard to real-world tasks. Such teacher- or self-assessments are made on the basis of a detailed picture of the learner's language ability built up during the course concerned. They are attractive because they can help to focus both learners and teachers on an action-oriented approach. (Council of Europe, 2001: 180)

The attractiveness and concrete nature of the descriptors for communicative activities acted like the tip of the iceberg, hiding the depths of the competences and strategies that come into play in each action. It was the sort of logic WYSIWYG (What You See Is What You Get) that we are familiar with in the new technology domain. Fundamentally it remained at the level of *description* rather than moving to the level of *interpretation*. This move requires another support, one that enables teachers to develop assessment criteria and to transform non-systematic impressions into well-grounded judgements. The descriptors provided in CEFR Chapter 5 are this tool: they are a starting point for the development of assessment criteria. 'The descriptors presented in this chapter [CEFR Chapter 5] help the teacher explain and categorize what can be deduced or inferred from the performance. They also make it possible to define a competence profile' (Piccardo, 2014a: 46). In fact, it is not one particular performance that is important but rather the competences that are generalisable and the way learners/social agents are able to mobilise them.

This issue of focusing only on descriptors of communicative activities has been worsened by the profusion of ELPs that were made available to practitioners immediately after the publication of the CEFR. They certainly served a noble purpose, that of making the CEFR 'system' more accessible and user-friendly to teachers. However, they were meant primarily for learners, so they were necessarily user-oriented and not teacher-oriented. Thus, teachers misunderstood that the tool had a deliberately limited scope in seeking to bring the CEFR to learners. This is the main reason why the ELPs contributed *de facto* to hiding the need for the complementarity of the two types of descriptors for fostering proficiency among learners, and the professionalism that CEFR-informed assessment requires.

Let us see in more detail the reasons why this complementarity is so crucial in the AoA. We saw that the AoA expands the common notion of task by reasoning – and planning – in terms of scenarios and projects. This scenario or project is also a way of making assessment more meaningful. As we said, scenarios necessarily develop through steps or sub-tasks, which in turn allow learners/social agents to engage in relevant communicative activities and speech acts. However, the scenario/project calls for a global assessment, which includes different dimensions, linguistic, pragmatic and, at a more general level, aspects such as the capacity to work in a group, to plan ahead, to act strategically, to reorient action, etc. – in a word, all that contributes to the successful accomplishment of the culminating task, of the project itself.

It is objectively much more challenging to assess such a complex endeavour as a project, an action-oriented task, than assessing single activities as traditionally has been the case, or even than assessing tasks more limited in scope such as those used in CLT or TBLT. However, one of the principles of the AoA being curriculum alignment, assessment needs to be coherent with the way the language is used and thus learned, Therefore, in the same way that we explained that culminating tasks (also called macro-tasks) can (and need to) be subdivided into sub-tasks, assessment can come into play at different moments, with different functions: the global assessment being at the end of the scenario. However, the main point is not to assess different competences separately one after the other and give a grade. Nor is it to assess the different communicative activities independently from the context and the learner, and in relation to a norm. The idea is for the teacher (and learner in the case of self-assessment) to be able, from the action that the learner/user accomplishes, to infer the degree of proficiency achieved in terms of both the different communicative activities performed *and* the competences developed, both linguistic and general. This is where the establishment of clear stand-alone criteria that we mentioned earlier becomes crucial, so that teachers can prepare and use targeted grids/rubrics and checklists that allow them to collect reliable data and make informed, reasoned judgements. In turn, this helps them make learners aware of the way in which they mobilise their competences and accomplish tasks. This new awareness then accompanies them towards a higher, more sophisticated way to accomplish the same type of tasks, and thus to progress in their proficiency.

Working with scenarios, it is not a question of not assessing knowledge of the language, as some might think. It is a question of assessing this knowledge differently, through the learner's ability to mobilize such knowledge in the communicative situation within the context of a task to be fulfilled. (Bourguignon, 2006: 69, our translation)

To summarise, the impact of an AoA assessment using appropriate, transparent criterion-descriptors on the culture of classroom assessment can be listed as follows:

- increased awareness of the complexity involved in assessment and of the different aspects that need to be taken into account;
- differentiation between proficiency assessment and marking/grading, which had previously been confused;
- an understanding of the importance of including both spoken interaction and spoken production in relation to assessing speaking;
- the value of providing profiled grades, which gave a sense of achievement, rather than a single mark, which could be demotivating;
- the value and effectiveness of awareness-raising with learners, particularly the communication of the criteria used for assessment, self-assessment in relation to them and consequent sharing of the responsibility for progress and assessment;
- a new vision of error, expressed best by a teacher in France as *erreur constructible* [errors that one can construct upon];
- an appreciation of assessment as a support to learning, as opposed to summative, formal grades. (Piccardo, 2013c: 193–196)

The CEFR in general and the AoA in particular are concerned with improving the effectiveness of teaching and learning, and assessment places a crucial role in this process. In a dynamic view of the curriculum (Graves, 2008: See Section 5.1.3), the primary function of assessment is to serve learning and the secondary function is to provide data for the teacher to fine tune and improve their pedagogical know-how. As we discussed in Section 5.2.8, assessment is not an add-on: it is the driving force.

7.2 From Theory to Practice: Working with a Scenario

Although the main aim of this book is to cast light on the theoretical underpinnings and conceptual tenets of the AoA, it seems important to complete this chapter by providing some highlights in relation to its practical dimension. This will help readers to get a better sense of the implications that the action-oriented perspective has on the teaching and learning process. We would like to emphasise, though, that this section only intends to provide the gist of how to translate the tenets of the AoA into practice and should not be interpreted as a hands-on section that can be followed like a recipe. First of all, it is limited to a few examples, and secondly, it lacks the necessary comprehensiveness and detailed guidance that hands-on material would require. What we intend to offer here is more a way of fleshing out some of the theoretical and conceptual discussion of the previous chapters, an opportunity to remind readers that the aim of research in SLE is to improve practice. Nonetheless, as we said, one of the characteristics of the AoA is that it views teachers as professionals engaged in a dynamic process of self-development, and that it adopts a complex perspective of learning that refuses opposition and even dissociation of theory and practice. In particular, it rejects the current business-oriented metaphor in teacher education, according to which 'learning to teach has become a matter of mastering a set of narrow *competencies:* lesson planning, questioning mode, test construction, assessment strategies' (Davis & Sumara, 1997: 105, our emphasis: see discussion of competencies as opposed to competences in Chapter 2). Thus, we think that this section can be useful to researchers and practitioners alike and help the collective intelligence of those engaged in SLE at different levels and in different roles.

We said that one of the main innovations of the AoA is the adoption of a project-oriented perspective and the organisation of teaching and learning through action-oriented scenarios. We will list here a series of examples of scenarios and then we will discuss how these can be used in practice.

Level A1: *Holiday Wish List*

Your most anticipated holiday is here! Your family from overseas are coming to spend two weeks with your family over the winter break. Your parents have been very busy with work and have asked for your help with the holiday shopping by purchasing gifts for all the members of your family. They would like each person to receive an article of clothing, along with another gift. You can spend $50 per person. Think about the likes and dislikes of each member of your family and what gifts might be most suitable. Then, when you arrive at the department store, ask a sales associate for help by describing the members of your family, including their size, and responding to the sales associate's suggestions. When you are finished, email your parents to let them know your shopping trip was successful!

Level A1: *A Weekend Away*

You are planning to spend the weekend with your cousins, who live two hours away. Sunday is the birthday of one of your cousins. To get to your cousins' place, you and one of your parents will take the train. He or she asks you to pack your backpack, reminding you that you don't have to take everything, as your cousins will have many of the things you need such as towels, toothpaste, and soap. However, you have already assembled lots of things and your backpack isn't very big.

In addition, each of you wants to bring a birthday present for your cousin, and these presents have to be packed somewhere. Each of you will have to bring a backpack and make sure that it isn't too full. Your task is to:

- Create a list of the things that you want to take.
- Discuss this list with one of your friends, asking for help to decide what to take and what to leave at home.
- Together with a friend, choose a nice gift for your cousin that is not too big so that it will fit in your backpack and that is typical of your region/community (and you need to be ready to explain to your cousin why it is typical of your region/community).
- Get your backpack ready and answer questions from your Mum or Dad, who want to make sure that you have everything you need.

Level A2: Our Family History

Your school has organised a community celebration on Canadian history over the past 60 years. Each class will work on a different aspect (economic development, social trends, lifestyle, etc.) and submit a maximum of three student productions to a final jury. Your class has been assigned the social and historical development of Canada, a major part of which is families and immigration. The goal of the celebration is to inform others of the diversity of Canadian experience.

For this task, you will create your family tree and describe your family's life.

(1) With the help of your family, you will create a portrait of your family today (language[s] spoken, traditions, your immigration story). This can be in any form you prefer, mixing visuals and words and using a variety of media tools.
(2) You will have five minutes to present this work to the class, explaining your family tree and how it represents Canada and Canadians.
(3) The class will choose three posters to give to the school principal to be posted in the gym.
(4) As a class, you will prepare a final letter to the principal explaining why you have chosen these three posters.

Level B1: Launching a Language Blog

Your principal has noticed that there are fewer and fewer students signing up for language courses at your school and in your community. Next week, your language class will be launching a new blog to help promote a language throughout the school and beyond. The blog's *homepage will include a statement outlining the purpose of the blog and a list of the benefits of learning an additional language. In the blog, you will also showcase what you've been doing in class (using pictures, sound clips, comments, etc.) and make your blog as appealing as possible to prospective students. This can include features such as past events, details of upcoming events, a list of target language songs and artists, bios of popular athletes/actors. To promote the blog, carry out a live interview in front of the class during which a student host will ask you about this exciting new project. The audience will have a chance to ask you questions and try out the blog before its official launch!*

Level B1 and B2: *Humane Livestock Farming*

With your Science teacher, you have learned about the problem of intensive farming, or factory farming, of livestock. You were really struck by this problem and you discovered that many of your fellow students didn't know about it or didn't think it was a problem. You decide to take action.

Phase A. Prepare a presentation illustrating the key aspects of the problem. Create a two-page pamphlet that will make readers aware of the problem. Include statistics, studies on the advantages and disadvantages of intensive farming, excerpts of interviews with stakeholders, and photographs of intensive farming. Your pamphlet will summarise the key points of your presentation, which you will present to the entire school during the end of year exhibition.

Phase B. Next, you decide to write a letter to the managers of various supermarket chains, asking them to carry more meat and poultry that has not been produced intensively and to make consumers aware of the problem. You attach a copy of your pamphlet to the letter.

Level B2: *"Nuit Blanche"*

The municipal government is looking to sponsor a major art installation for Toronto's [or local city of choice] upcoming Nuit Blanche, a free, 12-hour, city-wide art exhibit featuring hundreds of artists from around the world.

With the intention of inspiring understanding between cultural and linguistic communities, the city is asking for proposals for an interactive art installation that combines a celebration from one of the local cultures (e.g. Valentine's Day in Canada) with elements from a similar or different celebration from one or two other cultures (e.g. New Year's Eve in Thailand).

Your group has decided to submit a proposal for an interactive art installation. You will work on researching celebrations in various languages/cultures, design an event which meets the submission guidelines, write a proposal, and receive feedback from other artists in the class.

C1 level: "Two-Eyed Seeing": Integrating Culturally Different Views in Environmental Studies

As informed citizens of your country, you have been asked by a local university or college to help plan a unique and ground-breaking 12-week intensive study abroad course for 2nd or 3rd year environmental biology students that was inspired (in part) by the writings and knowledge of environmental biologist, Robin Wall Kimmerer. The course you develop will have students visit three countries outside of Canada to learn from various sources about the local climate, biology and environmental practices. As this program is still in its planning stages, it is important that your course attracts a good number of students so that the program can continue. Your work will be presented and discussed at a curriculum developers meeting and, if successful, could lead to a collaboration with Wall Kimmerer.

These are some examples of action-oriented scenarios that can be used in class. The levels have been provided as an indication, as these scenarios have been developed and piloted for those levels. However, the levels of scenarios and tasks are flexible, since they can be adapted for lower or more advanced level students. We have provided in an appendix a template for developing scenarios that has been created within the Language and Cultural Diversity Reinvented (LINCDIRE) project. LINCDIRE is an international partnership of different institutions aiming to foster language innovation, on the principles of the AoA, plurilingualism, the integration of technologies and the cross-fertilisation in education of western humanistic views and indigenous epistemologies. This template presented in the appendix has been slightly modified by eliminating the section concerning the indigenous epistemologies as it is not relevant for the scope of this book. More information on the LINCDIRE project can be found on its website: www.lincdireproject.org. Scenario templates from two other projects are also provided as appendices.

We will hereafter briefly explain the process of working with scenarios and discuss some of its implications.

As one can see, scenarios are blueprints for projects and they contain one (or more) culminating, action-oriented tasks that provide the necessary coherence to the entire scenario. Users/learners are working towards a precise goal and each task implies the creation of some form of artefact (it can be a written or an oral text, or a multimedia product involving some other semiotic code(s), like pictures or graphics, etc.).

It is evident, even after reading the scenarios quickly, that none of them can be done in one or two lessons. In fact, each of these scenarios requires chunking down into a series of steps through which users/learners will mobilise their competences in order to engage in different communicative activities and in turn, by performing these activities, they will construct and broaden different competences, both linguistic and general. As we said, the strategic component plays a fundamental role here at two levels: in the sense of acting strategically in order to complete the task and in the sense of using all available communication strategies to perform the different communicative activities.

Faced with the instructions of these scenarios, users/learners start a process during which they think of what exactly is required from them, what strengths and resources they can draw on and, finally, what their weaker points are and how they can improve them or compensate for the gaps. With this in mind they start planning their actions.

On their side, teachers need to have in mind both the big picture, i.e. the long-term objectives, and the more detailed medium and short term objectives that they are targeting in their pedagogic action. Thus, planning a solid and well-articulated scenario is the most fundamental step in the AoA. It starts, in a sense, with adopting a posture a little like that which a scriptwriter would adopt: to see, to figure out, what might happen during the culminating task, what artefact(s) could result from the project, what scope the learners' work and engagement would have. After that the idea is to write a brief but clear description of the scenario. This will be the basis for the next steps.

As each scenario is a complex endeavour, it requires a form of signposting so that both users/learners and teachers know what they are aiming towards and where they are in the process. As we suggested above, 'can-do' descriptors, in particular the extended set provided in the CEFR Companion Volume, serve precisely this purpose. The teacher needs to purposefully choose from the wealth of descriptors that the CEFR Companion Volume presents those that he/she will be using throughout the scenario. As we said earlier, descriptors serve a double purpose: (a) to make the curriculum visible by setting objectives, and (b) to provide transparency in assessment. Thus, once a teacher has clear in mind what the main goals of the scenario are, he/she will proceed to selecting specific descriptors. The descriptors will be of different nature:

- Those which describe the performance (descriptors of communicative activities, focusing on the *WHAT*), and
- Those which help to interpret the performance (descriptors of competences, focusing on the *HOW*).

The former will be more student-oriented and can be used also for self- or peer-assessment; the latter will be more teacher-oriented and will help the teacher target the right level of difficulty but also support students in the improvement of their proficiency.

As we saw, the vision of competences in the CEFR is a plural one, encompassing both general and communicative language competences. The latter in turn include linguistic, sociolinguistic and pragmatic competences. The choice of the descriptors needs to be balanced in order to cover these different aspects and not be reduced to strictly grammatical or lexical competences. Furthermore, as we explained, other crucial aspects come into play in the process of language learning. The AoA aims to foster plurilingualism, a strategic attitude, and the ability to mediate communication, concepts and texts, thus targeted descriptors for these aspects need also to come into play (see Section 6.4).

Selecting descriptors is a delicate and crucial phase that requires a thorough consideration of what can realistically be achieved at the targeted level and what needs to be prioritised not only in relation to the specific task but also in relation to the broader long-term syllabus, so that learners are effectively accompanied in their process of language acquisition and a balanced development of the different aspects of language and communication is fostered. The time spent by the teacher in this selection phase is certainly not wasted as the set of selected descriptors will accompany all the actors involved, throughout the scenario/project work, and will be crucial to providing the necessary transparency:

> In the action-oriented approach, the learner must be aware of [the] goal and the nature of the task that he or she must accomplish. The learner must understand what the accomplishment of this task entails in terms of language activities and non-language activities. The learner must be aware of his or her needs, strengths, and weaknesses with respect to this task — in other words, what he or she already knows and already knows how to do — and what he or she still needs to learn in order to maximize the likelihood of success accomplishing the task. (Piccardo, 2014: 18)

By making a selection of relevant descriptors available to the user/learner from the beginning, this kind of awareness is fostered. Needless to say, the descriptors may be adapted to fit the specific needs of the scenario. These same descriptors will be used to create the final rubrics/grids, both those for teacher assessment and those for self/peer-assessment.

Once the relevant descriptors have been selected (and if necessary adapted), teachers (and learners) need also to think about the prior knowledge required for accomplishing the task(s). Again this is a selective process, the idea is really to identify prerequisites without which the users/learners would be unable to complete the scenario. The aim is to identify any necessary language that the learners might not have, which could be dealt with in a short targeted phase to fill the gap. Finally, other potential stumbling blocks need to be identified (for instance in the case of working with technologies, any technical issues that might occur, or issues related to the specific composition or layout of the class, etc.). This phase should be written down in a clear and structured way, as it will serve as a reference document not just now for the scenario, but also beyond it, in relation to the whole syllabus. Also, most importantly, they will be crucial to inform the next phase, designing the scenario workflow.

Once the first phase (descriptor selection) is completed, it is time to think about how the scenario can be realistically broken down into sub-tasks/steps and to plan these different steps, so that learners are accompanied in their learning trajectory and offered the right opportunities to engage in a coherent and appropriate series of communicative activities through which they will develop their competences and improve their proficiency.

Although the role of the learners is enhanced in the AoA as they are expected to be actively involved in their learning process, the role of the teacher remains more crucial than ever. It is the teacher who creates that *landscape of affordances* that we have mentioned and also helps learners to perceive these affordances, to act upon them, and subsequently to capitalise on the action through a reflective phase, both metalinguistic and metacognitive. It is during the cycle of the scenario work that the teacher also needs to be alert and accompany the learning process in the most unobtrusive but at the same time effective way possible. He/she will provide the necessary resources and support, orchestrate the phases of plenary, group, and individual work, decide if and when a short intervention on his/her part is necessary – for instance on a point of grammar or a socio-pragmatic aspect or a vocabulary-related issue that might emerge and need immediate treatment in order to avoid jeopardising the flow of the action. Helpful questions to guide this process are, for instance: What happens at each step? Who does what? Which resources will the teacher and the learners need? etc. Each sub-task should help learners build the competences they will need to move towards the culminating task.

The chunking down of the scenario into steps or sub-tasks represents the marked path that facilitates the learners' action and the process of constructing their proficiency. First comes the decision about the time to allocate to the scenario in order to maximise learners' chances to accomplish the culminating, action-oriented task. This is dependent both on the scenario itself and also on the characteristics of the context (class, individual learners, institution, material conditions, etc.), on the time constraints and on the available resources and facilities. Again this needs to be seen as a decision presenting some room for adjustment while being acted out.

Once the series of steps has been laid down, each of them is also planned in terms of activities envisaged, necessary resources, possible work methodology and mediational means. It is a good idea to try to provide an internal coherence to each of the steps, which can boost learners' sense of achievement. Something as simple as providing a title for each of the sub-tasks can be helpful for both teachers and learners.

In the process of detailed planning, a back and forth with the scheme produced in phase one is essential. In fact, each step/sub-task should help learners build the competences they will need to move towards the culminating task. So one needs to refer to the communicative activities and competences selected when describing the scenario and to think about how the different steps can be designed to focus on the descriptors chosen. During this planning phase, as the full picture of what the task will look like becomes clearer, it might be necessary to complete or slightly adjust some of the choices made during the initial planning phase, especially referring to time, resources and potential stumbling blocks.

One important point during the detailed planning of the different steps is to reflect on how they can contribute to learners' overall development in terms of both communicative language competences and strategies, and also in terms of sensibilisation to the plurilingual dimension and to the mediational aspects of any learning. Thus, it is advisable to have a sort of scenario overview that helps to make sure that these aspects have been integrated in a coherent and balanced way. As can be seen in the appendix, an overview table can help this reflection moment. In accordance with the backward design principle of the AoA that we highlighted throughout the book, it is advisable to start with the culminating task (Part 4 in Appendix 1) and proceed backwards. The idea is to check off all the relevant dimensions for the culminating task first and then do the same for the sub-tasks. Proceeding in this manner will help notice any inconsistencies in the detailed planning. For example, one might notice that the culminating task focuses on oral interaction but oral interaction has not really been covered in any sub-task. Or, several sub-tasks may focus on pragmatic competence but this is not core to the culminating task. Again, as a consequence of this reflective phase, some aspects of the previous two phases (descriptor selection; planning sub-tasks) might need to be adjusted.

Finally, the last part of the planning and development of the task is the preparation of an observation checklist, a self-assessment checklist, and finally assessment grids/rubrics.

As we repeatedly said in this book, planning and assessment are strictly linked and the descriptors are the backbone of the entire work on action-oriented tasks. Thus, in making the grid/rubric one must make sure that the selected descriptors are used. Assessment is a data collection process: on the basis of collected data decisions are made concerning assessment and, if required, grading purposes. Thus, an important aspect is a guided observation of what exactly happens during the learning process. For this reason observation checklists are extremely useful.

As we have said, the roles of the teacher and the learner are complementary in assessment. Thus, a teacher-oriented observation checklist should be used by teachers alongside a student-oriented self-assessment checklist used by learners. An assessment-oriented grid/rubric will complete the set of assessment tools. Needless to say the student-oriented checklist will look slightly different from the teacher-oriented checklist, in particular, the former should be written in a way that learners can understand. Any educational jargon should be avoided, for instance, instead of the category name, 'Communicative Activities', the learners' checklist could read: 'What I can do in the language I am learning'. The descriptors will also need to be reworded to make them clearer for learners. Finally, a separate document, an assessment grid/rubric designed for summative assessment is needed. However, even this grid/rubric could be adapted for formative assessment at some point during the scenario (e.g. parts relevant to the particular sub-task), before being used as is for final summative assessment.

Once all these parts of the document are completed, a final revision phase is appropriate in order to make sure of the completeness and coherence of the ensemble. Needless to say, during the implementation of the scenario things don't necessarily go according to plan, and often such unplanned occurrences are particularly relevant learning moments and should not be underestimated. The planning document remains a living thing and can certainly be updated while learners and teachers work through the scenario. The scenario does not exist until it is enacted.

To summarise, the cyclical process of working with scenarios unfolds according to the following principles:

(1) Use backward design.
(2) Select the relevant descriptors for your task.
(3) Develop the sub-tasks and lesson plans.
(4) Balance the task/scenario.
(5) Create your observation and assessment tools.
(6) Review the scenario.
(7) Enact the scenario.
(8) Regularly observe, if necessary adjust during implementation, and assess.
(9) Revise the scenario for future use.

Finally, the accurate, detailed and explicit planning of scenarios and tasks needs to be seen as a way of keeping track of the learning and teaching process. More importantly, it is a way of constructing all the building blocks for the syllabus. The sum of all the pieces of the puzzles enable teachers and learners alike to have a clear sense of their learning path and their progress in the language.

As mentioned before, several projects have recently exploited the scenario concept and the availability of descriptors to create teaching modules related to the user/learner's real-life needs. Naturally these projects have developed different models for their scenario template. Some models use descriptors, others just describe situations. Some models suggest descriptors just for communicative language activities whilst others also propose using descriptors for communicative language strategies and competences. Some models include a list of enabling objectives, in terms of aspects of communicative language competence, plus perhaps strategies, whilst others stay at the more macro level of defining only situations, leaving it to the teacher to diagnose the enabling needs. Some give a suggested sequence of implementation activities, whilst others define just the objectives. Three different scenario templates that all use CEFR descriptors are given in the appendices.

With regard to the implications of implementing a scenario, all teachers have their own individual style, and learners recognise and appreciate this. Therefore giving advice on how to go about things inevitably borders on the inappropriate. Nevertheless, the list of tips below may be useful, at least to stimulate reflection:

- Ensure your scenario (a) has a clear frame, which includes clearly defined parameters for the product – but also (b) leaves enough latitude for learners/users to create their own goals, make their own choices and take ownership. Remember that: 'There has to be enough predictability and security for learners not to feel lost and bewildered ... but there must also be enough room to innovate and move in novel directions for learners to develop autonomy and fuel their intrinsic motivation' (van Lier, 2007: 53) and that the younger the learners the more framing, predictability and scaffolding they require.
- Ensure that the instructions are clear, short and complete.
- Plan the culminating task for a time you know that almost all learners will be there.
- At lower levels, encourage learners to use all their linguistic resources (including L1) while they are working out how to approach the task.
- Encourage higher level groups to adopt a conscious language policy: when they will work in which language? When it will be a

'free-for-all?' Allow them to decide to work in the 'target language' (process) yet produce the product in another language, or vice versa, or to use a variety of languages, if they wish.

- If groups are taking some time to get moving, don't take over the action in frontal teaching: go around and help get them up and running.
- Don't be afraid to skip a phase, an activity/sub-task aimed to practice an enabling competence, if you realise an 'off-the-shelf' scenario is too big for the time available.
- Take the opportunity in earlier scenarios to train on 'how to do group work.' The descriptors for *mediating concepts* from the CEFR Companion Volume may help here.
- If technology is involved, find out who in the class is good with it and harness their talent as 'trouble-shooters' to be on first call for any 'crises.'
- Don't interrupt the action – learn to do nothing; teachers often get a bad conscience when they do nothing for more than a few minutes. Learn to leave groups in peace.
- Be consistent in how you use body language or where and how you sit or stand – so learners/users recognise what operating mode the class is in: when they can ask you things, when they should just get on with it.
- Observe without dominating. If you take notes, do so naturally, sitting down.
- If you take notes, note good strategies and language use – not just problems.
- Have a palette of strategies for when you will give language input. You might pre-teach/revise specific language they will clearly need – or put this on a handout. It could be that learners come over to you where you are sitting; it could be that you circulate constantly. There could be a 'language clinic' at some point – perhaps a different lesson – when you go over points that have come up in different groups for the benefit of the whole class. There could be a report session in which learners, rather than you, present such new language they used.
- Don't make your assessment instruments too complicated: 10 descriptors well-observed are better than a long checklist. Different sections or columns for different aspects help to frame your observation.
- Check that learner versions of your assessment instruments are simple to understand and age-appropriate. Maybe ask a colleague to look at them before you use them.

8 Conclusion

As we said at the beginning of this book, to some extent the AoA was a practice in search of a theory. This may sound exaggerated but in reality it is not. Although it is true that several of the theoretical positions taken by the AoA were hinted at in the CEFR in 2001, as we have shown, the time was not yet ripe at the end of the 1990s to give full substance to the AoA, which, at the time it was announced, was more a programmatic wishlist than a theoretically informed and coherent methodological shift. As was the case for the concept of mediation, though, the CEFR proved forward-looking in the way it anticipated major changes of perspective in applied linguistics and language education in general. Since that time there has been a fertile debate in different human and social sciences that has proved particularly enlightening for education in general. There has also been a wealth of studies in applied linguistics that all broaden the theoretical horizon of SLE. With reference to the CEFR, while in the English-speaking literature scholarly discussion has tended to underestimate its potential, focusing mainly on the view of progression in second language acquisition presented in the CEFR illustrative descriptor scales (e.g. Alderson, 2007; Hulstijn, 2007; Hulstijn *et al.*, 2010), a discussion around the theoretical basis and implications of the AoA as a second language pedagogy emerged in the continental literature (e.g. Puren, 2002, 2004, 2009; Beacco, 2007; Lion-Olivieri & Liria, 2009; Rosen, 2009; Richer, 2008, 2009, 2012, 2017). Meanwhile, practitioners in many different contexts have developed the AoA on the ground, thus feeding back into the discussion around concepts and theories.

Some twenty years down the road we are now in a position in which we are able to fit all the pieces of the puzzle together. We have now acquired the necessary distance to complete and extend the CEFR, as has been the case with the CEFR Companion Volume. In addition, we are also ready to both interrogate the different theories that in one way or another have contributed to the shaping of the AoA and to see their interconnections and synergies, as well as their potential to inform innovation in language classrooms. This book has tried to capture all this and to cast light on the AoA by providing a theoretical rationale and conceptual underpinnings. It has also aimed to situate the AoA historically within the long and challenging development of SLE. No innovation happens without the context being ready to make room for it, and this applies to the AoA too. By grounding the emergence and shaping of the AoA over these last two decades within the development of theories and methodologies in SLE and beyond, this book contextualises the AoA within a broader theoretical framework, which as we have said calls for a broad metatheory.

This book has therefore sought to theorise the underpinnings of the AoA and to explain why, as for example Bourguignon (2006), Puren (2002, 2009) and Richer (2009) argue, the AoA cannot be seen as synonymous with TBLT, as is sometimes assumed. We have shown in Chapter 2 the way in which the AoA and CEFR have a view of competence as situated action that aligns with theoretical positions in linguistics (e.g. Austin, 1962; Hymes, 1972; Halliday, 1973, 1975, 1978), communication theory (e.g. Wiemann, 1977), and in particular, as Richer clearly argues in his work (2009, 2012, 2017), in the world of work – *sociologie du travail* (Le Boterf, 2010; Zarifian, 2001). In Chapter 3, we showed the way in which a wide variety of concepts and theories align with and/or have contributed to the AoA's development, particularly Halliday's systemic approach and concept of situated meaning potential and the ecological perspective that has to some extent developed from it. We discussed the crucial concepts of agency, theory of action, situated cognition, communities of practice, collective intelligence, etc. and the way they all align with and have contributed to the AoA. Above all, we acknowledged the debt to sociocultural theory and the central place in the AoA of the concepts of mediation and plurilingual/pluricultural competence, showing why, in the light of recent societal developments and the richer place afforded to interculturality in SLE, these concepts have recently been more fully conceptualised in the CEFR Companion Volume (North & Piccardo, 2016a, 2016b) and operationalised in descriptors (Council of Europe, 2018). Finally, as we explained at the end of Chapter 3, such a colourful, ecological framework also requires an overarching theory, and we agree with van Lier (2004) that complexity theories, in particular DST, provide this.

What does all this mean for SLE? In our view, the synthesis of current learning theories offered by the AoA enables the fundamental paradigm shift that CLT called for, but was unable to provide, mainly due to the rather limited view of SLE that informed CLT. Even if nobody can deny that the move towards the communicative era was a welcomed and necessary first step to go beyond the simplistic perspective offered by many methods beforehand, CLT still adopted a linear paradigm. CLT moved from studying 'the language' to learning how to communicate, in the sense of learning the language now in order to be able to communicate in the future. However, it was not language use in the sense of acting together with others in and through language(s) and by so acting, learning the language(s), learning how to act in that (those) language(s), and learning how to act with the 'other'. Firstly, it was a view that tended to highlight declarative and instrumental language use and the conventional meaning of words as codified in dictionaries based on monolingual native speaker usage rather than pragmatic, situated speaker meaning. Secondly, it was one that maintained a strict separation between the structure of the target language and the psychological and emotional dimensions. In other words one studied 'pure' words, expressions and structures without taking into account their symbolic nature, with the connection between language and thought or that between language and identity being given little attention. Thus, the CLT perspective had intrinsic limits that would not allow it to stretch beyond a certain point. The considerable societal changes of the last two decades have made those limits clear. This helps to explain why CLT has lost its power to innovate and also why in curricula and textbooks which claim to be communicative, more traditional methodologies tend to resurge in disguise. One must certainly acknowledge the great innovation that CTL underwent through TBLT and the great contribution that this development has brought to SLE. However, the foundations of the entire communicative turn were limited to preparing learners to communicate with the foreigner passing by (Puren, 2009) and have not substantially changed.

This is even more problematic in today's globalised world of 'liquid modernity' (Baumann, 2000) than it was 20 years ago when the AoA first made its appearance on the scene. Today, teachers tend to be increasingly confronted with learners who have differing linguistic and cultural identities, differing world views and 'cartographical' tools that they have collected during their life trajectories. These users/learners are not some kind of neutral beings, but people with personalities, identities and stories that have developed in specific temporal, geographical and cultural conditions, with which they continue to be connected in a dynamic relationship. All these different combinations and changes in today's sociological landscape urgently need an ecologically-oriented pedagogy that acknowledges that users/learners from different horizons, functioning in different geographical and cultural contexts are able to work together in the pursuit of a shared goal, a goal in which the use of languages is not purely instrumental, but rather a subjective, *creative* experience. As we discussed in Section 3.4, Halliday documented the fact that the creative function of language is acquired well before the transactional function which so much of SLE focuses on. Play is the root of all learning and as Richer's humanistic model of competence shows (see Figure 2.1) competence is reinforced and developed through the satisfaction and pleasure that comes from exercising it. In this sense we can apply Piccardo's (2005a) definition of creativity to the entire language learning process:

> A faculty – intrinsic to human nature and likely to develop – of rich and original production and reproduction, personal reconstruction of concepts and data, autonomous and non-banal use of all different kinds of elements (including texts, images, music ...), plus free association and disassociation, all within a framework of play and pleasure. (Piccardo, 2005a: 32)

It is a fundamental misconception to think that, because the CEFR and CEFR Companion Volume present learning aims in a hierarchy of scales, the thinking behind them or the AoA is linear or unidimensional. Quite the contrary. The aim of offering some 80 scales – and presenting them as illustrative of the even broader galaxy that is language use – is precisely to demonstrate just how varied aims in SLE can be. And of course, progress in one area, where the users/learner is motivated and invests time and energy, spills over into other areas through the development of transversal competences, the strengthening of self-esteem, the ability to project oneself, to relate to and collaborate with others, as well as through other aspects of *savoir-être* – the key competence in a humanistic view of education.

The central tenet of the AoA it to see users/learners as 'social agents' interpreting the world in relation to their internal mental context and the external social dimension, and acting strategically to accomplish tasks. In line with theories of situated action, situated cognition and sociocultural theory, action-oriented tasks invite learners to act as language users, rather than as just language learners, i.e. to engage in a process of self-regulation by planning how to cope with the challenge presented, checking hypotheses and reframing these based on experience in a cyclical manner. This involves taking the initiative, exerting agency, and different forms of mediation. The process involves, from both learners and teachers, setting a goal to reach in a task/project, the user/learner gauging what he/she lacks in order to reach it, and monitoring progress towards the goal, with feedback during and afterwards with adjustments made accordingly. In a complex task/project, discourse is seen as both (a) mediation process (constructing knowledge and facilitating that process) and (b) as a meta-cognitive tool for planning, evaluation, reconfiguration/revision.

Action-oriented tasks give users/learners the opportunity to engage in action – to come up with a well-defined outcome, to create an artefact: a visible product. It is during the *process* of developing the product that the learners mediate and (pluri)language i.e. exploit different linguistic and semiotic resources to communicate and (co)construct meaning, and so acquire new language. This is why action-oriented tasks can be equated with projects. And project work is a perspective that is valid from the lower levels, when users/learners are developing the ability to communicate, all the way to the highest levels. It is no coincidence that professional further training tends to be task and project-based. In SLE, users/learners at the A-levels find in collaborative projects an enhanced sense of achievement and purpose in their learning trajectory; on the other hand C-level users/learners need a stimulating, challenging context in which to engage personally and creatively with the language and invest in the production of something concrete, whether it is a performance or an artefact, whether it involves their professional/academic life or the world of the imagination, if they are to acquire a feel for the conative layers of meaning in the language. Familiarity with certain types of scripts/genres can be exploited in a creative way in tasks related to identity and experiences. Users/learners, especially less self-confident ones, will undertake challenging tasks provided that the work proceeds in an iterative fashion and they thus have the opportunity to be imperfect especially in their first tries – without being assessed on accuracy. Encouraging learners to use all of their linguistic repertoire and to codeswitch and experiment with different languages, will help them see connections, common roots, etc.

The product will result from an iterative process of drafting or rehearsal. It is during this process that focus on form is most likely to occur, and the immediate, situated nature of the work should help users/learners to better remember the new language knowledge gained. The final version, written or performed, should be assessed in relation to quality criteria. Here tasks should be situated so that learners learn to adopt different genre styles in artefacts and appropriate register and tone in the case of a performance. In terms of results, teachers should not expect regular, linear progress from individual work, because of natural 'U-shaped learning curves' (Larsen-Freeman & Cameron, 2008: 129), but should insist that groups pool resources to correct drafts.

CoPs and situated learning both suggest that learners can learn a lot from each other as well as from the teacher. Collaborative group work is an effective way to multiply sources of mediation. Cooperation leads to creating, innovating and inventing. However, a group needs personal engagement of identity, partnerships and a sense of community for this to function well. CI theory and SCT suggest that effective co-construction of meaning is dependent on and intrinsically related to the social dimension in this way. Descriptors for *mediating concepts* can help users/learners become more aware of how to build on each other's ideas. Descriptors for *mediating communication* can make users/learners aware of the depth and delicate nature of the communication process and its crucial role in the success of cooperative work.

Such active participation in a group presupposes motivation and emotional engagement. The belief that one can be successful (self-efficacy) is strengthened by experiences of previous success, the chance to compare one's performance with those of others (= peer assessment), and verbal encouragement (= support from the teacher).

Situated experience is a central concept in the AoA, which aligns with the cognitive position that learning takes place in a meaningful context. The teacher needs to provide *dynamic learning situations*. Experience with CoPs suggests that collaborative tasks and projects in small groups that are oriented towards learners' interests, related to everyday experience, that may involve an element of fieldwork outside school can be very effective dynamic learning situations. These dynamic experiences, rich in affordances, should be challenging because language growth occurs at the edge of a learner's comfort zone, at the border between order and chaos. An iterative process of drafting or rehearsal is advisable because people do not manage a masterly performance first time around. For the same reason, assessment in earlier phases should take the form of feedback and feedforward, encouraging attempts to use more complex language, not discouraging linguistic experimentation by penalising error. This may well require a radical shift of emphasis in the assessment culture of the institution, away from marks towards the creation of artefacts that learners can be proud of, perhaps building on the concepts of identity texts and language portfolios. This is linked to another important concept in CoPs: success should be given recognition and published.

To summarise: the move towards an action-oriented, ecological, complex perspective is a move away from the linear, computer metaphor of language learning towards a view of language being constructed in interaction and collaboration. This view completely contradicts traditional approaches in which language is taught in order to be later applied. Language is no longer seen as separate from the individual and the social context. The increased importance given to collaboration and to the role of others in language learning also implies a move beyond a focus on functional exchanges, as in the communicative approach, to a perspective involving collaboration in the construction of new knowledge. Rather than receiving 'inputs', learners should be exposed to a rich landscape of affordances through a series of complex tasks that invite them to engage in a creative process, deploying and stretching all their resources to do so. Language needs to emerge in a rich social context of language use, in which users/learners feel free to use language as modelling clay, which they can shape to create and express new meaning, receive support from peers and teachers, both in the process of construction and in the reflection. As Davis and Sumara state, learning is 'occasioned' rather than 'caused' (1997). They stress that: 'As others have suggested (e.g. Lave & Wenger, 1991; Vygotsky,

1962, 1978) all of our "understandings" are situated and co-emerge with complex webs of experience' (1997: 115). Thus, although there are no causal relationships between actions, the crucial role of the teacher resides in the notion of occasioning: 'By occasioning actions, the teacher participates in, but does not determine, student learning' (1997: 115).

What are the implications of all this for institutions and teachers? As Slattery reminds us, in a traditional, linear perspective:

> ... teachers and learners would ... find security in a 'minimal curriculum' that isolates disciplines and departments, separates knowledge from the learner, seeks meaning apart from context, judges learning on memorization, suppresses and annihilates differences, and immortalizes the competitive victor. (2013: 288)

In fact, the greatest challenge for an institution is to successfully encourage and support teachers to get out of that secure zone, to adopt a complex perspective rather than a simple linear one in the way in which they approach their work.

However, encouraging is not enough. The role of the institution is also to make space for teachers to adopt such a complex perspective. Teachers are called on to play a more challenging but much more rewarding role than simply that of applying a curriculum in precisely the way that is prescribed by the institution. They are called on to work towards objectives and to adopt the most effective strategies and modalities in order for the users/learners to achieve those objectives. Thus, a curriculum needs to be a blueprint, a set of guiding principles rather than a straightjacket of contents to be checked off on a list. The core distinction between (a) curriculum, seen as broader guidelines that ensure coherence across levels and classes, and (b) syllabus, that is the contextualised operationalisation of those guidelines into pedagogical actions, is crucial in the AoA. Needless to say, curriculum and syllabus are not the same thing, even though they must operate in synergy. This requires a shared vision and collaboration both vertically throughout the institution and horizontally among language teachers, seen as a community of practice.

As in all complex systems, a well organised school system will demonstrate coherence at the different levels, with recognisable patterns being iterated at these different levels of class, school, school district and even overall school system, as with fractals, one of the core concepts of complexity theories. CAS are self-similar at different scales: agency of learners will be modelled and fostered through agency of teachers. Thus institutions need to help teachers in their professional self- and peer development. At the same time, they also need to initiate and foster a culture of quality, with clear procedures and accountability at the different levels (Piccardo *et al.*, 2017, 2019a, 2019b). This is not at odds with complexity, quite the contrary. Clear procedures and a culture of accountability (which is not a synonym for standardised tests, but rather with the introduction of transparency in goal setting and evaluation criteria) liberate space and energy for teachers to exert and develop their agency in the shaping of their syllabuses. Needless to say, to be successful, such change has to happen across the learning of all languages – because when learning an L3, the users/learners should be able to profit from their experience with previous languages, similarities between languages and transversal discourse competence. The ultimate goal is in fact an overall language education, which encompasses and goes beyond the learning of any specific language. Not only do teachers of different languages need to be able to network and exchange ideas and know-how, but above all they need to plan together. Consequently, the approach to assessment also needs to be consistent across languages.

The two related concepts of *alignment* (of curriculum, teaching, assessment) and *backward design*: defining outcomes and working backwards from them to create task/project-based modules, are particularly important for institutions. All this starts with defining the educational philosophy, the place of multiple identities, the valuing of plurilingual resources and the overall educational, societal aims – in practical concrete terms. What types of learning experiences should learners have? What are the key competences that they should acquire? How is a plurilingual perspective to be operationalised? How will learners record and/or document their plurilingual profiles, their multiple identities?

The aim of language education is to enable users/learners to learn how to mean: how to recognise and use the meaning potential in communicative situations relevant to them. 'Can do' descriptors define what a person could mean in a particular type of situation and can thus be useful for (a) curriculum planning and (b) module/scenario and task/project planning. Once the more concrete curriculum aims have been defined with descriptors, teachers can use the descriptors to plan their modules, to tell users/learners what is happening and why, to organise tasks and materials, for assessment, to report results, etc. Concrete goals (e.g. descriptors selected in relation to a specific task/project) work better than vaguely defined aims. Planning backwards requires a triangulation of the learners' personal interests and strengths/weaknesses, with the objectives defined by the descriptors, and the materials and/or expertise available. This is not simple, it is complex. Teachers may need awareness-raising and training to do this effectively. They will need to understand the difference between the two types of descriptors (of activities: WHAT learners can do/aspects of competence: HOW well they can do it).

A number of university language centres and specialised language institutes (notably members of the Eaquals and UNIcert schemes) have reoriented their curricula towards a proficiency approach. However, this represents a CEFR-informed approach; an AoA requires changes to the actual pedagogy itself in addition to the changes in the way the curriculum is identified and organised.

Any change to pedagogy will be more successful if it involves a programme of teacher education through continuous professional development in which a substantial number of teachers are involved from an early stage in giving input to and feedback on the development of both curriculum and resources. But to set up any teacher education programme, the institution needs a clear idea of what changes to pedagogy are implied in the AoA. We come here full circle: the AoA represents a paradigm shift not only in methodological terms, but also as it makes visible the need for all the actors in language education to work in a synergic, interdependent way. Interest in linguistic and cultural diversity, seeing it as an ordinary characteristic of everyday life and language and hence acquiring an open attitude to norms are not given for granted, they are constructed daily through personal involvement and investment. Creating the conditions for this to happen is the responsibility of every single actor, from learners to teachers to institutions, to the society at large. In an ideal world all this would change together. However, more realistically, change in one of the nested CAS will involve change in all other CAS and new balances, which in turn will be temporary and open to yet new changes and innovation. The AoA with its broad, solid, theoretical and conceptual basis can greatly facilitate this process. It can contribute to opening the classroom doors to the world, achieving the goal of the dynamic, holistic and whole-person language education that is necessary in our ever-changing societies.

Appendix 1: LINCDIRE Action-oriented Scenario Template

Part 1: Scenario Description

1) **Title:**

2) **Overview:**

3) **Target learners:**

4) **Languages**
   - **Main target language:**
   - **Other language(s) involved:**

5) **CEFR Level:**

6) **Main goal(s) (by the end of the scenario, students will be able to...):**
   -

8) **Communicative language activities expressed through Can Do statements: (circa 4-6)**
   -

9) **Communicative competences expressed through Can Do statements: (max 6 in total)**
   Linguistic (grammar/vocabulary/phonology)
   -

   Pragmatic and sociolinguistic (functional/discourse, register/contextual appropriacy)
   -

   Sociocultural (proximity convention, directness/indirectness)
   -

10) **Plurilingual/Pluricultural dimension:** (max 2)
   -

11) **Mediation:** (max 4)
   -

12) **Ability to learn:** (max 4)
   -

13) Prior knowledge required:

14) Time for scenario completion (steps + culminating task):

Step 1 (title):

Step 2 (title):

...

...

Culminating Task (Proposal presentation & reflection session):

Total:

15) Resources:

  •

16) Potential Stumbling Blocks:

NB: a selection of the 'can-do' descriptors indicated at points 8), 9), and 10) should form the basis for compiling the appropriate observation checklist for the culminating task (part 4: Observation Checklist).

Part 2: My Scenario Planner*

*This table is intended to provide teachers with an overview of the scenario development. It shows the balance and distribution of the focus in the different steps.

Step	Communicative Language Activities[1]					Communicative Competences			Mediation	Ability to learn	Pluri-dimension[2]	Notes
	L	SP	SI	R	W	WI	Linguistic	Pragmatic/ Sociolinguistic	Sociocultural				
1 (title)													
2 (title)													
3 (title)													
4 (title)													
Culminating Task:													

[1] L = Listening; SP = Spoken Production; SI = Spoken Interaction; R = Reading; W = Writing; WI = Written Interaction
[2] Specify where Plurilingual (PL) and/or Pluricultural (PC) dimensions fit in

Part 3: Scenario Development*

*This tool is meant to explain the development of the different phases of the scenario: it will include notes on how to proceed, types of activities, who does what, reference to specific resources used at a specific moment.

The column on the left helps you to break down the scenario development into manageable teaching/learning chunks, therefore you may choose to enter either the # of each step or, if you feel it more useful, to indicate the time units you are usually working with (e.g. 70' ....)

Step	What happens	Resources (if any)
1	(title) •	
2	(title) •	
3	(title) •	
4	(title) •	
5	Culminating task: •	

Part 4: Observation Checklist (to be used for culminating task)

By the end of this task: _____ :

name of student

	by him/herself	with help	not yet
Communicative language activities			
•			
•			
•			
Communicative competences			
•			
•			
•			
Plurilingual and pluricultural competences			
•			
•			
Ability to learn			
•			
•			
Mediation			
•			
•			
•			

Use the CEFR-related bank of descriptors to customise the rubric according to the outcomes/enabling competences established for your task. You can adapt the original descriptors to fit the task better.

Part 5: Language Learning Self-Assessment Checklist

Scenario: .... [provide the title]

These are the things I will be able to do by the end of this scenario (the teacher will insert the descriptors, he/she may want to tweak/simplify their formulation to make them more transparent for students, and more age appropriate too):

	by myself	with help	not yet
What I can do in the language I am learning			
•			
•			
•			
Quality of the language I use			
•			
•			
•			
•			
I am plurilingual (PL) and pluricultural (PC)			
•			
My ability to learn			
•			
Mediation			
•			
•			
•			
My space for free reflection			

Appendix 2: CASLT Scenario Template
(Source: Hunter, Cousineau, Collins & Hook, forthcoming)

SCENARIO – (title)		
Domain:		**Level:**
Authentic Resources Used During the Scenario:	**Expected Learning Outcomes (e.g., Overall Expectations):**	**Assessment Opportunities:** For Learning – As Learning – Of Learning –
ACTION-ORIENTED TASK		
Description:	**Checklist:** ☐ Learners are 'social agents' in an authentic social context ☐ Action is purposeful with real-world application ☐ There is a clearly communicated goal to be accomplished that results in a product or outcome ☐ Learning is supported by authentic, real-life texts and experiences ☐ There are conditions and constraints that promote critical and creative thinking ☐ Learners draw upon their existing and newly developed competences ☐ Learners make choices and think and act strategically	
Descriptors: *Expressed through can-do statements* **Language Activities and Strategies Needed to Complete the Task** **Language Competences Needed to Complete the Task**		

Note: General Competences (i.e. declarative knowledge, skills and know-how, existential competence, and ability to learn) are always combined with language competences (i.e. linguistic, sociolinguistic and pragmatic) to complete a task. Although there are not descriptor scales for general competences, they are an important component of language proficiency.

SUB-TASKS		
Description of Sub-tasks to Build Identified Competences:	Language Activities Used:	Competences Stressed:

Appendix 3: Eaquals Scenario Template

(Source: North, Ortega & Sheehan 2010; Eaquals & CIEP, 2014)

Part 1: Scenario Overview

TITLE: _____

DOMAIN	CONTEXT	TASKS	ACTIVITIES	TEXTS

LEVEL		
CAN-DOS*	(descriptor)	
CRITERIA* (quality of language) (criteria name)	...	
	...	
	...	

COMPETENCES		
STRATEGIC		
PRAGMATIC	Functional	
	Discourse	
LINGUISTIC	Grammatical	
	Lexical	
	Phonological	

* Taken verbatim from the CEFR. Portfolio or school's adapted descriptors.

Part 2: Implementation

COMPETENCE. T(S)	LEARNING CONTEXT	ACTIVITY		MATERIALS
			Engage	
			Study	
			Activate	

References

Abbs, B., Ayton, B. and Freebairn, I. (1975) *Strategies*. London: Longman.

Abutalebi, J. and Green, D. (2007) Bilingual language production: The neurocognition of language representation and control. *Journal of Neurolinguistics* 20, 242–275.

ACTFL (American Council on the Teaching of Foreign Languages) (2012) *ACTFL Proficiency Guidelines*. www.actfl.org/publications/guidelines-and-manuals/actfl-proficiency-guidelines-2012 (accessed 08 March 2018).

Aden, J. (2010) L'empathie, socle de la reliance en didactique des langues-cultures [Empathy, the basis of connection in language teaching]. In J. Aden, T. Grimshaw and H. Penz (eds) *Enseigner les langues-cultures à l'ère de la complexité: Approches interdisciplinaires pour un monde en reliance [Teaching Languages and Cultures in the Era of Complexity: Interdisciplinary Approaches in a Connected World]* (pp. 23–44). Bruxelles: Peter Lang, Coll.GramR.

Adesope O., Lavin, T., Thompson, T. and Ungerleider, C. (2010) A systematic review and meta-analysis of the cognitive correlates of bilingualism. *Review of Educational Research* 80 (2), 207–245.

Ahearn, L.M. (2001) Language and agency. *Annual Review of Anthropology* 30, 109–137.

Alhadeff-Jones, M. (2008) Three generations of complexity theories: Nuances and ambiguities. *Educational Philosophy and Theory* 40 (1), 66–82.

Ahmed, S. (2004) *The Cultural Politics of Emotion*. New York: Routledge.

Alderson, J.C.A (1983) Who needs jam? Response to Harrison. In A. Hughes and D. Porter (eds) *Current Developments in Language Testing* (pp. 87–92). London: Academic Press.

Alderson, J.C.A. (1991) Bands and scores. In J.C.A. Alderson and B. North (eds) *Language Testing in the 1990s* (pp. 71–86). London: Macmillan/Modern English Publications: British Council.

Alderson, J.C.A. (ed.) (2002) *Case Studies in the Use of the Common European Framework*. Strasbourg: Council of Europe. www.coe.int/en/web/common-european-framework-reference-languages/documents (accessed 08 March 2018).

Alderson, J.C.A (2007) The CEFR and the need for more research. *The Modern Language Journal* 91 (4), 659–662.

Alderson, J.C.A. and North, B. (eds) (1991) *Language Testing in the 1990s*. London: Macmillan/Modern English Publications: British Council.

Alderson, J.C.A. and Urquhart, S. (1984) *Reading in a Foreign Language*. Harlow: Longman.

Alexander, R. (2008) Culture, dialogue and learning: Notes on an emerging pedagogy. In N. Mercer and S. Hodgkinson (eds) *Exploring Talk in Schools* (pp. 99–114). London: Sage.

Alladi, S., Bak, T.H., Duggirala, V., Surampudi, B., Shailaja, M., Shukla, A.K., Chaudhuri, J.R. and Kaul, S. (2013) Bilingualism delays age at onset of dementia, independent of education and immigration status. *Neurology* November 6, 2013. Doi: 10.1212/01.wnl.0000436620.33155.a4.

Allan, K. (1997) Speech act theory: Overview. In P.V. Lamarque and R.E. Asher (eds) *Concise Encyclopaedia of the Philosophy of Language* (pp. 454–467). Oxford: Pergamon Press.

Androutsopoulos, J. (2006) Multilingualism, diaspora, and the internet: Codes and identities on German-based diaspora websites. *Journal of Sociolinguistics* 10 (4), 520–547.

Anthony, E.M. (1963) Approach, method and technique. *English Language Teaching* 17, 63–57.

Anzaldúa, G. (1999) *Borderlands/La Frontera* (2nd edn). San Francisco, CA: Aunt Lute Books.

Ardoino, J. (2000) *Les avatars de l'éducation [Educational Avatars]*. Paris: Presses Universitaires de France.

ARG (Assessment Reform Group) (1999) *Assessment for Learning: Beyond the Black Box*. Cambridge: University of Cambridge, School of Education.

Arnold, J. (1999) *Affect in Language Learning*. Cambridge: Cambridge University Press.

Arnold, J. and Brown, H.D. (1999) A map of the terrain. In J. Arnold (ed.) (1999) *Affect in Language Learning* (pp. 1–24). Cambridge: Cambridge University Press.

Arnott, S., Brogden, L.M., Faez, F., Peguret, M., Piccardo, E., Rehner, K., Taylor, S.K., Wernicke, M. (2017) Implementing the Common European Framework of Reference for Languages (CEFR) in Canada: A research agenda. *The Canadian Journal of Applied Linguistics* 20 (1), 31–54.

Arrizón, A. (2006) *Queering Mestizaje: Transculturation and Performance*. Ann Arbour: University of Michigan Press.

ATESL: Alberta Teachers of English as a Second Language (2016) Enhancing Intercultural Communicative Competence. A Resource based on the ATESL Adult ESL Curriculum Framework: Adapted from the intercultural knowledge and skills strand of the Massachusetts curriculum framework. https://www.atesl.ca/documents/1484/ICCResourceEbook.pdf (accessed 09 February 2019).

Athanasopoulos, P. (2011) Cognitive restructuring in bilingualism. In A. Pavlenko (ed.) *Thinking and Speaking in Two Languages* (pp. 29–65). Bristol: Multilingual Matters.

Athanasopoulos, P., Bylund, E. and Casasanto, D. (2016) Introduction to the special issue: New and interdisciplinary approaches to linguistic relativity. *Language Learning* 66 (3), 482–486.

Atkinson, D. (ed.) (2011) *Alternative Approaches to Second Language Acquisition*. New York: Routledge.

Atkinson, D., Churchill, E., Nishino, T. and Okada, H. (2007) Alignment and interaction in a sociocognitive approach in second language acquisition. *The Modern Language Journal* 91, 169–188.

Auer, P. (1995) The pragmatics of code-switching: A sequential approach. In L. Milroy and P. Muysken (eds) *One Speaker, Two Languages* (pp. 115–135). Cambridge: Cambridge University Press.

Auger, N. and Louis, V. (2009) Approche par les tâches, perspective actionnelle du FLE: quelles tâches possibles? [A task-based approach, an action-oriented perspective on French as a foreign language. What tasks are possible?] In E. Rosen (ed.) (pp. 102–110).

Austin, J.L. (1962) *How to do Things with Words*. Oxford: Clarendon Press.

Ausubel, D., Novak, J.D. and Hanesian, H. (1978) *Educational Psychology: A Cognitive View* (2nd edn). New York: Holt, Rinehart and Winston.

Bachelard, G. [1934] (2003) *Le nouvel esprit scientifique [The New Scientific Spirit]*. Paris: Presses Universitaires de France.

Bachman, L.F. (1990) *Fundamental Considerations in Language Testing*. Oxford: Oxford University Press.

Bachman, L.F. and Palmer A.S. (1996) *Language Testing in Practice*. Oxford: Oxford University Press.

Backus, A., Gorter, D., Knapp, K., Schjerve-Rindler, R., Swanenberg, J., ten Thije, J.D. and Vetter, E. (2013) Inclusive multilingualism: Concept, modes and implications. *European Journal of Applied Linguistics* 1 (2), 179–215.

Bak, T.H., Vega-Mendoza, M. and Sorace, A. (2014) Never too late? An advantage on tests of auditory attention extends to late bilinguals. *Frontiers in Psychology 5*. doi: 10.3389/fpsyg.2014.00485.

Baker, C. (1988) *Key Issues in Bilingualism and Bilingual Education*. Clevedon: Multilingual Matters.

Baker, C. (2001) *Foundations of Bilingual Education and Bilingualism* (3rd edn). Clevedon: Multilingual Matters.

Bakhtine, M. (1984) *Esthétique de la création verbale [The Aesthetic of Verbal Creation]*. Paris: Gallimard.

Balboni, P.E. (2015). *Le sfide di Babele: Insegnare le lingue nelle società complesse [The Challenges of Babel: Teaching Languages in Complex Societies]*. (4th edn.) Torino: UTET Università.

Bandura, A. (1989) Human agency in social cognitive theory. *American Psychologist* 44, 1175–1184.

Bandura, A. (2001) Social cognitive theory: An agentic perspective. *Annual Review of Psychology* 52, 1–26.

Barnes, D. and Todd, F. (1977) *Communication and Learning in Small Groups*. London: Routledge and Kegan Paul.

Barrett, M. (2016) *Competences for Democratic Culture – Living Together as Equals in Culturally Diverse Democratic Societies*. Strasbourg: Council of Europe.

Bartning, I., Martin, M. and Vedder, I. (2010) Communicative proficiency and linguistic development: intersections between SLA and language testing research. *Eurosla Monographs Series, 1*. European Second Language Association. www.eurosla.org (accessed 08 March 2018).

Bauman, Z. (1992) *Intimations of Postmodernity*. New York/London: Routledge.

Bauman, Z. (2000) *Liquid Modernity*. Cambridge: Polity.

Beacco, J-C. (2007) *L'approche par compétences dans l'enseignement des langues [The Competence-Oriented Approach in Language Teaching]*. Paris: Didier.

Beacco, J-C. and Byram, M. (2007a) *From Linguistic Diversity to Plurilingual Education: Guide for the Development of Language Education Policies in Europe*. Strasbourg: Council of Europe. www.coe.int/en/web/common-european-framework-reference-languages/documents (accessed 08 March 2018).

Beacco, J-C. and Byram, M. (2007b) *From Linguistic Diversity to Plurilingual Education: Guide for the Development of Language Education Policies in Europe. Executive Version*. Strasbourg: Council of Europe. www.coe.int/en/web/common-european-framework-reference-languages/documents (accessed 08 March 2018).

Beacco, J-C. and Porquier, R. (2008) *Niveau A2 pour le français:un référentiel [Level A2 for French: a Reference Level Descriptor]*. Paris: Didier.

Beacco, J-C., Porquier, R. and Bouquet, S. (2004) *Niveau B2 pour le français: un réferentiel [Level B2 for French: a Reference Level Descriptor]*. Paris: Didier (2 volumes).

Beacco J-C, Byram, M., Cavalli, M., Coste, D., Egli Cuenat, M., Goullier, F. and Panthier, J. (2015) *Guide for the Development and Implementation of Curricula for Plurilingual and Intercultural Education*. Strasbourg; Council of Europe. www.coe.int/en/web/common-european-framework-reference-languages/documents (accessed 08 March 2018).

Beacco, J-C., De Ferrari, M., Lhote, G. and Tagliante, C. (2005) *Niveau A1.1 Pour le français/Référentiel DILF [Level A1.1. for French: a Reference Level Descriptor DILF]*. Paris: Didier.

Beacco, J-C., Krumm, H-J, Little, D. Thalgott, P., Council of Europe (eds) (2017) *The Linguistic Integration of Adult Migrants. Some Lessons from Research/ L'intégration linguistique des migrants adultes. Les enseignements de la recherche*. Berlin/Boston: de Gruyter.

Beacco, J-C., Porquier, R. and Bouquet, S. (2007) *Niveau A1 pour le français: Un réferentiel [Level A1 for French: a Reference Level Descriptor]*. Paris: Didier.

Bell, D.M. (2003) Method and postmethod: Are they really so incompatible? *TESOL Quarterly* 37, 325–336.

Beltrán, J. and Lin, R. (2017) Exploring the possibilities of scenario-based assessment: an introduction. *Teachers College, Columbia University Working Papers in Applied Linguistics and TESOL* 17(2), i–ii.

Benesch, S. (2012) *Considering Emotions in Critical English Language Teaching. Theories and Praxis.* New York: Routledge.

Bento, M. (2012) Pour une définition de l'action dans la perspective actionnelle en France [For a definition of action in the action-oriented perspective in France]. *Synergies Canada* 5, 1–9. https://journal.lib.uoguelph.ca/index.php/synergies/article/view/1591 (accessed 10 March 2018).

Bergeron J., Desmarais L. and Duquette L. (1984) Les exercices communicatifs: un nouveau regard [Communicative exercises: a new perspective. *Etudes de Linguistique Appliquée [Studies in Applied Linguistics]* 56, 38–47.

Berthoud, A-C. (ed.) (1996) Acquisition des competences discursives dans un contexte plurilingue [The acquisition of discourse competence in a plurilingual context]. *VALS/ASLA: Bulletin Suisse de Linguistique Appliquee [Swiss Bulletin of Apllied Lingustiques]*, 64. ISSN-1023-2044.

Berthoud, A-C., Grin, F. and Lüdi, G. (2013) *Exploring the Dynamics of Multilingualism: The DYLAN project.* Amsterdam: John Benjamins.

Bialystok, E. (2001) *Bilingualism in Development: Language, Literacy, and Cognition.* Cambridge: Cambridge University Press.

Bialystok, E. (2009) Bilingualism: The good, the bad, and the indifferent. *Bilingualism: Language and Cognition* 12 (1), 3–11.

Bialystok, E., Craik F.I. and Freedman M. (2007) Bilingualism as a protection against the onset of symptoms of dementia. *Neuropsychologia* 45, 459–464.

Bialystok, E., Craik, F.I. and Luk, G. (2008) Cognitive control and lexical access in younger and older bilinguals. *Journal of Experimental Psychology: Learning, Memory and Cognition* 34, 859–873.

Bickes, H. (2004) Bilingualismus, Mehrsprachigkeit und Mentales Lexikon – Evolutionsbiologische, soziokulturelle und kognitionswissenschaftliche Perspektiven [Bilingualism, plurilingualism and mental lexicon - Perspectives from evolutionary biology, sociocultural and cognitive sciences]. *Fremdsprachen lehren und lernen [Learning and Teaching Foreign Languages]* 33, 27–51.

Biggs, J. (2003) *Aligning Teaching and Assessment to Curriculum Objectives: Imaginative Curriculum Project. LTSN Imaginative Curriculum Guide IC022.* York: Higher Education Academy.

Biggs, J. and Tang, C. (2011) *Teaching for Quality Learning at University.* Maidenhead: McGraw-Hill and Open University Press.

Black, P.J. and Wiliams, D. (1998) *Inside the Black Box: Raising Standards through Classroom Assessment.* London: King's College London School of Education.

Blömeke, S., Gustafsson, J-E. and Shavelson, R.J. (2015) Beyond dichotomies: Competence viewed as a continuum. *Zeitschrift für Psychologie [Journal of Psychology]* 223, 3–13. doi.org/10.1027/2151-2604/a000194.

Bloom, B.S. (1968) Learning for mastery. Instruction and curriculum. Regional education laboratory for the Carolinas and Virginia, topical papers and reprints, Number 1. *Evaluation comment* 1 (2), 2, 1–12.

Bloom B.S. and Krathwohl D.R. (1956) *The Classification of Educational Goals, by a Committee of College and University Examiners.* New York: Longman.

Bloomfield, L. (1914) *Introduction to the Study of Language.* New York: Holt.

Bloomfield, L. (1933) *Language.* Chicago: University of Chicago Press.

Borg, S. (2006) The distinctive characteristics of foreign language teachers. *Language Teaching Research* 10 (1), 3–31. Doi: 10.1191/1362168806lr182oa.

Bourguignon, C. (2006) De l'approche communicative à l' « approche communicaction-nelle »: une rupture épistémologique en didactique des langues-cultures [From the communicative approach to the "communicactional approach": an epistemological break in the teaching of languages and cultures]. *Synergies Europe* 1, 58–73. http://gerflint.fr/Base/Europe1/Claire.pdf (accessed 08 March 2018).

Bourguignon, C. (2010) *Pour enseigner les langues avec les CERCL- clés et conseils [Teaching Languages with the CEFR: Keys Points and Tips]*. Paris: Delagrave.

Bowes, C.A and Flinders, D.J. (1990) *Responsive Teaching: An Ecological Approach to Classroom Patterns of Language, Culture, and Thought*. New York: Teachers College Press.

Breen, M.P. and Candlin, C.N. (1980) The essentials of a communicative curriculum in language teaching. *Applied Linguistics* 1 (2), 89–112.

Brewer, S.S. (2018) Cultivating language skills from the inside-out: A focus on memory. In J. Mackay, M. Birello and D. Xerri (eds) *ELT Research in Action: Bridging the Gap between Research and Classroom Practice* (pp. 45–47). Faversham: IATEFL.

Brincker, M. (2014) Navigating beyond "here and now" affordances – on sensorimotor maturation and "false belief" performance. *Frontiers in Psychology* 5 (12). doi. org/10.3389/fpsyg.2014.01433.

Brindley, G. (1986) *The Assessment of Second Language Proficiency: Issues and Approaches*. Adelaide: National Curriculum Resource Centre.

Brindley, G. (1989) *Assessing Achievement in the Learner-Centred Curriculum*. Sydney: Macquarie University. NCELTR Research Series (National Centre for English Language Teaching and Research).

Brockmann, M., Clarke L. and Winch, C. (2008) Knowledge, skills, competence: European divergences in vocational education and training (VET) – the English, German and Dutch cases. *Oxford Review of Education* 34 (5), 547–567.

Broch H. (2005) *Logique d'un monde en ruine, Six essais philosophiques [The Logic of a World in Ruins: Six Philosophical Essays]*. Paris/Tel-Aviv: Editions de l'éclat.

Brown D. (2007) *Principles of Language Learning and Teaching* (5th edn). White Plains NY: Pearson Longman.

Brown, G. and Yule, G. (1983) *Teaching the Spoken Language*. Cambridge: Cambridge University Press.

Brown, G., Anderson, A., Shilock, R. and Yule G. (1984) *Teaching Talk: Strategies for Production and Assessment*. Cambridge: Cambridge University Press.

Brown, J.S., Collins, A. and Duguid, P. (1989) Situated cognition and the culture of learning. *Educational Researcher* 18 (1), 32–42.

Brumfit, C.J. (1981) Notional syllabuses revisited: A response. *Applied Linguistics* 2, 90–92.

Brumfit, C.J. (1984) *Communicative Methodology in Language Teaching: The Roles of Fluency and Accuracy*. Cambridge: Cambridge University Press.

Brumfit, C.J. (2001) *Individual Freedom in Language Teaching*. Oxford: Oxford University Press.

Burton, D. (1980) *Dialogue and Discourse; A Sociolinguistic Approach to Modern Drama Dialogue and Naturally Occurring Conversation*. London: Routledge and Kegan Paul.

Butjes, D. and Byram, M. (1990) *Mediating Languages and Cultures*. Clevedon: Multilingual Matters.

Bygate, M., Skehan, P. and Swain, M. (eds) (2001) *Researching Pedagogic Tasks: Second Language Learning, Teaching and Testing*. London: Longman.

Byram, M. (1997) *Teaching and Assessing Intercultural Communicative Competence*. Clevedon: Multilingual Matters.

Byram, M. (2006) *Language and Identities. Intergovernmental Conference: Languages of Schooling: Towards a Framework for Europe*. Strasbourg, 16–18 October

2006. Strasbourg: Council of Europe. https://rm.coe.int/16805c5d4a (accessed 08 March 2018).

Byram M. (2008) *From Foreign Language Education to Education for Intercultural citizenship*. Clevedon: Multilingual Matters.

Byram M. (2009) *Multicultural Societies, Pluricultural People and the Project of Intercultural Education*. Strasbourg: Council of Europe. https://rm.coe.int/multicultural-societies-pluricultural-people-and-the-project-of-interc/16805a223c (accessed 08 March 2018).

Byram, M. and Parmenter, L. (eds) (2012) *The Common European Framework of Reference: The Globalisation of Language Policy*. Bristol: Multilingual Matters.

Byram, M. and Wagner, M. (2018) Making a difference: Language teaching for intercultural and international dialogue. *Foreign Language Annals* 51, 140–151.

Byram, M. and Zarate, G. (1996) Defining and assessing intercultural competence: Some principles and proposals for the European context. *Language Teaching* 29 (4), 239–243.

Byram, M., Barrett, M. Ipgrave, J., Jackson, R. and Méndez García, C. (2009) *Context, Concepts and Theories of the 'Autobiography of Intercultural Encounters'*. Strasbourg: Council of Europe. www.coe.int/t/dg4/autobiography/Source/AIE_en/AIE_context_concepts_and_theories_en.pdf (accessed 08 March 2018).

Byram, M., Golubeva, I., Hui, H. and Wagner, M. (eds) (2017) *From Principles to Practice in Education for Intercultural Citizenship*. Bristol: Multilingual Matters.

Byram, M., Gribkova, B. and Starkey, H. (2002) *Developing the Intercultural Dimension in Language Teaching: A Practical Introduction for Teachers*. Strasbourg: Council of Europe. www.scribd.com/document/338011483/Developing-the-Intercultural-Dimension-in-Language-Teaching-pdf (accessed 08 March 2018).

Byram, M., Zarate G. and Neuner, G. (1996) *Sociocultural Competence in Language Learning and Teaching*. Strasbourg: Council of Europe.

Byrnes, H. (2007) Perspectives: (Issue on the CEFR). *The Modern Language Journal* 91 (4), 641–685.

Canagarajah, S. (2007) The ecology of global English. *International Multilingual Research Journal* 1 (2), 89–100.

Canagarajah, S. (2009) The plurilingual tradition and the English language in South Asia. *AILA Review* 22, 5–22.

Canagarajah, S. (2011a) Codemeshing in academic writing: Identifying teachable strategies of translanguaging. *The Modern Language Journal* 95 (3), 401–417.

Canagarajah, S. (2011b) Translanguaging in the classroom: Emerging issues for research and pedagogy. In L. Wei (ed.) *Applied Linguistics Review* 2, 1–27). Berlin: De Gruyter Mouton.

Canagarajah, S. (2013) *Translingual Practice: Global Englishes and Cosmopolitan Relations*. London and New York: Routledge.

Canagarajah, S. (2018) Materializing 'competence': Perspectives from international STEM scholars. *The Modern Language Journal* 102 (2), 268–291. doi: 10.1111/modl.12464.

Canagarajah, S., and Liyanage, I. (2012) Lessons from pre-colonial multilingualism. In M. Martin-Jones, A. Blackledge, and A. Creese (eds) *The Routledge Handbook of Multilingualism* (pp. 49–65). London: Routledge.

Canale, M. (1983) On some dimensions of language proficiency. In J.W. Oller (ed.) (pp. 333–342).

Canale, M. (1984) On some theoretical frameworks for language proficiency. In C. Rivera (ed.) *Language Proficiency and Academic Achievement* (pp. 28–40). Clevedon: Multilingual Matters.

Canale, M. and Swain, M. (1980) Theoretical bases of communicative approaches to second language teaching and testing. *Applied Linguistics* 1 (1), 1–47.

Candelier, M., de Pietro, J-F., Facciol, R., Lorincz, I., Pascual, X. and Schröder-Sura, A. (2011) *CARAP–FREPA: A Framework of Reference for Pluralistic Approaches to Languages and Cultures*. Strasbourg: Council of Europe. http://carap.ecml.at/ (accessed 08 March 2018).

Candlin, C.N. (1987) Towards task-based language learning. In C.N. Candlin and D.F. Murphy (eds) *Language Learning Tasks: Lancaster Practical Papers in English Language Education 7* (pp. 5–22). Hemel Hempstead: Prentice Hall International and Lancaster University.

Caré, J-M. and Debyser F. (1995) *Simulations globales [Global Simulations]*. Sèvres: Centre international d'études pédagogiques (CIEP).

Carrasco Perea, E. (ed.) (2010) Intercompréhension(s): repères, interrogations et perspectives. *Synergies Europe 5*. https://gerflint.fr/Base/Europe5/europe5.html (accessed 08 March 2018).

Carroll, B.A. (2017) A learning-oriented assessment perspective on scenario-based assessment. *Teachers College, Columbia University Working Papers in Applied Linguistics and TESOL 17*(2), 28–35. https://academiccommons.columbia.edu/doi/10.7916/D8XD2CNC (accessed 30 September 2018).

Carson, L. (2012) The role of drama in task-based learning: Agency, identity and autonomy. *Scenario Journal for Drama and Theatre in Foreign and Second Language Education 6* (2), 46–59.

Castellotti, V. (2002) Qui a peur de la notion de compétence? [Who is afraid of the notion of competence?] In V. Castellotti and B. Py (pp. 9–18).

Castellotti, V. and Py, B. (eds) (2002) *La notion de compétence en langue [The Notion of Competence in Language]*. Lyon: ENS Editions.

Cazden, C. (2018) *Communicative Competence, Classroom Interaction, and Educational Equity. The Selected Works of Courtney B. Cazden*. New York: Routledge.

Celce-Murcia, M. (1991) Language teaching approaches: An overview. In M. Celce-Murcia (ed.) *Teaching English as a Second or Foreign Language* (2nd edn) (pp. 3–11). Boston, MA: Heinle and Heinle Publishers.

Celce-Murcia, M. (2007) Rethinking the role of communicative competence in language teaching. In A.A. Soler and M.P. Safont Jorda (eds) *Intercultural Language Use and Language Learning* (pp. 41–57). Berlin: Springer.

Celce-Murcia, M., Dörnyei, Z. and Thurrell, S. (1995) Communicative competence: A pedagogically motivated model with content specifications. *Issues in Applied Linguistics 6* (2), 5–35.

Cenoz, J. (2009) *Towards Multilingual Education: Basque Educational Research from an International Perspective*. Bristol: Multilingual Matters.

Cenoz, J. (2013) Defining multilingualism. *Annual Review of Applied Linguistics 33*, 3–18. doi: 10.1017/S026719051300007X.

Cenoz, J. and Gorter, D. (2011) A holistic approach to multilingual education: Introduction. *The Modern Language Journal 95*, 339–343. doi:10.1111/j.1540-4781.2011.01204.x.

Champney, H. (1941) The measurement of parent behaviour. *Child Development 12* (2), 131–166.

Cho, K., Piccardo, E., Lawrence, G. and Germain-Rutherford, A. (2018) LINguistic and Cultural DIversity REinvented (LINCDIRE): Integrating western and indigenous perspectives to redefine language education practices. *The Language Educator* March/April 2018, 44–48.

Chomsky, N. (1965) *Aspects of the Theory of Syntax*. Cambridge MA: The MIT Press.

Chomsky, N. (1975) *Reflections on Language*. London: Temple Smith.

Chomsky, N. (1980) *Rules and Representations*. Oxford: Blackwell.

Chomsky, N. (1992) *Language and Thought*. Wakefield: Moyer Bell.

Cilliers, P. (1998) *Complexity and Postmodernism: Understanding Complex Systems*. London and New York: Routledge.

Cilliers, P. (2005) Knowledge, limits and boundaries. *Futures 37*, 605–613. doi: 10.1016/j.futures.2004.11.001.

Clapham, C. (1996) *The Development of IELTS: A Study of the Effect of Background on Reading Comprehension. Studies in Language Testing 4*. Cambridge: Cambridge University Press.

Clark, J.L. (1987) *Curriculum Renewal in School Foreign Language Learning*. Oxford: Oxford University Press.

Coïaniz A. (2001) *Apprentissage des langues et subjectivité [Subjectivity and the Learning of Languages]*. Paris: L'Harmattan.

Cole, M. (1996) *Cultural Psychology: A Once and Future Discipline*. Cambridge: Belknap Press.

Cook, V.J. (1991) The poverty-of-the-stimulus argument and multi-competence. *Second Language Research* 7 (2), 103–117.

Cook, V.J. and Wei, L. (2016) *The Cambridge Handbook of Linguistic Multicompetence*. Cambridge: Cambridge University Press.

Corder, P. (1981) *Error Analysis and Interlanguage*. Oxford: Oxford University Press.

Coste, D. (2014) Plurilingualism and the challenges of education. In P. Gromes and H. Wu (eds) (pp. 15–32).

Coste, D. and Cavalli, M. (2015) *Education, Mobility, Otherness: The Mediation Functions of Schools*, Strasbourg: Council of Europe. www.coe.int/en/web/common-european-framework-reference-languages/documents (accessed 08 March 2018).

Coste D. and Hebrard, J. (1991) Vers le plurilinguisme? [Towards plurlngualism?] *Le Français dans le Monde: Recherches et Applications [French in the World: Research and Applications]*. Paris: Hachette.

Coste, D., Courtillon, J., Ferenczi, V., Martins-Baltar, M., Papo, E. and Roulet, E. (1976) *Un niveau-seuil [A Threshold Level]*. Strasbourg: Conseil de l'Europe.

Coste, D., Di Pietro, J-F and Moore, D. (2012) Hymes et le palimpseste de la compétence de communication: tours, détours et retours en didactique des langues [Hymes and the palimpsest of communicative competence: turns, detours and returns in language pedagogy]. *Langage et Société [Language and Society]* 139, 103–123.

Coste, D., Moore, D. and Zarate, G. (1997) *Compétence plurilingue et pluriculturelle. Vers un Cadre Européen Commun de référence pour l'enseignement et l'apprentissage des langues vivantes.* Études préparatoires. Strasbourg: Council of Europe. Reprinted in English (2009) as *Plurilingual and Pluricultural Competence. Studies towards a Common European Framework of Reference for Language Learning and Teaching.* Strasbourg: Council of Europe. www.coe.int/en/web/common-european-framework-reference-languages/documents (accessed 08 March 2018).

Coulthard, M. (1977) *An Introduction to Discourse Analysis*. London: Longman.

Council of Europe (1992) *Transparency and Coherence in Language Learning in Europe: Objectives, Assessment and Certification. Symposium held in Rüschlikon, 10–16 November 1991: Report.* Strasbourg. Council of Europe.

Council of Europe (1996) *Modern Languages: Learning, Teaching, Assessment. A Common European Framework of Reference. Draft 2 of a Framework Proposal.* CC-LANG (95) 5 rev. IV. Strasbourg: Council of Europe.

Council of Europe (2001) *Common European Framework of Reference for Languages: Learning, Teaching, Assessment*, Cambridge: Cambridge University Press. www.coe.int/en/web/common-european-framework-reference-languages/ (accessed 08 March 2018).

Council of Europe (2009) *Relating Language Examinations to the Common European Framework of Reference for Languages: Learning, Teaching, Assessment (CEFR)*. Strasbourg: Council of Europe. www.coe.int/en/web/common-european-framework-reference-languages/tests-and-examinations (accessed 08 March 2018).

Council of Europe (2018) *Common European Framework of Reference for Languages : Learning, Teaching, Assessment. Companion Volume with New Descriptors.*

Strasbourg: Council of Europe. https://rm.coe.int/cefr-companion-volume-with-new-descriptors-2018/1680787989 (accessed 08 March 2018). The definitive ISBN version will be published in print and online in early 2020; page numbers will change.

Cowley, S.J., Gahrn-Andersen, R. (2018) Simplexity, languages and human languaging, *Language Sciences* doi.org/10.1016/j.langsci.2018.04.008.

Creese, A. and Blackledge, A. (2010) Translanguaging in the bilingual classroom: A pedagogy for learning and teaching? *The Modern Language Journal* 94 (1), 103–115.

Csikszentmihalyi M. (1996) *Creativity*. New York: Harper Perennial/Harper Collins Publishers.

Csikszentmihalyi, M. (2015) *The Systems Model of Creativity. The Collected Works of Mihaly Csikszentmihalyi*. Dordrecht: Springer.

Cummins, J. (2008) Teaching for transfer: challenging the *two solitudes* assumption in bilingual education. In J. Cummins and N.H. Hornberger (eds) *Encyclopedia of Language and Education. Bilingual Education* Vol. 5 (pp. 65–75). New York: Springer. 10.1007/978-0-387-30424-3_116.

Cummins, J. (2017) Teaching minoritized students: Are additive approaches legitimate? *Harvard Educational Review* 87 (3), 404–425.

Cummins, J. and Early, M. (2010) *Identity Texts: The Collaborative Creation of Power in Multilingual Schools*. Stoke-on-Trent, Staffordshire: Trentham Books Ltd.

Cummins, J., Hu, S., Markus, P. and Montero, M.K. (2015) Identity texts and academic achievement: Connecting the dots in multilingual school contexts. *TESOL Quarterly* 49 (3), 555–581.

Dacrema, N. (2012) Il 'caso Austria'. In I. Putzu I and G. Mazzon (eds) *Lingue, letterature nazioni: Centri e periferie tra Europa e Mediterraneo* (pp. 294–346). Milan: Franco Angeli.

Dam, L. (ed.) (2001) Learner autonomy: new insights. *AILA Review* 15.

Damasio, A.R. (1994) *Descartes' Error: Emotion, Reason, and the Human Brain*. New York: Putnam.

Damasio, A.R. (1999) *The Feeling of What Happens: Body and Emotion in the Making of Consciousness*. New York: Harcourt Brace.

Damasio A.R. (2003) *Looking for Spinoza: Joy, Sorrow and the Feeling Brain*. New York: Harcourt Brace.

Daniels, H. (2001) *Vygotsky and Pedagogy*. London: Routledge Falmer.

Davies, A. (1989) Communicative competence as language use. *Applied Linguistics* 10 (2), 157–170.

Davis, B. (2008) Complexity and education: Vital simultaneities. *Educational Philosophy and Theory* 40 (1), 50–65.

Davis, B. and Sumara, D.J. (1997) Cognition, complexity, and teacher education. *Harvard Educational Review* 67 (1), 105–126.

Davis, B. and Sumara, D.J. (2005) Challenging images of knowing: Complexity science and educational research. *International Journal of Qualitative Studies in Education* 18 (3), 305–321.

Debyser, F. and Yaiche, F. (1986) *L'immeuble [The Building]*. Paris: Hachette.

de Bot, K. (2016) Multi-competence and dynamic/complex systems. In V. Cook and L. Wei (eds) *The Cambridge Handbook of Linguistic Multi-competence* (pp. 125–141). Cambridge: Cambridge University Press.

de Bot, K., Lowie, W. and Verspoor, M. (2007) A dynamic systems theory approach to second language acquisition. *Bilingualism: Language and Cognition* 10 (1), 7–21.

de Jong, J.H.A.L., Mayor, M. and Hayes, C. (2016) *Developing Global Scale of English Learning Objectives aligned to the Common European Framework. Global Scale of English Research Series*. London: Pearson. https://www.pearson.com/content/dam/one-dot-com/one-dot-com/english/TeacherResources/GSE/GSE-WhitePaper-Developing-LOs.pdf (accessed 08 March 2018).

de Mauro, T. (1977) Il plurilinguismo nella società e nella scuola italiana [Plurilingualism in the Italian culture and school]. In R. Simone and G. Ruggiero (eds) *Aspetti sociolinguistici dell'Italia contemporanea. [Sociolinguistic Aspects of Contemporary Italy] Atti dell'VIII Congresso Internazionale di Studi (Bressanone, 31 maggio-2 giugno 1974)* Vol. I. Pubblicazioni della SLI 10/1 (pp. 87–101). Roma: Bulzoni Editore.

de Montmollin, M. (1996) Savoir travailler. Le point de vue de l'ergonome [The ability to work seen from an ergonomic perspective]. In J-M. Barbier (ed.) *Savoirs théoriques et savoirs d'action [Theoretical Knowledge and Capacity for Action]* (pp. 189–199). Paris: Presses Universitaires de France.

de Terssac, G. (1992) *Autonomie dans le travail [Autonomy at Work]*. Paris: Presses Universitaires de France.

de Terssac, G. and Chabaud, C. (1990) Référentiel opératif commun et fiabilité [Common operational reference points and their reliability]. In J. Leplat and G. de Terssac (eds) *Les facteurs humains de la fiabilité dans les systèmes complexes [Human Reliability Factors in Complex Systems]* (pp. 110–139). Toulouse: Octarès Editions.

Debyser, F. (1986) *Simulations globales: L'immeuble [Global Simulations: The Building]*. Paris: Hachette. (New edition, 1996).

Defert, J-J. (2012) Appréhender la complexité. Enjeux et raisonnances dans le domaine culture [Understanding complexity: issues and resonances in the cultural domain] *International Journal of Canadian Studies/Revue internationale d'études canadiennes*, 45–46, 307–329. Retrieved from http://id.erudit.org/iderudit/1009908ar.

Degache, C. (ed.) (2003) Intercomprehension en langues romanes. Du développement des compétences de compréhension aux interactions plurilingues, de Galatea à Galanet [Intercomprehension in Romance languages. From the development of comprehension competences to plurilingual interactions: from Galatea to Galanet]. *Lidil* 28.

Del Barrio, M.M. (ed.) (2015) *La enseñanza de la intercomprensión a distancia [Distance Teaching of Intercomprehension]*. Madrid: Universidad Complutense de Madrid. http://eprints.ucm.es/35033/1/ense%C3%B1anza%20valido.pdf (accessed 08 March 2018).

Delamare le Diest, F. and Winterton, J. (2005) What is competence? *Human Resource Development International* 8 (1), 27–46.

Deleuze, G. and Guattari, F. (1987) *A Thousand Plateaus*. Minneapolis: University of Minnesota Press.

Deming, W.E. (1986) *Out of the Crisis*. Cambridge, MA: MIT, Center for Advanced Engineering Studies.

Dendrinos, B. (2006) Mediation in communication, language teaching and testing. *Journal of Applied Linguistics* 22, 9–35.

Dendrinos, B. (2013) Testing and teaching mediation. Directions in English Language Teaching, Testing and Assessment. Athens: RCeL publications https://rcel2.enl.uoa.gr/directions/issue1_1f.htm (accessed 20 June 2019).

Denyer, D. (2009) La perspective actionnelle définie par le CECR et ses répercussions dans l'enseignement des langue [The action-oriented perspective and its repercussions in language teaching]. In M.L. Lions-Olivieri and P. Liria (eds) (pp. 141–156).

Dewaele, J.M. and Wei, L. (2013) Is multilingualism linked to a higher tolerance of ambiguity? *Bilingualism: Language and Cognition* 16 (1), 231–240.

Di Pietro, R.J. (1987) *Strategic Interaction: Learning Languages through Scenarios*. Cambridge: Cambridge University Press.

Dickinson, L. (1987) *Self Directed Learning*. Oxford: University Press.

Díez-Bedmar, M.B. (2017) Fine-tuning descriptors for CEFR B1 level: insights from learner corpora. *ELT Journal*. ccx052, https://doi.org/10.1093/elt/ccx052.

Doidge, N. (2007) *The Brain that Changes Itself*. New York: Viking Press.

Doise, W. and Mugny, G. (1997) *Psychologie sociale et développement cognitif [Social Psychology and Cognitive Development]*. Paris: Armand Colin.

Dolz, J. (2002) L'énigme de la compétence dans l'éducation [The enigma of competence in education]. In V. Castellotti and B. Py (pp. 83–104).

Doyé, P. (2004) A methodological framework for the teaching of intercomprehension. *Language Learning Journal* 30 (1), 59–68.

Doyé, P. (2005) *Intercomprehension: Guide for the Development of Language Education Policies in Europe: From Linguistic Diversity to Plurilingual Education. Reference Study*. Strasbourg: Council of Europe. https://rm.coe.int/intercomprehension/1680874594 (accessed 08 March 2018).

Durham Immigration Portal (2016) *Durham Immigration Portal: Exploring the Region of Durham through Task-based Learning*. www.durhamimmigration.ca/en/work-and-study/resources/Living-in-English_Discovering-Durham.pdf (accessed 08 March 2018).

Eaquals and CIEP (2015) *Inventaire linguistique des contenus clés des niveaux du CECRL [Linguistic Inventory of Core Content at the CEFR Levels]*. Sévres: CIEP. www.eaquals.org/wp-content/uploads/Inventaire_ONLINE_full.pdf (accessed 08 March 2018).

Edge, J. (2001) (ed.) *Action Research*. Alexandria, VA: TESOL.

Egan, K. (2002) *Getting It Wrong from the Beginning: Our Progressive Inheritance from Herbert Spencer, John Dewey, and Jean Piaget*. New Haven, CT: Yale University Press.

Ehrmann, M. (1999) Ego boundaries and tolerance of ambiguity in second language learning. In J. Arnold (ed.) *Affect in Language Learning*. Cambridge: Cambridge University Press.

Ellis, N.C. (2006) Cognitive perspectives on SLA: The associative-cognitive CREED. *AILA Review* 19, 100–121.

Ellis, N.C. (2014) Cognitive and social language use. *Studies in Second Language Acquisition* 36, 397–402. doi:10.1017/S0272263114000035.

Ellis, N.C. and Larsen-Freeman, D. (eds) (2009) *Language as a Complex Adaptive System*. Chichester, West Sussex; Malden, MA: Wiley-Blackwell.

Ellis, R. (1989) Are classroom and naturalistic acquisition the same? A study of classroom acquisition of German word order rules. *Studies in Second Language Acquisition* 11, 305–328.

Ellis, R. (1992) Learning to communicate in the classroom: A study of two language learners' requests. *Studies in Second Language Acquisition* 14 (1), 1–23.

Ellis, R. (2003) *Task-based Language Learning and Teaching*. Oxford: Oxford University Press.

Ellis, R. (2009) Task-based research and language pedagogy. In K. van den Branden, M. Bygate and J. M. Norris (eds) (pp. 109–30). Originally published, 2000, in *Language Teaching Research* 4, 193–220.

Ellis, R. (2018) *Reflections on Task-based Language Teaching*. Bristol: Multilingual Matters.

Engel, D., Woolley, A.W., Jing, L.X., Chabris, C.F. and Malone, T.W. (2014) Reading the mind in the eyes or reading between the lines? Theory of Mind predicts collective intelligence equally well online and face-to-face. *PLoS ONE* 9, 12. doi.org/10.1371/journal.pone.0115212.

Engeström, R. (1995) Voice as communicative action. *Mind, Culture, and Activity* 2 (3), 192–215, doi: 10.1080/10749039509524699.

Engeström, Y. (1999) Activity theory and individual and social transformation. In Y. Engeström, R. Miettinen and R. Punamäki (eds) *Perspectives on Activity Theory: Learning in Doing: Social, Cognitive and Computational Perspectives* (pp. 19–38). Cambridge: Cambridge University Press. doi:10.1017/CBO9780511812774.003.

European Commission (2006) Lifelong Learning – Key Competences. Summary of Recommendation 2006/962/EC on key competences for lifelong learning. http://eur-lex.europa.eu/legal-content/EN/TXT/?uri=LEGISSUM:c11090 (accessed 08 March 2018).

European Commission (2009) *Study on the Contribution of Multilingualism to Creativity. Compendium Part One. Multilingualism and Creativity. Final Report: Towards an Evidence-base.* http://www.dylan-project.org/Dylan_en/news/assets/StudyMultilingualism_report_en.pdf (accessed 08 March 2018).

European Parliament (2006) Recommendation of the European Parliament and the Council of 18th December 2006 on Key Competences for Lifelong Learning (2006/962/EC). http://eur-lex.europa.eu/legal-content/EN/TXT/?uri=celex:32006H0962 (accessed 08 March 2018).

Færch, C. and Kasper, G.K. (1983) Plans and strategies in foreign language communication. In C. Færch and G.K. Kasper (eds) *Strategies in Interlanguage Communication* (pp. 20–60). Harlow: Longman.

Figueras, N. (2012) The impact of the CEFR. *English Language Teaching Journal* 66 (4), 477–485.

Filliettaz, L. (2002) *La parole en action [The Word in Action].* Genève: Éditions Nota Bene.

Filliettaz, L. (2004) Le virage actionnel des modèles du discours à l'épreuve des interactions de service [The actional turn in models of discourse on the basis of evidence from service encounters]. *Langage et Société [Language and Society]* 107 (1), 31–54.

Filliettaz, L. and Bronckart, J-P. (eds) (2005) *L'analyse des actions et des discours en situation de travail. Concepts, methodes et applications [The Analysis of Actions and Talk in Work Situations].* Louvain: Peeters, BCILL.

Forsberg, F. and Bartning, I. (2010) Can linguistic features discriminate between the communicative CEFR-levels? A pilot study of written L2 French. In I. Bartning, M. Martin and I. Vedder (eds) (pp. 133–158).

Foster, P. and Skehan, P. (1996) The influence of planning and task type on second language performance. *Studies in Second Language Acquisition* 18, 299–323.

Freadman, A. (2014) Fragmented memory in a global age: The place of storytelling in modern language curricula. *The Modern Language Journal* 98 (1), 373–385.

Freeman, D. (2002) The hidden side of the work: Teacher knowledge and learning to teach. A perspective from North American educational research on teacher education in English language teaching. *Language Teaching* 35, 1–13. doi:10.1017/S0261444801001720.

Friedman, R. and Rogers, K. (1998) Introduction. In R. Friedman and K. Rogers (eds) *Talent in Context: Historical and Social Perspectives on Giftedness* (pp. xv–xxiv). Washington, DC: American Psychological Association. doi:10.1037/10297-000.

Fries, C. (1945) *Teaching and Learning English as a Foreign Language.* Ann Arbour: University of Michigan Press.

Fulcher, G. (1993) The construction and validation of rating scales for oral tests in English as a foreign language, PhD thesis, University of Lancaster.

Fulcher, G. (1996) Does thick description lead to smart tests? A data-based approach to rating scale construction. *Language Testing* 13 (2), 208–238.

Fulcher, G. (2004) Deluded by artifices? The Common European Framework and harmonization. *Language Testing Quarterly* 1 (4), 253–266.

Furlong, A. (2009) The relation of plurilingualism/culturalism to creativity: A matter of perception. *International Journal of Multilingualism* 6 (4), 343–368.

Gadamer, H-G. (1990) *Truth and Method.* New York: Continuum.

Galaczi, E.D. and Weir, C.J. (eds) (2013) *Exploring Language Frameworks: Proceedings of the ALTE Krakow Conference, July 2011.* Cambridge, Studies in Language Testing Series: Cambridge University Press.

Gallagher, S. (2009) Philosophical antecedents to situated cognition. In P. Robbins and M. Aydede (eds) *The Cambridge Handbook of Situated Cognition* (pp. 35–51). Cambridge: Cambridge University Press.

Gallagher, S. (2015) Seeing things in the right way: How social interaction shapes perception. In M. Doyon and T. Breyer (eds) *Normativity in Perception* (pp. 117–127). Basingstoke: Palgrave MacMillan.

Gallagher, S. and Hutto, D. (2008) Understanding others through primary interaction and narrative practice. In J. Zlatev, T. Racine, C. Sinha and E. Itkonen (eds) *The Shared Mind: Perspectives on Intersubjectivity* (pp. 17–38). Amsterdam: John Benjamins.

Gallagher, S., Martínez, S., and Gastelum, M. (2017) Action-space and time: Towards an enactive hermeneutics. In B. Janz (ed.) *Place Space and Hermeneutics* (pp. 83–96). Dordrecht: Springer.

García, O. (2009) *Bilingual Education in the 21st Century: A Global Perspective.* Oxford: Wiley-Blackwell.

García, O. and Lin, A. (2016) Translanguaging and bilingual education. In O. García, A. Lin and S. May (eds) *Bilingual and Multilingual Education. Encyclopedia of Language and Education 5.* New York: Springer. doi: 10.1007/978-3-319-02324-3_9-1.

García, O. and Wei, L. (2014) *Translanguaging: Language, Bilingualism and Education.* Basingstoke: Palgrave Macmillan.

García, O., Bartlett, L. and Kleifgen, J. (2007) From biliteracy to pluriliteracies. In P. Auer and L. Wei (eds) *Handbook of Applied Linguistics, Vol. 5: Multilingualism* (pp. 207–228). Berlin: Mouton de Gruyter.

García, O., Johnson, S. and Seltzer, K. (2017) *The Translanguaging Classroom. Leveraging Student Bilingualism for Learning.* Philadelphia: Caslon.

Germain, C. (1993) Évolution de l'enseignement des langues: 5000 ans d'histoire *[The Evolution of Language Teaching: 5,000 Years of History].* Paris: CLE international.

Gibson, J.J. (1986) *The Ecological Approach to Visual Perception.* Hillsdale, NJ: Erlbaum (original work published 1979, New York: Psychology Press).

Gipps, C.V. (1994) *Beyond Testing: Towards a Theory of Educational Assessment.* London: Falmer Press.

Glaboniat, M., Müller, M., Rusch, P., Schmitz, H. and Wertenschlag, L. (2005) *Profile deutsch A1 – C2. Lernzielbestimmungen, Kannbeschreibungen, Kommunikative Mittel [German Profile A1–C2. Definition of Learning Objectives, Can-Do Statements, Communicative Resources].* München: Langenscheidt.

Glaser, R. (1963) Instructional technology and the measurement of learning outcomes: Some questions. *American Psychologist* 18 (8), 519–521.

Glaser, R. (1994a) Instructional technology and the measurement of learning outcomes: Some questions. *Educational Measurement: Issues and Practice* 13 (4), 6–8.

Glaser, R. (1994b) Criterion-referenced tests: Part 1. Origins. *Educational Measurement: Issues and Practice* 13 (4), 9–11.

Glăvenau, V.P. (2010) Principles for a cultural psychology of creativity. *Culture and Psychology* 16, 147–163.

Glăvenau, V.P. (2012) What can be done with an egg? Creativity, material objects and the theory of affordances. *The Journal of Creative Behavior* 46 (3), 192–208.

Glăvenau, V.P. (2013) Rewriting the language of creativity: The five A's framework. *Review of General Psychology* 17 (1), 69–81.

Gleick, J. (1987) *Chaos: Making a New Science.* New York: Penguin Books.

Glenberg, A.M. and Goldberg, A.B. (2011) Improving early reading comprehension using embodied CAI. *Instruction Science* 39, 27–39.

Glenberg, A.M. and Kaschak, M.P. (2002) Grounding language in action. *Psychnomic Bulletin and Review* 9 (3), 558–565.

Glenberg, A.M., Gutierrez, T., Levin, J.R., Japuntich, S. and Kaschak, M.P. (2004) Activity and imagined activity can enhance young children's reading comprehension. *Journal of Educational Psychology* 96 (3), 424–436.

Goffman, E. (1963) *Stigma; Notes on the Management of Spoiled Identity*. Englewood Cliffs, N.J.: Prentice-Hall.

Goffman. E. (1967) *Interaction Ritual*. New York: Doubleday.

Goffman E. (1972) On face-work: an analysis of ritual elements in social interaction. In J. Lever and S. Hutchinson (eds) *Communication in Face to Face Interaction* (pp. 319–347). Harmondsworth: Penguin Books. Originally published 1955.

Goffman, E. (1976) Replies and responses. Language in Society 5 (3), 257–313.

Good, T.L. and Brophy, J.E. (1990) *Educational Psychology: A Realistic Approach* (4th edn). New York: Longman.

Good, T.L. and Brophy, J.E. (1995) *Contemporary Educational Psychology*. White Plains, NY: Longman.

Gosling, J. (1981) Kinesics in discourse. In M. Coulthard and M. Montgomery (eds) *Studies in Discourse Analysis* (pp. 158–183). London: Routledge and Keegan Paul.

Goullier, F. (2007a) *Council of Europe Tools for Language Teaching: Common European Framework and Portfolios*. Paris: Didier/Council of Europe.

Goullier, F. (2007b) In Council of Europe *The Common European Framework of Reference for Languages (CEFR) and the Development of Language Policies: Challenges and Responsibilities*. Intergovernmental Language Policy Forum, Strasbourg, 6-8 February 2007: Report (pp. 29–37). Strasbourg: Council of Europe

Goullier, F., Beacco, J-C., Sheils, J., and Fleming, M. (2016) *The Language Dimension in All Subjects – A Handbook for Curriculum Development and Teacher Training*. Strasbourg: Council of Europe. https://book.coe.int/en/language-policy/7119-the-language-dimension-in-all-subjects-a-handbook-for-curriculum-development-and-teacher-training.html (accessed 08 March 2018).

Graves, K. (2008) The language curriculum: A social contextual perspective. *Language Teaching* 41 (2), 147–181.

Grebe, P. and Drosdowski, G. (1963) *Duden Etymologie: Herkunftswörterbuch der Deutschen Sprache [Duden Etymology: Dictionary of Word Origins for the German Language]*. Mannheim: Bibliographisches Institut.

Green, A. (2012) *Language Functions Revisited: Theoretical and Empirical Bases for Language Construct Definition Across the Ability Range*. Cambridge: Cambridge University Press.

Grice, H.P. (1975) Logic and conversation. In P. Cole and J. Morgan (eds) *Syntax and Semantics. Vol. 3: Speech Acts* (pp. 41–58). New York: Academic Press.

Gromes, P. and Wu, H. (2014) *Plurilingual Education: Policies – Practices – Language Development*. Amsterdam/Philadelphia: John Benjamins.

Guilford, J-P. (1967) *The Nature of Intelligence*. New York: McGraw-Hill.

Gumperz, J.J. (1982) *Discourse Strategies*. Cambridge: Cambridge University Press.

Gumperz, J.J. (1984) *Communicative Competence Revisited*. Berkeley (CA): University of California Press, Berkeley Science Report Series.

Habermas, J. (1970) Towards a theory of communicative competence. In H.P. Dreitzel (ed.) *Recent Sociology 2* (pp. 115–148). New York: Macmillan.

Hakuta, K., Bialystok, E. and Wiley, E. (2003) Critical evidence: A test of the critical-period hypothesis for second-language acquisition. *Psychological Science* 14 (1), 31–38.

Halliday, M.A.K. (1973) *Explorations in the Functions of Language*. London: Edward Arnold.

Halliday, M.A.K. (1975) *Language How to Mean. Explorations in the Development of Language*. London: Edward Arnold.

Halliday, M.A.K. (1978) *Language as Social Semiotic: the Social Interpretation of Language and Meaning*. London: Edward Arnold.

Halliday, M.A.K. (1989) *Spoken and Written Language*. Oxford: Oxford University Press.

Halliday, M.A.K. (2002) Applied linguistics as an evolving theme. Plenary address to the Association Internationale de Linguistique Appliqué, Singapore, December 2002.

Halliday, M.A.K. (2007) Applied linguistics as an evolving theme. In J. Webster (ed.) *Language and Education: Collected Works of M.A.K. Halliday* (pp. 1–19). London: Continuum.

Harley, B. Allen P. Cummins J. and Swain M. (1990) Response by the DBP Project members to the discussion papers of Bachman and Schachter. In B. Harley, P. Allen, J. Cummins and M. Swain (eds) *The Development of Second Language Proficiency* (pp. 50–54). Cambridge: Cambridge University Press.

Harmer, J. (2001) *How to Teach English*. (3rd edn). Harlow: Pearson.

Harris, R. (2001) *The Language Myth in Western Culture*. Routledge: London.

Hawkins, A. (1999) Foreign language study and language awareness. *Language Awareness* 8 (3), 124–142.

Hawkins, E.W. (1984) *Awareness of Language: An Introduction*. Cambridge: Cambridge University Press.

Hawkins, J. and Filipovic, L. (2012) *Criterial Features in L2 English: Specifying the Reference Levels of the Common European Framework*. Cambridge: Cambridge University Press.

Herman, J.L., Aschbacher, P.R. and Winters, L. (1992) *A Practical Guide to Alternative Assessment*. Alexandria, VA: Association for Supervision and Curriculum.

Herdina, P. and Jessner, U. (2002) *A Dynamic Model of Multilingualism: Changing the Psycholinguistic Perspective*. Clevedon: Multilingual Matters.

HKEAA (Hong Kong Examinations and Assessment Authority) (no date) *Hong Kong Diploma of Secondary Education Examination. English Language Level Descriptors. Speaking Descriptors*. www.hkeaa.edu.hk/DocLibrary/HKDSE/Subject_Information/eng_lang/LevelDescriptors-ENG-Speaking.pdf (accessed 08 March 2018).

Hoijer, H. (1954) The Sapir-Whorf hypothesis. In H. Hoijer (ed.) *Language in Culture: Conference on the Interrelations of Languages and Other Aspects of Culture* (pp. 92–105). Chicago, IL: University of Chicago Press.

Holec, H. (1981) *Autonomy and Foreign Language Learning*. Oxford: Pergamon (originally published 1979, Strasbourg: Council of Europe.)

Horowitz, E. (2001) Language anxiety and achievement. *Annual Review of Applied Linguistics* 21, 112–127.

Howatt, A.P.R. (1984) *History of English Language Teaching*. Oxford: Oxford University Press.

Hulstijn, J. (2007) The shaky ground beneath the CEFR: Quantitative and qualitative dimensions of language. *The Modern Language Journal* 91 (4), 663–666.

Hulstijn, J.H., Alderson, J.C.A. and Schoonen, R. (2010) Developmental stages in second-language acquisition and levels of second-language proficiency: Are there links between them? In I. Bartning, M. Martin and I. Vedder (eds) (pp. 11–20).

Hunter, D., Cousineau, D., Collins, G. and Hook, G. (forthcoming) *Action-oriented Approach: Handbook*. Ottawa: Canadian Association of Second Language Teachers.

Hunter, D., Piccardo, E. and Andrews, A. (2017) *Synergies: Settlement, Integration and Language Learning/Synergies: Établissement, intégration et apprentissage de la langue*. Durham District School Board, Continuing Education. www.ddsb.ca/school/dce/Programs/learnenglish/synergies/Pages/default.aspx (accessed 08 March 2018).

Huta, A. (2013) The Common European Framework of Reference. In C.A. Chapelle (ed.) *The Encyclopedia of Applied Linguistics*. Oxford: Wiley-Blackwell. doi: 10.1002/9781405198431.wbeal0157.

Hymes, D.H. (1972a) On communicative competence. In J.B. Pride and J. Holmes (eds) *Sociolinguistics* (pp. 269–93). Harmondsworth: Penguin.

Hymes, D.H. (1972b) Models of the interaction of language and social life. In J.J. Gumperz and D.H. Hymes (eds) *Directions in Sociolinguistics: The Ethnography of Communication* (pp. 35–71). New York: Holt, Rinehart and Winston.

Hymes, D.H. (1974) *Foundations of Sociolinguistics: An Ethnographic Approach.* Philadelphia: University of Pennsylvania Press.

Hymes, D.H. (1986) Models of interaction of language and social life. In J.J Gumperz and D.H. Hymes (eds) *Directions in Sociolinguistics* (pp. 52–65). Oxford: Basil Blackwell.

IELTS (no date) *Speaking Band Descriptors (public version).* www.ielts.org/-/media/pdfs/speaking-band-descriptors.ashx?la=en (accessed 08 March 2018).

ILR (Interagency Language Roundtable) (no date) *Interagency Language Roundtable Descriptions of Language Proficiency: Introduction.* www.govtilr.org/Skills/ILRscale1.htm (accessed 08 March 2018).

INCA Project (2004) *Intercultural Competence Assessment. INCA Assessor Manual.* https://ec.europa.eu/migrant-integration/librarydoc/the-inca-project-intercultural-competence-assessment (accessed 08 March 2018).

Indurkhya, B. (2013) Computers and creativity. In T. Veale, K. Feyaerts and C. Forceville (eds) *Creativity and the Agile Mind* (pp. 61–79). Berlin/Boston: De Gruyter Mouton.

Instituto Cervantes (2007) *Niveles de referencia para el Español: Plan curricular del Instituto Cervantes.* Madrid: Biblioteca Nueva.

Isaacs, T. (2016) Assessing speaking. In D. Tsagari and J. Banerjee (eds) *Handbook of Second Language Assessment* (pp. 131–146). Berlin: De Gruyter Mouton.

John-Steiner, V. (1992) Creative lives, creative tensions. *Creativity Research Journal* 5, 99–108.

Johnstone, B. and Marcello, W. (2010) Dell Hymes and the ethnography of communication. In R. Wodak, B. Johnstone and P. Kerswill *The Sage Handbook of Sociolinguistics* (pp. 1–17). London: Sage. http://citeseerx.ist.psu.edu/viewdoc/download?doi=10.1.1.657.1418&rep=rep1&type=pdf (accessed 08 March 2018).

Jolly, B. (2012) Shining light on competence. *Medical Education* 46, 343–348. doi: 10.1111/j.1365-2923.2011.04203.x.

Jones, K. (2009) Culture and creative learning: A literature review. Newcastle: Creativity, Culture and Education. https://www.creativitycultureeducation.org//wp-content/uploads/2018/10/CCE-lit-review-83.pdf (accessed 08 March 2018).

Jones, L. (1982) *Simulations in Language Teaching.* Cambridge: Cambridge University Press.

Jones, N. and Saville, N. (2009) European language policy: Assessment, learning and the CEFR. *Annual Review of Applied Linguistics* 29, 51–63.

Jørgensen, J.N., Karrebæk, M.S., Maden, L.M. and Møller, J.S. (2011) Polylanguaging in superdiversity. *Diversities* 13 (2), 24–37. www.unesco.org/shs/diversities/vol13/issue2/art2 (accessed 08 March 2018).

Karp, I. (1986) Agency and social theory: A review of Anthony Giddens. *American Ethnologist* 13 (2), 131–37.

Käufer, S. and Chemero, A. (2015) *Phenomenology: An Introduction.* Cambridge: Polity Press.

Kelly, M. (2009) *LanQua: Language Network for Quality Assurance: Progress report – Public part.* https://www.ecml.at/Portals/1/5MTP/CEFR%20Matrix/documents/LanQua-Final-Report-Public-Part.pdf (accessed 08 March 2018).

Kelly, M. and Grenfell, M. (2004) *European Profile for Language Teacher Education.* www.lang.soton.ac.uk/profile/report/MainReport.pdf (accessed 08 March 2018).

Kennedy, D., Hyland, A. and Ryan, N. (2009) Learning outcomes and competences. In D. Kennedy, A. Hyland, N. Ryan, V. Gehmlich and A. Balissa (eds) *Using Learning*

Outcomes: Best of the Bologna Handbook (Vol. 33, pp. 59–76). Berlin: DUZ Medienhaus. https://www.researchgate.net/publication/285264101_Learning_outcomes_and_competencies (accessed 08 March 2018).

Kharkhurin, A.V. (2012) *Multilingualism and Creativity*. Bristol: Multilingual Matters.

Kharkhurin, A.V. (2014) Creativity 4in1: Four-criterion construct of creativity. *Creativity Research Journal* 26, 338–352.

Kharkhurin, A.V. (2016) Multi-competence as a creative act: Ramifications of the multi-competence paradigm for creativity research and creativity fostering education. In V. Cook and L. Wei (eds) *Cambridge Handbook of Linguistic Multi-Competence* (pp. 420–444). Cambridge: Cambridge University Press. doi:10.1017/CBO9781107425965.020.

Kibbee, D.A. (2010) *Chomskyan (R)evolutions*. Amsterdam: John Benjamins.

Kim, Y, J., Engle, D., Williams Woolley, A., Yu-Ting Lin, J., McArthur, N. and Malone, T.W. (2017) What makes a strong team? Using collective intelligence to predict team performance in League of Legends. Paper given at the 20th ACM Conference on Computer-Supported Cooperative Work and Social Computing (CSCW 2017) February 25–March 1, 2017, Portland, OR.

King, J. and Chetty, R. (2014) Codeswitching: Linguistic and literacy understanding of teaching dilemmas in multilingual classrooms. *Linguistics and Education* 25, 40–50.

Klein, W. (1986) *Second Language Acquisition*. Cambridge: Cambridge University Press.

KMK (Kulturministerkonferenz) (2003) *Bildungsstandards für die erste Fremdsprache (Englisch/Französische) für den Mittleren Schulabschluss [Educational Standards for the First Foreign Language (English/French) for Lower Secondary School Certificates].* www.kmk.org/fileadmin/Dateien/veroeffentlichungen_beschluesse/2003/2003_12_04-BS-erste-Fremdsprache.pdf (accessed 08 March 2018).

KMK (Kulturministerkonferenz) (2012) *Bildungsstandards für die fortgeführte Fremdsprache (Englisch/Französische) für die Allgemeine Hochschulreife [Educational Standards for the First Foreign Language (English/French) for for Upper Secondary School Certificates].* www.kmk.org/fileadmin/Dateien/veroeffentlichungen_beschluesse/2012/2012_10_18-Bildungsstandards-Fortgef-FS-Abi.pdf (accessed 08 March 2018).

Kolb, E. (2016) *Sprachmittlung: Studien zur Modellierung einer komplexen Kompetenz [Linguistic Mediation: Studies to Model a Complex Competence].* Münster: Münchener Arbeiten zur Fremdsprachen-Forschung, Waxmann.

Khubchandani, L.M. (1997) *Revisualizing Boundaries: A Plurilingual Ethos*. New Delhi, India: Sage.

Kramer, R. (2007) How might action learning be used to develop the emotional intelligence and leadership capacity of public administrators? *Journal of Public Affairs Education* 13 (2), 205–230.

Kramsch, C. (1986) From language proficiency to interactional competence. *The Modern Language Journal* 70 (4), 366–372.

Kramsch, C. (1993) *Context and Culture in Language Teaching*. Oxford: Oxford University Press.

Kramsch, C. (2000) Social discursive construction of self in L2 learning. In J.P. Lantolf (ed.) (pp. 133–154).

Kramsch, C. (ed.) (2002) *Language Acquisition and Language Socialization. Ecological Perspectives*. New York: Continuum.

Kramsch, C. (2004) Language, thought, and culture. In A. Davies and C. Elder (eds) *Handbook of Applied Linguistics* (pp. 235–261). Oxford: Oxford University Press.

Kramsch, C. (2008) Ecological perspectives on foreign language education. *Language Teaching* 41 (3), 389–408. https://doi.org/10.1017/S0261444808005065.

Kramsch, C. (2009) *The Multilingual Subject. What Language Learners Say About Their Experience and Why It Matters*. Oxford: Oxford University Press.

Kramsch, C. (2011) The symbolic dimensions of the intercultural. *Language Teaching* 44, pp. 354–367. doi:10.1017/S0261444810000431.

Kramsch, C. (2014) Teaching foreign languages in an era of globalization: Introduction. *The Modern Language Journal* 98 (1), 296–311. doi: 10.1111/j.1540-4781.2014.12057.x 0026-7902/14/296–311.

Kramsch, C. and Whiteside, K. (2008) Language ecology in multilingual settings. Towards a theory of symbolic competence. *Applied Linguistics* 29 (4) 1, 645–671. https://doi.org/10.1093/applin/amn022.

Krashen, S.D. (1981) *Second Language Acquisition and Second Language Learning.* Oxford: Pergamon Press.

Kravchenko, A.V. (2016) Two views on language ecology and ecolinguistics. *Language Sciences* 54, 102–113.

Krumm, H-J. (2003) Sprachenpolitik und Mehrsprachigkeit. [Linguistic policy and plurilingualism] In B. Hufeisen and G. Neuner (eds) *Mehrsprachigkeitskonzept – Tertiärsprachenlernen – Deutsch nach Englisch [Plurilingualism-Concept: Tertiary education – German after English]* (pp. 35–49). Strasbourg: Council of Europe Publishing.

Krumm, H-J. and Jenkins, E-M. (2001) *Kinder und ihre Sprachen – lebendige Mehrsprachigkeit.Sprachenporträts – gesammelt und kommentiert von Hans-Jürgen Krumm [Children and their Languages - Vibrant Multilingualism: Language Portraits Collected and Commented on by Hans-Jürgen Krumm]*. Vienna, Austria: Eviva Verlag.

Kumaravadivelu, B. (2001) Toward a postmethod pedagogy. *TESOL Quarterly* 35, 537–560. doi:10.2307/3588427.

Kumaravadivelu, B. (2003) *Beyond Methods: Macrostrategies for Language Teaching.* New Haven: Yale University Press.

Lacoste, M. (1995) Paroles d'action sur un chantier [Words of action on a pathway]. In D. Véronique and R. Vion (eds) *Des savoir-faire communicationnels [Communicative Skills]* (pp. 451–461). Aix-en-Provence: Presses Universitaires de Provence.

Lado, R. (1961) *Language Testing*. London: Longman.

Lado, R. (1964) *Language Teaching: A Scientific Approach*. New York: McGraw-Hill.

Lahire, B. (1998) *L'Homme pluriel. Les ressorts de l'action [Plural Man: The Springboards of action]*. Paris: Nathan.

Lantolf, J.P. (ed.) (2000) *Sociocultural Theory and Second Language Learning.* Oxford: Oxford University Press.

Lantolf, J.P. (2007) Sociocultural theory: A unified approach to L2 learning and teaching. In J. Cummins and C. Davison (eds) *International Handbook of English Language Teaching* (pp. 692–701). New York: Springer.

Lantolf, J.P. (2011) The sociocultural approach to second language acquisition: Sociocultural theory, second language acquisition, and artificial L2 development. In D. Atkinson (ed.) (pp. 24–47).

Lantolf, J. P. (2014) A bridge not needed. *Studies in Second Language Acquisition* 36, 368–374. doi: 10.1017/S0272263114000035.

Lantolf, J.P. and Poehner, M. (2014) *Sociocultural Theory and the Pedagogical Imperative in L2 Education: Vygotskian Praxis and the Research/Practice Divide.* New York: Routledge.

Lantolf, J.P., Kurtz, L. and Kisselev, O. (2016) Understanding the revolutionary character of L2 development in the ZPD: Why levels of mediation matter. *Language and Sociocultural Theory* 4 (2), 153–171.

Larsen-Freeman, D. (1997) Chaos/complexity science and second language acquisition. *Applied Linguistics* 18 (2), 141–165.

Larsen-Freeman, D. (2002) Language acquisition and language use from a chaos/complexity theory perspective. In C. Kramsch (ed.) (33–46).

Larsen-Freeman, D. (2007) On the complementarity of Chaos/Complexity Theory and Dynamic Systems Theory in understanding the second language acquisition process. *Bilingualism: Language and Cognition* 10 (1), 35–37.

Larsen-Freeman, D. (2011) A complexity theory approach to second language development/acquisition. In D. Atkinson (ed.) (pp. 48–72).

Larsen-Freeman, D. (2017) Complexity theory: The lessons continue. In L. Ortega and Z.H. Han (eds) *Complexity Theory and Language Development: In Celebration of Diane Larsen-Freeman* (pp. 11–50). Amsterdam and Philadelphia: John Benjamins.

Larsen-Freeman, D. and Anderson, M. (2011) *Techniques and Principles in Language Teaching* (3rd edn). Oxford: Oxford University Press.

Larsen-Freeman, D. and Cameron, L. (2008) *Complex Systems and Applied Linguistics.* Oxford: Oxford University Press.

Lasnier, J.-C., Morfeld, P., North, B., Serra Borneto, C. and Spaeth, P. (2003) *A Guide for the Evaluation and Design of Quality Language Learning and Teaching Programmes and Materials. A project related to the European Commission's White Paper 'Teaching and learning. Towards the learning society,' objective 4, 1st support measure.* Brussels: European Commission. https://www.ecml.at/Portals/1/5MTP/CEFR%20Matrix/documents/Quality-Guide-EN.doc (accessed 20 June 2019).

Lave, J. and Wenger, E. (1991) *Situated Learning: Legitimate Peripheral Participation.* Cambridge: Cambridge University Press.

Le Bianic, T. (2001) Genèse de la notion de compétence en sociologie du travail. Séminaire de thèse du 9 mai 2001 [The Genesis of the notion of competence in the sociology of work]. Note de travail – Document séminaire LEST CNRS – UMR 6123. Aix-en-Provence: Université de Provence/Université de la Méditerranée (Accessed 08 March 2018).

Le Boterf, G. (1994) *De la compétence – Essai sur un attracteur étrange [Competence: A Strange Attractor].* Paris: Les Éditions d'Organisation.

Le Boterf, G. (2010) *Construire les compétences individuelles et collectives: Agir et réussir avec compétence [Constructing Individual and Collective Competences: Act and Succeed with Competence]* (2nd edn). Paris, Eyrolles: Éditions d'Organisation, originally published 2000.

Legutke, M. and Thiel, W. (1982) Airport. *Westermanns Pädagogische Beiträge [Westermann's Pedagogical Contributions]* 34, 288–299.

Le Moigne, J-L. (1996) Complexité. In D. Lecourt (ed.) *Dictionnaire d'histoire et philosophie des sciences [Dictionary of the History and Philosphy of Science]* (pp. 205–215). Paris, Presses Universitaires de France.

Le Moigne, J-L. (2003) *Le constructivisme. Modéliser pour comprendre [Constructivism: Modellng in order to gain Understanding] (vol. 3).* Paris : L'Harmattan).

Le Moigne J-L. (2006) *La théorie du système général. Théorie de la modélisation [General Systems Theory: The Theory of Modelling].* Paris: Presses Universitaires de France. Previous editions 1997 and 1994. www.mcxapc.org/inserts/ouvrages/0609tsgtm.pdf (accessed 08 March 2018).

Le Moigne J-L. (2012) *Les épistémologies constructivistes [Constructivist Epistomologies].* Paris: Presses Universitaires de France.

Lenz, P. and Schneider, G. (2004) A bank of descriptors for self-assessment in European Language Portfolios. Strasbourg: Council of Europe. www.coe.int/en/web/common-european-framework-reference-languages/bank-of-supplementary-descriptors (accessed 08 March 2018).

Lenz, P. and Studer, T. (2007) *Lingualevel. Instrumente zur Evaluation von Fremdsprachenkompetenzen 5. bis 9. Schuljahr [Lingualevel: Foreign Language Assessment Tools: 5th to 9th School Years].* Bern. Schulverlag. www.lingualevel.ch (accessed 08 March 2018).

Leontiev, A.N. (1979) The problem of activity in psychology. In J. Wetsch (ed.) *The Concept of Activity in Soviet Psychology* (pp. 37–71). Armonk, NY: Sharpe Publishers.

Leplat, J. (1991) Compétence et ergonomie [Competence and ergonomy]. In R. Amalberti, M. de Montmollin and J. Theureau (eds) *Modèles en analyse du travail [Models in the Analysis of Work]* (pp. 263–278). Liège: Mardaga.

Leung, C. and Scarino, A. (2016) Reconceptualizing the nature of goals and outcomes in language/s education. *The Modern Language Journal*, 100 (Supplement 2016), 81–95. doi: 10.1111/modl.12300.

Levinson, S.C. (1983) *Pragmatics*. Cambridge: University Press.

Levy, D. and Zarate, G. (2003) *La médiation et la didactique des langues et des cultures* [Mediation and the Teaching of Languages and Cultures]. *Le Français dans le Monde. Recherches et Applications [French in the World: Research and Applications]*. Paris: CLE international.

Levy, P. (2010) From social computing to reflexive collective intelligence: The IEML research program. *Information Sciences* 180 (1), 71–94. https://www.researchgate.net/publication/222651189_From_social_computing_to_reflexive_collective_intelligence_The_IEML_research_program (accessed 20 June 2019).

Lewin, K. (1952) *Field Theory in Social Science: Selected Theoretical Papers by Kurt Lewin*. London: Tavistock.

Lewis, G., Jones, B. and Baker, C. (2012) Translanguaging: Developing its conceptualisation and contextualisation. *Educational Research and Evaluation* 18 (7), 655–670.

Liddicoat, A.J. and Scarino, A. (2013) *Intercultural Language Teaching and Learning*. Oxford: Wiley Blackwell.

Liddicoat, A.J. and Zarate, G. (2017) Intercultural Mediation/médiation interculturelle: A plurilingual exploration: Symposium introduction. AILA conference, Rio de Janeiro, 25 July 2017.

Li, P. and Grant, A. (2016) Second language learning success revealed by brain networks. *Bilingualism: Language and Cognition* 19 (4), 657–644.

Lightbown, P.M. (1985) Great expectations: Second-language acquisition research and classroom teaching. *Applied Linguistics* 6, 153–18.

Lincke, K. (1912) *Lehrbuch der Englischen Sprache für höhere Lehranstalten: Zweiter Teil: Zweites und drittes Jahr (Obertertia und Untersekunda) [English Language Coursebook for Higher Education Institutes: Second Part: Second and Third Years (Upper third and Lower second)]*. Frankfurt am Main: Verlag von Moritz Diesterweg.

Lindemann H-J. (2002) The principle of action-oriented learning. In GIZ (Gründer- und Innovationszentrums) (ed.) Linking German TVET with Anglo-Saxon CBET, International Workshop – Weimar GTZ, 2002. www.halinco.de/html/docde/HOL-prinzip02002.pdf (accessed 08 March 2018).

Lions-Olivieri, M-L. and Liria, P. (eds) (2009) *L'approche actionnelle dans l'enseignement des langues. Douze articles pour mieux comprendre et faire le point [The Action-oriented Approach in Language Teaching: Twelve Articles to Better Understand the State-of-the-art]*. Paris: Difusión-Maison des langues.

Liskin-Gasparro, J.E. (1984) The ACTFL proficiency guidelines: A historical perspective. In T.V. Higgs (ed.) *Teaching for Proficiency, the Organising Principle* (pp. 11–42). Lincolnwood (Ill.): National Textbook Company.

Liskin-Gasparro, J.E. (2003) The ACTFL proficiency guidelines and the oral proficiency interview: A brief history and analysis of their survival. *Foreign Language Annals* 36 (4), 483–490.

Little, D. (1991) *Learner Autonomy 1: Definitions, Issues and Problems*. Dublin: Authentik.

Little, D., Dam, L. and Legenhausen, L. (2017) *Language Learner Autonomy: Theory, Practice and Research*. Bristol: Multilingual Matters.

Little, D. and Erickson, G. (2015) Learner identity, learner agency, and the assessment of language proficiency: Some reflections prompted by the Common European Framework of Reference for Languages. *Annual Review of Applied Linguistics* 35, 120–139. doi: 10.1017/S0267190514000300.

Long, M.H. (1985) A role for instruction in second language acquisition: Task-based language teaching. In K. Hyltenstam and M. Pienemann (eds) *Modelling and Assessing Second Language Acquisition* (pp. 77–79). Clevedon: Multilingual Matters.

Long, M.H. and Crookes, G. (1991) Three approaches to task-based syllabus design. *TESOL Quarterly* 26 (1), 27–55.

Long, M.H. and Crookes, G. (1992) *Three Approaches to Task-based Syllabus Design*. Oxford: Oxford University Press.

Long, M.H. and Crookes, G. (1993) Units of analysis in syllabus design: The case for task. In G. Crookes and S.M. Gass (eds) *Tasks in a Pedagogical Context: Integrating Theory and Practice* (pp. 9–54). Clevedon: Multimedia Matters.

Loveday, L.J. (1982) *The Sociolinguistics of Learning and Using a Non-native Language*. Oxford: Pergamon.

Lowe, P. (1985) The ILR proficiency scale as a synthesising research principle: the view from the mountain. In C.J. James (ed.) *Foreign Language Proficiency in the Classroom and Beyond*. Lincolnwood (Ill.): National Textbook Company.

Lubart, T. (1999) Creativity across cultures. In A. Sterneberg (ed.) *Handbook of Creativity* (pp. 339–350). Cambridge: Cambridge University Press.

Lubart, T. (with Mouchiroud, C., Tordjman, S. and Zenasni, F.) (2003) *Psychologie de la créativité [Psychology and Creativity]*. Paris: Armand Collin.

Lüdi, G. (2011) Vers de nouvelles approches théoriques du langage et du plurilinguisme. *Travaux Neuchâtelois de Linguistique* 53, 47–64.

Lüdi, G. (2014) Dynamics and management of linguistic diversity in companies and institutes of higher education: Results from the DYLAN project. In P. Gromes and H. Wu (eds) *Plurilingual Education: Policies – Practices – Language Development* (pp. 113–138). Amsterdam/Philadelphia: John Benjamins.

Lüdi, G. and Py, B. (2009) To be or not to be ... a plurilingual speaker. *International Journal of Multilingualism* 6 (2), 154–167.

Lüdi, G. and Py, B. (1986/2003) *Être bilingue [Being Bilingual]*. Bern: Peter Lang.

Lüdi, G., Höchle Meier, K. and Yanaprasart, P. (2016) *Managing Plurilingual and Intercultural Practices in the Workplace: The Case of Multilingual Switzerland*. Amsterdam: John Benjamins.

Lussier, D., Ivanus, D., Chavdarova Kostova, S., Golubina, K., Skopinskaja, L., Wiesinger, S. and de la Maya Reamar, G. (2007) *Guidelines for Assessing Intercultural Communicative Competence*. Strasbourg: European Centre for Modern Languages/Council of Europe Publications.

Lyotard, J-F. (1979) *La condition postmoderne: Rapport sur le savoir [The Postmodern Condition: A Report on the State of Knowledge]*. Paris: Éditions de Minuit.

MacNamara, T. (2011) Managing learning: Authority and language assessment. *Language Teaching* 44 (4), 500–515.

MacNamara, T. and Roever, C. (2006) *Language Testing: The Social Dimension*. Oxford: Basil Blackwell.

MacSwan, J. (ed.) (2014) *Grammatical Theory and Bilingual Codeswitching*. Cambridge: MIT Press.

MacSwan, J. (2017) A multilingual perspective on translanguaging. *American Educational Research Journal* 54 (1), 167–201. doi: 10.3102/0002831216683935.

Maddux, W., Adam, H. and Galinsky, A. (2010) When in Rome ... Learn why the Romans do what they do: How multicultural learning experiences facilitate creativity. *Personality and Social Psychology Bulletin* 36 (6), 731–741.

Mager, R.F. (1962) *Preparing Instructional Objectives*. Palo Alto (CA): Feardon Publishers.

Makoni, B. and Makoni, S. (2010) Multilingual discourses on wheels and public English in Africa: A case for 'vague linguistic.' In J. Maybin and J. Swann (eds) *The Routledge Companion to English Language Studies* (pp. 258–270). London and New York: Routledge.

Makoni, S. and Pennycook, A. (2007) *Disinventing and Reconstituting Languages.* Clevedon: Multilingual Matters.

Malafouris, L. (2015) Metaplasticity and the primacy of material engagement. *Time and Mind* 8 (4), 351–371.

Malicka, A. and Levkina, M. (2012) Measuring task complexity: Does EFL proficiency matter? In A. Shehadeh and C.A. Coombe (eds) *Task-Based Language Teaching in Foreign Language Contexts: Research and Implementation* (pp. 43–67). Amsterdam: John Benjamins Publishing.

Malinowski B. (1946) The problem of meaning in primitive languages. Supplement 1. In C.K. Ogden and I.A. Richards (eds) *The Meaning of Meaning* (pp. 296–336) (8th edn). Harcourt: Brace and World.

Mandelbrot, B. (1983) *The Fractal Geometry of Nature.* New York: Freeman.

Marginson, S. and Dang, T.K.A. (2017) Vygotsky's sociocultural theory in the context of globalization. *Asia Pacific Journal of Education* 37 (1), 116–129. http://dx.doi.org/10.1080/02188791.2016.1216827.

Marinova-Todd, S.H., Marshall, D.B. and Snow, C.E. (2000) Three misconceptions about age and L2 learning. *TESOL Quarterly* 34 (1), 9–34.

Marshall, S. and Moore, D. (2016) Plurilingualism amid the panoply of lingualisms: addressing critiques and misconceptions in education. *International Journal of Multilingualism.* (pp. 1–16) http://dx.doi.org/10.1080/14790718.2016.1253699.

Martin, M., Mustonen, S., Reiman, N. and Seilonen, M. (2010) On becoming an independent user. In I. Bartning, M. Martin and I. Vedder (eds) *Communicative Proficiency and Linguistic Development: Intersections Between SLA and Language Testing Research* (pp. 57–80). Amsterdam: Eurosla.

Martin-Jones, M. and Romaine S. (1985) Semilingualism: A half-baked theory of communicative competence. *Applied Linguistics* 6, 105–117.

Martyniuk, W. (ed.) (2010) *Relating Language Examinations to the Common European Framework of Reference for Languages: Case studies and Reflections on the Use of the Council of Europe's Draft Manual.* Cambridge: Cambridge University Press.

Martyniuk, W. and Noijons, J. (2007) Executive summary of results of a survey on the use of the CEFR at national level in the Council of Europe Member States. Paper given at the intergovernmental Language Policy Forum 'The Common European Framework of Reference for Languages (CEFR) and the development of language policies: challenges and responsibilities,' Strasbourg, 6–8 February 2007.

Masciotra, D., Roth, W-M., and Morel, D. (2007) *Enaction: Towards a Zen Mind in Learning and Teaching.* Rotterdam: Sense Publishers.

Masciotra, D. and Morel, D. (2011) *Apprendre par l'expérience active et située: la méthode ASCAR* [Learning through Active Situated Experience: The ASCAR Method]. Québec: Presses de l'Université du Québec.

Matsuo, C. (2012) A critique of Michael Byram's intercultural communicative competence model from the perspective of model type and conceptualization of culture. *Fukuoka University Review of Literature and Humanities* 44, 347–380.

Maturana, H. and Varela, F. (1980) *Autopoiesis and Cognition: The Realization of Living.* Dordrecht: Kluwer.

May, S. (2014) *The Multilingual Turn: Applications for SLA, TESOL and Bilingual Education.* New York: Routledge.

McLaughlin, B. and Harrington, M. (1989) Second language acquisition. *Annual Review of Applied Linguistics* 10, 122–134.

Melo-Pfeifer, S. (2012) Intercomprehension between romance languages and the role of English: A study of multilingual chat-rooms. *International Journal of Multilingualism* 11 (1), 1–18.

Merleau-Ponty, M. (1962) *Phenomenology of Perception*. London: Routledge.

Mignolo, W.D. (2000) *Local Histories/Global Designs: Coloniality, Subaltern Knowledges, and Border Thinking*. Princeton, NJ: Princeton University Press.

Miller, R. (2011) *Vygotsky in Perspective*. New York: Cambridge Press.

Miller, C., Hoggan, J., Pringle, S. and West, C. (1988) *Credit Where Credit's Due. Report of the Accreditation of Work-based Learning Project*. Glasgow. SCOTVEC.

Mingers, J. (2001) *Can Social Systems be Autopoietic?* Coventry: Warwick Business School.

Mitchell, C.B. and Vidal, K.E. (2001) Weighing the ways of the flow: Twentieth century language instruction. *The Modern Language Journal* 85 (1), 26–38.

Morin, E. (1977) *La méthode. I. La nature de la nature [The Method: The Nature of Nature]*. Paris: Seuil.

Morin, E. (1990/2005) *Introduction à la pensée complexe [Introduction to Complex Thought]*. Paris: ESF.

Morin, E. (2001) *L'humanité de l'humanité [The Humanity of Humanity]*. Paris: Seuil.

Morin, E. (2004) *Pour entrer dans le XXIe siècle [Entering into the 21st Century]*. Paris: Points.

Morin, E. (2005) *Introduction à la pensée complexe [Introduction to Complex Thought]*. Paris: Éditions Seuil. Originally published 1990, Paris: ESF.

Morin, E. and Le Moigne, J.-L. (1999) *L'intelligence de la complexité [The Intelligence of Complexity]*. Paris: L'Harmattan.

Moirand, S. (1982) *Enseigner à communiquer en langue étrangère [Teaching to Communcate in a Foreign Language]*. Paris: Hachette.

Montuori, A. and Purser, R. (1997) Social creativity: The challenge of complexity. Translation of "Le dimensioni sociali della creatività." *Pluriverso* 1, 78–88.

Moore, D. and Gajo, L. (2009) Introduction: French voices on plurilingualism and pluriculturalism: Theory, significance, and perspectives. *International Journal of Multilingualism* 6, 137–153.

Morris, J.F. (1966) *The Art of Teaching English as a Living Language*. London: Macmillan.

Morrow, K. (ed.) (2004) *Insights from the Common European Framework*. Oxford: Oxford University Press.

Mouchiroud, C. and Zenasni, F. (2013) Individual differences in the development of social creativity. In M. Taylor (ed.) *The Development of Imagination* (pp. 387–402). New York: Oxford University Press.

Muñoz, C. and Singleton, D. (2011) A critical review of age-related research on L2 ultimate attainment. *Language Teaching* 44 (1), 1–35.

Nation, I.S.P. and Macalister, J. (2010) *Language Curriculum Design*. New York: Routledge.

National Standards in Foreign Language Education Project (1999) *Standards for Foreign Language Learning in the 21st Century*. Yonkers, NY: National Standards in Foreign Language Education Project.

Negishi, M., Takada, T. and Tono, Y. (2013) A progress report on the development of the CEFR-J. In E.D. Galaczi and C.J. Weir (eds) *Exploring Language Frameworks: Proceedings of the ALTE Krakow Conference, July 2011* (pp. 135–163). Cambridge, Studies in Language Testing Series: Cambridge University Press.

Nerenz, A. and Spinelli, E. (2003) Learning scenarios: Integrating curriculum and assessment. In K. H. Cárdenas and M. Klein (eds) *Traditional Values and Contemporary Perspectives in Language Teaching*. 2003 report of the Central States Conference on the Teaching of Foreign Languages (pp. 115–132). Valdosta, GA: Lee Bradley.

Neuner-Anfindsen, S. and Meima, E. (2016) MAGICC: A project of the EU lifelong learning programme: Modularising multilingual and multicultural academic communication competence. *European Journal of Applied Linguistics* 4 (2), 341–347. doi: 10.1515/eujal-2016-0008 (accessed 08 March 2018).

Neuner, G.R. and Hunfeld, H. (1993) *Methoden des fremdsprachlichen Deutschunter-richts: Eine Einführung (Fernstudienangebot Deutsch als Fremdsprache). Fernstudiene-inheit 4 [Foreign Language Teaching Methods for German: An Introduction. (Distance Learning Offer: German as a Foreign Language. Distance Learning Unit 4.* Berlin: Langenscheidt.

Neuner, G.R. Schmidt, R., Wilms, H. and Zirkel, M. (1979) *Deutsch Aktiv l. Lehrbuch [Active German: 1st Coursebook].* Berlin and Munich: Langenscheidt.

Nicolis, G. (1995) *Introduction to Nonlinear Science.* Cambridge: Cambridge University Press.

Niemeier, S. and Dirven, R. (2000) *Evidence of Linguistic Relativity.* Amsterdam: John Benjamins.

Norris, J. and Ortega, L. (2000) Effectiveness of L2 instruction: A research synthesis and quantitative meta-analysis. *Language Learning* 50, 417–528.

North, B. (1986) Activities for continuous communicative assessment. Unpublished MA Phase 3 project English Language Research Dept., Birmingham.

North, B. (1991) Standardisation of continuous assessment grades. In J.C.A. Alderson and B. North (eds) (pp. 167–177).

North, B. (1992) European Language Portfolio: Some options for a working approach to design scales for proficiency. In Council of Europe (1992) (pp. 158–174), reprinted in Schärer and North.

North, B. (1994) *Perspectives on Language Proficiency and Aspects of Competence: a Reference Paper Defining Categories and Levels.* Strasbourg: Council of Europe CC-LANG (94) 20.

North, B. (1995) The development of a common framework scale of descriptors of language proficiency based on a theory of measurement. *System* 23 (4) 445–465.

North, B. (1997) Perspectives on language proficiency and aspects of competence. *Language Teaching* 30, 92–100.

North, B. (2000) *The Development of a Common Framework Scale of Language Proficiency.* New York: Peter Lang.

North, B. (2008a) Levels and goals – Central frameworks and local strategies. In B. Spolsky (ed.) *The Handbook of Educational Linguistics* (pp. 220–232). Malden MA and Oxford UK: Blackwell.

North, B. (2008b) The CEFR levels and descriptor scales. In L. Taylor and C.J. Weir (eds) *Multilingualism and Assessment: Achieving Transparency, Assuring Quality, Sustaining Diversity. Proceedings of the ALTE Berlin Conference, May 2005* (pp. 21–66). Cambridge: Cambridge University Press.

North, B. (2010) The educational and social mpact of the CEFR. In L. Taylor and C.J. Weir (eds) *Language Testing Matters: Investigating the Wider Social and Educational Impact of Assessment. Proceedings of the ALTE Cambridge Conference, April 2008* (pp. 357–377). Cambridge: Cambridge University Press.

North, B. (2014) *The CEFR in Practice.* Cambridge: Cambridge University Press.

North, B. (2014) Putting the Common European Framework of Reference to good use. *Language Teaching* 47 (2), 228–249. doi: 10.1017/S0261444811000206.

North, B. and Panthier, P. (2016) Updating the CEFR descriptors – The context. *Research Notes* 63, 16–23.

North, B. and Piccardo, E. (2016a) Developing illustrative descriptors of aspects of mediation for the Common European Framework of Reference (CEFR). Strasbourg, France: Council of Europe. www.coe.int/en/web/common-european-framework-reference-languages/documents (accessed 08 March 2018).

North, B. and Piccardo, E. (2016b) Developing illustrative descriptors of aspects of mediation for the Common European Framework of Reference (CEFR): A Council of Europe project. *Language Teaching* 49, 455– 459. doi: 10.1017/ S0261444816000100.

North, B. and Piccardo, E. (2019) Developing new CEFR descriptor scales and expanding the existing ones: Constructs, approaches and methodologies. In J. Quetz and H. Rossa (2019) (eds) The Common European Framework of Reference, Illustrative Descriptors, Extended Version 2017. Special issue of *Zeitschrift für Fremdsprachenforschung* (ZFF) 30 (2), 142–160.

North, B. and Schneider, G. (1998) Scaling descriptors for language proficiency scales. *Language Testing* 15 (2), 217–262.

North, B., Angelova, M., Jarocsz, E. and Rossner R. (2018) *Language Course Planning.* Oxford: Oxford University Press.

North, B., Ortega, Á. and Sheehan, S. (2010) *British Council – EAQUALS Core Inventory for General English.* London: British Council/EAQUALS, ISBN 978-086355-653-1. www.eaquals.org (accessed 08 March 2018).

Nunan, D. (1989) *Designing Tasks for the Communicative Classroom.* Cambridge: Cambridge University Press.

Nunan, D. (2004) *Task-based Language Teaching.* Cambridge: Cambridge University Press.

Nunan, D. (2005) Important tasks of English education: Asia-wide and beyond. *Asian EFL Journal* 7 (3), 5–8.

Nunn, R. (2006) Designing holistic units for task-based learning. *Asian EFL Journal* 8 (3), 69–93.

Oatley, K and Jenkins, J. (1996) *Understanding Emotions.* Cambridge, MA: Blackwell.

O'Dwyer, F., Hunke, M., Imig, A., Nagai, N., Naganuma, N. and Schmidt, M.G. (eds) (2017) *Critical, Constructive Assessment of CEFR-informed Language Teaching in Japan and Beyond.* Cambridge: Cambridge University Press.

O'Malley, J.M. and Chamot, A.U. (1990) *Learning Strategies in Second Language Acquisition.* Cambridge: Cambridge University Press.

O'Malley, J.M., Chamot, A.U. and Walker, C. (1987) Some applications of cognitive theory to second language acquisition. *Studies in Second Language Acquisition* 9 (3), 287–306.

OECD (2005) The definition and selection of key competences. Executive summary. www.oecd.org/pisa/35070367.pdf (accessed 08 March 2018).

OECD (n.d.) Recognition of Non-formal and Informal Learning. www.oecd.org/edu/skills-beyond-school/recognitionofnon-formalandinformallearning-home.htm (accessed 08 March 2018).

Oller, J.W. (ed) (1983) *Issues in Language Testing Research.* Rowley, MA: Newbury House.

Oller, J.W. (1983a) Evidence for a general proficiency factor. In Oller (ed.) (pp. 3–10), originally published in 1976.

Oller, J.W. (1983b) A Consensus for the Eighties? In Oller (ed.) (pp. 351–6).

Ontario Ministry of Education (2010) Growing success: Assessment, evaluation and reporting in Ontario schools. First edition, covering Grades 1-12. www.edu.gov. on.ca/eng/policyfunding/growSuccess.pdf (accessed 08 March 2018).

Ontario Ministry of Education (2013) The Ontario curriculum: French as a foreign language: Core French (Grades 4–8); Extended French (Grades 4-8); French Immersion (Grades 1–8). www.edu.gov.on.ca/eng/curriculum/elementary/fsl18-2013curr.pdf (accessed 08 March 2018).

Orioles, V. (2004) Plurilinguisme: modèles interprétatifs, terminologie et retombées institutionnelles [Plurilingualism: interpretative models, terminologie and institutional impact]. *Revue Française de Linguistique Appliquée [French Review of Applied Linguistics]* 2 (IX), 11–30.

Orman, J. (2013) New lingualisms, same old codes. *Language Sciences* 37, 90–98.

Oscarson, M. (1979) *Approaches to Self-assessment in Foreign Language Learning.* Oxford: Pergamon.

Oscarson, M. (1984) *Self-assessment of Foreign Language Skills: A Survey of Research and Development Work.* Strasbourg: Council of Europe.

Otheguy, R., García, O. and Reid, W. (2015) Clarifying translanguaging and deconstructing named languages: A perspective from linguistics. *Applied Linguistics Review* 6 (3), 281–307.

Otsuji, E. and Pennycook, A. (2010) Metrolingualism: Fixity, fluidity and language in flux. *International Journal of Multilingualism* 7 (3), 240–254.

Oxford, R.L. (1990) *Language Learning Strategies: What Every Teacher Should Know.* Boston MA: Heinle and Heinle.

Parizzi, F. and Spinelli, B. (2009) *Profilo della Lingua Italiana [Profile of the Italian Language].* Firenze: La Nuova Italia.

Pavlenko, A. (2006) *Emotions and Multilingualism.* Cambridge: Cambridge University Press.

Pavlenko, A. and Lantolf, J.P. (2000) Second language learning as participation and the (re) construction of selves. In J.P. Lantolf (ed.) (pp. 155–177).

Peal, E. and Lambert, M. (1962) The relationship of bilingualism to intelligence. *Psychological Monographs* 76 (546), 1–23.

Pearson (2017) *Global Scale of English (GSE): Learning Objectives and Other GSE Resources.* https://www.pearson.com/english/en/about/gse/learning-objectives.html (accessed 08 March 2018).

Pennycook, A. (2017) Translanguaging and semiotic assemblages. *International Journal of Multilingualism* 14 (3), 269–282. https://doi.org/10.1080/14790718. 2017.1315810.

Perani, D., Abutalebi, J., Paulesu, E., Brambati, Paula, C., Stefano F., and Fazio, F. (2003) The role of age of acquisition and language usage in early, high-proficient bilinguals: An fMRI study during verbal fluency. *Human Brain Mapping* 19 (3), 170–182.

Pérez, E. (1999) *The Decolonial Imaginary: Writing Chicanas into History.* Bloomington and Indianapolis: Indiana University Press.

Perrenoud, Ph. (1997) *Construire des compétences dès l'école [Constructing competence from School onwards.]* Paris: E.S.F.

Piaget, J. (1950) *The Psychology of Intelligence.* London: Routledge and Kegan Paul.

Piaget, J. (1969) *Psychologie et pédagogie* [Psychology and Pedagogy]. Paris: Denoël.

Piccardo, E. (2005a) *Créativité et technologies de l'information et de la communication dans l'enseignement/apprentissage des langues étrangères* [Creativity and Information Technologies and the Teaching/Learning of Foreign Languages]. Milano: Arcipelago Edizioni.

Piccardo, E. (2005b) *Complessità e insegnamento delle lingue straniere: Ripensare un paradigma* [Complexity and the teaching of foreign languages: Rethinking a paradigm]. *RILA (Rassegna Italiana di Linguistica Applicata)* 37 (2–3), 75–92.

Piccardo, E. (ed.) (2006) La richesse de la diversité: recherches et réflexions dans l'Europe des langues et des cultures [The richness of diversity: Research and reflections in the Europe of languages and cultures]. *Synergies Europe, 1.* http://ressources-cla.univ-fcomte.fr/gerflint/Europe1/europe1.html (accessed 08 March 2018).

Piccardo, E. (2010a) L'enseignant: un stratège de la complexité [The teacher: A strategist of complexity]. In G. Baillat, D. Niclot and D. Ulma (eds) *La formation des enseignants en Europe: Approche comparative [Teacher Education in Europe: A Comparative Approach]* (pp. 79–98). Brussels: De Boeck.

Piccardo, E. (2010b) From communicative to action-oriented: New perspectives for a new millennium. *CONTACT TESL Ontario* 36 (2), 20–35.

Piccardo, E. (2012a) Médiation et apprentissage des langues: Pourquoi est-il temps de réflechir à cette notion? [Mediation and learning languages: Why is it time to reflect on this notion?] *ELA: Études de Linguistique Appliquée [Studies in Applied Linguistics]* 167, 285–297.

Piccardo, E. (2012b) Multidimensionality of assessment in the Common European Framework of References for languages. (CEFR). *Les Cahiers de l'ILOB/OLBI Working Papers* 4, 37–54.

Piccardo, E. (2013a) Plurilingualism and curriculum design: Towards a synergic vision. *TESOL Quarterly* 47 (3), 600–614.

Piccardo, E. (2013b) Évolution épistémologique de la didactique des langues: la face cachée des émotions [The epistemological evolution of language teaching: the hidden face of emotions]. *Lidil* 48, 17–36.

Piccardo, E. (2013c) Assessment recollected in tranquillity: the ECEP project and the key concepts of the CEFR. In Galaczi and Weir (eds) *Exploring Language Frameworks. Proceedings of the ALTE Kraków Conference* (pp. 187–204). Cambridge: Cambridge University Press.

Piccardo, E. (2014a) From Communicative to Action-oriented: a Research Pathway. https://transformingfsl.ca/en/resources/from-communicative-to-action-oriented-illuminating-the-approaches/ within the website of the project From Communicative to Action-oriented: Illuminating the Approaches funded by the Government of Ontario and the Government of Canada/Canadian Heritage (accessed 08 February 2019).

Piccardo, E. (2014b) The impact of the CEFR on Canada's linguistic plurality: A space for heritage languages? In P. Trifonas and T. Aravossitas (eds) *Rethinking Heritage Language Education* (pp. 183–212). Cambridge: Cambridge University Press.

Piccardo, E. (2015) Sprachenunterricht im Zeichen der Komplexität: Rückblick und Ausblick [Language teaching in the time of complexity: Looking back and looking forwards]. In H. Drumbl and A. Hornung (eds) *Beiträge der XV Internationalen Tagung der Deutschlehrerinnen und Deutschlehrer Bozen, 29. Juli – 03.August 2013 [Proceedings of the XV International Congress of German Teachers, Bozen, 29th July to 3rd August, 2013]* (pp. 69–92). Bolzano: Bozen-Bolzano University Press.

Piccardo, E. (2016a) La diversité culturelle et linguistique comme ressource à la créativité [Cultural and linguistic diversity as a resource for creativity]. *Voix plurielles [Plural Voices]* 13 (1), 57–75.

Piccardo, E. (2016b) Créativité et complexité: quels modèles, quelles conditions, quels enjeux? [Creativity and complexity: which models, which conditions, which issues?] In I. Capron Puozzo (ed.) *La créativité en éducation et en formation. Perspectives théoriques et pratiques [Creativity in Education and training: Theoretical and Practical Perspectives]* (pp. 47–64). Bruxelles: de Boek.

Piccardo E. (2017) Plurilingualism as a catalyst for creativity in superdiverse societies: A systemic analysis. *Frontiers. Psychology* 8: 2169.doi: 10.3389/fpsyg.2017.02169.

Piccardo, E. (2018) Plurilingualism: vision, conceptualization, and practices. In P. Trifonas and T. Aravossitas (eds) *Springer International Handbooks of Education. Handbook of Research and Practice in Heritage Language Education* (pp. 1–19). New York, NY: Springer International Publishing (doi:10.1007/978-3-319-38893-9_47-1).

Piccardo, E. and Galante, A. (2018) Plurilingualism and agency in language education. The role of dramatic action-oriented tasks. In J. Choi and S. Ollerhead. *Plurilingualism in Teaching and Learning* (pp. 147–164). New York: Routledge.

Piccardo, E. and Hunter, D. (2017) Settlement, integration and language learning: Possible synergies. A task-based, community-focused program from the Region of Durham (Ontario, Canada). In In J-C Beacco *et al.* (eds) (pp. 175–180).

Piccardo, E. and North, B. (in press) Plurilingualism: A developing notion. Creating and validating descriptors for the CEFR to describe plurilingual and pluricultural competence. In S.M.C. Lau and S. Stille (eds) *Plurilingual Pedagogies: Critical and Creative Endeavors for Equitable Language (in) Education*. New York, NY: Springer International Publishing.

Piccardo, E. and Puozzo, I. (2012) La créativité pour développer la compétence plurilingue déséquilibrée [Creativity as a means to develop unbalanced plurilingualism]. In G. Alao, M. Derivry-Plard, E. Suzuki and S. Yun-Roger (eds) *Didactique plurilingue et pluriculturelle: L'acteur en contexte mondialisé [Plurilingual and Pluricultural Pedagogy: the Agent in a Globalised World]* (pp. 23–38). Paris: Editions des archives contemporains.

Piccardo, E. and Puozzo, I. (2015) Introduction. From second language pedagogy to the pedagogy of 'plurilingualism': A possible paradigm shift?/De la didactique des langues à la didactique du plurilinguisme: un changement de paradigme possible? *The Canadian Modern Language Review/La Revue Canadienne des Langues Vivantes* 71 (4), 317–323.

Piccardo, E., Berchoud, M., Cignatta, T., Memntz, O. and Pamula, M. (2011b) *Pathways Through Assessment, Learning and Teaching in the CEFR*. Graz, Austria: European Centre for Modern Languages: ISNBN: 978-92-871-7159-7.

Piccardo, E., Czura, A., Erickson, G. and North, B. (2019a) QualiMatrix: A Quality Assurance Matrix for CEFR Use. www.ecml.at/ECML-Programme/Programme2016-2019/QualityassuranceandimplementationoftheCEFR/tabid/1870/language/en-GB/Default.aspx (accessed 08 March 2018).

Piccardo, E., Germain-Rutherford, A., and Clement, R. (eds) (2011a) Adopter ou adapter le Cadre européen comun de référence est-il seulement européen? [Adopt or adapt the Common European Framework of Reference - is it European?] *Synergies Europe*, 6. https://gerflint.fr/Base/Europe6/Europe6.html (accessed 08 March 2018).

Piccardo, E., North, B. and Maldina, E. (2017) QualiCEFR: A quality assurance template to achieve innovation and reform in language education through CEFR implementation. *Proceedings of the 6th International ALTE Conference. Learning and Assessment: Making the Connections. Bologna, Italy, 3–5 May 2017* (pp. 96–103). http://events.cambridgeenglish.org/alte2017-test/perch/resources/alte-2017-proceedings-final.pdf (accessed 08 March 2018).

Piccardo, E., North, B., Maldina, E. (2019b) Promoting innovation and reform in language education through a quality assurance template for CEFR implementation. *Canadian Journal of Applied Linguistics/Revue Canadienne de Linguistique Appliquée* 22 (1), 103–128.

Piccardo, E., Payre-Ficout, C., Germain-Rutherford, A. and Townshend, N. (2018) LINCDIRE: une approche actionnelle pour des compétences plurilingues et pluriculturelles [LINCDIRE: An action-oriented approach for plurilingual and pluricultural competences]. *Les Langues Modernes [Modern Languages]* 1, 67–76.

Piepho, H-E. (1979) *Kommunikative Didaktik des Englischunterrichts Sekundarstufe I: Theoretische Begründung und Wege zur Praktischen Einlösung eines Fachdidaktischen Konzepts [Communicative English Language Teaching in Lower Secondary: Theoretical Justifications and Ways Towards Practical Implementation of Pedagogic Concepts]*. Limburg: Frankonius Verlag.

Pikkarainen, E. (2014) Competence as a key concept of educational theory: A semiotic point of view. *Journal of Philosophy of Education* 48 (4), 621–636.

Pinho, A.S. (2015) Intercomprehension: A portal to teachers' intercultural sensitivity. *Language Learning Journal* 43 (2), 148–164.

Piribauer, G., Atzlesberger, U., Greinix, I., Ladstätter, Mittendorfer, F., Renner, H. and Steinhuber, B. (2015) *Plurilingualism: Designing and Implementing Plurilingual Oral Exams: Framework for the Austrian Upper Secondary Level Oral Leaving Examination at Colleges for Higher Vocational Education*. Vienna: CEBS (Center for Vocational Languages).

Poehner, M.E. (2016) Sociocultural theory and the dialectical-materialist approach to L2 development: Introduction to the special issue. *Language and Sociocultural Theory* 3 (2), 133. doi:10.1558/lst.v3i2.32869.

Poehner, M.E. and Swain, M. (2016) Development as cognitive-emotive process. *Language and Sociocultural Theory* 3 (2), 219–241.

Polanyi, M. (1962) *Personal Knowledge*. Chicago, IL: University of Chicago Press.

Polanyi, M. (1966) *The Tacit Dimension*. Chicago, IL: University of Chicago Press.

Porcelli, G. (2005) La glottodidattica come scienza interdisciplinare [Language teaching methodology as an interdisciplinary science]. *Synergies France 4*, 121–130.

Porto, M. (2012) Academic perspectives from Argentina. In M. Byram and L. Parmenter (eds) (pp. 129–138).

Porto, M. and Yulita, L. (2017) Language and intercultural citizenship education for a culture of peace. In M. Byram, I. Golubeva, H. Hui and M. Wagner (eds) (pp. 199–224).

Prabhu, N.S. (1984) Procedural syllabuses. In T.E. Read (ed.) *Trends in Language Syllabus Design* (pp. 272–80). Singapore: Singapore University/RELC.

Prabhu, N.S. (1987) *Second Language Pedagogy*. Oxford: Oxford University Press.

Prasad G. (2014) Portraits of plurilingualism in a French International School in Toronto: Exploring the role of the visual methods to access students' representations of their linguistically diverse identities. *Canadian Journal of Applied Linguistics* 17 (1), 55–71.

Puozzo Capron, I. (2014) *Le sentiment d'efficacité personnelle d'élèves dans un contexte plurilingue. Le cas du français au secondaire en Vallée d'Aoste [The Feeling of Self-efficacy of Students in a Plurilingual Context. The Case of the Aosta Valley]*. Berne: Peter Lang.

Puozzo Capron, I. and Piccardo, E. (2014) Pour une évaluation créative en classe de langues [For creative assessment in the language classroom]. In M-T. Maurer-Feder (ed.) *L'enseignant au sein du dispositif d'enseignement/apprentissage de la langue étrangère [The Teacher in the Teaching/Learning of Foreign Language]* (pp. 91–100). Besançon: ADCUEFE.

Puren, C. (2002) Perspectives actionnelles et perspectives culturelles en didactique des langues-cultures: vers une perspective co-actionnelle co-culturelle. *Les Langues Modernes* 3, 55–71.

Puren, C. (2004) L'evolution historique des approches en didactique des langues-cultures ou comment faire l'unité des "unités didactiques" [The historical evolution of approaches in the pedagogy of languages and cultures – or how to unite 'teaching units'], Congrès Annuel de l'Association pour la Diffusion de l'Allemand en France (ADEAF) [Annual Conference of the Association for the Diffusion of German in France], École Supérieure de Commerce de Clermont-Ferrand, 2–3 Novembre 2004, France.

Puren, C. (2006) De l'approche communicative à la perspective actionnelle [*From the communicative approach to the action-oriented perspective*]. *Le Français dans le Monde* 347, 37–40.

Puren, C. (2009a) La nouvelle perspective actionnelle et ses implications sur la conception des manuels de langue [The new action-oriented perspective and its implications for the conceptualisation of language teaching course books]. In M-L. Lions-Olivieri and P. Liria (eds) (pp. 119–137).

Puren, C. (2009b) Conclusion-synthèse : variations sur la perspective de l'agir social en didactique des langues-cultures étrangères [Conclusion-synthesis: Variations on the perspective of social action in language-culture teaching pedagogy]. In E. Rosen (ed.) *Le Français dans le Monde, Recherches et Applications, numéro spécial 45 [French in the World: Special Issue 45* (pp. 154–167).

Pyrko, I., Dörfler, V. and Eden, C. (2017) Thinking together: What makes communities of practice work? *Human Relations* 70 (4), 389–409.

Quetz, J. and Vogt, K. (2009) Bildungsstandards für die erste Fremdsprache: Sprachenpolitik auf unsicherer Basis [Educational standards for the first foreign language: Language policy on an insecure basis]. *Zeitschrift für Fremdsprachenforschung [Journal for Foreign Language Research]* 20 (1), 63–89.

Rampton, B. (1995) *Crossing: Language and Ethnicity Among Adolescents*. London: Longman.

Reed, E.S. (1995) The ecological approach to language development: Radical solution to Chomsky's and Quine's problems. *Language and Communication* 15 (1), 1–25.

Reed, E.S. (1996) *Encountering the World: Towards an Ecological Psychology*. New York: Oxford University Press.

Rehbein, J., ten Thije D.J. and Verschik, A. (2012) Lingua receptiva (LaRa) – Remarks on the quintessence of receptive multilingualism. *The International Journal of Bilingualism* 16 (3), 248–264.

Richards, J.C. (2013) Curriculum approaches in language teaching: Forward, central and backward design. *RELC Journal* 44 (1), 5–33.

Richards, J.C and Rodgers, T.S. (1986) *Approaches and Methods in Language Teaching: A Description and Analysis*. Cambridge: Cambridge University Press.

Richer, J-J. (2008) Le français sur objectifs spécifiques (F.O.S.): une didactique spécialisée? [French for specific purposes (FSP): a specialised pedagogy?] *Synergies Chine [Synergies China]* 3, 15–30.

Richer, J-J. (2009) Lectures du Cadre: continuité ou rupture? [Readings of the CEFR: continuity or rupture?]. In M-L. Lions-Olivieri and P. Liria (eds) (pp. 13–48).

Richer, J-J. (2012) *La didactique des langues interrogée par les compétences [Language Pedagogy put to the Question from the Perspective of Competences]*. Bruxelles: EME and InterCommunications sprl.

Richer, J-J. (2017) Quand le monde du travail peut venir en renfort de la didactique des langues. ... [When the world of work can come to reinforce language pedagogy]. *Revue TDFLE 70 La pensée CECR. [TDFLE Review 70: The CEFR Concept]* 1–34. http://revue-tdfle.fr/revue_publi.id_publi-36.html (accessed 08 March 2018).

Richterich, R. and Chancerel, J.L. (1980) *Identifying the Needs of Adults Learning a Foreign Language*. Oxford: Pergamon. (Reprint of 1978 publication with same name, Strasbourg: Council of Europe).

Richterich, R. and Suter, B. (1981) *Cartes sur table [Cards on the Table]*. Paris: Hachette.

Rietveld, D.W. and Kiverstein, J. (2014) A rich landscape of affordances. *Ecological Psychology* 26 (4), 325–352.

Rivenc, P. and Boudot, J. (1962) *Voix et images de France, 1er Degré [Voices and Images of France: 1st Level]*. Paris: CREDIF/Didier.

Rivers, W. (1983) *Communicating Naturally in a Second Language: Theory and Practice in Language Teaching*. Cambridge: Cambridge University Press.

Robinson, P. (2001) Task complexity, task difficulty, and task production: Exploring interactions in a componential framework. *Applied Linguistics* 22, 27–57.

Robinson, P. (2007) Task complexity, theory of mind, and intentional reasoning: Effects on L2 speech production, interaction, uptake and perceptions of task difficulty. *International Review of Applied Linguistics* 45, 193–213.

Roegiers, X. (2000) *Une pédagogie de l'intégration. Compétences et intégration des acquis dans l'enseignement [A Pedagogy of Integration: Competences and the Integration of Knowledge Gained from Teaching]*. Bruxelles: De Boeck.

Rosen, E. (ed.) (2009) La perspective actionnelle et l'approche par les tâches en classe de langue [The action-oriented perspective and the task-based approach in the language classroom]. *Le Français dans le Monde, Recherches et Applications, numéro spécial 45 [French in the World: Special Issue 45]*.

Rumelhart, D.E. and McClelland, J.L. (1986) On learning and the past tenses of English verbs. In J.L. McClelland, D.E. Rumelhart and the PDS Research Group (eds) *Parallel Distributed Processing: Explorations in the Microstructures of Cognition. Vol. 2 Psychological and Biological Models*. Cambridge (MA): MIT Press.

Saad, C.S., Damian, R.I., Benet-Martinez, V., Moons, W.G. and Robins, R.W. (2013) Multiculturalism and creativity: Effects of cultural context, bicultural identity, and ideational fluency. *Social Psychological and Personality Science* 4, 369–375.

Salamoura, A. and Saville, N. (2011) *English Profile: Introducing the CEFR for English, Version 1.0, April 2011*. Cambridge: UCLES/CUP.

Savignon, S.J. (1972) *Communicative Competence: An Experiment in Foreign Language Teaching*. Philadelphia: Center for Curriculum Development.

Savignon, S.J. (1983) *Communicative Competence: Theory and Classroom Practice*. Reading MA: Addison-Wesley.

Savignon, S.J. (2002) Communicative language teaching: Linguistic theory and classroom practice. In S.J. Savignon (ed.) *Interpreting Communicative Language Teaching: Contexts and Concerns in Teacher Education* (pp. 1–27). New Haven and London: Yale University Press.

Sawyer, K.R. (2003) Emergence in creativity and development. In K.R. Sawyer (ed.) *Creativity and Development* (pp. 12–60). New York: Oxford University Press.

Sawyer, K.R. (2012) *Explaining Creativity: The Science of Human Innovation*. New York: Oxford University Press.

Sbisà, M. (2007) How to read Austin. *Pragmatics* 17 (3), 461–473. doi: 10.1075/prag.17.3.06sbi.

Scalzo, R.A. (1998) L'approccio comunicativo. Oltre la competenza comunicativa [The communicative approach: Beyond communicative competence]. In C. Serra Borneto (ed.) *C'era una Volta il Metodo [Once Upon a Time There Was The Method]* (pp. 137–171). Roma: Carrocci.

Schärer, R. and North, B. (1992) *Towards a Common European Framework for Reporting Language Competency*, Washington D.C.: NFLC Occasional Paper, National Foreign Language Center.

Schegloff, E. (1972) Sequencing in conversational openings. In J. Lever and S. Hutchinson (eds) *Communication in Face to Face Interaction* (pp. 374–405). Harmondsworth: Penguin Books.

Schegloff E and Sacks H. (1973) Opening up closings. *Semiotica* 8, 289–327.

Schleiss, M. and Hagenow-Caprez, M. (2017) fide – On the way to a coherent framework. In J-C Beacco *et al.* (eds) (pp. 169–174).

Schmidt, R.W. (1990) The role of consciousness in second language learning. *Applied Linguistics* 11 (2), 129–158.

Schmidt, R.W. (2001) Attention. In P. Robinson (ed.) *Cognition and Second Language Instruction* (pp. 3–32). Cambridge: Cambridge University Press.

Schneider, G. and North, B. (2000) *Fremdsprachen können: was heisst das? Skalen zur Beschreibung, Beurteilung und Selbsteinschätzung der fremdsprachlichen Kommunikationsfähigkeit. [Knowing a Foreign Language: What does that Mean? Scales for the Description, Assessment and Self-assessment of Foreign Language Communicative Proficiency]*. Chur/Zürich: Nationales Forschungsprogramm 33: Wirksamkeit unserer Bildungssysteme [National Research Programme 33: Effectiveness of Our Education System]/Verlag Rüegger.

Schneider, G., North, B. and Koch, L. (2000) *A European Language Portfolio*. Berne: Berner Lehrmittel- und Medienverlag.

Schneuwly B. (2008) Vygotski, l'école et l'écriture [Vygotsky, school and writing]. *Cahiers des sciences de l'éducation [Working Papers in Educational Science]* 118. Geneva: Université de Genève.

Schroeter, K. (2008) *Competence literature review*, www.cc-institute.org/docs/default-document-library/2011/10/19/competence_lit_review.pdf (accessed 08 March 2018).

Schulz, D. and Griesbach, E. (1955) *Deutsche Sprachlehre für Ausländer [German Language Course for Foreigners]*. Munich: Hueber Verlag.

Schumann J.H. (1997) *The Neurobiology of Affect in Language*. Boston: Blackwell.

Schumann, J.H. (1999) A neurobiological perspective on affect and methodology in second language learning. In J. Arnold (ed.) *Affect in Language Learning* (pp. 28–42). Cambridge: Cambridge University Press.

Searle, J.R. (1969) *Speech Acts: An Essay in the Philosophy of Language*. Cambridge: Cambridge University Press.

Searle, J.R. (1975) Indirect speech acts. *Syntax and Semantics* 3, 59–82.

Searle, J.R. (1976) The classification of illocutionary acts. *Language in Society* 5 (1), 1–24.

Selinker, L. (1972) Interlanguage. *IRAL* 10 (3), 209–31.

Serra Borneto C. (ed.) (1998) *C'era una Volta il Metodo [Once Upon a Time There Was The Method]*. Roma: Carrocci.

Sickinger, P. and Schneider, K.P. (2014) Pragmatic competence and the CEFR: Pragmatic profiling as a link between theory and language use. *Linguistica* 54 (1), 113–127.

Sinclair, J.McH. (1983) Planes of discourse. In S.N.A. Rizvil (ed.) *The Two-fold Voice: Essays in Honour of Ramesh Mohan*. Salzburg: Salzburg Studies in English Literature, University of Salzburg.

Sinclair, J.McH. and Brazil, D. (1982) *Teacher Talk*. Oxford: Oxford University Press.

Sinclair, J.McH. and Coulthard, R.M. (1975) *Towards an Analysis of Discourse: The English Used by Teachers and Pupils*. Oxford: Oxford University Press.

Skehan, P. (1995) Analysability, accessibility and ability for use. In G. Cook and S. Seidlhofer (eds) *Principle and Practice in Applied Linguistics: Studies in Honour of H.G. Widdowson* (pp. 91–106). Oxford: Oxford University Press.

Skehan, P. (1996) A framework for the implementation of task-based instruction. *Applied Linguistics* 17, 38–62.

Skehan, P. (1998) *A Cognitive Approach to Language Learning*. Oxford: Oxford University Press.

Skehan, P. (2001) Tasks and language performance assessment. In M. Bygate, P. Skehan and M. Swain (eds) *Researching Pedagogic Tasks: Second Language Learning, Teaching and Testing* (pp. 167–185). London: Longman.

Skehan, P. and Foster, P. (1995) Task type and task processing conditions as influences on foreign language performance. *Thames Valley University Working Papers in English Language Teaching* 3, 139–188.

Skehan, P. and Foster, P. (2001) Cognition and tasks. In P. Robinson (ed.) *Cognition and Second Language Instruction* (pp. 183–205). Cambridge: Cambridge University Press.

Skinner, B.F. (1938) *The Behavior of Organisms: An Experimental Analysis*. Oxford, England: Appleton-Century.

Skinner, B.F. (1957) *Verbal Behavior*. New York: Appleton Century Crofts.

Skutnabb-Kangas, T. (1981) *Bilingualism or Not: The Education of Minorities*. Clevedon: Multilingual Matters.

Slattery, P. (2013) *Curriculum Development in the Postmodern Era: Teaching and Learning in an Age of Accountability* (3rd edn). New York: Routledge.

Smith, F. (1985) A metaphor for literacy: Creating worlds or shunting information? In D. Olson, N. Torrance and A. Hildyard (eds) *Literacy, Language and Learning, the Nature and Consequences of Reading and Writing*. Cambridge: Cambridge University Press.

Smith, M.K. (1996) Competence and competencies. In *The Encyclopaedia of Informal Education*. http://infed.org/mobi/what-iscompetence-and-competency/ (accessed 08 March 2018).

Spada, N.M. (1997) Form-focused instruction and second-language acquisition: A review of classroom and laboratory research. *Language Teaching* 30, 73–87.

Spinelli, E. and Nerenz, A. (2004) Learning scenarios: The new foreign language curriculum. *CLEAR News* 8(1), 1–6. http://clear.msu.edu/spring-2004-learning-scenarios-the-new-foreign-language-curriculum/ (accessed 30 September 2018).

Spinoza, B. (1981) *The Ethics* (G. Eliot trad.). New York: Joseph Simon Publisher. (Original published in 1677).

Spolsky, B. (1989) *Conditions for Second Language Learning: Introduction to a General Theory*. Oxford: Oxford University Press.

Spolsky, B. (2008) Historical and future perspectives. In E. Shohamy and N.H. Hornberger (eds) *Encyclopedia of Language and Education – Vol. 7, Language Testing and Assessment* (2nd edn) (pp. 445–454). New York: Springer.

Stathopoulou, M. (2013) The linguistic characteristics of KPG written mediation tasks across levels. In N. Lavidas, T. Alexiou and A.M Sougari (eds) *Major Trends in Theoretical and Applied Linguistics: Selected Papers from the 20th ISTAL*. London: Versita de Gruyter.

Stern, H.H. (1983) *Fundamental Concepts of Language Teaching*. New York: Oxford University Press.

Stern, H.H. (1992) *Issues and Options in Language Teaching*. Oxford: Oxford University Press.

Sternberg, R.J., and Lubart, T. (1995) *Defying the Crowd: Cultivating Creativity in an Age of Conformity*. New York: Free Press.

Stevick, E.W. (1980) *A Way and Ways*. Rowley, MA: Newbury House.

Stratilaki, S. (2005) Vers une conception dynamique de la compétence plurilingue: quelques réflexions six ans après [Towards a dynamic conceptualisation of plurilingual competence: What reflections six years afterwards?]. In M.A. Mochet (ed.) *Plurilinguisme et apprentissages – Mélanges Daniel Coste [Plurilingualism and Learning-Different Contributions of Daniel Coste]*. Série Hommages [Hommge Seres] (pp. 155–168). Ecole Normale Supérieure – Lettres et Sciences humaines, Lyon.

Swain, M. (2006) Languaging, agency and collaboration in advanced language proficiency. In H. Byrnes (ed.) *Advanced Language Learning: The Contribution of Halliday and and Vygotsky* (pp. 95–108). London-New York: Continuum.

Swain, M. (2013) The inseparability of cognition and emotion in second language learning. *Language Teaching* 46 (2), 195–207. doi:10.1017/S0261444811000486.

Swain, M. and Lapkin, S. (2013) A Vygotskian sociocultural perspective on immersion education. The L1/L2 debate *Journal of Immersion and Content-Based Language Education* 1 (1), 101–129.

Swain, M., Kinnear, P. and Steinman, L. (2015) *Sociocultural Theory in Second Language Education: An Introduction Through Narratives* (2nd edn). Bristol: Multilingual Matters.

Swales, J.M. (1990) *The Genre Analysis: English in Academic and Research Settings*. Cambridge: Cambridge University Press.

Swan, M. (2005) Legislation by hypothesis: The case of task-based instruction. *Applied Linguistics* 26 (3), 376–401.

Sweet, H. (1899/1964) *The Practical Study of Languages: A Guide for Teachers and Learners*. London: Dent. Also published London: Oxford University Press: 1964. (Cited in Stern, 1983: 317).

Szabo, T. and Goodier, T. (2017) Collated representative samples of descriptors of language competences developed for young learners: Resource for educators. Version 1 developed through Eurocentres consultancy for the Council of Europe. Strasbourg, France: Council of Europe. www.coe.int/en/web/common-european-framework-reference-languages/bank-of-supplementary-descriptors (accessed 08 March 2018).

Tajfel, H. and Turner, J. (2001) An integrative theory of intergroup conflict. In M.A. Hogg and D. Abrams (eds) *Intergroup Relations: Essential Readings* (pp. 94–109). Philadelphia: Psychology Press.

Takala, S. (2013) The CEFR in use: Some observations of three Nordic countries. In N. Figueras (ed.) The impact of the CEFR in Catalonia. *APAC Monographs* 9, 9–18.

Tarone, E. (1980) Communication strategies, foreigner talk and repair in interlanguage. *Language Learning* 30, 417–431.

Tarone, E. (1983) Some thoughts on the notion of "communication strategy". In K. Faerch and G. Kasper (eds) *Strategies in Interlanguage Communication* (pp. 63–68). Harlow: Longman. Originally published in *TESOL Quarterly* 1981.

Tellier, M. (2008) The effect of gestures on second language memorisation by young children. *Gesture* 8 (2), 219–235.

ten Thije, J.D., Gooskens, C., Daems, F., Cornips, L. and Smits, M. (2017) Lingua receptiva: Position paper on the European Commission's Skills Agenda. *European Journal of Applied linguistics* 5(1), 141–146. https://doi.org/10.1515/eujal-2017-0003 (accessed 11 May 2016).

The Douglas Fir Group (2016) A transdisciplinary framework for SLA in a multilingual world. *The Modern Language Journal* 100 Supplement (1), 19–47. doi: 10.1111/modl.12301.

Thelen, E. and Smith, L. (1994) *A Dynamic Systems Approach to the Development of Cognition and Action*. Cambridge, MA: MIT Press.

Thierry, G. and Wu, Y.J. (2007) Brain potentials reveal unconscious translation during foreign-language comprehension. *Proceedings of the National Academy of Sciences* 104 (30), 12530–12535.

Thornbury, S. (2016) Communicative language teaching in theory and practice. In G. Hall (ed.) *The Routledge Handbook of English Language Teaching* (pp. 224–237). London: Routledge.

Titone R. (1968) *Teaching Foreign Languages: An Historical Sketch*. Washington DC: Georgetown University Press.

Trim, J.L.M. (1995) Résumé of Report of Modern Languages Programme. In C. Brumfit (ed.) *The Work of the Council of Europe and Second Language Teaching* (pp. 1–22). London: Modern English Publications/British Council.

Trim, J.L.M. (ed.) (2001) *Common European Framework of Reference for Languages: Learning, Teaching, Assessment (CEFR): A Guide for Users*, Strasbourg: Council of Europe. www.coe.int/en/web/common-european-framework-reference-languages/documents (accessed 08 March 2018).

Trim, J.L.M. (2007) *Modern Languages in The Council of Europe: 1954–1997: International co-operation in support of lifelong language learning for effective communication, mutual cultural enrichment and democratic citizenship in Europe*. Strasbourg: Council of Europe, Language Policy Division.

Trim, J.L.M. (2012) The Common European Framework of References for Languages and its background: A case study of cultural politics and educational influences. In M. Byram and L. Parmenter (eds) *The Common European Framework of Reference: The Globalisation of Language Policy* (pp. 14–34). Bristol: Multilingual Matters.

Tudor, I. (2001) *The Dynamics of the Language Classroom*. Cambridge: Cambridge University Press.

Tudor, I. (2003) Learning to live with complexity: Towards an ecological perspective on language teaching. *System* 31, 1–12.

UNESCO (2009) UNESCO world report: Investing in cultural diversity and intercultural dialogue. http://unesdoc.unesco.org/images/0018/001847/184755e.pdf (accessed 08 March 2018).

Valsiner, J. and Rosa, A. (2007) Contemporary socio-cultural research: Uniting culture, society, and psychology. In J. Valsiner and A. Rosa (eds) *The Cambridge Handbook of Sociocultural Psychology* (pp. 1–20). Cambridge: Cambridge University Press.

van Avermaet, P. and Gysen, S. (2006) From needs to tasks: Language learning needs in a task-based perspective. In K. van den Branden (ed.) *Task-based Language Education: From Theory to Practice* (pp. 17–46). Cambridge: Cambridge University Press.

van den Branden, K. (2006) Introduction: Task-based language teaching in a nutshell. In K. van den Branden (ed.) *Task-based Language Education: From Theory to Practice* (pp. 1–16). Cambridge: Cambridge University Press.

van den Branden, K. (ed.) (2006) *Task-based Language Education: From Theory to Practice.* Cambridge: Cambridge University Press.

van den Branden, K. and van Avermaet, P. (1995) Taakgericht onderwijs: theoretische uitgangspunten. In VON-werkgroep NT2 (eds) *Taakgericht Taalonderwijs: een Onmogelijke Taak?* (pp. 9–20). Deurne: Wolters-Plantyn.

van den Branden, Bygate, M. and Norris, J.M. (2009) Task-based language teaching: Introducing the Reader. In K. van den Branden, M. Bygate and J.M. Norris (eds) *Task-based Language Teaching: A Reader* (pp. 1–13). Amsterdam: John Benjamins.

van den Branden, K., Bygate, M. and Norris, J.M. (eds) (2009) *Task-based Language Teaching: A Reader,* Amsterdam: John Benjamins.

van Ek, J.A. (1975) *The Threshold Level in a European Unit/credit System for Modern Language Learning by Adults.* Strasbourg: Council of Europe.

van Ek, J.A. (1986) *Objectives for Foreign Language Teaching, Volume I: Scope.* Strasbourg: Council of Europe.

van Ek, J.A. and Trim, J.L.M. (2001a) *Waystage.* Cambridge: Cambridge University Press.

van Ek, J.A. and Trim, J.L.M. (2001b) *Threshold 1990.* Cambridge: Cambridge University Press.

van Ek, J.A. and Trim, J.L.M. (2001c) *Vantage.* Cambridge: Cambridge University Press.

van Geert, P. (1994) *Dynamic Systems of Development. Change between Complexity and Chaos.* Herthfordshire: Harverster Wheatsheaf.

van Lier, L. (1988) *The Classroom and the Language Learner.* Harlow: Longman.

van Lier, L. (1997) Approaches to observation in classroom research: Observation from an ecological perspective. *TESOL Quarterly* 31, 783–787.

van Lier L. (2000) From input to affordance: Social-interactive learning from an ecological perspective. In J.P. Lantolf (ed.) (pp. 245–259).

van Lier L. (2002) An ecological-semiotic perspective on language and linguistics. In C. Kramsch (ed.) (pp. 140–164).

van Lier, L. (2004) *The Ecology and Semiotics of Language Learning.* Dordrecht: Kluwer Academic.

van Lier L. (2007) Action-based teaching, autonomy and identity. *Innovation in Language Teaching and Learning* 1 (1), 1–19.

van Lier, L. (2010) The ecology of language learning: Practice to theory, theory to practice. *Procedia Social and Behavioral Sciences* 3, 2–6.

Varela, F.G., Maturana, H.R., and Uribe, R. (1974) Autopoiesis: The organization of living systems, its characterization and a model. *Biosystems* 5 (4), 187–196.

Varela, F., Thomson, E. and Rosch, E. (1991) *The Embodied Mind: Cognitive Science and Human Experience.* Cambridge, MA: MIT Press.

Verdelhan-Bourgade, M. Verdelhan, M. and Dominique, P. (1982) *Sans frontières [Without Frontiers].* Paris: CLE International.

Ventola, E. (1979) The structure of casual conversation in English. *Journal of Pragmatics* 3, 267–298.

Vernant, D. (1997) *Du discours à l'action [From Discourse to Action].* Paris: Presses Universitaires de France.

Vernon, P.E. (ed.) (1970) *A Review of "Creativity."* Harmondsworth: Penguin.

Vertovec, S. (2007) Super-diversity and its implications. *Ethnic and Racial Studies* 30 (6), 1024–1054. doi: 10.1080/01419870701599465.

Vetter, E. (2012) Exploiting receptive multilingualism in institutional language learning: The case of Italian in the Austrian secondary school system. *International Journal of Bilingualism* 16 (3), 348–365.

Vietör, W. (1882/1886) Der Sprachunterricht muss umkehren! Ein Beitrag zur Überbürdungsfrage [Language teaching must turn back! A contribution to the discussion of the overload issue]. In W. Hüllen (ed.) (1979) *Didaktik des englisch*

Unterrichts [English Teaching Pedagogy] (pp. 9–31). Darmstadt: Wissenschaftliche Buchgesellschaft.

Vogel, S. and García, O. (2017) Translanguaging. *Oxford Research Encyclopedia of Education. Subject: Languages and Literacies.* doi: 10.1093/acrefore/9780190264093.013.181.

Vollmer, H.J. (1981) Why are we interested in "general language proficiency?" In J.C. Alderson and A. Hughes (eds) *Issues in Language Testing, ELT Documents 111.* (pp. 152–176). London: British Council.

Vollmer, H.J. (2003) Ein gemeinsamer europäischer Referenzrahmen für Sprachen: Nicht mehr, nicht weniger [A common European framework of reference for languages: Not more, not less]. In K.-R. Bausch, H. Christ, F.G. Königs, and H.-J. Krumm (eds), *Der Gemeinsame Europäische Referenzrahmen für Sprachen in der Diskussion [Common European Framework of Reference in Discussion]. Arbeitspapiere der 22. Frühjahrskonferenz zur Erforschung des Fremdsprachenunterrichts [Working Papers of the 22nd Spring Conference on Language Teaching Research]* (pp. 192–206). Tübingen: Narr.

von Bertalanffy, L. (1950) An outline of general system theory. *British Journal for the Philosophy of Science* 1, 114–129.

von Bertalanffy, L. (1968) *General System Theory: Foundations, Development, Applications.* New York: George Braziller.

Vygotsky, L.S (1962) *Thought and Language.* Cambridge, MA: MIT Press.

Vygotsky L.S. (1978) *Mind in Society: The Development of Higher Psychological Processes.* Cambridge, MA: Harvard University Press.

Vygotsky, L.S. (1981) The genesis of higher mental functions. In J.V. Wertsch (ed.) *The Concept of Activity in Soviet Psychology* (pp. 144–188). Armonk, N.Y.: M.E. Sharpe.

Vygotsky, L.S. (1986) *Thought and Language.* (A. Kozulin, Trans. and Ed). Cambridge, MA: MIT Press.

Vygotsky, L.S. (1999 [1927]) *La signification historique de la crise en psychologie [The Historical Significance of the Crisis in Psychology].* Paris: Delachaux et Niestlé.

Waldrop, M.M. (1992) *Complexity: The Emerging Science at the Edge of Order and Chaos.* New York: Simon and Shuster.

Walqui, A. (2006) Scaffolding instruction for English language learners: A conceptual framework. *The International Journal of Bilingual Education and Bilingualism* 9 (2), 159–180.

Wandruska, M. (1979) *Die Mehrsprachigkeit des Menschen. [The Plurilingualism of the Human Being].* Stuttgart: Kohlhammer.

Waters, A. (2011) Advances in materials design. In M.H. Long and C.J. Doughty (eds) *The Handbook of Language Teaching* (pp. 311–326). Oxford: Wiley-Blackwell.

Weaver, W. (1948) Science and complexity. *American Scientist* 36, 536–544.

Webb, N. (2009) The teacher's role in promoting collaborative dialogue in the classroom. *British Journal of Educational Psychology* 78 (1), 1–28.

Wei, L. (2011) Multilinguality, multimodality, and multicompetence: Code- and modeswitching by minority ethnic children in complementary schools. *The Modern Language Journal* 95 (3), 370–384.

Weir, C. (2005) *Language Testing and Validation: An Evidence-based Approach.* Basingstoke: Palgrave Macmillan.

Wenger, E. (1998) *Communities of Practice: Learning, Meaning and Identity.* New York: Cambridge University Press.

Wenger, E. (2006) Communities of Practice: A brief introduction. http://wenger-trayner.com/introduction-to-communities-of-practice/ (accessed 08 March 2018).

Wenger E. (2010) Communities of practice and social learning systems: The career of a concept. In C. Blackmore (ed.) *Social Learning Systems and Communities of Practice* (pp.179–198). Springer: London.

Wertsch, J.V. (1998) *Mind as Action*. New York: Oxford University Press.

Widdowson, H.G. (1978) *Teaching Language as Communication*. Oxford: Oxford University Press.

Widdowson, H.G. (1979) *Explorations in Applied Linguistics*. Oxford: Oxford University Press.

Widdowson, H.G. (1984) *Explorations in Applied Linguistics 2*. Oxford: Oxford University Press.

Widdowson, H.G. (1989) Knowledge of language and ability for use. *Applied Linguistics* 10 (2), 128–137.

Wiemann, J.M. (1977) Explication and test of a model of communicative competence. *Human Communication Research* 3, 195–213.

Wiemann, J.M. and Backlund, P. (1980) Current theory and research in communicative competence. *Review of Educational Research* 50 (1), 185–199.

Wiggins, G. and McTighe, J. (2005) *Understanding by Design* (2nd edn). Alexandria, VA: Association for Supervision and Curriculum Development.

Wilds, C.P. (1975) The oral interview test. In B. Spolsky and R. Jones (eds) *Testing Language Proficiency* (pp. 29–44). Washington D.C.: Center for Applied Linguistics.

Wilkins, D.A. (1976) *Notional Syllabuses*. Oxford: Oxford University Press.

Wilkins, D.A. (1978) Proposal for levels definition. In J.LM. Trim *Some Possible Lines of Development of an Overall Structure for a European Unit/Credit Scheme for Foreign Language Learning by Adults* (pp. 71–78). Strasbourg: Council of Europe.

Wilkinson, C. (1992) Strategies for testing strategic competence: An examination of possibilities. *IATEFL Silver Jubilee Conference Report*, 76–77.

Williams, C. (1996) Secondary education: Teaching in the bilingual situation. In C. Williams, G. Lewis and C. Baker (eds) *The Language Policy: Taking Stock*. Llangefni (Wales): Canolfan Astudiaethau Iaith.

Willis, J. (1983) Spoken discourse in the EFL classroom, unpublished MA thesis, University of Birmingham.

Willis, J. (1996) *A Framework for Task-Based Learning*. Harlow: Longman.

Willis, D. and Willis, J. (2007) *Doing Task-based Teaching*. Oxford: Oxford University Press.

Wolff, D. (2003) Content and language integrated learning: A framework for the development of learner autonomy. In D. Little, J. Ridley and E. Ushioda (eds) *Learner Autonomy in the Foreign Language Classroom: Teacher, Learner, Curriculum and Assessment* (pp. 198–210). Dublin: Authentik.

Wood, D., Bruner, J., & Ross, G. (1976) "The role of tutoring in problem solving". *Journal of Child Psychology and Psychiatry and Allied Disciplines* 17, 89–100.

Wood, D.J., Bruner, J.S., and Ross, G. (1976) The role of tutoring in problem solving. *Journal of Child Psychiatry and Psychology* 17 (2), 89–100.

Woodruffe, C. (1991) Competent by any other name. *Personnel Management* 23 (9), 30–33.

Woolley, A.W., Chabris, C.F., Pentland, A., Hashmi, N. and Malone, T.W. (2010) Evidence for a collective intelligence factor in the performance of human groups. *Science* 330, 686.

Wright, S. (2000) *Community and Communication: The Role of Language in Nation Building and European Integration*. Clevedon: Multilingual Matters.

Wright, S. (2001) Language and power: Background to the debate on linguistic rights. *International Journal on Multicultural Societies* 3 (1), 44–54.

Wylie, E. and Ingram, D. (1995) *Australian Second Language Proficiency Ratings (ASLPR). General Proficiency Version for English*. Brisbane: Griffith University.

Yaiche, F. (1996) *Les simulations globales. Mode d'emploi [Global Simulations: How to Use Them]*. Paris: Hachette.

Zarate, G. (2003) Identities and plurilingualism: Preconditions for the recognition of intercultural competences. In M. Byram (ed.) *Intercultural Competence* (pp. 84–117). Strasbourg: Council of Europe.

Zarate, G., A., Gohard-Radenkovic, A., Lussier, D. and Penz, H. (2004) *Cultural Mediation in Language Learning and Teaching*. Graz: European Centre for Modern Languages.

Zarate, G., Levy, D. and Kramsch, C. (2008) *Précis du plurilinguisme et du pluriculturalisme. [Summary of Plurilingalism and Pluriculturalism]*. Paris: Contemporary Publishing International SARL.

Zarifian, P. (2001) *Objectif compétence [Objective: Competence]*. Paris: Éditions Liaisons.

Zenasni, F., Besançon, M. and Lubart, T. (2008) Creativity and tolerance of ambiguity: An empirical study. *Journal of Creative Behavior* 42 (1), 61–73.

Index